BLOOD NARRATIVE

NEW AMERICANISTS   A series edited by Donald E. Pease

BLOOD NARRATIVE

Indigenous Identity in American Indian and Maori

Literary and Activist Texts CHADWICK ALLEN

Duke University Press   Durham and London   2002

© 2002 Duke University Press

All rights reserved

Printed in the United States of

America on acid-free paper ∞

Designed by C. H. Westmoreland

Typeset in Adobe Garamond with Lithos

display by Keystone Typesetting, Inc.

Library of Congress Cataloging-

in-Publication Data appear on the

last printed page of this book.

Some material reprinted with permission

from *Narrative* 6, no. 3 (October 1998).

Copyright 1998 by the Ohio State

University. All rights reserved.

FOR MY FAMILY

CONTENTS

ACKNOWLEDGMENTS

Traveling to Aotearoa/New Zealand and studying Maori language, culture, literature, and activism shaped and focused this project. I am pleased to acknowledge the research support I received from a Sheldon Travelling Fellowship from Harvard University in 1987–88, from an IIE Fulbright Fellowship in 1994, and, in the summer of 1998, from the College of Humanities at Ohio State University.

My first introductions into Kiwi life and into te ao Maori came from the staff and students at St. John's College, the combined Anglican and Methodist seminary, in Auckland. I owe a special gratitude to Muru Walters and Russel Gaskin, to the friends who invited me into their homes (and into the homes of their unsuspecting relatives), and to the folks at the City Mission in Christchurch. During my Fulbright year, I was welcomed onto Waipapa Marae by the staff, students, and faculty in the Department of Maori Studies at Auckland University. Ko aku mihi ki a koutou katoa. I have fond memories of conversations with Hineira Woodard, Jane McRae, Ruth Wiki, and many others there, as well as with Witi Ihimaera in the Department of English. I am especially grateful to Ranginui Walker for inviting me to present my early work at the Maori Studies Seminar Series and for generously allowing me access to his private files on the World Council of Indigenous Peoples; to Hugh Kawharu and Margaret Mutu for challenging me to think deeply about the Treaty of Waitangi and about key Maori concepts; and to Anne Salmond for her guidance, inspiration, and warm friendship. I want to thank the staff at the New Zealand National Archives for their assistance in locating editorial materials related to the journal *Te Ao Hou*, and Jenny Gill, the director of Fulbright New Zealand, for her enthusiastic support of my research.

Many mentors encouraged the beginnings of this project when I was in graduate school; first among them was my fellow Oklahoman Carter Revard at Washington University in St. Louis. Among those at the University of Arizona to whom I am indebted are Barbara Babcock and Larry Evers for their years of unfailing support and for their insights into American Indian literatures and theory; Michelle Grijalva, Jane Hill, and Joan Dayan helped shape my early thinking on this project and lent me their time and expertise when they had plenty of other things to do. My colleagues Alesia Garcia and Maureen Salzer allowed me to talk endlessly about my ideas and made my early writing process immeasurably saner. I owe a special debt of gratitude to Annette Kolodny, not only for her consistent and careful guidance into the profession but also for the inspiration of her brilliance, the example of her amazing drive and commitment, and the generosity of her friendship. She is a role model I aspire to live up to.

As this project developed into a book, Dick Pearce, Jim Phelan, Steve Fink, Georgina Dodge, Leigh Gilmore, and, heroically, Debra Moddelmog gave their time and energy to discussing my ideas and reading drafts of chapters. Daniel Littlefield facilitated last minute research at the American Native Press Archives. My gratitude also goes out to my students, who helped me to develop my thinking about postcolonial theory, and to the anonymous readers at *American Literature* and *American Quarterly*, who helped me to better articulate my arguments about blood memory and treaty discourse. Joel Tobin was a patient listener and sounding board when I needed feedback the most.

The writing of this book would not have been possible without the continuing love and support of my parents, Sue and Richard Allen, and my grannie, Marie Holder, whose stories and example sustain me even when I'm far away from southern Oklahoma.

INTRODUCTION

Marking the Indigenous in

Indigenous Minority Texts

Improvisation is a vital element of cultural resistance; it determines the survival of a people, enhances the continuity of their spirit, the essence of their art.—Ngahuia Te Awekotuku (Maori), *Mana Wahine Maori*

Survival is imagination, a verbal noun, a transitive word. —Gerald Vizenor (Chippewa), "Crows Written on the Poplars"

Some readers will recognize the primary title of this book as a version of Kiowa author N. Scott Momaday's signature trope *memory in the blood* or *blood memory*, which achieves tropic power by blurring distinctions between racial identity (blood) and narrative (memory).[1] By echoing Momaday, I mean to evoke the complicated, multiperspectivist, and sometimes controversial maneuvers that are employed by indigenous minority writers and activists when they attempt to render contemporary indigenous minority identities as literary and activist texts. An earlier version of the title expanded Momaday's trope into the yoked form *blood as narrative/narrative as blood* in an effort to indicate a fluid movement between the key terms. But the reversed similes also suggested that the potential effects of blurring distinctions between blood and narrative are limited to a set of comparisons. As we shall see, simple comparison is rarely the effect of either Momaday's provocative juxtaposition or the many other maneuvers developed by indigenous minority activists and writers to assert indigenous identities in contemporary texts.

In the broadest sense, this study investigates the construction of indigeneity within the context of a deep and enduring settler colonization. More specifically, it analyzes a number of the narrative tactics developed by writers and activists who self-identify as American Indian or New Zealand Maori to mark their identities as persistently distinctive from those of dominant European-descended settlers and as irrevocably rooted in the particular lands these writers, activists, and their communities continue to call home. I limit my focus, further, to the early contemporary period (World War II through the 1970s), an era of dramatic social transformations and unprecedented textual production. Critics have largely avoided indigenous minority texts produced in the first half of the early contemporary period; political engagement and stylistic innovation are less obvious in these texts than in those published after 1968. But the "improvisational" and "transitive" discursive practices described by Te Awekotuku and Vizenor as the basis for contemporary indigenous survival and resistance began in the 1940s, 1950s, and early 1960s, and it was then that they first became visible to diverse audiences.[2] I emphasize narrative tactics in order to engage Michel de Certeau's model for these types of maneuvers—provisional, opportunistic, and creative—that enable disenfranchised peoples like indigenous minorities to realize practical kinds of power, including the power to make their voices heard by multiple audiences.[3] One of the aims of this project in comparative literary and cultural studies, then, is to articulate the rhetorical complexity of indigenous minority writing in First World settler nations like the United States and Aotearoa/New Zealand.[4] Another, related aim is to develop a better sense of the distinct dynamics of the particular form of (post)coloniality experienced by indigenous minorities like American Indians and New Zealand Maori in the post–World War II era.[5]

Why compare literary and activist texts produced by contemporary American Indians and New Zealand Maori? The first answer is that the comparison sets each group's discursive practices in relief, suggesting avenues for analysis and theory that are less obvious when texts produced by either group are considered on their own. American Indians and Maori share much in their responses to settler colonialism and in their assertions of indigenous identity. This is not surprising. Both groups experienced a dramatic population decline after initial contact with Europeans and the introduction of European diseases and military technology, and in both countries settler colonialism culminated in a series of violent land wars and land confiscations in the mid- and late nineteenth century. Neither Maori nor American Indian populations began to recover from the devastation of the contact era until the second half of the twentieth century, after World War II, the point at which this study begins. As those born after the war came of age in the 1960s and 1970s, both Maori and American Indians produced an explosive "renaissance" that forever altered their countries' national literatures and politics and that invigorated international efforts at creating indigenous coalitions.

However, it is also their significant differences within broadly similar histories that make these groups, their experiences, and their contemporary discursive practices especially productive for comparison. Aotearoa/New Zealand is considerably smaller than the United States in both its geographical area and its total contemporary population, and, as a group of South Pacific islands, it is relatively isolated compared to the United States. The European colonization of Aotearoa/ New Zealand began two centuries later than it did in North America, and it was a more rapid process: Captain James Cook first landed in New Zealand in 1769, and the British invasion was seriously under way, via neighboring Australia, by the 1820s. Because of different geographies and different histories of colonial settlement, Maori are today a smaller population than American Indians in absolute terms but a much larger percentage of the total population of their contemporary nation, about 15 percent of 3.7 million compared to less than 1 percent of over 260 million.[6] Like American Indians, Maori did not conceive of themselves as a single cultural or ethnic group until Europeans described them as such, and their locally defined identities have persisted into contemporary times. As a group, however, diverse Maori iwi (peoples or "tribes") more closely resemble each other in terms of their common Polynesian language, culture, and genealogy than do the diverse American Indian nations spread across the continental United States and Alaska. The relative visibility of Maori within the national population coupled with their relative cultural homogeneity has meant a greater Maori presence in national politics and dominant discourses. Finally, both American Indians and Maori were engaged as treaty "partners" by imperial and settler governments. But where American Indian nations negotiated nearly four hundred separate treaties with the United States, Maori negotiated a single treaty with Great Britain's colonial representative. As I explain in detail below, this difference provides an important entry for theorizing about the forms of (post)colonial hybridity at work in contemporary indigenous minority texts.

But, less expectedly, the comparison also highlights the often hidden context of colonialism that is still operative within the United States: it reveals how that context has affected—and continues to affect—the narrative tactics of literary and activist texts produced by those individuals and communities who insist on identifying themselves not as American but as American Indian. Given that American Indians (along with Alaska Natives and Native Hawaiians) constitute less than 1 percent of the total U.S. population and have little say in the design or enforcement of U.S. laws, current demographic and political realities tend to obscure the ongoing history of colonialism in the United States, the persistent presence and distinctiveness of its indigenous peoples, and the unique legal and moral relationships forged between indigenous peoples and the federal government through treaties and other binding agreements. Moreover, both the development of postcolonial theory and the rise of multiculturalism in the last quarter of the twentieth century have also tended to obscure the ongoing colonized status of indigenous peoples in the United States. So-called orthodox postcolonial theory has drawn almost exclusively from the experiences of populations in Southeast Asia, Africa, and the Caribbean; when critics have examined British settler colonies like New Zealand, Australia, and Canada, they have focused the majority of their attention on the continuing psychological effects of the colonial past on European settlers and their descendants—not on the material or psychological circumstances of these nations' indigenous minorities. For a variety of reasons, including its early independence from Britain and its own history as an imperial power in offshore territories like the Philippines, the United States has been included in studies of "settler colonies" only rarely, with little attention paid to American Indians or their textual production. Although various multiculturalist projects have brought a greater number of American Indian texts into the American literary canon, they have often done so by leveling distinctions between peoples indigenous to what is now the United States and other nondominant U.S. "minorities." The distinctiveness of American Indian identity is elided in what one recent academic commentary on multiculturalism describes as "the dominant social understanding of the United States as a society of immigrants."[7] I take up these issues of the relationships among indigenous minority status, postcolonial theory, and multiculturalism in greater detail in the separate introductions to part 1 and part 2. My point here is that, unlike typical postcolonial or multicultural approaches, the comparison with Maori in Aotearoa/New Zealand refocuses critical attention on American Indians as both colonized and indigenous.

A recent example highlights the power of this comparison. At the new Museum of New Zealand Te Papa Tongarewa, which opened in Wellington in 1998, both the ongoing distinction between indigenous peoples and European settlers and the significant ongoing relationship between these groups and their descendants are positioned at the structural center of the building and thus at the conceptual center of the contemporary settler nation—something not to be encountered in any nationally representative museum in the United States. The striking design of the museum in Wellington reflects a conception of Aotearoa/New Zealand as a bicultural nation, made up of "the Tangata Whenua, people here by right of first arrival," and "the Tangata Tiriti, people here by right of the Treaty [of Waitangi]."[8] Display space at the museum is divided into Tangata Whenua galleries on one side and Tangata Tiriti galleries on the other; the layouts of each wing reflect the differing settlement patterns of indigenous Maori and Pakeha (European) settlers. These contrasting physical spaces meet in a central Wedge zone, a symbolic "point of cleavage" meant to suggest both a coming together and a separating, as well as the fluidity of movement between these divergent meanings of the verb "to cleave." The Wedge houses the museum's permanent exhibit on the Treaty of Waitangi, which includes large-scale replicas of the conflicting Maori and English language versions of Aotearoa/New Zealand's founding charter and multiple Maori and Pakeha voices that interpret the Treaty's relevance for the contemporary nation and its diverse peoples.[9] Although this conception of Aotearoa/New Zealand is not uncontested, in many ways the new museum stands as a monument to efforts made over the last two decades by both Maori and Pakeha to heal old wounds from a turbulent history of racial conflict and aggressive attempts by dominant settlers to impose a British-derived monoculture. As an American visitor accustomed to the marginalization of indigenous peoples in representations of the United States, I found the innovative architecture of "Te Papa" and the high visibility of the progressive politics that undergird its design nothing less than breathtaking. More to the point, the new structure and the provocative concept of its design are suggestive of the national impact of Maori writing and activism in the early contemporary period. And they draw attention to possible models for the representation of indigeneity in the United States, such as a paradigm of treaty partners or of fluid movement between separation and alliance.

Blood Narrative is organized to foreground a comparative methodology, and both part 1 (World War II–1960s) and part 2 (1960s–1970s) move from materials produced by Maori toward materials produced by American Indians. The several visits I made to Aotearoa/New Zealand between 1987 and 1998 to study contemporary Maori language, literature, and political activism, including a full year in 1994 working with faculty and students in the Department of Maori Studies at Auckland University, suggested a rich comparative context for better understanding the rhetorical complexity and the particular dynamics of (post)coloniality evident in American Indian literature and activism. In limiting my focus to the period I consider early contemporary, that is, the period that begins with the onset of World War II and ends—or, more accurately, is transformed—sometime during the early 1980s, I concentrate on the less well known but formative period that set the stage for the innovative, better-known work of indigenous minority writers who emerged in the final quarter of the twentieth century.

For New Zealand Maori and for American Indians, as for so many communities around the globe, the early contemporary period was an era of rapid change, affecting everything from local economies and political structures to national residency patterns and birthrates to international travel, communication, and coalition. Both Maori and American Indians fought on behalf of their contemporary nations during World War II and joined their nations' war support efforts in remarkable numbers. The events of the war and the formation of the United Nations at its end spurred these men and women to pursue their longstanding efforts to assert cultural and political distinctiveness with renewed vigor. During the war years and in the first decades of the war's aftermath, Maori and American Indians worked largely within dominant discourses in their efforts to define and to assert viable contemporary indigenous identities. But by the late 1960s and early 1970s, when the children of World War II veterans came of age, both New Zealand and the United States felt the effects of an emerging indigenous renaissance, marked by dramatic events of political and cultural activism and by unprecedented levels of literary production. By the mid-1970s, Maori and American Indians were part of a burgeoning international indigenous rights movement, signaled by, among other events, the formation and first general assembly of the World Council of Indigenous Peoples (WCIP).

Writers and activists who identified as Maori or American Indian in this period produced, appropriated, and/or revalued both indigenous and nonindigenous discourses for their contemporary purposes; they also created, appropriated, reclaimed, refashioned, and/or juxtaposed powerful tropes, emblematic figures, and distinctive genre conventions in their efforts to represent the increasing complexity of contemporary indigenous minority identities. The primary concern of *Blood Narrative* is to better understand Maori and American Indian discursive practices and their effectiveness for various audiences, to better understand, that is, how indigenous minority writers and activists *mark* and thus construct contemporary indigenous identities as distinct from settler and other nonindigenous identities in their particular nations and in the larger global context.

Some Preliminary Terminology

Indigenous peoples can be defined as those populations that were already resident when Europeans or other colonizers invaded, occupied, and/or settled their traditional territories. Such a general definition of indigeneity—"original inhabitants"—is of limited use, however, when applied to examples of colonial relations in specific geographical locations and during specific historical periods. Distinctions can be drawn, for instance, among, one, indigenous peoples who have remained majority populations in their homelands; two, indigenous peoples who were dislocated to foreign territories, where they may have displaced other indigenous peoples (becoming, in effect, settlers themselves) and where they may have become either majority or minority populations; and, three, indigenous peoples who have become minorities in lands they once controlled. New Zealand Maori and

American Indians fall into the last category of indigenous minorities, along with Alaska Natives and Native Hawaiians in the United States, First Nations peoples in Canada, and Aboriginal peoples and Torres Strait Islanders in Australia. Other, perhaps less obvious indigenous minorities include Smaller Peoples in the Russian Federation, Sami in the Scandinavian countries, and Ainu in Japan.

There has been increasing debate over whether the circumstances under which indigenous minorities live in First World settler nations like Aotearoa/New Zealand and the United States are best described as "colonialism," "postcolonialism," "internal colonialism," "para-colonialism," "domestic imperialism," or something else. I take up this debate in some detail in the introduction to part 1, and there I offer a justification for my own use throughout the book of the term *(post)colonial,* which employs parentheses to emphasize the irony of an often-asserted post-colonial situation (where the hyphenated "post-" implies "beyond") that is never quite one for indigenous minorities. I want to note here that additional generalizing labels have been affixed to indigenous minorities along these different lines, some generated by indigenous peoples themselves, including the relatively politically neutral terms "original nations," "domestic nations," or "nations within," and the more overtly politically radical terms "internal colonies" and "captive" or "occupied" nations. Some Maori activists, for example, designate New Zealand as "Occupied Aotearoa." In Canada, both indigenous peoples and settlers currently use the term "First Nations" to refer collectively to American Indian, Inuit, and Métis peoples; some U.S. American Indians employ it as well. This term is notable for its implications of historic memory coupled with its relative political neutrality: "First Nations" suggests both prior occupancy of territory and prior political organization (and thus self-determinacy) without overtly carrying accusations of violence or theft against majority populations of European-descended settlers in Canada or the United States.

In the international arena, two generalizing labels for indigenous peoples have come into common currency. "First Peoples" is a United Nations term that is applied to indigenous peoples in all parts of the world, whether they are majority or minority populations, while "Fourth World" is a more politically radical term that is often, though not always, limited to indigenous minorities. Both terms acknowledge indigenous status—claims of deep historical, cultural, and spiritual ties to specific lands—as a legitimate rationale for collective political identity at local, national and, potentially, international levels. But unlike the term "First Peoples," "Fourth World" serves to distinguish the particular historical contexts and contemporary concerns of indigenous minorities from those of the majority indigenous populations of so-called developing or Third World nations, as well as from those of the majority-settler First World populations that now occupy and control most of the traditional territories claimed by indigenous minorities like Maori and American Indians.[10] It is for this reason that I employ "Fourth World" as a general term for indigenous minority peoples.

The Fourth World condition is marked by a perennial struggle between "native" indigeneity and "settler" or "New World" indigeneity. Stated briefly, aboriginal inhabitants of what are now First World nations have been forced to compete for *indigenous* status with European settlers and their descendants eager to construct new identities that separate them from European antecedents. Indigenous minority assertions of prior claims to land, resources, languages, and cultures—above all, of the right to maintain some level of cultural and political distinctiveness—appear to threaten settlers' constructions of an available New World and to call into question settlers' attempts to assert their own cultural distinctiveness from Europe.[11] This is a struggle over definitional control (who will be allowed to define themselves as "indigenous") in which the stakes continue to be high: the right to claim tangible resources such as land, minerals, timber, and fisheries, as well as the right to claim intangible but nonetheless highly valuable political, social, and symbolic resources such as authenticity and legitimacy. And it is a struggle over definitional control that continues to be regulated by tensions among the contradictory desires of dominant settlers to identify with indigenous peoples, to supersede them, and to eradicate them completely, either through absorption or genocide. This complex struggle has, at least in part, motivated settlers' calls for all inhabitants of their nations to behave as one people, to self-identify as part of a dominant culture and to speak a dominant language. The same complex struggle has motivated politically and militarily dominant settlers either to invalidate claims of native status through acts of legislation (for example, requirements of blood quantum, endogamous marriage, or patrilineal descent, or the granting/imposition of national citizenship) or to deny indigenous claims to collective rights guaranteed by international law by unilaterally redefining indigenous peoples and nations as "populations," "groups," "societies," "persons," and "ethnic minorities."[12] As settlers' projects for establishing cultural authenticity and national legitimacy have developed over time, claims of native indigeneity often have been ignored.

The Occasion of Indigeneity

In her seminal 1975 analysis *Hui: A Study of Maori Ceremonial Gatherings*, New Zealand anthropologist Anne Salmond argues persuasively for taking an "occasional" approach to the study of "formal Maori culture" and postcontact Maori identity, rather than trying to analyze the contemporary Maori situation as an integrated whole (210). Drawing on Erving Goffman's theories of the "significance of situations as frames for action" (3), Salmond points out that "in contact situations everywhere, minority groups maintain their distinct identities in episodic sub-cultures, which carry over from one special occasion to the next" (210). I extend Salmond's idea of the significance of Maori cultural "occasions" in order to analyze diverse performances of indigenous identity within and alongside the larger performance of the contemporary settler nation.[13]

Salmond's description of "contact situations" is somewhat limited by its clear division between indigenous- and settler-controlled spaces. According to Salmond, the contemporary marae (Maori community facility) is "a last outpost of traditional culture," where "*Maoritanga* [Maoriness or Maori identity] comes into its sharpest definition, whereas in other situations, especially in the cities, it plays at best a background role" (210). A more refined assessment becomes possible by engaging Homi Bhabha's notion of the performativity of all cultural engagements, where "the social articulation of difference, from the minority perspective, is a complex, on-going negotiation," as well as by engaging Mary Louise Pratt's definition of "contact zones": "social spaces where cultures meet, clash, and grapple with each other, often in contexts of highly asymmetrical relations of power."[14] These theories help articulate the fact that the contemporary marae is not simply a bastion of "traditional" Maori culture located away from the contact zones and cultural negotiations of the city, where non-Maori rules and values dominate. The contemporary marae, whether rural or urban, is also a complex contact zone itself, where Maori meet not only other Maori, with whom they may or may not share common experiences, traditions, and views, but also a diverse range of Pakeha (Europeans), as well as migrant or immigrant Pacific Islanders, various individuals of mixed blood and mixed heritage, and, increasingly, non-European and non-Polynesian immigrants and tourists. Maori rules and values may dominate on the marae but, as at other locations in the contemporary settler nation, they do not dominate free from the potential oppo-sition—or free from the potential appropriation—of racial or cul-tural outsiders. In diverse social spaces with asymmetrical relations of power, including the marae, Maori individuals and communities negotiate the potential and situational forms and meanings of contem-porary Maori identity through various modes of cultural performance. As Te Awekotuku states succinctly, "Creativity was a potent weapon in political battle [within precontact Maori society and, in the contact era, between Maori and Pakeha]—and it has remained so" (164). Much the same can be said of the complex cultural negotiations performed at contemporary American Indian tribal and pan-tribal social, religious, political, academic, or activist events, which are as diverse as the closed conferences of elders conducted during the meeting of the Wabanaki Confederacy held in Maine and the public dances staged for tourists during the Gallup Ceremonial held in New Mexico. In the new mil-lennium, such negotiations increasingly occur as well in cyberspace.

Salmond's paradigm of minority cultural "episodes" and "occasions" can be expanded to include events of political and cultural activism and, broadly defined, literary and activist texts. For these purposes it is useful to conceive of events of indigenous protest as both instances of ethnopolitical conflict and performances of ethno-drama.[15] Activist events—demonstrations, marches, and occupations—employ ideolog-ical interpretive frames such as "Kotahitanga" (Unity), "Red Power," or "nationalism" that help assign meaning to movement participation and to specific protest activities.[16] Designed to highlight ethnic differences between the majority settler population and the particular indigenous minority people, these events also tend to have an immediately discern-able dramatic structure. They stage the "facts" of persistent indigenous presences and a version of contemporary indigenous "reality." They often also endeavor to make it possible for members of the dominant culture to see and/or to understand certain cultural and political "truths," such as the continuing importance of the ancestral land base to indigenous identity or the continuing relevance of historic treaties and other negotiated agreements. As drama, these events routinely mobilize powerful emblematic representations of Native identity, whether along tribal, pan-tribal, or pan-indigenous lines, that respond to the expectations—and that often are shaped by the expressed needs—of particular audiences.[17] Typically, in the period covered by the present study, the specific circumstances and the particular charismatic leaders of individual activist events could bring together a wide range of tribal groups, women and men, rural and urban individuals, and diverse radical and moderate protest factions only for a limited period of time, for a particular occasion or set of occasions, for a particular performance or set of performances.

Similarly, it is useful to conceive of indigenous minority texts as "occasions" for the performance of indigeneity, as "episodes" in the ongoing negotiation of contemporary indigenous minority identities. An occasional and episodic approach invites us to read particular literary and activist texts as responses to the multiple motivations for their creation and, potentially, as co-creators of the multiple contexts of their reception—local, national, and global—rather than to focus on their conformity or lack of conformity to a given set of standards for authenticity or aesthetic excellence. Navajo poet Luci Tapahonso explicitly compares her acts of writing to her "occasional" visits to the Navajo nation, and she describes her works as "enabling myself and other Navajos to sojourn mentally and emotionally to our home, Din-étah."[18] Tapahonso's statements suggest that there is often more than one text in play during public performances of indigenous minority identities and often more than one audience able to interpret the markers of indigeneity in contemporary texts.

The latter point was made dramatically clear to me during a "Maori concert" I attended in December 1994 at the renowned War Memorial Museum in Auckland.[19] Although I lived for almost a year within a block of the museum, I avoided the Maori concert regularly performed there until the week before my return to the United States. Given the museum's central location on the New Zealand tourist trail, I feared the concert would disappoint because it would not feel "authentic." As I predicted, the concert's sizable audience consisted of European and Asian tourists, most of whom had arrived at the museum on commercial tour buses. Also as I predicted, the concert's program of waiata (songs), waiata-a-ringa (action songs), and haka (chants with actions), while highly accomplished and entertaining, was designed to present mostly static images of the "traditional Maori," that is, the Maori before contact with Europeans. The performers wore "traditional" costumes, and no mention was made of the diverse lives that Maori people lead today. Unknown to me or to the other tourists, however, a local Maori school group arrived during the performance and was seated at the rear of the auditorium. At the performance's conclusion, amid the bustle of moving chairs and the chatter of several European and Asian languages, the Maori school group unexpectedly reframed the "text" of the concert. Suddenly, I became aware that much more had been at stake during the performance than simply welcoming foreign visitors, teaching cultural outsiders, or earning a few tourist dollars.

When the staged portion of the concert ended, the school group's leader, a Maori man, stood up at the back of the room and began to whaikorero (deliver a speech) in response to the performers' efforts. His group, about fifteen or twenty Maori adolescents and a Maori woman who was likely another teacher, arranged themselves behind him to stand in support. The Maori man's voice rang out over the tourists' conversations. In eloquent Maori, he formally addressed the concert troupe, acknowledging their considerable effort and telling them how important it is for Maori young people to have opportunities to see and hear these aspects of Maori culture and to see and hear them performed so well. Although the performers were caught off guard, they quickly assessed the situation and lined up below the stage to listen politely. The tourist audience, who had been told that the concert was over and that the performers would shake hands with them as they filed out of the auditorium, was visibly confused. Families and other small groups continued to converse; several individuals pushed their way past the Maori students to get to the door. Others openly expressed their discomfort. When the Maori man finished his speech, his group supported him by singing a waiata. In response, one of the male members of the concert troupe made a short speech in Maori; his group, now better organized, performed a short waiata to support their speaker. Only now, after this exchange of korero and waiata between manuhiri (guests) and tangata whenua (hosts), was the concert considered complete for these participants. The unexpected deployment of Maori language, dialogue between Maori speakers, and the recognizable conventions of whaikorero and waiata shifted the focus of the concert from a primarily "tourist" performance to a significantly "Maori" performance, serving distinctly Maori purposes. In effect, the occasion of the concert was reframed in terms of a Maori ethno-nationalist discourse. And once reframed, at least for certain readers, the concert could function as an activist event. The active presence of the Maori school group disrupted the "museumification" of Maori culture for tourist consumption, and it revealed the text of the staged concert as a potential force for galvanizing the younger generation's sense of its Maoritanga (Maori identity). Strikingly, this shift in the concert's interpretive ideological frame occurred not covertly but openly, literally over the heads of the tourist audience.

In the chapters that follow, I take an occasional approach in order to analyze indigenous minority texts as particular episodes in the ongoing negotiations and performances of post–World War II New Zealand Maori and American Indian identities as *indigenous* identities. Further, in order to highlight how the construction of indigenous identity in Aotearoa/New Zealand and the United States has been transformed over time, I organize each chapter in relation to the two overarching theoretical terms that emerge from my comparative analysis: first, what I call the blood/land/memory complex and, second, a specific manifestation of that complex, the discourse of treaties. I offer initial definitions for these terms below; in subsequent chapters, I refine and expand these definitions as I employ each term in specific analyses. In foregrounding the blood/land/memory complex and treaty discourse, it is not my intention to suggest that these terms can account for the construction of meaning in all contemporary Maori or American Indian texts. Analysis of oral literatures in English and indigenous languages and of various forms of local writing and publication, such as tribal or iwi newspapers, for instance, are mostly beyond the scope of the present study. Rather, I use these overarching terms to focus my analysis on two sets of related narrative tactics for asserting indigeneity that largely have been unexplored in recent scholarship on indigenous minority writing, the significance of which becomes especially clear within a comparative New Zealand Maori–American Indian framework.

Blood/Land/Memory:
Defining and Defending Indigenous Minority Identities

The intimate "and/or" juxtaposition of these three highly charged terms is meant to be suggestive of the Fourth World condition experienced by contemporary Maori and American Indians. *Blood, land,* and *memory* name primary and interrelated sites in the struggle over defining indigenous minority identities in Aotearoa/New Zealand and in the United States; they also name three primary and interrelated tropes or emblematic figures that contemporary indigenous minority writers and activists have developed in their works in the post–World War II era to counter and, potentially, to subvert dominant settler discourses.

Individually, each of these terms, along with the cluster of potential meanings it represents, has been and continues to be considered controversial. Discussions of indigenous "blood," for example, often raise disturbing issues of essentialism, racism, and genocide. These discussions also raise the vexed issue of how to define and certify contemporary indigenous identities in Aotearoa/New Zealand and in the United States given the demographic reality of large numbers of "mixed-blood" individuals and communities. Government officials, social scientists, and indigenous minority peoples themselves have disagreed over whether biological kinship, language, culture, group consciousness, community endorsement, personal declaration, or some combination of these "objective" and "subjective" criteria should be used to recognize "authentic" indigenous status. Discussions of indigenous "land" often raise equally disturbing issues of colonial reterritorialization: the historical and contemporary attempts to decode and recode indigenous lands so that they can be appropriated into the colonial power's economic and cultural systems.[20] And often they expose, more specifically, the ongoing colonial practices in New Zealand and the United States of forcibly expropriating resources from indigenous peoples for the benefit of settlers. Further, these discussions draw attention to continuing assaults on lands that remain under indigenous control (and to ongoing assaults on the people who inhabit those lands) through flooding for hydroelectric projects, mining, weapons testing, and hazardous waste disposal.[21] And discussions of indigenous "memory" often reveal the underlying disparities that still exist between indigenous and invading peoples' conceptions of history, as well as the underlying unequal power relations that determine whose version of history and whose methods of historiography are considered "legitimate" and "authentic" in various popular, academic, and legal contexts.

However disconcerting these issues may prove for particular audiences, including those U.S. scholars who have lamented the possible racist connotations, especially, in the indigenous (re)deployment of "blood," it is imperative that we contextualize the discursive appeal and symbolic power of these emblematic figures. What I call the blood/land/memory complex is an expansion of Momaday's controversial trope blood memory that makes explicit the central role that land plays both in the specific project of defining indigenous minority personal, familial, and communal identities (blood) and in the larger project of reclaiming and reimagining indigenous minority histories (memory). Like Momaday's trope, the blood/land/memory complex articulates acts of indigenous minority recuperation that attempt to seize control of the symbolic and metaphorical meanings of indigenous "blood," "land," and "memory" and that seek to liberate indigenous minority identities from definitions of authenticity imposed by dominant settler cultures, including those definitions imposed by well-meaning academics.[22] Throughout the book, I employ the blood/land/memory complex as a useful construct for analyzing assertions of indigenous identity and authenticity. Although other scholars have used these individual terms or their cognates to examine the construction of Native identity in American Indian texts, typically they have focused on one and excluded the others. I argue that these terms and their potential meanings must be examined together, as a complex set of interactions, so that we can better understand the ways Maori and American Indian writers and activists both juxtapose and integrate "real" and "imagined" genealogies, physical and metaphorical ancestral land bases, and narratives of "real" and "invented" histories in their constructions of viable contemporary indigenous identities. Moreover, I argue that the blood/land/memory complex, like Momaday's trope blood memory, names both the process and the product of the indigenous minority writer situating him- or herself within a particular indigenous family's or nation's "racial memory" of its relationship with specific lands.[23]

Indigeneity, Hybridity, and the Discourse of Treaties

In multicultural settler nations like the United States and Aotearoa/ New Zealand, the discourse of treaties stands out as a distinguishing feature of the discursive relationship between indigenous peoples and settler-invaders. The treaty-making process implicitly recognizes the sovereignty of indigenous nations; specific treaty documents explicitly vow that imperial or settler governments will uphold that sovereignty. Since it operates within a paradigm of nation-to-nation status, the discourse of treaties, like the discourse of declarations of war or declarations of independence, provides one of the few interpretive frames within which contemporary indigenous minority activists and writers can stage formal dialogue with dominant settler interests on (potentially) equitable terms. Because historic treaties recognize indigenous nations as sovereign, they continue to offer strong legal and moral bases from which indigenous minority peoples can argue for land and resources rights as well as articulate cultural and identity politics. By imposing one group's expectations on the other even as it envisions their reconciliation, the discourse of historic treaties is simultaneously pragmatic and idealistic. It therefore offers indigenous minority activists and writers a widely recognized symbol and a set of widely recognized statements through which they can not only express anger over past and present acts of colonial violence but, at the same time, continue to imagine the possibility of future peace. In other words, the indigenous minority appropriation of treaty discourse is a specific and powerful manifestation of the blood/land/memory complex.

I argue in the chapters that follow that the appropriation and redeployment of treaty discourse helps define the particular type of (post)colonial hybridity at work in many New Zealand Maori and American Indian texts produced in the post–World War II era. Analyses of Maori and American Indian mobilizations of treaty discourse force us to question the usefulness of theories of hybridity and mimicry that totalize the discursive strategies of various colonized and formerly colonized peoples. Much of so-called orthodox postcolonial theory emphasizes what it defines as an ambivalence inherent in colonial discourses; by revealing or exploiting this ambivalence, so the argument goes, "natives" or indigenous "subalterns" have been able to effectively de-center European colonial discourses from their positions of power and authority in India, Africa, and the Caribbean. As evidenced by the frequently cited, comprehensive study *The Empire Writes Back* (1989) by Bill Ashcroft, Gareth Griffiths, and Helen Tiffin, typical readings of postcolonial literary texts rightly celebrate the ways in which these works often deploy "a number of counter-discursive strategies, re-entering the western episteme at one of its most fundamental points of origination to deconstruct those notions and processes which rationalized the imposition of the imperial word on the rest of the world" (104). Although useful in a general sense, this theory of postcolonial hybridity offers no terms by which to account for the ways indigenous minorities like New Zealand Maori or American Indians might *re-recognize*, rather than deconstruct, the authority of particular colonial discourses, such as treaties, for their own gain.[24]

To take another well-known example, Homi Bhabha, in his influential essay collection *The Location of Culture* (1994), details historical and literary events in which dominant British discourses (and, in particular, the European book) are "displaced," "transformed," and "transfigured" in their "discovery" and "repetition" in colonial India, Africa, and the Caribbean. In its displacement through mimicry, Bhabha argues, the basis of colonial discourse—its "rules of recognition"—is "estranged." The thrust of Bhabha's complicated thesis is that this particular manifestation of hybridity, this process of displacement and estrangement, is paradigmatic of all indigenous resistance to dominating discourses. In Bhabha's formulation, "Hybridity [always] represents that ambivalent 'turn' of the discriminated subject into the terrifying, exorbitant object of paranoid classification—a disturbing questioning of the images and presences of authority" (113). Like Ashcroft, Griffiths, and Tiffin's version of postcolonial reading practices, Bhabha's model is attractively optimistic and extremely useful for understanding the disruptive potential of discursive hybridity.[25] It is untenable, however, as a generalization across diverse cultures and across diverse histories of colonial encounters. To look at only two potential examples, in Aotearoa/New Zealand and in the United States the (post)colonial hybridity of the indigenous minority encounter with treaty discourse—and, in particular, with the Euro-American "book" of treaty documents—operates differently and has opposite aims.

The dominant power in both New Zealand and the United States disavowed the discourse of treaties almost as soon as the ink was dry, arguing that the promises inscribed in treaty documents and the recognition of sovereignty inherent in the treaty-making process are not binding on the settler nation. Once disavowed, treaty documents and the events of treaty making could be transformed into mere abstractions—platitudes of good faith, understatements of treachery—with no concrete relevance. In contrast, Maori and American Indian appropriations and redeployments of treaty discourse work to re-recognize and, in the process, to revalue the discourse of treaties. Treaty documents are neither "transformed" nor "transfigured" by these activists and writers, and the authority inscribed in treaties is generally not questioned. Instead, this disavowed discourse is reified—reclaimed from impotent abstraction and once again rendered concrete. To rephrase Bhabha's definition of colonial mimicry as "almost the same, *but not quite,*" we might define indigenous re-recognition as "exactly the same, *but then some.*" Indigenous minority redeployments of treaty discourse insist that the dominant power remember the cross-cultural and cross-national agreements it forged with indigenous nations during previous eras; contradicting Bhabha, they reinstate and reinvigorate this colonial discourse's original powers of legal enforcement and moral suasion. Such redeployments work, therefore, as at the new Museum of New Zealand Te Papa Tongarewa, to re-center the discourse of treaties, to re-establish treaty documents as powerful and authoritative and as binding on the contemporary settler nation.

There are subtle but significant differences between how Maori and American Indian activists and writers redeploy the discourse of historic treaties in early contemporary texts. Maori activists and writers tend to mobilize the competing discourses of the bilingual Treaty of Waitangi as allegory. This strategy is made possible by the fact that, unlike in the United States, where the federal government's representatives negotiated nearly four hundred separate treaties with indigenous nations between 1788 and 1868, in Aotearoa/New Zealand the British Crown's representative negotiated a single written agreement, the Treaty of Waitangi, which was eventually "signed" by more than five hundred Maori rangatira or "chiefs."[26] However, there are four extant versions of the 1840 Treaty: three English-language versions, which are similar in content and which only a few rangatira signed, and one Maori-language version, which diverges from the English texts and on which the vast majority of rangatira inscribed their names or identifying marks. Although the Treaty was never ratified by the New Zealand Parliament, its brief contents are well known. Today, New Zealanders generally consider it their nation's founding document (or documents) and a charter for ongoing relations between Maori, the government, and Pakeha (European) settlers. Maori, moreover, have long considered the Treaty both a sacred covenant and an esteemed taonga, a "treasured possession" handed down from their ancestors.[27] As a result, Te Tiriti o Waitangi/the Treaty of Waitangi provides a "silent second text" against which contemporary Maori works can be read as allegory.[28] But because this silent second text speaks in two distinct, conflicting voices, the resultant allegory always explicitly rehearses the difficulty of reconciling the Treaty's divergent Maori- and English-language versions. However strongly a particular allegory might promote one version, it cannot suppress the other. Even in those works that never allude to treaty documents specifically, tension between competing Maori and Pakeha versions of the "truth" often is suggestive of treaty allegory. This effect is only enhanced in bilingual and dual-language texts.

In contrast, American Indian activists and writers tend to redeploy treaty discourse as metaphor and metonymy—but, strikingly, not as allegory. Since so many individual treaties were signed in the United States, neither the specific contents of any one treaty document nor the details of any particular treaty dispute are well enough known to provide the basis for allegory, especially for national audiences. Instead, American Indian activists and writers evoke the discursive characteristics of treaties as metaphors for Indian-White relations and inscribe treaty documents in their texts as metonyms for the promises made—and most often broken—by the federal government. American Indian activists and writers typically foreground the generalized contents and surface features of a treaty, including the physical characteristics of the document itself as well as the rhetorical and literary style, figures of speech, and narrative devices in and associated with its preamble and specific articles. This move is obviously strategic, since dominant Euro-American culture typically has foregrounded the context of treaties in order to disavow their discourse. Inevitably, both the U.S. government and White U.S. citizens have had to argue that treaty promises are politically retrograde, a discourse without contemporary meaning that was designed in the past to pacify Indians or ameliorate their inevitable subjugation. The dominant culture has had to foreground the idea that treaty documents were little more than bothersome formalities, or that they were ruses designed to deceive, or that, whatever the federal government's intentions at the time of signing, treaty promises are no longer practical for the nation. This appears especially true in discussions of those nearly two hundred mid-nineteenth-century treaties that were negotiated in the years spanning the large-scale removals of southeastern Indian nations to the Indian Territory west of the Mississippi River and the final large-scale "Indian wars" fought on the central, southern, and northern plains. Although such arguments are promoted as the exposure of important truths hidden behind the facades of actual treaty documents, their effect is not to reveal some politically neutral "truth" but rather to undermine the sovereignty of American Indian nations recognized in past eras. To counter this selective and defensive amnesia, American Indian activists and writers foreground, as I have suggested above, precisely those surface features of treaties that the dominant culture wishes to ignore. Both metaphoric and metonymic redeployments of treaty discourse draw attention to the idea that treaties are not only the founding discourse for peaceful relations between American Indian nations and the United States but also undeniable records of binding agreements, whatever the U.S. government may have intended at the time of signing or may desire today.

Despite tactical differences, both New Zealand Maori and American Indian writers and activists engage the discourse of treaties as one of the sanctioned discourses for inscribing stories about indigenous minorities in First World nations. But—and here is the critical maneuver—they refuse to engage, and even mock, the subsequent rules of recognition that have enabled the dominant culture to (mis)read treaty discourse as an enduring sign of Maori or Indian subjugation rather than as an enduring sign of compromise between mutually respected sovereignties. These writers' and activists' hard-won subversion is manifest in their re-recognition of a treaty discourse that acknowledges indigenous sovereignty and in their insistence on the continuing authority of that original recognition. Given the demographic and political realities of indigenous minorities, such maneuvers represent a deft set of tactics for facilitating activist occupation of significant sites of colonial discourse. Like physical occupations of confiscated lands, literary occupations of treaty discourse do not seek to disrupt or displace the dominant colonial narrative but rather to realign its contemporary consumption with the terms of the relevant past, to assert that it has an ongoing rather than a narrowly situated authenticity.[29]

Organization of the Book

The comparative methodology employed in *Blood Narrative* has necessitated a somewhat elaborate structure. Following this general introduction, the book is divided into two parts, each of which comprises an introduction and two chapters; the book ends with a separate chapter-length conclusion. Part 1 concentrates on the period from World War II through the early 1960s. The introduction to part 1 begins with an assessment of the usefulness of postcolonial theory for reading indigenous minority literary and activist texts. It then examines the relevant historical and social contexts during and in the early decades after World War II for Aotearoa/New Zealand and the United States, and sets up the central comparative argument of part 1. Chapter 1 investigates the primary site for Maori publication in this period, the government-sponsored journal *Te Ao Hou/The New World*, while chapter 2 investigates the early evolution of contemporary American Indian writing, with a particular focus on the work of Ruth Muskrat Bronson, Ella Cara Deloria, John Joseph Mathews, D'Arcy McNickle, and delegates to the 1961 American Indian Chicago Conference. Part 2 concentrates on the period of the 1960s through the end of the 1970s (with occasional forays into the 1980s to develop particular themes). The introduction to part 2 begins by assessing the usefulness of multiculturalist paradigms for reading indigenous minority texts. As in part 1, it then examines the relevant historical and social contexts in this period for Aotearoa/New Zealand and the United States and sets up the central comparative argument of part 2. Chapter 3 explores the narrative tactics developed in a wide range of literary and activist texts produced during the period of the so-called Maori renaissance, which began about 1970. Special attention is paid to works by Witi Ihimaera, Patricia Grace, Harry Dansey, Merata Mita, Keri Hulme, Apirana Taylor, and Bruce Stewart. Chapter 4 explores narrative tactics developed by an equally wide range of activists and writers during the period of the so-called American Indian renaissance, which began several years earlier, about 1964. Special attention here is paid to works by the activist group Indians of All Tribes, the Navajo nation, Vine Deloria Jr., Dallas Chief Eagle, James Welch, Leslie Marmon Silko, Joy Harjo, N. Scott Momaday, and Gerald Vizenor. The conclusion connects part 1 and part 2 and examines the beginnings of a larger international context for indigenous minority literary and activist texts. After chronicling the formation of the World Council of Indigenous Peoples (WCIP) in the mid-1970s and analyzing the WCIP's founding documents, the Conclusion links both the successes and the failures of the WCIP's narrative tactics to the emerging body of "indigenous theory" that has developed in the United States and Aotearoa/New Zealand since the 1970s.

As an appendix, I include an "Integrated Time Line," which covers the years from the beginning of World War II to 1980. I list national and international government actions, political activism, and publications relevant to American Indians, New Zealand Maori, and other Fourth World peoples. It is my hope that this appendix will serve as a map of what can seem a confusing international Fourth World situation. It is also my hope that this appendix, while not exhaustive, will help make visible the many conjunctions and coalitions among indigenous minority peoples that occurred during this period at the local, national, and global levels.

A Note on Maori Language

Except where I felt it would be useful for emphasis or clarity, I have chosen not to draw attention to Maori words, phrases, or passages with italics. My decision to give Maori language the same status as English follows the typical practice of contemporary authors in Aotearoa/New Zealand. For the sake of simplicity, I have chosen not to mark long vowels in Maori either with a macron (for example, Pākehā) or by doubling the vowel (for example, Paakehaa), except when vowel markings are part of a quotation. Contemporary writers are divided over which system works best, and some Maori writers prefer no vowel markings at all.

The Maori language was developed into a writing system by early

British missionaries. The written language consists of eight consonants (*h, k, m, n, p, r, t,* and *w*), two digraphs (*ng* and *wh*), and five vowels (*a, e, i, o, u*), each of which can be short or long. The consonants are pronounced similarly to their English counterparts, except that the *r* is slightly rolled. *Ng,* a nasalized *n,* is pronounced as in *singer* (but not as in *finger*). *Wh* is pronounced either as in *whale* or, more commonly in contemporary Maori speech, as a soft *f.* The vowels are pronounced as follows:

short *a* like *u* in "nut"	long *a* like *a* in "Chicago"
short *e* like *e* in "peck"	long *e* like *ai* in "pair"
short *i* like *i* in "pit"	long *i* like *ee* in "peep"
short *o* like *o* in "colt"	long *o* like *o* in "orb"
short *u* like *u* in "put"	long *u* like *oo* in "moon"

In Maori diphthongs, each vowel is sounded but usually glided over without a break.[30]

PART I

A DIRECTED SELF-DETERMINATION

The Maori people are facing social problems which have to be solved partly by the reiteration of certain ideas. These ideas are to help the integration of the Maori people with the community as a whole. . . . Te Ao Hou is a publicity medium with the above-mentioned aims. In fact, the reason for the existence of Te Ao Hou is to promote these objectives, and it is not justified for any other reason.—Memorandum from the Director, New Zealand Information Service, 20 March 1956

Philosophically speaking, the Indian wardship problem brings up basically the questionable merit of treating the Indian of today as an Indian, rather than as a fellow American citizen. . . . Following in the footsteps of the Emancipation Proclamation of ninety-four years ago, I see the following words emblazoned in letters of fire above the heads of the Indians—THESE PEOPLE SHALL BE FREE!
—Senator Arthur V. Watkins (R.-Utah), May 1957

IRREVERSIBLY, WORLD WAR II provoked both large- and small-scale changes in the lives of New Zealand Maori and American Indians. As has been both celebrated and lamented in the decades since, indigenous minorities responded to the contemporary call to arms in numbers far disproportionate to their small percentage of their nation's general population. In Aotearoa/New Zealand, large numbers of Maori men and women experienced the world outside their rural tribal communities—both within and outside the nation—for the first time through military and civilian defense service. When war broke out in 1939, "young men in their hundreds joined the Maori Battalion for service overseas."[1] At home, men and women joined the Maori War Effort Organization; many moved to the cities to work in munitions factories and other "essential industries." By war's end in 1945, when the total Maori population—men, women, and children—was estimated at only 100,000, over 17,000 Maori men had enlisted for military service and at least another 11,500 Maori men and women had worked in the agricultural and industrial war effort.[2] In the United States, American Indian men and women participated in the war with similar enthusiasm. An estimated 25,000 Indian men—or more than one-third of all eligible Indian men between the ages of eighteen and fifty—saw active duty in American fighting forces; over eight hundred Indian women served as nurses or in the military's auxiliary branches.[3] Other indigenous women either joined the Red Cross or the American Women's Voluntary Service or worked in their local communities to produce necessary provisions for American troops or to raise money.[4] Although there were isolated cases of resistance to the draft on grounds of citizenship or treaty disputes, Indians, like their Maori counterparts, overwhelmingly volunteered for military service.[5] In addition, also like their Maori counterparts, an estimated 40,000 Indian men and women willingly joined the industrial and agricultural war support effort, leaving their reservation homes for factory work—in cities like Los Angeles, Tulsa, Denver, and Albuquerque—or for work in shipyards, railroad gangs, coal and copper mines, sawmills, farming enterprises, and canneries around the country.[6] Quite suddenly, formerly isolated and economically disadvantaged indigenous minorities were integrated into the industries and institutions that were located at the strategic center of national life and at the emotional core of the dominant culture's sense of its own authenticity and legitimacy. And thus situated, they were able to earn, most for the first time, the financial resources required to purchase the tangible signs of that mainstream life.

Part I explores the construction of indigenous identity in New Zealand Maori and American Indian literary and activist texts in the early decades after the beginning of World War II. This was a period when indigenous minority writers and activists worked overwhelmingly either within the confines of or at some high level of compliance with dominant discourses. Given this context of political conservatism, it seems fair to ask, To what degree were indigenous minority writers and activists able to resist pressures to promote assimilation? Which discursive forms were most productive for advocating indigenous distinctiveness and indigenous opposition? Under conditions of institutionalized surveillance and ongoing supervision, was "opposition" possible as we recognize it today and, if so, how might we now distinguish between acts of complicity with dominant power and acts of contestation? American Indian writer and critic Gerald Vizenor challenges readers to consider specific historical and tribal contexts when deciding whether or not particular texts qualify as "resistance." He reassesses the romantic portrayals of camp life produced by Charles Eastman (Sioux) at the turn of the twentieth century, for example, as a "wise" resistance literature given the context of the recent massacre at Wounded Knee. Eastman, Vizenor writes, "celebrated peace and the romance of tribal stories to overcome the morose remembrance of the Wounded Knee Massacre [in 1890]. Could there have been a wiser resistance literature or simulation of survivance at the time?" Vizenor then asks, "What did it mean to be the first generation to hear the stories of the past, bear the horrors of the moment, and write to the future? What were tribal identities at the turn of the century?"[7] For the early contemporary period, we can ask, What did it mean to be the first generation to move in such large numbers into the "enemy territory" of the dominant society and its discourses? What were viable indigenous minority identities—and what were the public markers of those identities—in the first decades after entry into World War II?

To help answer these questions, it is useful, as Vizenor's analysis of

Eastman's turn-of-the-century tactics suggests, to distinguish between "direct" and "indirect" forms of political opposition. Unlike direct opposition, which openly confronts dominant power, an indirect or "symbolic" opposition works to rally indigenous minority peoples around emblematic representations of their communities and cultures without unduly provoking government sanction or negative public opinion. Indirect opposition thus can provide a relatively quiet but nonetheless essential period "preparatory" to a more direct "politics of embarrassment" conducted through public confrontation or shaming or to a "politics of rights" conducted through litigation.[8] In the first decades after entry into World War II, indirect opposition made tactical sense for both Maori and American Indians. As their populations began to recover from the devastating effects of the contact era, the impressive record of indigenous minority war service was a boon for positive public relations; it became a symbol of citizenship in the contemporary nation. But the positive image of patriotism had a potentially negative underside. It also could be promoted as evidence that indigenous minorities were ready, both as individuals and as communities, to give up separate identities, terminate distinctive status, and assimilate fully into the dominant society. Among Maori and American Indian peoples themselves, participation in the war provided useful skills and experiences for coping with a rapidly changing world, but it also became a symbol of indigenous minority strength, a reviving of a warrior tradition, with the potential to galvanize indigenous communities and to energize activism at local and national levels. During the first decades after entry into the war, indigenous minority writers and activists developed narrative tactics for a complex—if not always consistent—indirect opposition that attempted to balance arguments for building an inclusive national citizenship (that is, for becoming full-fledged citizens of their contemporary nations) with arguments for maintaining distinct indigenous identities.

Indigenous Minority Texts and Postcolonial Theories

When the United Nations was created in 1945, both the United States and Aotearoa/New Zealand signed on as charter members. Neither, however, interpreted the UN's 1948 Decolonization Mandate as applying to their nation's indigenous minorities.[9] Nonetheless, the creation of the UN and the signing of its 1948 mandate are a suggestive context for indigenous minority activism and writing in the early contemporary period.

There have been explicit calls to situate indigenous minority literatures within the contexts of colonialism and indigeneity at least since the early 1980s, when Acoma poet Simon Ortiz published his essay "Towards a National Indian Literature: Cultural Authenticity in Nationalism" (1981) and Maori filmmaker Merata Mita published her essay "Indigenous Literature in a Colonial Society" (1984). Such calls have become all the more frequent since the approach and passing of the 1992 Columbus quincentenary in the United States and the 150th anniversary of the signing of the Treaty of Waitangi in Aotearoa/New Zealand in 1990.[10] Thus far, arguments for designating these literatures as "colonial," "postcolonial," "paracolonial," "internally colonized," or something else have relied heavily on terminology developed by scholars who focus on materials produced by colonized or formerly colonized peoples in Africa, Southeast Asia, and the Caribbean or by Europeans and their descendants in the British settler colonies.[11] One popular source of definitions for these terms, among indigenous as well as nonindigenous scholars, has been *The Empire Writes Back* (1989) by Australian critics Bill Ashcroft, Gareth Griffiths, and Helen Tiffin. They argue that "the position of [indigenous] groups such as the Maoris, Inuit, and Australian Aborigines is a *special* one because they are *doubly marginalized*—pushed to the psychic and political edge of societies which themselves have experienced the dilemma of colonial alienation" (144, emphasis added). Their distinction is provocative and no doubt well intended; but the definition itself marginalizes indigenous minority peoples within a paradigm that privileges instead the "plight" of their oppressors. The notion of a double marginalization continues to prioritize a settler perspective: "your" oppression is a "special" case of "ours"—not a different case—and "we" all struggle against the same colonial legacy.

Both Louis Owens (Choctaw/Cherokee) and Arnold Krupat have employed *The Empire Writes Back* in order to align contemporary American Indian literature with other literatures written in English by "'natives' under colonial pressures."[12] Each argues that specific features of contemporary American Indian writing can be mapped onto models of "classic" postcolonial literatures. Owens locates contemporary American Indian literature within the second stage of the three-stage model for postcolonial literary production offered in *The Empire Writes Back*.[13] In his argument for distinguishing the ongoing "colonial" status of American Indian literatures from clearly "postcolonial" literatures produced in other parts of the world, Krupat employs the term "internal colonialism." Nevertheless, he situates contemporary American Indian literature within the model for the development of postcolonial African literature advanced by Kwame Anthony Appiah.[14] While Owens's and especially Krupat's efforts in this direction are important first steps for gauging the relevance of postcolonial theory for American Indian—or, more generally, Fourth World—literature, both run a considerable risk of simply grafting indigenous minority literatures onto existing postcolonial models, developed in response to radically different colonial and postcolonial histories, rather than pursuing rigorous independent study of indigenous minority literatures and their relevant contexts.

In their more recent work, Ashcroft, Griffiths, and Tiffin attempt to discipline supposedly wayward indigenous activists and writers for not following the techniques that orthodox postcolonial theory prefers, most prominently, ambivalence, hybridity, pastiche, and fragmentation.[15] They remark in *The Post-Colonial Studies Reader*, the anthology they edited in 1995, that "indigenous groups have so often fallen into the political trap of essentialism set for them by imperial discourse" (214). There is a degree of truth in this statement, especially if situated within specific contexts, but there is also an element of barely concealed paternalism. Indigenous minority discourses pose a problem for those orthodox postcolonial theories that designate "essentialism," "nativism," "nationalism," and so forth as anachronistic politics, because indigenous minority discourses often emphasize land and treaty rights and because they often insist on persistent racial, cultural, and linguistic distinctiveness despite other changes over time. They provoke charges of a retrograde "essentialism," in particular, because orthodox postcolonial critics often fail to understand how discourses that intersect with the controversial blood/land/memory complex, including the discourse of treaties, might appear cogent for indigenous minority activists and writers. A number of critics of orthodox postcolonial theory have argued, in other contexts, that nationalism, tribalism, and sovereignty are not simply matters of individual identity and the development of self-esteem or exercises in "word play."[16] But these terms have a particular resonance for indigenous minority writers and activists in the early contemporary period. Their right to assert an indigenous nationalism or sovereignty distinct from and potentially in opposition to that of settler-invaders had been not only historically suppressed but also perennially disavowed—and it continues to be disavowed today. In this Fourth World context, nationalism, tribalism, sovereignty, and even essentialism represent the subject matter of a "real" politics that remains at best imminent and provide the ground rules for access to real estate that has been long denied.[17]

Other critics offer distinctions among postcolonial labels that are more useful than Ashcroft, Griffiths, and Tiffin's for characterizing the contemporary Fourth World situation. Anne McClintock describes First World settler nations like Aotearoa/New Zealand and the United States as "breakaway settler colonies." Such nations are distinguished, McClintock argues, "by their formal independence from the founding metropolitan country, along with continued control over the appropriated colony (thus displacing colonial control from the metropolis to the colony itself)."[18] Eric Cheyfitz argues, more specifically, that "In the United States, [Anglo-American] imperialism since 1823 has taken the form of an *internal colonialism*, in which, through the institutional structure of the Bureau of Indian Affairs, first established in 1824, the federal government has assumed ultimate 'title' to Indian lands."[19] A similar argument can be made for Aotearoa/New Zealand by pointing to its 1840 Royal Charter, which "gave the [British-appointed] Governor power to survey the whole of New Zealand and divide it up into districts, counties, towns, townships, and parishes," as well as "instructed the Governor to make grants of 'waste land' to private persons for their use, or to corporate bodies in trust for public use," and by pointing to the subsequent establishment of the Native Affairs Department, later renamed the Department of Maori Affairs.[20] In both instances, the designation of internal colonialism is based on the breakaway settler colony's attempts, after winning its own independence from Britain, to continue the colonial project of systematically alienating aboriginal title to land. As I argue in the introduction, one of the consequences of this ongoing appropriation has been a competition between "native" and "settler" indigeneity.

The development of labels such as "breakaway settler colony" and "internal colonialism," although significant, have not produced systematic analyses of Fourth World literatures or theories about the production and reception of these literatures on their own terms and in their particular contexts. And, as Jace Weaver (Cherokee) argues, "there are potentially troubling aspects of post-colonial discourse that must be seriously debated before American Natives can determine whether it is useful to hop aboard the post-colonial bandwagon."[21] He points to the critiques of orthodox postcolonial theory made by Ella Shohat, Ruth Frankenberg, and Lata Mani to argue that if it is indeed true, as these critics charge, that postcolonial theory has tended to be "ahistorical, universalizing, [and] depoliticizing" on the one hand, and obsessively concerned with the "critique of dominant, Western philosophical discourse" on the other, then "Natives will want little part of it" (13). More recent critiques, such as E. San Juan Jr.'s *Beyond Postcolonial Theory* (1998), raise the additional suspicions that orthodox postcolonial theory's "indeterminacy," "deracinated sensibility," and "utopian idealisms" actually "serve the interests of the global status quo," "mystifyi[ng] the political/ideological effects of Western postmodernist hegemony and prevent[ing] change."[22] Chidi Okonkwo, in *Decolonization Agonistics in Postcolonial Fiction* (1999), charges that *The Empire Writes Back,* in particular, "must therefore be interpreted as a neocolonialist work inspired by Australia's strategic need to reposition itself in the post–Cold War global geopolitics of the New World Order."[23] So-called orthodox postcolonial theory is not, of course, the monolith that these and other critics sometimes make it out to be, and, although highly influential, its claims have stood neither unchallenged nor unchanged over the past quarter century. What these critiques demonstrate is that postcolonial theory can become counterproductive when it extends its (sometimes veiled) analysis of a local phenomenon into global abstractions. While orthodox postcolonial theory offers useful frameworks for inquiry and potential avenues for comparisons, especially as it is being critiqued and rewritten by critics such as San Juan and Okonkwo, there is no need to abdicate American Indian studies or indigenous minority studies more generally in favor of orthodox postcolonial theory's obsessions. There is still too much work to be done within the Fourth World itself.

A number of American Indian scholars point to potential alternatives. In particular, they direct our attention to theories for understanding the nature of contemporary indigenous *survival* and its textual representation within specific contexts. In "Towards a National Indian Literature: Cultural Authenticity in Nationalism" (1981), Simon Ortiz argues that "the crucial item that has to be understood" in the study of contemporary American Indian literature is "the way that Indian people have *creatively* responded to forced colonization" (66, emphasis added). In his critical 1987 essay "Colonialism and Native American Literature: Analysis," Jack D. Forbes (Powhatan/Delaware/ Saponi), contends that "Native American literature today must be regarded as a colonized and submerged literature," and he eschews any dominant model for postcolonial literary development. Forbes stresses the importance of a work's primary audience and how particular audiences—not academic critics—define "what literature consists of" for their communities (18). This is similar to the "occasional" approach I describe in the Introduction. For Forbes, a crucial element in identifying a work as both indigenous and worthy of analysis has to do with whether it "is internal to the [particular indigenous] culture" (19), rather than the work's language, genre classification, popularity with nonindigenous critics, and so forth. Consequently, Forbes considers nonfiction works, including tribal newspapers and pan-tribal journals, an essential component of contemporary indigenous "literature." He argues that one "impact of colonialism and the resultant struggle for liberation is that a great percentage of literature produced will be of a practical nature, concerned with problem-solving, political agitation, political theory, philosophy, strategy and tactics. Poetry and fiction may well be of this nature, along with songs, plays, et cetera, but the ordinary form used will be non-fiction" (20). This means that many texts in the potential indigenous minority "canon" will of necessity not display such techniques as hybridity, pastiche, and fragmentation— often considered the hallmarks of postcolonial writing—in any overt or self-conscious way. Forbes goes on to critique those American Indian novels most celebrated by critics identified with the dominant culture, including Momaday's *House Made of Dawn* and James Welch's (Blackfeet/Gros Ventre) *Winter in the Blood,* as "hardly . . . 'political,' " arguing that "the alienation depicted [in these novels] is only related to colonial conquest by means of the chance knowledgeability of a particular reader, not through anything in the texts" (20). Although

Forbes's dismissal of these and other critically acclaimed works is too categorical, his larger point is compelling. If we are to approach a fuller understanding of contemporary indigenous minority literatures and their development under conditions of ongoing and evolving colonialism, scholars must move beyond studies of the same handful of popular novelists and undertake the more difficult task of analyzing a much larger body of nonfiction and mixed-genre texts, whose oppositional strategies may be less subtle but also less easily recognized by scholars working exclusively with the analytical frameworks provided by orthodox postcolonial theory. A number of scholars have begun to move in this direction; in the present study, I engage in this more difficult task by juxtaposing well-known indigenous minority literary texts with lesser known nonfiction and, in particular, activist texts produced by American Indians and New Zealand Maori.

Indigenous minority survival and its representations within the context of deep settler colonization have become the central focus of the "indigenous theory" developed since the 1970s. This work suggests that colonial relations in which dominant power works to forcefully exclude indigenous peoples from the dominant social order while exploiting their labor and/or resources differ from colonial relations in which dominant power works to forcefully include indigenous minorities within the dominant society and thus to define them out of separate existence. Forceful colonial inclusion is marked not only by the commodification of land and the subsequent individuation of land ownership; it is also characterized by a history of relocation of individuals and families into the settler metropole (including the adoption of indigenous infants into settler families and the creation of boarding schools for indigenous children), attempts to terminate separate citizenship or other oppositional political status, mandatory education, mandatory language assimilation, the suppression of indigenous cultural and spiritual institutions, and so forth. A focus on forceful colonial inclusion helps to define more clearly the particular dynamics of the ongoing colonial status of contemporary indigenous minorities.

The dominant, European-derived culture in both the United States and Aotearoa/New Zealand typically has disavowed its persistent role as a colonizer in relation to indigenous peoples while foregrounding its own changing roles in relation to imperial Britain. Broadly speaking, in both countries the dominant settler culture popularly conceives its history as a clear and consistent movement away from the status of a British colony toward the status of a postcolonial sovereign state and independent First World nation. Indigenous peoples play a relatively minor role in this dominant paradigm. When they are considered beyond the period of first contact, they are conceived of either as impediments to settler progress (and therefore "bad" savages) or as the recipients of settlers' gifts of enlightened religion, proper government, and personal freedoms (making them "noble" or "redeemable" savages). Both of these popular conceptions mask the settler's role as colonizer. For members of the dominant culture, the relationship between their roles in relation to imperial Britain and in relation to indigenous peoples—the first foregrounded, the second disavowed—might be diagrammed thus:

colonial subject/colonizer → postcolonial settler/colonizer → First World citizen/colonizer

The persistent role of colonizer in relation to indigenous peoples is disavowed because it calls into question the supposed ethical victories of the dominant culture's transformations in relation to imperial Britain. Similarly, the roles of indigenous peoples in the United States and Aotearoa/New Zealand can be diagrammed using a related set of terms—one changing over time, one persistent—the first foregrounded by the dominant culture, the second largely disavowed:

indigenous citizen/colonized → colonial subject/colonized → postcolonial "ward" of the settler government/colonized → First World citizen/colonized

These diagrams are highly generalized and in no way illustrate the complexity of the histories of either colonizing settlers or colonized indigenous peoples. They do, however, illustrate an important point about the relationship between settlers and indigenous peoples in the United States and Aotearoa/New Zealand. Although over time other roles have transformed for both—and although these roles continue to evolve—the basic relationship between colonizer and colonized persists. At different times and in different places, the persistence of this relationship is manifested in different forms and in different public and private spheres: in reservation policies, in land rights legislation, in treaty violation claim settlements, in leasing agreements, in systems of blood quantum, in certification systems for indigenous art, in racial slurs, in the regulation of indigenous tourism and gaming operations, in sports team logos, and so on. Given the complexity and contingency of this ongoing relationship, throughout the book I employ the term *(post)colonial* to emphasize the irony of an often asserted post-colonial situation, such as the early decades after World War II, that is never quite one.

After the White Man's War

The Maori population grew rapidly after World War II. Coupled with shrinking land holdings, this population explosion meant that rural Maori were increasingly forced to migrate to urban centers like Auckland and Wellington to find housing and work. Whereas 90 percent of the Maori population had been rural in the decade preceding the war, by 1951 nearly 20 percent were urban.[24] The situation was similar in the United States. There was a postwar indigenous "baby boom," and by 1950 nearly 25 percent of all Indians lived in urban areas, up from less than 5 percent in 1940. But, as historian Alison Bernstein documents, "By 1950 the unemployment rate for urban Indians had reached fifteen percent, nearly three times that of whites."[25] The dominant culture in both Aotearoa/New Zealand and the United States had been comfortable with images of indigenous minorities as "fighting" men or as "working" men and women during the war, but it was much less comfortable with the economic and social realities of indigenous minority individuals and communities in the immediate postwar period. When soldiers returned home, their military paychecks soon disappeared. War factories were obliged to cut their workforces, and many managers preferred to hire veterans with backgrounds similar to their own rather than indigenous minorities. All too soon Maori and American Indians were back where they had been before the war economically, with the added difficulties of a rapidly increasing population and often radically changed personal expectations about their lifestyles, social opportunities, and political rights. More and more either lived permanently in urban areas—increasingly in the worst parts of cities—or migrated back and forth between urban areas and rural or reservation communities.

And in the towns and cities, greater numbers of Maori and American Indians were able to attend educational institutions, including universities, which promoted the formation of pan-tribal alliances.[26]

Maori Affairs: A Controlled Transformation

In Aotearoa/New Zealand, movements to build urban marae (community facilities), voluntary associations like the Maori Women's Welfare League, and university Maori student groups began to emerge as powerful social and political forces. To help facilitate even more migration to the cities, the Department of Maori Affairs developed in 1960 an official urban relocation program.[27] Over time, sizable constituencies for regional and national Maori political action began to coalesce. The national government did its best not only to control the pace of Maori migration but also to direct the development of contemporary Maori personal and communal identities. One of the mechanisms it devised to effect the desired outcomes was a Maori magazine.

There were calls for a national Maori journal for some time prior to 1952, when the Department of Maori Affairs published the first issue of *Te Ao Hou/The New World*. In 1940, for example, Professor I. L. G. Sutherland ended the influential essay collection he edited to mark the centennial of the signing of the Treaty of Waitangi, *The Maori People Today: A General Survey,* by asserting the great need for a national Maori forum. In his remarks, Sutherland defines Maoritanga (Maoriness or Maori identity) in terms of the marae, "a symbol for Maori community life" (421), and argues that marae are needed to develop Maori community life in urban settings, where increasing numbers of Maori are now living. He then laments the lack of effective communication in the Department of Maori Affairs and charges that this lack of communication is holding back Maori progress. Sutherland concludes by arguing for an official national publication "taking the form of a periodical news sheet for Maoris and those engaged in all branches of the Maori service" (439). Sutherland lays out a charter for the kind of publication he has in mind: "Such a news sheet could make clear to all such matters as general Government policy, give a brief and simple account of the progress of development schemes, of plans and progress in regard to housing and *marae* improvement. It could report important Maori gatherings, note development in regard to arts and crafts, be the medium for health propaganda, report progress in the Native schools and in general give information regarding all matters relating to the Maori people" (439). Sutherland notes that there are "precedents" for a publication of this type, most notably a U.S. publication produced monthly by the Office of Indian Affairs, *Indians at Work: A News Sheet for Indians and the Indian Service.*[28]

Whether through Sutherland's influence or through other channels, officials in Maori Affairs became aware of *Indians at Work* as a model for deploying a government-sponsored journal to help administer the social assimilation and political control of indigenous peoples living in a First World settler nation. In particular, they were drawn to the news sheet's primary message: through a program of regular "work" and Western "education," indigenous people receiving government benefits could be transformed into an ideal of independent, hard-working, productive "citizens." The Department of Maori Affairs files reveal that in 1950 the under-secretary wrote to the U.S. commissioner of Indian affairs, William A. Brophy, stating that he had "read back issues of 'Indians At Work,'" and noting that "It appears, from this material, that there is a considerable similarity between the work done by your office and the work of the Maori Affairs Department in NZ."[29]

Indians at Work had been created in 1933 by Brophy's predecessor John Collier. Collier began the "news sheet" almost immediately after taking office as commissioner of Indian affairs as part of his Emergency Conservation Work program, an Indian division of the Civilian Conservation Corps (CCC), which had been developed as a New Deal employment scheme designed to put more Americans to work and to promote much-needed soil conservation and reforestation. The original purpose of *Indians at Work*, then, was to advertise and promote Indian conservation work on the reservations. Collier also used the journal, especially his opening editorial, as a vehicle for critiquing federal Indian policies of the past and for advocating his own ideas for changing national policy in the future. There was little room in Collier's agenda for actual Indian voices, and no room for opposition to the dominant culture.[30]

Collier's primary aims for *Indians at Work* coincided with Sutherland's goals for a national Maori journal. Sutherland's subsequent influence is apparent in legislation affecting the Department of Maori Affairs after 1940 and, once the journal had been officially proposed in

1949, in the formulation of specific objectives for *Te Ao Hou*. After 1940 Sutherland argued that "with the passing of the older generation of Maori leaders, those with over-all comprehension and influence," it was important that the individual Maori today be well informed so that "he [can] feel as closely as possible his unity with his people and the relation of his people and all their activities to the life of the country as a whole."[31] In other words, contemporary Maori could both pursue traditional communal life—albeit on a larger, national scale—and modern national citizenship by developing as individuals. A national journal would help these individual Maori stay informed and integrate their lives into the larger (Pakeha) life of New Zealand.

These goals are echoed in New Zealand's 1945 Maori Social and Economic Advancement Act.[32] Two main thrusts of the act are particularly relevant to Sutherland's goals for *Te Ao Hou* and to the eventual launching of the journal in 1952. First, the act states that Maori are to be guided by the minister of Maori affairs and his staff officers in their "advancement" (12.a.i) as well as in their "maintenance" of Maori culture (12.a.v). Second, the act states that Maori tribal executives are to "collaborate" with various state departments and educational institutions in order to promote *the objectives of those departments and institutions* (12.b,c,d). Thus the authors of the act envisioned and hoped to enforce the collaborative guidance of Maori into mainstream New Zealand society. Even the continuation of Maori traditions was to be guided by the government's objectives. A 1951 memo detailing the purposes of the then-proposed national Maori journal developed the act's ideas further, advising Members of Cabinet that

> 1. The Maori people find it difficult to understand the fine details of the Government's Land Development, Housing and Welfare administration, and of the legislation especially affecting Maoris. . . . The press gives little space to such matters and it seems that the only effective way of providing the knowledge is by way of a regular periodical.
> 2. Such a periodical would further be needed to give guidance to the Maori Tribal Executives and Committees, and to explain the European ideas about such matters as health, education, household budgeting etc. It should raise the cultural standard and awareness of the Maori people generally by discussing Maori arts and crafts, etc. and providing reading material of general educational value.

It was hoped that, like *Indians at Work, Te Ao Hou*—as a regular and pervasive messenger of government policy disguised as "the people's book"—could play an important role in implementing the personal, cultural, and political "guidance" of Maori. As the journal developed over the years into a veritable Maori institution, the Department of Maori Affairs shifted the emphasis of its promotional rhetoric from guidance to welfare.[33] In 1957 the department stated in its annual report that *Te Ao Hou* "can be used as an agency for welfare work" to perform a number of "primary objectives": "1. Coverage of news about progressive Maori development. 2. Stimulation of activities that welfare generally aims to encourage. 3. Development of Maori in-born valuable gifts of self-expression through story-telling, poetry, description of tribal events."[34] Unlike *Indians at Work, Te Ao Hou* took advantage of what government officials saw as "Maori in-born valuable gifts of self-expression" and encouraged Maori contributions to the magazine. As I argue in chapter 1, it is precisely the active inclusion of diverse Maori voices that opened the possibility for galvanizing the Maori community and subverting dominant discourses in the pages of *Te Ao Hou.*

Indian Affairs: From the War to Termination

As World War II ended, the Bureau of Indian Affairs came under renewed and increasingly intense attack. Opponents of the BIA, many calling themselves "friends" of the Indians, argued that the Bureau's postwar goal, like that of the Department of Maori Affairs, should be to continue the process of assimilation that had been fostered by the war's demographic upheavals. In this climate, only two options were seriously entertained: "freedom" from federal services could be conducted on an individual basis, or it could be conducted on a tribal basis.[35] Collier, with his philosophy of corporate Indian progress, preferred the second option. His handpicked successor as commissioner of Indian affairs, William Brophy, began compiling a list of tribes considered suitable for "termination" of their federal supervision as early as 1946. In August 1953, the Eighty-third Congress passed House Concurrent Resolution 108, which singled out thirteen tribes for termination and bound the government "as rapidly as possible, to make the Indians . . . subject to the same laws and entitled to the same privileges and responsibilities as are applicable to other citizens of the United States, to end their status as wards of the United States, and to grant them all the rights and prerogatives pertaining to American citizenship." Furthermore, H.C.R. 108 resolved that Indians "should be freed from Federal supervision and control and from all the disabilities and limitations specially applicable to Indians." The most widely publicized termination struggle, fought by the Menominee Nation of Wisconsin, was initiated the next year, in 1954, when President Eisenhower signed into effect the Menominee Termination Bill.

The idea of Indian "freedom" on an individual basis was not wholly abandoned. In 1948 the BIA initiated an off-reservation job placement program for unmarried Navajo men that developed into a full-scale Relocation Program for both individuals and families in the early 1950s. By 1956, more than 5,000 Indians were involved annually.[36] Although relocation had devastating effects on particular individuals and families, it helped others to escape reservation poverty. And, in cities like Chicago and Los Angeles, the beginnings of a pan-Indian consciousness were promoted by the formation of pan-tribal communities around Indian Centers set up to help migrant Indians adjust to urban life.[37]

The intricate history of the era of termination and relocation has been well documented by historians Donald Fixico and Kenneth Philp. Philp emphasizes that Indian leaders were of diverse opinions about the potential effects of termination. For some, "federal withdrawal offered the hope that the government would honor its promise of self-rule under [the Indian Reorganization Act of 1934]"; others saw termination as "a unique opportunity for a claims settlement and per capita distribution of tribal assets."[38] Fixico concludes that the period from 1945 to 1960 "constituted one of the most crucial periods in the history of federal-Indian relations."[39] Despite the various hopes of Indian leaders, Fixico writes, "In everything that it represented termination threatened the very core of American Indian existence—its culture. The federal government sought to de-Indianize Native Americans" (183). As I argue in chapter 2, in a diverse array of texts American Indian activists and writers, most of whom were directly involved with national institutions such as the BIA, the Christian missions, or the academy, responded to this threat with a sense of its inevitability and yet refused to give over fully to the demands of dominant discourses.

As my brief summaries indicate, in the early decades after World War II the dominant culture in both Aotearoa/New Zealand and the

United States attempted to facilitate (and, so far as possible, to compel) a profound transformation: turning indigenous "communities of descent" based on kinship, shared culture, and connection to specific areas of land into Western-style "communities of assent" based on individual choice of association.[40] Literary critics have shown little interest in the works produced within this historical context and under these conditions of surveillance and supervision. This is especially true in Aotearoa/New Zealand, where mainstream scholars have dismissed early contemporary texts produced by Maori writers as "unsophisticated," "sentimental," or "nostalgic."[41] As chapter 1 and chapter 2 demonstrate, however, the first decades after World War II were an important preparatory period of indirect opposition to dominant discourses that attempted to direct an indigenous minority "self-determination" on nonindigenous terms. On the occasions of their performance, the narrative tactics of these texts, although relatively quiet, were far from unsophisticated; they questioned the assimilationist orthodoxy of their day and prepared the way for the more explosive tactics of the indigenous minority renaissance of the late 1960s and 1970s.

1

A MARAE ON PAPER

Writing a New Maori World in *Te Ao Hou*

The first thing any Maori community will do to show its vigor and
energy is to build a fine marae. One can be sure that where there is a
marae of a high standard, there is also usually a community which
takes a credible part in the pakeha side of life. . . . These ideas . . . are
proof that the Maori is not content to follow the past but has
adapted useful pakeha ideas freely in his own tribal life.
—"The Story of the Modern Marae," *Te Ao Hou*

Expunge his little title in that land and whatever you may do for
him you have made him a homeless wanderer from the tribal life
which is his being. . . the preservation of the Maori marae is imperative. . . . If Maoritanga is to persist it must have the venue of the
marae.—Very Rev. J. G. Laughton, "Maoritanga" *Te Ao Hou*

Beginning in 1952, New Zealand Maori could purchase at their local
newsstand or receive through the mails by subscription "he pukapuka
ma te iwi Maori," a book for the Maori people. Although Maori had
been producing local and regional newspapers in both English and
Maori languages for almost a century, the publication of *Te Ao Hou/
The New World* marked the appearance of the first Maori journal that
was truly national in scope.[1] The Department of Maori Affairs produced seventy-six issues of the magazine between 1952 and 1975, making *Te Ao Hou* a primary site for publishing information and opinions
of concern to the Maori community. It was also the only national
forum where contemporary writing by Maori authors could be displayed in either English or Maori: articles on history and traditional
arts, personal essays and reminiscences, short works of fiction and
poetry, and new works in traditional or modified genres. And, despite
the fact that it was produced under the auspices of several departments
of the New Zealand government and the specific guidance of three

Pakeha editors, during the years of its publication most Maori readers appear to have considered *Te Ao Hou* a "Maori" text and institution.[2] Certainly the government did its best to promote *Te Ao Hou* as essentially and even prescriptively Maori.

This chapter traces how the inclusion of diverse Maori voices in *Te Ao Hou* opened the possibility for subverting the government's assimilationist goals, even at the site of its own promotional discourse, during the roughly twenty-year period between the early 1950s and the late 1960s. Not surprisingly, the earliest Maori writing in *Te Ao Hou* appears more or less complicit with the stated goals of dominant power. It promotes the virtues of at least some level of assimilation into various aspects of Pakeha life, and it endorses a level of subordination of local Maori independence to the greater needs of the predominantly Pakeha nation. In this respect the early stories emulate the publicity films produced in the 1940s and early 1950s by the New Zealand National Film Unit. While these short films often promote the maintenance of Maori language and the development of Maori creative arts, they do so within a context of assumed (or enforced) assimilation to Pakeha standards of "hygiene" and to Pakeha methods for "homecrafts" and farming.[3] Distinctively Maori culture is relegated to those aspects that can benefit the Pakeha economy, especially the growing tourist trade. One of the dramas produced by the Film Unit in 1951, for instance, a nineteen-minute, black-and-white film titled "Aroha," creates a fictional "university student and descendant of Maori chiefs," Aroha, in order to narrate the contemporary Maori's "struggle to find a full and satisfactory life combining European with Maori ways."[4] The film is subtitled "A Story of the Maori People," and the opinions of its progressive female protagonist are meant to guide the nation's best and brightest rangatahi (young people) toward assimilation. "Why should I bury myself here in the country," the well-educated Aroha laments, "just because I'm a Maori?" At the same time, however, whether or not it was the intention of the Film Unit, "Aroha" inscribes the rural Maori community, situated on its traditional land base, as a welcoming and still viable refuge from the Pakeha world.

On closer inspection, the early stories published in *Te Ao Hou* also inscribe the viability of the rural Maori community, in charge of its own "progress," as an alternative to Pakeha-controlled assimilation. While such inscriptions represent at best an indirect opposition to

Pakeha mandates, focused inward and on galvanizing the community rather than outward and on demanding reform, their presence complicates the too easy dismissal of these early stories as fully compliant with dominant discourses. As one might expect, texts published in *Te Ao Hou* in the mid- and late 1960s question the goals of dominant power more openly than the early stories, and they more openly counter Pakeha ideals. In their strategic deployments of Maori language and in their development of emblematic figures for a persistent and distinctive Maori identity, these stories anticipate the innovative tactics of "renaissance" fiction published after 1970. Before turning to the Maori voices published in *Te Ao Hou*, however, I will begin with an analysis of the magazine's dominant metaphor, "a marae on paper," which was developed in a series of early editorials. With its allusions to treaty discourse and to the blood/land/memory complex, the idea of a marae on paper had a lasting impact on the development of early contemporary Maori writing.

Dualing Discourses/Nga Korero E Paparua Ana

Under the editorial guidance of Erik Schwimmer, an enthusiastic young officer in the Department of Maori Affairs sympathetic to indigenous causes, *Te Ao Hou*'s inaugural issue appeared in the midst of the dramatic social, economic, and demographic changes that followed World War II.[5] The magazine's sixty-four pages contain some twenty essays that address contemporary concerns, plus a Maori crossword puzzle, a book review, and a summary of "Sport among the Maori people." Schwimmer announces in his editorial that "For the first issue, the Editor has had to write a good deal himself to start the ball rolling" (1). The majority of these articles are in English; only a small minority are rendered in both English and Maori versions, printed in dual columns per page. In later issues a small number of articles appear as Maori texts without translation.

In his first dual-language editorial, printed on pages one and two in separate versions, Schwimmer lays out his early hopes for *Te Ao Hou* and launches what will become its central metaphor. For the bilingual reader, the editorials provide a set of approximate but not identical English and Maori interpretive frames for reading the new magazine:

Te Ao Hou should become like a "marae" on paper, where all questions of interest to the Maori can be discussed.

Ano te ahua o tenei pukapuka he "Marae" hei whakawhaititanga i nga whakaaro Maori.[6]

In English, Schwimmer deploys *marae* (community facilities or meeting place) as an abstract term designating a mode of discussion and exchange that can take place in writing—in this context, an ideal of openness and inclusiveness appropriate to Maori and Pakeha alike—rather than as a concrete term denoting a locus of interactions among a living kin-group, their land base, and their ancestors. He expresses his intentions in terms of conditional futurity ("should become"), emphasizing *Te Ao Hou*'s potential as text ("a marae on paper") for answering questions or discussing issues he considers national in scope. In Maori, the implications of Schwimmer's idea of how *Te Ao Hou* might function as a marae are somewhat different. There is no mention of a marae on *paper,* and the verb is not explicitly conditional. Rather, "this book" (tenei pukapuka) is to have the "shape" or "form" (te ahua) of a marae for the purpose (hei) of "compressing" or "cataloging" (whakawhaititanga; literally, to cause to be put into a small place) diverse Maori "opinions" and "feelings" (nga whakaaro Maori).[7] In other words, *Te Ao Hou* is to take on the semblance of a marae in order to carry out one of the marae's primary functions, the staging of hui (gatherings) for the purpose of building consensus.

The connotations of *marae* are wider than either a mode of discussion or a locus of interactions among kin-group, land, and ancestors. Although Schwimmer may or may not have intended to evoke these wider connotations, both Maori and knowledgeable Pakeha were no doubt aware of them and considered their implications for *Te Ao Hou.* Ample evidence indicates that officials in Maori Affairs worried over the potential of a "marae" to subvert their intention that the magazine serve as an official "voice" of the government.[8] In fact, in a 1954 memo the minister of Maori Affairs states, "At the outset the magazine was intended to assist the promotion of the objectives of the Government. . . . I am given to understand that the magazine is now being regarded as the 'marae of the Maori people' where diverse subjects and thought are brought for discussion. This was never intended." It seems crucial, therefore, to briefly explore the wider connotations of the term *marae.*

Anthropologists of both Maori and Pakeha descent have observed— and Maori, generally, have insisted—that the marae stands at the center of contemporary Maoritanga, whether conceived in terms of specific iwi (tribal) and hapu (clan) identities or in terms of pan-tribal "Maori culture." In the past, *marae* referred exclusively to the open yard directly in front of the wharenui (meeting house), known as the marae atea, and was used for the performance of rituals on behalf of the community. Today, *marae* refers to all the buildings and open spaces in a Maori community facility. Typically, a contemporary marae contains a carved meeting house (whare whakairo) that represents and embodies the community's principal ancestor, an open courtyard in front of the house (marae atea), and a dining hall (whare kai). Rural marae also typically include an adjacent cemetery (urupa). A marae may belong to a tribal group (iwi), clan (hapu), or extended family (whanau), who are responsible for its physical and spiritual upkeep. In urban areas and on many university and school campuses, marae both large and small have been built to meet the needs of pan-iwi Maori immigrants and students. Other contemporary marae are sponsored by various Christian denominations. The marae is the favored site for important hui of all kinds, especially tangi (funeral ceremonies).

Often the marae is described in anthropological or social science discourses as a symbol of Maori "group identity," which acts "as a bridge to the past as well as a useful community centre in the present."[9] Maori and other New Zealanders describe the marae as "the only area in our New Zealand way of life that endorses Maori values and traditions to their fullest."[10] As a "Maori public place," the marae and the activities performed there are seen as asserting within the larger European-descended community the continuing integrity, relevance, and beauty of Maori language, ritual, architecture, arts, and community values. In Maori terms, the marae is "te turangawaewae o te iwi," the standing place of the people, or the place from which the people receive their standing or identity.[11] The marae and its buildings, especially the carved ancestral house (whare tipuna), connect the kingroup that "belongs" to a particular piece of earth (tangata whenua, land people, the people of the land) to their ancestors (tipuna) and to the gods (atua). The symbolic connotations of *marae* thus exemplify the complicated set of interactions designated by the blood/land/memory complex.

The meeting house itself carries several names, each emphasizing one of its many functions on the marae: whare nui (big house), whare puni (guest or sleeping house), whare hui (meeting house), whare runanga (council house), whare tipuna (ancestral house). As the ancestral house, the whare's architecture incarnates the notable, often legendary ancestor—male or female—from whom the group who owns the house acknowledges its descent. The carved head (koruru) or figure (tekoteko) at the apex of the whare's roof represents the ancestor for whom the whare is named. The roof's ridgepole (tahuhu) represents his backbone and main line of descent. The bargeboards fronting the roof's gable (maihi), often elaborately carved, are the ancestor's arms outstretched in welcome; the front porch is the ancestor's brain (roro). Inside the whare, the rafters (heke) represent the ancestor's ribs and descent lines. The interior walls, often decorated with carved wood slabs (poupou) that represent more recent family or tribal ancestors, are the principal ancestor's chest and belly. Moreover, the structure of the house also represents the period of creation when Papatuanuku (the Earth Mother), who is represented by the floor, and Ranginui (the Sky Father), who is represented by the roof, were separated from their marital embrace by their children, who are represented by the whare's posts (poupou) stretching between them. To be inside the whare tipuna on one's home marae is to be surrounded and protected, literally, by one's ancestors and by the gods. The meeting house is considered "ancestral" not because of the antiquity of its physical structure or particular ornaments—the age of its materials—but rather because it physically embodies ancestors in contemporary times. The house and the ancestor whom it incarnates "live" so long as they are kept up; during whaikorero (speech making) on the marae, the house is addressed as a living elder. The regular maintenance and periodic rebuilding of meeting houses ensures that important cultural skills, particularly woodcarving, tukutuku panelling, kowhaiwhai scroll painting, and their attendant rituals, are passed on to the next generation.

For Schwimmer to inaugurate the first issue of *Te Ao Hou* as a marae, then, was of no small significance. The English version of his first editorial, especially, reframes and textualizes this highly charged icon of "traditional" Maori culture and symbol of contemporary Maoritanga. The layout Schwimmer designed for *Te Ao Hou* attempts to reproduce in the reading experience, as far as possible, some of the attributes of a "real" visit to a physical marae. The editorial, for instance, can be read as a formal welcome (powhiri) to visitors coming onto the "marae on paper," with the inaugural editorial serving as an invitation announcing the opening of a new marae. In the fourth issue, Schwimmer augmented the magazine's format with an obituaries column and a table of contents. The obituaries, "Haere Ki O Koutou Tipuna," are placed at the beginning of the issue, following the editorial; read as part of a welcome onto a marae, the column formally recognizes the dead before the magazine addresses the business of the day. The table of contents, immediately following, then provides an agenda for the magazine's "hui." In his third editorial, Schwimmer asserts that *Te Ao Hou* can play a role in preserving traditional literary forms and indigenous knowledges by keeping them "alive" through use. In effect, each issue rebuilds the "marae on paper" with new texts. Maori are encouraged to pass on their knowledge by contributing manuscripts to the paper marae; younger Maori can participate in the marae's upkeep and acquire new skills through their reading. Schwimmer devotes his ninth editorial to the topic of Maori education; he acknowledges the educational role of the marae and states that it is the policy of *Te Ao Hou* to encourage the cultural development of Maori children "by providing suitable material, both in English and in Maori, for their study." As on a physical marae, where children participate in adult activities, *Te Ao Hou* will scatter material for younger readers throughout issues, rather than create a separate children's section.[12]

But what might it mean, more precisely, to create "a marae on paper"? What role might such a marae play in the lives of increasingly urban Maori people? In his first editorial, Schwimmer argues that "a true Maori world is slowly shaping itself to stand beside the Pakeha world. The Maori, in general, earns his living in the same way as the Pakeha. Life on the marae, sports, haka, arts and crafts therefore have to wait until times of leisure and relaxation. Yet, if these recreational and artistic interests are developed, they will make life in a predominantly Pakeha world more satisfying. They can, in fact, be the basis of a Maori culture in which his identity will be preserved."[13] In this view, Maori culture is no longer vital and pervasive but consists primarily of "recreational and artistic interests." It has been transformed, in other words, from an iwi-specific, land-based communal culture of descent into a pan-iwi, individuated culture of assent. Maori interests can—

and, by implication, must—be set aside in order to earn a living in a "predominantly Pakeha world." In his fourth editorial Schwimmer reiterates this idea as the promotion of "traditional" culture within the "practical and commonsense" context of contemporary New Zealand. The marae and the life potentially lived there are relegated to "times of leisure and relaxation." Once Maori culture is defined in this manner, as a list of separable, nonessential activities and interests, alternatives to the physical marae can be devised for achieving Maori "leisure." "A marae on paper" allows individual access to "life on the marae, sports, haka, arts and crafts" by making them conveniently available as text. And as text, they can be "enjoyed" alone, in the privacy of individually owned Maori homes.

The subtle gaps between the English and Maori versions of Schwimmer's first editorial are metonymic of persistent linguistic and cultural differences in Aotearoa/New Zealand. And they are evocative of the conflicting discourse of the bilingual Treaty of Waitangi. Indeed, in the above quotation Schwimmer's English version reflects the treaty discourse typically deployed by the national government and members of the dominant culture. Partnership is described in terms of Pakeha superiority, and a Western style of individualism is imposed on Maori even as communal activities are idealized. For bilingual readers, Schwimmer's Maori version offers a subtle counter to the English by imagining the magazine as a space for interactions among Maori and thus as a space for the potential contestation of Pakeha discourses. This observation raises a general point about the mobilization of treaty discourse in Aotearoa/New Zealand. For activist purposes, successful redeployments of treaty discourse depend on an audience's knowledge of the Maori version of the Treaty of Waitangi, its differences from the English version, and the subtle interplay among those differences. For attentive and actively bilingual readers, the dual-language text of Schwimmer's editorial not only solicits the production of that type of interplay—that is, the reader's creation of a bilingual and bicultural intertext—but also thematizes the back-and-forth translation involved when one reads across dual-language discourse.

Schwimmer's formula for creating "a true Maori world" makes it plain that, however sympathetic he and other individual bureaucrats might have been toward Maori interests, *Te Ao Hou* was designed as part of the policy of the Department of Maori Affairs to encourage the "progressive adjustment" of the Maori "to our modern world."[14] As such, one of the magazine's official purposes was the social assimilation, described as the "social progress," of Maori people. Careful readers sensed this mission from the beginning. One early reviewer remarked that "The danger facing this journal is, of course, that it will become chiefly a medium for official propaganda and apologetics, a trap it shows signs of falling into from the start." But the reviewer remarked further that "The twin aims of reconciling this adaption [of Maori lives more fully to European ways] with the retention of other Maori ways is one held by many thoughtful Maoris today. Their hope is a future somewhere between assimilation and separatism."[15] "A marae on paper," by providing a potential space for resistance to the government's ideals, offered the possibility for realizing this kind of compromise—or for realizing a more radical form of opposition. What if contributors took seriously the Maori version of Schwimmer's first editorial? Could *Te Ao Hou* in fact become a "Maori" space—a marae— for bringing together, codifying, and representing the diversity of contemporary Maori thought?

I Waenganui I Te Tautukunga Me Te Pakanga/ Between Compliance and Contestation

In the thirty-seven issues under Schwimmer's editorial control between 1952 and 1961, *Te Ao Hou* published forty-eight pieces of original short fiction. The majority of these are written for an adult audience, although, responding to the editor's call for suitable material for young Maori, there are stories for children as well, including several designated as "bedtime stories." Of the forty-eight stories, thirty-six were printed in English; six were printed as dual-language texts; and six were printed in Maori with no translation. The last, a series of stories detailing the exploits of the character Tawhaki, were written by Hirini Moko/Sidney Moko Mead (Maori and English versions of the author's name), who is described in issue 28 (September 1959) as "the only living author, as far as we know, who writes short stories in the Maori language" (22). Because of the popularity of these stories, Mead continued the series with two dual-language texts.

Many of the stories published during Schwimmer's editorship were submitted to one of the five literary competitions he staged in order to increase submissions from readers.[16] The editorial and the judge's commentary that followed each competition helped construct a paradigm for contemporary Maori writing very similar to the paradigm promoted by the Department of Maori Affairs for contemporary Maori identity: sympathetic to indigenous culture but nonetheless Pakeha-centered. After the fourth literary competition, reported in issue 27 (June 1959), competition judge and highly regarded poet Alistair Campbell specified the criteria used in selecting the winning entry for the English language category, the story "Goodbye" written by an author identified only as Tirohia, which translates into English as either "to be looked at" or the imperative "Look!" Campbell's comments echo both the advertisement for the first literary competition announced in issue 5 (spring 1953) and Schwimmer's subsequent editorials: what is desired and later praised is the representation of "the everyday situation" of the Maori and the Maori "real." That the dominant Pakeha culture should define these key terms for Maori is left implicit; the subtext to the editor's and the competition judge's printed statements is an argument that contemporary Maori writers should assist in the inevitable subordination of their community to Pakeha New Zealand—if not its outright assimilation. The Maori "everyday" and the Maori "real" ought to look very much like their Pakeha counterparts.

Tirohia's prize-winning story appears to satisfy these criteria. "Goodbye" is a character sketch of a young Maori in transition. As Tuhou, whose name translates as "new one," prepares to leave his family in the rural north to attend university in a city on the South Island, he weighs his locally focused childhood against the more nationally focused adulthood he desires. Tuhou represents a new generation of Maori eager to embrace modernity and to reject previous generations' disabling superstition and provincialism. Desire for "freedom" from the past and from the rural land base is thematized along a clearly gendered genealogical binary. Both Tuhou's grandfather and his father view his departure as fulfilling their own thwarted aspirations as young men. In contrast, Tuhou's grandmother, who believes that "The Maori belongs on his land," worries that "the city [is] an evil or a luxury . . . created by the Pakeha for the Pakeha only" (16); Tuhou's mother passed away in the city when he was a small boy, forcing his father's return to the farm. In the end, though it has been "hard" to say goodbye, Tuhou does, leaving the feminized Maori "country" for a masculine Pakeha "world." However, there is more to this brief sketch than Pakeha realism. Despite its assimilation plot, "Goodbye" nonetheless inscribes pro-Maori land rights and back-to-the-land positions in the thoughts, dialogue, and actions of Tuhou's grandmother. Moreover, the story's final image suggests the possibility that Tuhou may return home at a later date, after he has matured: "He felt very lonely as he gazed out of the [bus] window—almost like a love bird on a long migration to another country. He had left the nest" (16). Like a migratory love bird, Tuhou also may in later life return to the rural Maori land base to build a nest of his own.

The adult fiction published in *Te Ao Hou* during the early period of Schwimmer's editorship, including "Goodbye," is striking in its representation of the Maori "everyday" and the Maori "real," for it differs significantly from representations published by Maori authors during the so-called Maori renaissance. Absent in these early stories are direct references to British colonialism or its continuing legacy of racism in Aotearoa/New Zealand. And there are few references to a distinctive or imminent Maori spirituality, a hallmark of renaissance fiction. Instead, these early stories focus on the practical, often personal difficulties of cultural change in rural areas, small towns, and urban centers. Maori identity is neither "traditional" nor assimilated, neither assured nor under direct attack, but in a process of becoming something as yet undefined. Clear battle lines over identity have yet to be drawn in these stories, and there are few representations of evil Pakeha or of an evil Pakeha government; in fact, there are relatively few representations of Pakeha at all. The focus here is introspective, on Maori thinking about themselves and their communities, even when situated well within "enemy" territory. Many stories, for instance, narrate young protagonists' archetypal experiences of experimentation with the novelties of urban life. But rather than confront a world exclusively Pakeha, these characters establish migrant communities in the cities. Identity ("blood") and history ("memory") remain relatively secure; the recurring theme that links these meditations on Maori identity outward to contemporary Pakeha New Zealanders or to the legacy of British colonialism is land. Throughout the stories, as in "Goodbye," diminishing land holdings, coupled with a growing population of rangatahi (young adults), is an impetus for migration to urban centers and for innovation in Maori lifestyles. Yet the overwhelming majority of these stories simultaneously assert both the continuing viability of the rural land base in supporting "traditional" culture and the real possibility of a successful return to that land base should individuals either not succeed in the urban world or choose to leave it. Rural Maori physical and social geography remains a welcoming stronghold of a viable Maoritanga.

The two stories featured in issue 28 (September 1959) are typical of Maori short fiction in this period. "Yielding to the New," written by Arapera Blank, tells the story of a young woman, Marama, who leaves her large family and rural community to attend university in the city, where she studies anthropology among predominantly Pakeha classmates but socializes with a growing community of other Maori students. "Dreamer's Return," written by Mason H. Durie, tells the story of Boy Heru, a young Maori who has "crossed the ranges," leaving his rural community of Te Kohatu to try his luck in the city, where he works and carouses with other young Maori men. In both stories young adult protagonists experiment with the potential benefits and temptations of the city; prompted by Pakeha, Marama and Boy are forced to meditate on what it means to continue to identify culturally as Maori. Both stories record the creation of migrant Maori communities in the cities and a confidence that, despite this urban migration, rural life will endure as a locus of Maori cultural integrity, providing a ready site of personal renewal for those young people who have left but wish to return. And both stories reveal the tensions created between older and younger generations of Maori in the contemporary context of rapid social, demographic, and economic changes taking place in postwar Aotearoa/New Zealand. Read together, "Yielding to the New" and "Dreamer's Return" reveal as well the tension between rangatahi who choose to remain in the predominantly Pakeha cities and those who decide to return to the predominantly Maori rural villages. Neither decision is foregrounded as culturally correct. Each is a potentially viable strategy for personal survival and advancement, and even the choice of remaining in an urban area is not threatening, ultimately, to the survival of the rural community. What is foregrounded, instead, is the decision-making process itself, a rumination on personal identity and Maoritanga based in experiences of experimentation and initiation that are safeguarded by the continued existence of a rural Maori land base.

The narrative tactics deployed in these stories are also typical of Maori writing in *Te Ao Hou* during this period. Blank and Durie use Maori language sparingly—generally common words or phrases, greetings, and proper names—and they tend to set Maori language apart with quotation marks. None of the words or phrases, however, is glossed in the text. Although they do not render either story inaccessible to non-Maori speakers, these few words and phrases are metonymic of a persistent Maori linguistic and cultural difference. Furthermore, non-Maori speakers are withheld access to the significance of proper names. Since *Te Ao Hou* did not mark vowel length during Schwimmer's editorship, many Maori names are fruitfully ambiguous. In "Yielding to the New," *Marama* translates into English as the noun "moon" or "month," which might suggest the cycle of changes she undergoes in the story, while *Maarama* translates into English as the adjective "light," "clear," or "easily understood," which might suggest her movement toward knowledge and a clearer understanding of her social position in contemporary Aotearoa/New Zealand. In "Dreamer's Return," *Heru* translates into English as the noun "comb for the hair," which can be read as a joke in the story, since several characters comment that Boy Heru was "due for a good hair cut long ago." *Heru* also translates as the verb "to begin to flow," which can be read as a metaphor for Boy's decision to leave the alienating city and return home. The Maori place-names in "Dreamer's Return" also are potentially significant. *Te Kohatu*, Boy's home village, translates into English as "the stone" or "the rock," suggesting a place that is steady, both physically and metaphorically solid; *kohatu* is used to translate the biblical "rock of ages." *Mariu*, the town where Boy's Pakeha hospital-mate Charlie lived for a time when he was a young man, translates into English as "to look upon favorably," corresponding to Charlie's nostalgia for the life he knew among Maori in the past.

Durie's use of prophetic dreams/visions is a narrative tactic that more overtly challenges the conventions of Western realism, potentially contesting a dominant Pakeha construction of "everyday" life with a Maori alternative. Boy, who is in the hospital recovering after an accident, dreams of returning to his family and friends in Te Kohatu. In his dream he stands on a hill dressed in his "flash outfit" from the city. When his friends and family recognize him, they call out for Boy "to go down." He runs toward them, but they begin to laugh and point "as if something was wrong with [him]" and then move away. Frustrated, Boy at first strikes out. It is only when he performs a "colonial striptease" that Boy is reintegrated into the Maori community:

> I took off my shoes and threw them, then my socks and coat and short[s] till I had nothing on. They stopped laughing now and just looked.
>
> Next minute someone threw me an old pair of trousers—no knees in them and all ripped at the cuffs[,] but I put them on. You know, as soon as I had them on I was okay. I felt like a kid again and laughed and ran towards them. They slapped me on the back and kissed me and made a real fuss. We all laughed now and walked down to the sea[,] trampling my new clothes into the sand. (20)

Boy's colonial striptease is similar in function to the "sovereign striptease" that American Indian writer and scholar Gerald Vizenor enacts in his mixed-genre text "Socioacupuncture: Mythic Reversals and the Striptease in Four Scenes."[17] Vizenor describes the striptease as "a metaphor" and argues that "in the metaphor are mythic strategies for [indigenous] survival" (84). The ritual of striptease allows indigenous characters to strip off the colonizer's fixed images of indigenous identity and to expose "the pale inventors of the tribes" (91). Early in "Dreamer's Return," the hospital matron's dominant discourse fixes Boy Heru into a taxonomy of denigrated Maori identity ("disgusting I say") for which British colonialism bears no responsibility ("Ah well, not our fault"); later, Boy describes himself in similar terms, as trapped in an economy of Pakeha images (18, 19). The colonial striptease works as a strategy of Maori survival, allowing Boy to remove himself from a Pakeha taxonomy of identity based on materialism and individualism, asserting in its place a value system based on community solidarity. Significantly, the strategy is not complete until, at the end of the story, Boy makes a successful physical return to Te Kohatu, "no bag in his hand" (21).

In contrast, the more recognizable dream/vision experienced by Charlie invites a sentimental rather than a political reading. As he lies dying, Charlie dreams of his return to the village of Mariu, "where he had been brought up as a lone Pakeha among Maori friends": "Now he was walking over to the meeting house. Three old Kuias were sitting contentedly on the veranda smoking pipes. . . . Charlie walked over to them, held out his hand and was greeted with a hongi. He stood beside them and entered in the conversation. He was back at last" (21). Charlie returns specifically to the community's meeting house, where he is greeted by the kuia (women elders), who call the dead onto the marae during tangi (funeral ceremonies). Charlie's sentimental desire to return to the Maori life of the past balances Boy's colonial striptease with a Pakeha "reality," potentially undermining its political message. In this way Durie's competing dreams rehearse the Fourth World struggle between "native" indigeneity and "settler" or "New World" indigeneity. Attachments to specific lands and specific communities become enmeshed in a larger ideological conflict that comes into its sharpest focus when mapped onto Aotearoa/New Zealand's competing Pakeha and Maori traditions of Treaty interpretation. Charlie's dream rehearses the Pakeha argument that attachments to specific lands and communities marked "indigenous" are merely sentimental; they are attachments that can be satisfied by the *idea* of return. Boy's dream rehearses the Maori argument that attachments to indigenous lands and communities are spiritually and psychologically potent; the benefits they provide to indigenous peoples can be achieved only by actual physical return.

Ka Korero Ke Te Pukapuka Maori/
The Maori Magazine Speaks Differently Than Expected

During Margaret Orbell's editorship from March 1962 to March 1966, *Te Ao Hou* published a larger number of dual-language texts, and its short fiction more openly engaged in oppositional politics. It is unclear to what degree, if any, though, Orbell's presence affected the content of *Te Ao Hou*'s fiction. An academic rather than a bureaucrat, Orbell went on to become one of Aotearoa/New Zealand's leading scholars and translators of classical Maori. During her four years as editor she increased the number of translations of nineteenth- and early-twentieth-century Maori texts published in each issue. And she improved *Te Ao Hou*'s overall production values: her husband, the artist Gordon Walters, assisted with design, and he increased the amount and enhanced the quality of the magazine's art work.[18] *Te Ao Hou* also received a new logo. Foregoing direct translation, Orbell replaced the secondary title "The New World" with "The Maori Magazine." She moved the obituaries column to the back pages and discontinued the editorial. During these years no reference was made to "a marae on paper," and no other central metaphor was launched for the magazine.

Shifts in style and content of the short fiction suggest, however, that during the mid-1960s *Te Ao Hou* in fact became an increasingly vibrant "marae" in touch with contemporary concerns. The stories that Orbell published consciously narrate Maori confrontations with Pakeha racism; most often, such confrontations are staged in domestic settings, in Maori and Pakeha homes, and between individuals. The stories also directly address the issue of miscegenation, narrating the experiences of mixed-blood Maori identified by the stories' authors as "quartercaste" and "mongrel." At the same time, these more outward-looking stories often inscribe a Maori need for Pakeha affirmation and validation of things Maori. As in the earlier period, no single perspective is privileged. But the level of tension has clearly risen, and battle lines over Maori identity are beginning to be drawn.

The two stories published in issue 38 (March 1962), for instance, set up a dialectic of possible responses to Pakeha interest in Maori culture. Both "The Visitors," written by Hineira, and the dual-language story "Show Us the Way/Whakaaturia Mai Te Huarahi," written by Sidney Moko Mead/Hirini Moko, narrate Pakeha visits to Maori homes.[19] Hineira's humorous sketch of rural life, presented as a single English-language text, offers a positive depiction of how Pakeha can help Maori better appreciate their own cultural heritage and also become more modern. The narrator's mother and father are edified by their visit from a well-educated Pakeha couple; they pick up new skills and increase their social standing among their neighbors. At the story's end, the young narrator reevaluates her sense of her own Maoritanga, since the family's prized representation of classic Maori identity, a portrait of their "arrogant," tattooed ancestor, has been validated from the outside: the visiting Pakeha recognizes him as the illustrious "chief" depicted in a painting housed in the national museum.

In contrast, Mead's meditation on contemporary New Zealand politics offers a subtle challenge to the assumption of Pakeha superiority, especially in the intertext created when bilingual readers read *across* his English and Maori versions rather than read them sequentially. As in

"The Visitors," the Maori narrator in "Show Us the Way" worries about what a Pakeha guest will think of his home and family. Once the Pakeha arrives, however, the narrator, Rapa, focuses exclusively on his and his workmate Bill's conversation. At first Rapa reports that he is happy, because he feels "this Pakeha . . . is easy to please" (15). But soon Bill stops "glancing at the portraits of our children and ancestors hanging on the walls"—representations of a specific Maori family—and the conversation turns to "the Maori people" in general. As the discussion shifts from the immediate domestic sphere to the larger, national sociopolitical sphere, Rapa becomes less at ease. Bill asserts that "your Maori customs are pulling you people back" (15) and then argues specifically that tangi (funeral ceremonies) and hui (gatherings) should be abolished: they waste time and money. "Their greatest sin," Bill argues, "is that they separate us, making us go our separate ways. . . . We should really go together for we are one people—New Zealanders" (16). Bill argues further: "Let us regard the Maori and Pakeha people as one. Let us have the same laws, the same customs and similar thoughts. Let us do away with the special Maori members of parliament, let us put an end to the Maori Affairs Department so we will all be the same. Let there be one set of rules to be observed by everyone. If this is not done we will continue to be separated as we are now. Our differences will divide us and cause friction" (17). Bill's arguments bring together a litany of Pakeha complaints against the continuation of Maori traditions and political structures based on the Treaty of Waitangi. His patronizing tone represents as well typical Pakeha attitudes toward the ability of Maori to make important social, economic, and cultural decisions for themselves. At each point Bill asks, "Now Rapa, what do you think about my thoughts on the matter?" And at each point Rapa responds, "Yes, perhaps you are right." For his friend, Rapa plays the "good" Maori, agreeing with the Pakeha assessment of his culture. But Rapa, whose name translates into English as a noun meaning "canoe stern" or "blade of a paddle" and as a verb meaning "to seek," is in his own mind unsure. In his interior monologue he counters each of Bill's specific points, detailing to himself and to the reader the social and spiritual necessities of tangi (funeral ceremonies), the cultural and political importance of hui (gatherings), and the potential for personal and spiritual renewal in the practice of Maori oral and artistic traditions.

In analyzing Bill's assertion that Maori and Pakeha are "one people," Rapa reasons to himself:

> The essence of [Bill's] argument for unity is that we should leave behind, throw out and abandon our Maori customs.
>
> The politicians are the culprits who give voice to the idea that we are one people. They are the ones who publish to the world that we live together in brotherhood and goodwill. To my way of thinking this is the dream of a seer. The idealistic longings of people who go to church. (17)

Rapa's concise analysis points to the competition between native and settler indigeneity in Aotearoa/New Zealand. Maori assertions of the right to remain distinct are interpreted by Pakeha individuals like Bill and by the national government as threats to New Zealand's cultural authenticity, national legitimacy, and positive international image.

Although Rapa arrives at no definite conclusions—he is still "seeking"—the implications of his debate with Bill are clear, and they stand in stark contrast to the Maori acquiescence to Pakeha interests narrated in "The Visitors." In Mead's shift from a narrowly domestic to a broader sociopolitical focus, Pakeha are exposed as desiring nothing less than to mandate the abolition of Maori cultural practices, including tangi (funeral ceremonies), and to enforce that mandate through the strong arm of government. Furthermore, the point-for-point counters that Rapa offers for each of Bill's arguments evoke the competing discourses of the Treaty of Waitangi. For the bilingual reader, that evocation is even more pronounced in the subtle interplay between Mead's side-by-side Maori and English texts.

The presence of the "other" language in the dual-language text suggests the presence of additional meaning unavailable to the monolingual reader. Separated by a narrow gap of white space, the columns of Maori and English are metonymic of linguistic and cultural difference; for both English- and Maori-only readers, the absolute authority of either version by itself is undermined. As with the Treaty of Waitangi, only the bilingual reader has full access to all of the text's potential meanings: Maori, English, and the two combined. Read sequentially, Mead's Maori and English versions, like those of the Treaty, are close approximations of each other. Differences become apparent, however, when one reads back and forth across the gap. No matter how accurate the translation, there are discrepancies between the culturally defined connotations of Maori and English expressions. And, less expectedly, there are indications of the power of dual-language texts to challenge dominant discourses, for at key moments, the interplay between Mead's versions suggests that Rapa and Bill's debate is being conducted on two potentially opposed levels. On one level there is a Pakeha-style discourse on the asserted faults of Maori traditions and the necessity of creating adequate national policy to correct these faults, lest the nation suffer socially and economically. Lying behind this discourse, as it does behind the English versions of the Treaty of Waitangi, is an assumption of Pakeha sovereignty over the whole of Aotearoa/New Zealand and all her people(s)—an assumption that does not appear in the Maori-language version.

A brief comparison of the Treaty's documents will make this difference clear. In both versions, Queen Victoria acknowledges the unruly nature of British settlers while extolling the virtues of Great Britain and the monarchy. She argues in the preamble that she desires to establish a "Civil Government"/"Kawanatanga" in order to protect Maori and their property from her British subjects who are now living in New Zealand and to protect these same British subjects from each other. In the Maori version, the queen describes her emigrant subjects as "e noho ture kore ana," living without law. But the English and Maori versions diverge in the first article. In English, the Maori chiefs "cede to Her Majesty the Queen of England absolutely and without reservation all the rights and powers of *Sovereignty* . . . over their respective Territories as the sole Sovereigns thereof." In Maori, nga rangatira "ka tuku rawa atu ki te Kuini o Ingarangi ake tonu atu—te *Kawanatanga* katoa o o ratou w[h]enua," that is, the chiefs "give absolutely to the Queen of England for ever the complete *government* over their land" (emphasis added).[20] Controversy over the first article erupts in the chasm between British understandings of "sovereignty" and possible Maori understandings of "kawanatanga"/government at the time of signing. *Kawanatanga* was derived from *kawana,* a transliteration into Maori of the English word *governor.* Most scholars of Maori language agree that Maori in 1840, who had never experienced any form of supra-tribal authority, could have had no understanding of kawanatanga as meaning what the British understood by sovereignty—absolute authority vested in the sovereign, here specifically Queen Victoria and by extension her governmental institutions and representatives.

Moreover, in the Maori version's second article, the British queen guarantees not only to the chiefs but also to Maori hapu (sub-tribes) and all Maori people of New Zealand "te tino rangatiratanga o o ratou w[h]enua o ratou kainga me o ratou taonga katoa," that is, "the unqualified exercise of their chieftainship over their lands, villages and all their treasures." As noted Maori scholar I. H. Kawharu explains, tino rangatiratanga, the unqualified exercise of chieftainship, "would emphasize to a chief the Queen's intention to give them complete control according to *their* customs. 'Tino' has the connotation of 'quintessential.'"[21] Given that Maori were numerically, economically, and militarily dominant in Aotearoa/New Zealand in 1840, and given the queen's reasoning in the Treaty's preamble, the rangatira who signed the Treaty had no reason to believe they had given over to the British Crown and its representatives anything but the right to govern the newly arrived Pakeha traders and settlers, that is, the right to extend the force of British law to British subjects who had left their own country for New Zealand. For over a century following Maori population decline, Pakeha, who quickly became the majority, proceeded to develop New Zealand as a British nation, claiming authority through the English versions of the Treaty.[22] Maori, however, never forgot what had been promised them in Te Tiriti.[23] Rapa's internal monologue voices that tradition. Dominant discourse is countered through redirection rather than outright challenge or dismissal. As in de Certeau's model for tactics, Rapa's specific points depart from Bill's assumption of Pakeha sovereignty without ignoring either that concept or the source of its authorization. The activist potential of Rapa's response lies in its appropriation of Bill's assumption of sovereignty and its redeployment of that assumption as tino rangatiratanga.

On another level, the interplay between the English and Maori versions in Mead's text is suggestive of a metadiscourse on the power of dominant discourses like the English versions of the Treaty of Waitangi to affect—and potentially to destroy—Maori lives. Consider the following passage from Rapa's interior response to Bill's ideas:

Ko te whakaaro kei te whakararuraru i a au inaianei, ko teenei. Mehemea e hee ana te whakatakoto *kupu* hei arahi i a taatau, ko taatau anoo ka	What troubled me most was this. Supposing the *policy* laid down to guide us was wrong, all of us would be murdered, our children and our grandchildren. Who

koohurutia, ko aa taatau
tamariki, ko a taatau mokopuna.
Maa wai e whakatakoto nga
kupu? Ma taatau anoo, maa ngaa
taangata maarama raanei o te iwi
Paakehaa? Ki te hee, riro maa wai
taatau e koohuru?

should lay down a *policy*? Should
we ourselves, or should we rely
on the enlightened members of
the Pakeha people? And if it
should be wrong, who would be
responsible for our decimation?
(18, emphasis added)

In English, Rapa considers the nature and effects of "policy," and he questions who should lay down official policy affecting the Maori community; but, in Maori, Rapa considers the nature and effects of "texts"—kupu, anything said or written—and he questions who should lay down texts affecting his people, their children, and grandchildren. The discrepancy in translation is striking; it is also idiosyncratic, suggesting that the juxtaposition of "kupu" and "policy" is intended to create an additional level of meaning. Typically, *policy* is translated into Maori as "kaupapa" (rule, basic idea, topic, plan, scheme, proposal), which Mead does not employ here. As a noun *kupu* traditionally covers "anything said," including all verbal texts or messages, as well as single words. *Kupu* also can be used as a verb meaning "to speak." In contemporary times, as a noun *kupu* covers "anything written" as well as "anything said," which I translate as "text."[24] The gap between *policy* and *kupu* juxtaposes the idea of "laying down policy" in order to promote (and enforce) assimilation with the idea of "laying down words" in order to write a new text for Maori lives. The interplay between the discourse on policy and the discourse on kupu raises, further, the complicated issue of the power of language and representation to affect the real lives of individuals and communities, an issue often avoided in discussions of how Pakeha policies will affect the lives of politically subordinate Maori. This reading is only strengthened if we note that Bill's name is a homonym, both in English and in its Maori transliteration, Pire, for a *bill/pire,* that is, for a draft of a proposed law.[25] In both versions of Mead's story, what is at stake in the struggle over the power to create representations (the power to lay down words) and the power to enforce representations (the power to lay down policy) is the continuation of the Maori nation: the potential "murder"—koohuru, to kill by stealth or treachery—of contemporary Maori, their children, and grandchildren.

The two levels of Rapa and Bill's debate, the overt discussion of appropriate national policy and the less obvious metadiscourse on the power of representation, open a space for contesting dominant discourses. They also push beyond typical definitions of hybridity and polyvocality. Considered separately, both versions of "Show Us the Way/Whakaaturia Mai Te Huarahi" qualify as "hybrid" texts. In Bakhtin's terms, both can be read as linguistic hybrids in that each, while ostensibly a single-language text, "contains mixed within it two utterances, two speech manners, two styles, two 'languages,' two semantic and axiological belief systems."[26] Maori words—haka, tangi, hui—erupt in the English text; transliterations of English words—motokaa (motor car), Pire (Bill), Niu Tirini (New Zealand)—rub up against "traditional" words in the Maori text. Maori and Pakeha narrative conventions overlap and blend together: dialogue, interior monologue, quotation and citation of a published source, whaikorero (oratory), moteatea (lament), and karakia (chant and prayer) appear in each. As Bakhtin demonstrates, this "double-voicing" of the linguistically hybrid text undoes any singular, authoritative discourse. In Homi Bhabha's terms, both versions can also be read as culturally hybrid. This is especially true of the English version, where the traces of Maori language and culture provide "an active moment of challenge and resistance against a dominant cultural power."[27] The cultural hybridity of the English version interrogates dominant Pakeha discourse from within the text itself. The Maori version, however, must be acknowledged as culturally hybrid, too. While I would not argue that the traces of English language and Pakeha culture either challenge or resist politically subordinate Maori cultural power, they do challenge and resist any romantic or nativist notions of the purity—linguistic or cultural—of contemporary indigenous forms. In other words, Mead's Maori version displays the fact that, like the multi-texted Treaty of Waitangi, contemporary Maori language exists within and is a product of contact history.

For bilingual readers able to read back and forth across the two versions of Mead's story, a third hybrid text emerges in the space between the Maori and the English. In this third text—what might be called "te korero i waenganui/the text between"—the production of meaning is linguistically palimpsestic and overtly bicultural. Here the notion of hybridity accrues additional connotations: the text between Mead's English and Maori versions creates meaning(s) through complementarity and a bidirectional echo effect. English words and phrases reverberate across the white space as imperfect Maori counterparts; Maori language reverberates back with its own authority, altering, calling into question the authority of the English; and so on through the back-and-forth process of reading across versions. Each echo potentially doubles back on itself, taking on additional meanings and undermining others. Since each version already has embedded in it traces of the other language and culture, reverberations across the versions create meanings through more pronounced multiple collisions of the English and Maori languages and Pakeha and Maori cultures already encoded in each text. Given the particular linguistic skills of individual bilingual readers, no two reverberations will sound exactly the same.

Language becomes layered in the third text as in a palimpsest. Juxtapositions like "kupu" and "policy" invite the creation of additional meaning in the course of reading through the layers of words and phrases. The third text creates a more overt dialogue between the English and Maori versions that is notable for the fact that it does not prioritize one version over the other; rather, the third text encourages bilingual and bicultural study of the dual-language text as a whole. It provides a subtle but clear allegory for the need to engage the whole of the multi-texted Treaty of Waitangi when making important decisions about national policy. And it makes a subtle but clear statement that bilingualism and biculturalism represent the best possibilities for creating a shared world of meaning in contemporary Aotearoa/New Zealand.

Although complicated, mobilizations of treaty discourse during this period are less burdened emotionally than other manifestations of the blood/land/memory complex, especially in representations of racial mixing. For while the interactions of divergent texts can be rendered as a site for activism and the production of theory, ruminations on the enduring power of Maori "blood" and "memory" resist easy abstraction, even when individual texts appear to reduce racial mixing and its effects to simple terms. In issue 28 (September 1959), for instance, Schwimmer published an essay by Maori writer Harry Dansey titled "Of Two Races," which attempts to define the general attributes and specific problems of mixed-blood New Zealanders. Dansey distinguishes in particular the "brown Pakeha"—who looks Maori "but accentuates the European side of his character"—and the "white Maori" —"who is European in appearance but who is by nature a Maori" (7). Dansey argues that the mixed blood has a special role to play in Aotearoa/New Zealand as an intermediary moving back and forth between Maori and Pakeha. He even argues that citizens of mixed blood are "truer New Zealanders than those of full blood of either of the other races" (6). Dansey concludes his essay by asserting that in their racial mixing New Zealanders have inherited "both [a] heavy burden and [an] inestimable privilege" (8).

The story published during Schwimmer's editorship that most directly addresses the issue of mixed blood is "The Best of Both Worlds," printed in issue 31 (June 1960) and written by Barry Mitcalfe, a student of Maori language and traditional literatures who is racially Pakeha. But Mitcalfe's vision of racial mixing in Aotearoa/New Zealand counters Dansey's sense of optimism and national mission. The title is ironic: the young mixed-blood protagonist, Matiu Saxton, appears to have inherited only the worst of the Maori and Pakeha worlds represented in his bilingual name, which juxtaposes a Maori transliteration of Matthew with an obvious pun on Anglo-Saxon. Identified as racially Maori, Matiu is rejected by the Pakeha girl he desires. In his frustration, he emulates the Pakeha father he has never met, rejecting and then abandoning his Maori mother. The story presents neither harmony between the races nor the possibility of someone's achieving a viable contemporary identity as a mixed-blood New Zealander; it ends with the mixed-blood protagonist lost and directionless. Perhaps most significantly, Mitcalfe represents mixed-blood identity as emotionally unstable, similar to the extreme version of the "brown Pakeha" described by Dansey. Though Matiu's mother welcomes him unconditionally, he is psychologically unable to live comfortably as a Maori.

Two stories published under Margaret Orbell's editorship counter Mitcalfe's bleak vision by asserting strategies for incorporating mixed-blood individuals firmly within contemporary Maori culture. Both "Back to the Mat" by Mikaere Worthington, published in issue 40 (September 1962), and "To the Race—A Son" by R. Denness, published in issue 48 (September 1964), narrate the adoption of mixed-blood protagonists into Maori families and their rise to positions of leadership in Maori communities. Although either story might be dismissed as the conventional fantasy of the "wannabe" tribe, in Maori terms neither protagonist is an "outsider" wanting in: each possesses an identifiable and publicly recognized genealogical link to a Maori community. The transformations enacted in these narratives are therefore rituals not only of initiation and incorporation but also of salvage and reclamation. The genealogical link, even if through only a single line of descent, renders these characters authentically Maori and appropriate for inclusion and adoption. Subsequently, their interest in things Maori and/or their displayed potential for leadership renders them appropriate to lead the community in a context of changing demographics and in a political and economic climate that is increasingly complex. The other side of this, of course, is the implication that a single line of Maori descent renders these characters inappropriate for inclusion, adoption, or leadership in the Pakeha community. For *Te Ao Hou*'s original audience, no doubt the latter was read as an indictment of Pakeha racism.

Several maneuvers stand out in these writers' particular mobilizations of "blood" and "memory." Like Boy Heru in "Dreamer's Return," the "quarter-caste" protagonist of "Back to the Mat," Jim Mac-Laren, discovers his true purpose in life while in the hospital recovering from a near-fatal accident. In the bed next to Jim's lies a young Maori man, Rua, dying of leukemia. Rua's name translates into English as both "store for provisions" and "grave"; moreover, it suggests the phrase *rua totoe*, an expression used for a family dying out.[28] Rua initiates Jim into Maori language and culture, and his death provides the impetus for Jim to join and eventually lead Rua's rural Maori community. On his deathbed, Rua gifts Jim with a greenstone tiki (a neck pendant carved from nephrite jade) as a sign of Jim's transformation and of his new role as a proxy for the full-blood Rua. Tiki (also called hei-tiki) make up a category of carvings that resemble the human form. They personify "primeval man," the first human offspring of the god Tane, and such carvings can serve as "dwelling places for ancestral spirits" or as "vehicles of gods and other supernatural entities."[29] Some tiki represent particular ancestors and are given personal names. Like other pieces of carved greenstone, hei-tiki are considered taonga, treasured heirlooms, and their spiritual value increases with successive ownerships.[30] Rua's gift of the tiki serves as a visible sign of Jim's full entrance into Maori culture and, significantly, Maori whakapapa (genealogy). That Rua gives Jim the tiki on his deathbed symbolizes, further, Jim's death as a troubled "quarter caste" and his rebirth as Maori.

Jim expresses his personal revelation in terms of feeling the "Maori blood" of his grandmother stirring within him, and he vows to reclaim a Maori "memory": "I would make Rua's people my people, I would study their history and dedicate myself to their welfare. Now that I had a mission in life my paralysis seemed to disappear . . ." (12–13). Later, Jim's transformation is completed with formal adoption into Rua's Tuhoe tribe, marriage to a local woman, and a name change. His sense of mission is confirmed by a Tuhoe elder: "An old tohunga [spiritual leader] stands up and says that such a thing was forecast by his father years ago, that a part-Maori, part-Pakeha, with a greenstone tiki would lead his people back to happiness" (14–15). The narrative ends with a utopian vision of Jim leading an economically and culturally viable Tuhoe tribe within the context of a successfully bicultural nation, a nation in which "every New Zealander whether Maori or Pakeha or a bit of both will have the best of both worlds" (15).

Similarly, in "To the Race—A Son" a Maori elder confirms the indigenous identity and the leadership qualities of a young mixed blood. The elder says of the sandy-haired boy, "He's got the makings of a good leader. Born a mongrel, but with the right teachings and background he'll have the qualities of a pure breed" (7). In choosing the boy to succeed him, the elder, a high-born Ariki (leader), relinquishes the claim of his bloodline: "You don't know it yet boy, but you are going to rise above me, and those of us who have the arrogance to boast and live in the glory of our ancestors. . . . The title of leadership is mine through birth, but not through striving. I don't deserve it; give it to someone who does" (7). At the end of the story, the old man states plainly: "I'm glad you have Pakeha blood in you, boy" (9).

Perhaps most interesting—and, at first, most disturbing—is that both narratives enact the "dying out" of full-blood Maori. Although these enactments reflect unfortunate demographic realities, they are not presented in an elegiac or a pessimistic tone. Unlike the majority of the stories published during Schwimmer's editorship, these texts confront head-on the demographic situation of contemporary Aotearoa/New Zealand and attempt to imagine practical solutions to the problem of how to maintain a distinctly Maori culture for an increasingly mixed-blood Maori population. What emerges from Worthington's and Denness's narratives is a definition of indigenous identity as recognized Maori descent through *any* bloodline. Strategically, this solution asserts an exclusively Maori control over how contemporary Maori identity is to be defined.

He Karanga Ki Te Mahi/A Call to Action

The short fiction published during *Te Ao Hou*'s final years—under Joy Stevenson's editorship—mark the observable beginnings of the so-called Maori renaissance. Two of the renaissance's most prolific and important writers, Patricia Grace and Witi Ihimaera, began publishing during this period. Their early works shaped contemporary Maori writing in English, and their more recent works continue to influence both Maori writing and the larger bodies of New Zealand and Commonwealth literatures. Because of their importance to the later period, I discuss their work in chapter 3. In addition, during this period battle lines over the definition of contemporary Maori identity began to be drawn more sharply. A short article published in issue 62 (March-May 1968), "Maori-Tanga" by P. W. Hau, makes plain that the time for hesitant, deferential debate over the relevance of Maori culture has passed. Hau explicitly calls for a return to Maori traditions and Maori language in order to ensure their survival into the future. In particular, Hau urges the adult generation to take the place of its kaumatua (elders). It is time for Maori adults to assume their responsibilities, Hau and others increasingly assert, to take up the mantle of cultural leadership and set proper examples for young people. A story published in issue 56 (September 1966) narrates a positive response to this call and brings together, perhaps for the first time in contemporary Maori fiction, the theme and the emblematic figure that would become dominant in Maori writing published after 1970: the physical and spiritual return to the Maori land base and Maori spiritual traditions linked specifically to the whare tipuna, the ancestral house, on the protagonist's home marae. In "The Homecoming," written by J. H. Moffatt, the whare tipuna is inscribed as a touchstone of Maori identity, an emblematic link between contemporary rangatahi (young men and women) and their tipuna (ancestors), an important manifestation of the blood/land/memory complex.

"The Homecoming" narrates one of the possible endings to the stories of experimentation with the Pakeha world outside rural Maori villages begun in the previous decade in stories like "Yielding to the New" and "Dreamer's Return." The protagonist has returned to his home marae to attend his father's tangi (funeral). Bob appears to be almost a "stranger" to his people, and, faced with his father's death, he feels ashamed of his lack of Maori knowledge. But the local people do not judge him; they welcome him back with sympathy and reassurance, seeing much "in this young man . . . that they had known in his father." With the people's strength behind him, Bob is able to re-imagine during the tangi, which is held on the marae, his years away from the community as part of an ongoing Polynesian tradition of adventure and experimentation. From a Pakeha perspective, he looks back into the past in order to move forward into the future. But, from a Maori perspective, Bob stands in the present and fixes his eyes on the past (visible in front of him), looking there for solutions to present and future problems. Having reoriented his understanding of his life, Bob decides to remain "home."[31]

Moffatt mobilizes the emblematic force of the whare tipuna in the story's final image: "A new strength and a calmness came into his soul. Looking around the meeting house at the silent people, he said in a voice he could barely control, 'Thank you, thank you.' Quietly sobbing, he leant against the carved wall panel, his tears dropping from the defiant wooden face into the dust. Ropert Pipito Jones had come home" (7). The "silent people" can refer either to the living Maori elders attending the tangi or to the likenesses of Bob's ancestors carved into the meeting house's poupou (wooden wall slabs)—or to both. Bob presses his face to the carved face of one of his "defiant" ancestors in the traditional greeting of hongi (pressing of noses, sharing of breath). Within this embrace his tears fall literally from the eyes of his ancestor into the "dust," the land, his whenua. As discussed above, the ancestral house embodies a Maori kin-group's principal ancestor and his or her descent lines. When Bob returns to his home marae for his father's tangi, he returns not only to his family and community but also to the site, the spiritual locus, of his Maori ancestry in contemporary times, kept alive through the maintenance of the carved house and the performance of community-based ritual. Like the living elders who welcome him home unconditionally, the carved figures of Bob's ancestors offer him communion. Moffatt engages the emblematic force of the blood/land/memory complex when Bob's tears become indistinguishable from the ancestor's tears and then fall into the dust, linking them both to the Maori land base. One of the Maori words for land, whenua, is also the word for placenta or afterbirth. According to Maori custom, a newborn's afterbirth is buried on the grounds of its home marae, thereby returning its whenua (placenta) to the whenua (land) of its ancestors and asserting the child's rights as a member of the tangata whenua (people of the land). Bob's return to his "dust" is a return to his first and ancestral home, his turangawaewae, the place from which he derives his standing in the world.

It is instructive to juxtapose "The Homecoming" and other stories discussed above with one of the few articles published in *Te Ao Hou* that openly critiques government policy. Titled "Maoritanga" and written by the Very Reverend J. G. Laughton, a Maori minister, the article was published in two parts in issues 8 and 9 in 1954. Laughton offers an extended definition of contemporary Maoritanga divided into five parts that, together, evoke the interactions of the blood/land/memory complex: (1) Maori language, which Laughton sees as the cornerstone of Maori identity; (2) Maori art, which he sees as representing distinguishably indigenous accomplishments; (3) Maori community life, which he considers "the very blood" of Maori life, centered on the marae; (4) the religious nature of Maori life; and (5) Maori land, which Laughton defines as the vital link to tribal life. As long as the land remains under Maori control, Laughton writes in issue 9, Maori will "always [have] the tribe to go back to" (17). As can be seen in the explicit argument of "Maoritanga," the stories published in *Te Ao Hou* work to define Maori cultural "tradition" not as a set of fixed ideas or artifacts but rather as an interpretive process grounded in Maori language, art, community life, and, especially, land. Read as a group, the stories develop a matrix of interpretive models for viable contemporary Maori identities that neither privilege notions of a "pure," precontact Maori culture nor dismiss evidence of long-term contact with Pakeha settlers. Authenticity is linked to the ultimate endurance of the community and its values rather than to "pure" bloodlines or the uninterrupted continuation of "pure" cultural forms.

Over time, the stories shift from being narratives of archetypal migration away from rural Maori communities to being narratives of archetypal return. Throughout, however, the rural Maori community remains a viable locus of Maori identity and culture. Although it is most often represented as diminished in both population and tangible resources, particularly land, the rural Maori village and its values nevertheless are represented as still competing, albeit indirectly, with the Pakeha city as the focal point of a contemporary Maori identity. Like Maori language in *Te Ao Hou*'s dual-language texts, the rural Maori village and its inhabitants offer through symbolic opposition a counter to dominant Pakeha discourse, asserting the continuing value of Maori traditions and Maori community in the face of large-scale migration to urban areas and the government's official policies of assimilation. By the end of *Te Ao Hou*'s long run, the journal had pushed the politics of the representation of the rural Maori village to a new level of direct engagement by clearly asserting the possibility of educated rangatahi returning to the Maori land base and continuing the spirit—if not the exact practices—of Maori traditions. That possibility is made manifest through communion with Maori ancestors in the whare tipuna on the protagonist's home marae. In "The Homecoming," the "marae on paper" for the first time explicitly asserts the essential spiritual and political functions of marae proper: connecting living kin with powerful ancestors and providing a place for both a diverse range of individuals and the community as a whole to stand.

It is not clear that when Schwimmer published "The Story of the Modern Marae" in *Te Ao Hou* issue 2, he understood the possible activist and literary implications of linking the "vigor" and "energy" of a contemporary Maori community to its building of a "fine marae." During the Maori renaissance, which is the subject of chapter 3, the theme of returning "home" to the marae and the emblematic figure of the ancestral house became central in representations of indigenous identity in the work of such writers as Witi Ihimaera, Patricia Grace, Keri Hulme, Apirana Taylor, and Bruce Stewart. By accepting the invitation to help build a "marae on paper," early contemporary Maori writers were able to lay the groundwork for a literary and political renaissance even within the confines of a government-controlled publication. In *Te Ao Hou*'s pages these writers explored, set, and challenged the early parameters in the battle over the representation of contemporary Maori identity.

2

INDIAN TRUTH

Debating Indigenous Identity after

Indians in the War

> Through[out] the Solomons, in the Marianas, at Peleliu, Iwo Jima, and almost every island where Marines have stormed ashore in the war, the Japanese have heard a strange language gurgling through the earphones of their radio listening sets—a voice code which defies decoding.—Sgt. Murrey Marder, "Navajo Code Talkers"

> Why aren't the Indians free? The policy of segregation and special treatment is deeply rooted in the past. . . . It is time for the people to demand that this evil be reformed.—O. K. Armstrong, "Set the American Indians Free!"

In the autumn of 1945, two publications anticipated the dynamics of the post–World War II debate over the parameters of contemporary American Indian rights and the meaning of contemporary indigenous identity in the United States: *Indians in the War* and "Set the American Indians Free!" In November, the Office of Indian Affairs (OIA) released its memorial pamphlet *Indians in the War.* Supervised by John Neihardt, who had become the OIA's director of information, this fifty-four-page pamphlet honors Indian recipients of the Award for Valor and commemorates the extensive range of Indian service in a series of new and reprinted articles.[1] Depictions of assimilation are balanced against depictions of an enduring cultural distinctiveness, and the articles highlight the two icons that are today most commonly associated with the unique contributions by Indians to the war effort: Ira Hayes, a Pima from Arizona, who served as a Marine paratrooper and who is credited with helping to raise the American flag on the summit of Mount Suribachi on Iwo Jima, and the Navajo "code talkers," whose "hidden" language is celebrated as a U.S. secret weapon that secured the Pacific theater.[2] Accompanying the articles are photographs of Indian men and women in action, their families aiding the war back home, and, to illustrate the article titled "Ceremonial Dances in the Pacific," Indian Marines dressed in improvised ceremonial costume— "colored cloth," "paint," "chicken feathers, sea shells, coconuts, empty ration cans and rifle cartridges"—dancing for U.S. victory on a beach in the Solomon Islands. The pamphlet's centerpiece is a substantial (although incomplete) list of nearly five hundred Indian soldiers, sailors, and airmen who lost their lives in battle. Twenty-seven photographs border the names of these honored dead; in each, a young serviceman smiles confidently. A separate tally lists Indian men wounded in action and features an additional thirty-six portraits. The pamphlet's cover illustration links its contemporary project to classic images from the nineteenth century. Captioned "Burial of a Brave," the drawing depicts a scaffold burial in a southwestern landscape, and it invites readers to locate the commemoration of contemporary Indian "braves" in a familiar tradition of imperialist nostalgia and popular representation. In the foreground, a feathered Indian stands poised beneath the platform, ready to sacrifice a paint pony so that the fallen warrior will have a mount for the spirit world. Other spotted horses stand in the middle distance, one ridden by a grieving Indian, while buzzards circle in the clear sky above.[3] We are meant to participate in a historical reenactment.

In August, the *Reader's Digest* published "Set the American Indians Free!," a polemical essay by O. K. Armstrong that drew the immediate condemnation of the American Association on Indian Affairs and other "friends of the Indians."[4] Armstrong's six-page article is accompanied by a line drawing in which a three-dimensional portrait of a uniformed American (presumably Indian) soldier is superimposed over a ghostly, two-dimensional outline of his befeathered warrior ancestor. The celebrated *American* of the present supersedes the memorialized *Indian;* we are meant to witness a metamorphosis. In language charged with the rhetoric of "freedom," Armstrong argues that Indian servicemen "demand full rights of citizenship" for themselves and their reservations (47). Even in 1945, his specific points would have sounded familiar to many *Digest* readers: federal Indian policies remain unnecessarily paternalistic, breeding dependency and isolation rather than the desired independence and assimilation; the cost of maintaining Indians as permanent "wards" of the government continues to rise, reaching unsustainable levels; Indians do not have full access to reservation lands (that is, they cannot freely sell tribal lands to non-Indians); and, moreover, the Indians possess "more acres by far than they ever use" (50). What is new in Armstrong's version of the perennial argument for "releasing" Indians from their federally defined status is how it employs a celebration of Indians' experiences in World War II as evidence of both their need and their readiness for "emancipation."

Read together, *Indians in the War* and "Set the American Indians Free!" suggest two strong ideological poles that would pull at Indians and non-Indians alike after U.S. entry into World War II. *Indians in the War* is a compelling and comfortable document for most White audiences of the time—as well as for some Indian audiences—because it foregrounds cherished images of fallen warriors fulfilling what is perceived as their particular destiny: responding to instinctive calls to honor and martyrdom that mark Indians as racially or culturally distinctive but that ultimately serve the dominant culture's desired ends. In this sense, *Indians in the War* is a subtle, perhaps final statement of John Collier's cultural philosophy and of the policies he supervised from 1933 to 1945 as commissioner of Indian affairs.[5] "Set the American Indians Free!" was also compelling reading for dominant audiences—and, given Armstrong's citations of support from Indian servicemen and political leaders, compelling reading as well for certain Indian audiences—though for quite opposite reasons. "Set the American Indians Free!" holds up Indian military service as evidence not of a racial or cultural distinctiveness but rather of a basic similarity among all patriotic citizens. Armstrong's rhetoric of "emancipation" and civil equality soon would be heard in congressional debates and public battles over the institution of already proposed termination and relocation policies designed to promote Indian integration into mainstream American life.

As in Aotearoa/New Zealand, in the early decades after the country's entry into World War II, indigenous writers and activists in the United States worked largely within or at some level of compliance with dominant discourses. This chapter examines how American Indian writers and activists developed paradigms for contemporary indigenous identities within a discursive space that assumed the inevitability of their assimilation. Like their Maori counterparts who wrote for the government-sponsored journal *Te Ao Hou,* Indian writers and activists in this period offered at best an indirect opposition to dominant ideology. In line with *Indians in the War,* the major works produced by Indian writers from the war years into the early 1960s celebrate idealized representations of the Indian past. And in line with "Set the American Indians Free!" they argue that Indian experience is human experience—and often quintessentially "American" experience— in a specific context. The nonfiction work of Ruth Muskrat Bronson (Cherokee), the nonfiction and fictional works of Ella Cara Deloria (Sioux) and D'Arcy McNickle (Cree/Salish), the philosophical and autobiographical work of John Joseph Mathews (Osage), and the activist writing produced by delegates to the 1961 American Indian Chicago Conference (AICC) confront what is seen as the inevitability of assimilation by attempting to balance representations of a distinctive indigenous past with arguments for a basic similarity between Indians and other Americans.

Individual writers mobilized the blood/land/memory complex to different degrees in order to argue that Indians could maintain *some level* of distinctly indigenous identities and *some level* of ties to indigenous lands and cultures. In the documents produced by delegates to the AICC, it becomes clear that, during the period as a whole, Indian writers and activists appropriated and redeployed a weak version of treaty discourse. They launched activist assertions of the blood/land/ memory complex but immediately revised these statements in terms of the dominant discourses of civic, political, and Christian equality. In effect, they purposefully understated the tension between separation and supervision that lies at the heart of U.S.-Indian treaty discourse in order to avoid unnecessarily challenging the audiences they hoped to persuade. Although these maneuvers may have represented a practical approach to tactics for the period, they frustrated the younger generation, who, by the early 1960s, openly expressed a loss of faith in the ability of the federal government and its representatives of any racial background to solve Indian problems and who openly denounced the assimilating influence of the Christian missions. Eventually fed up with the tactics of the World War II generation, during the so-called American Indian renaissance these younger men and women, like their counterparts in Aotearoa/New Zealand, would become increasingly outspoken and increasingly militant in their own activism and writing.

No Braver Yanks

A little-known example of how Indian writers maneuvered the uneasy border between compliance and contestation during the war era is a long poem written by William A. Riegert (Chippewa), published in 1946 in the *South Dakota Historical Collections* (22:26–27).[6] Alison Bernstein, a historian, quotes two lines from the poem as evidence of Indian integration during the war and as proof that Indian and White soldiers "came to accept one another as equals and friends."[7] It is true that Riegert's poem celebrates Indian participation in the war. However, its pointed title—"What Are We, 'The American Indian,' Fighting For?"—is suggestive of larger themes of exposing the dominant culture's history of violent discrimination against Indians before the war and continued indifference of the United States, even after Indian sacrifice, to Indian calls for "the same freedom" enjoyed by Whites. The poem mobilizes the blood/land/memory complex and offers a complicated thesis on Indian heroism, loyalty, and "integration":

WHAT ARE WE, "THE AMERICAN INDIAN," FIGHTING FOR?

To secure THEE forever, in our isolation and decay
To make of us only common clay
To mould at thy will, then cast and despise.
To mould again and again, and then our demise.
Or, to live for Eternity and the will to be free,
To live in peace with God and thee?
Did you not land on our shores—seeking freedom and peace,
Did we not succor you from famine and disease,
Did you not live and repay us with greed,
Did you not constitute, excluding Indians in your Deed,
Did you not entreaty and break at your will,
Did you think of your past and go on to your fill?
AMERICA, WE CHERISH AND LOVE YOU, OUR NATIVE LAND
Where honorably we surrendered, each Tribe and Band:
Tecumseh and Sitting Bull, many others you recall
Fought YOU, the aggressor, till they did fall.

But not in vain, God Forbade, till time presents this thought
Remember Tinker and Waldron, how, and for whom they fought.
And thousands of others have filled your ranks,
Shoulder to shoulder are no braver Yanks.
What are we fighting for around the world,
It is the Stars and Stripes forever unfurled,
It is Italy, France, Russia, China and England's future,
Are we any less than they, because of our nature?
We are now a Smith, a Jones, or Takes Him Standing,
Like your Smiths and Jones on some foreign landing.
We bind each other's wounds and eat the same ration.
We dream of our loved ones in the same nation.
Cannot our rights be equal, in peace as in war,
What more can you ask, that we would be fighting for?
How many wars then, by your side must we fight,
How long must you ponder to see our right,
When will your handclasp be firm and secure,
When will your voice call, to reassure
The right to live, the same freedom for all
The RIGHT of our BIRTHPLACE, When-Will-You-Call?

The *South Dakota Historical Collections* notes that Riegert's poem was read aloud before the Pierre, South Dakota, Kiwanis Club in October 1945 by Luke Two-Tails Gilbert, a Cheyenne River Sioux who in 1940 had been elected chairman of the Black Hills Sioux Nation Council and who in 1945 was also serving as a member of the first executive council of the National Congress of American Indians. These details suggest that Riegert's work was known among Indian leaders and that at least some of them endorsed his views. One can only imagine the impact an impassioned reading of the poem might have had on the assembled members of the Kiwanis Club.

In a tone of controlled anger, Riegert's poem attempts to answer the surprisingly complex question of its title. The poem juxtaposes a concise summary of the social and economic conditions faced by Indians in the early 1940s—many feel they are treated as "clay" to be molded by the changing fancy of the government—with a condensed version of their significant contact history and with an emotionally charged description of Indian service during the war.[8] Along the way, the poem poses a series of difficult questions and compares U.S. ideals of "freedom and peace" inscribed in the Constitution and forged in treaties with the realities of the contemporary nation. Dividing the poem is an exclamation that asserts Indians' indigenous rights to U.S. soil: "AMERICA, WE CHERISH AND LOVE YOU, OUR NATIVE LAND." The exclamation is repeated in the final line, which argues that Indians claim "freedom" from "isolation and decay" not as a gift of White charity but as a birthright guaranteed by indigenous status. The poem insists that Indians fought in past wars against intruding Whites and continue to fight in the present war alongside White fellow Americans for the same reason. The aim is not, as both *Indians in the War* and "Set the American Indians Free!" argue, to fulfill the goals of the dominant culture. Instead, American Indians fight for their "NATIVE LAND" and the "RIGHT" of their "BIRTHPLACE." Indigeneity, rather than assimilation, is the compelling call to arms.

Other educated Indians also saw the positive portrayal of Indian participation in the war as an opening for public relations efforts and for at least some degree of activism. In 1944, eighty Indians from twenty-seven states and representing more than fifty tribes met in Denver, Colorado, to form the National Congress of American Indians (NCAI).[9] Their number included D'Arcy McNickle, who had worked in the Bureau of Indian Affairs since 1936, other BIA employees, tribal council members like Luke Two-Tails Gilbert, religious leaders, and a wide range of Indian professionals. These men and women were not a "radical" group.[10] Their primary goal was to present a unified voice to the American public and to the federal government in order to lobby for treaty rights on behalf of tribes and for full citizenship rights on behalf of individuals. To that purpose, the NCAI worked, as historian Thomas Cowger observes, to create "an institutional expression" of a common, intertribal identity "as a single ethnic group"; at the same time, the NCAI also emphasized "the citizenship of Indians in separate nations" (6, 11). Throughout the postwar period, the apparent conflict between the assertion of a viable tribal identity and the assertion of a viable pan-Indian identity frustrated the dominant culture and U.S. lawmakers, who would have preferred a choice by Indians of one identity or the other; the same issue caused tension among Indian individuals and communities, who were of diverse opinions about the advantages and disadvantages of different citizenships.[11] To promote the assertion of both identities, the NCAI developed at their annual conventions emblematic figures of "Indianness" that marked both the specific indigeneity and the ethnic unity of American Indians. One marker was the "Treaty of Peace, Friendship, and Mutual Assistance" created for the 1948 convention in Sante Fe, New Mexico. The NCAI appropriated and redeployed the dominant discourse of treaties, with its recognition of nation-to-nation status, in order to assert that the organization represented a coalition of united indigenous nations that were in a unique relationship, individually and collectively, with the United States. Delegates re-signed the treaty at each subsequent convention.[12]

Causing the Ghosts to Linger, but Not Stay: Revising the Blood/Land/Memory Complex

The NCAI argued, Bernstein points out, "that Indians, unlike any other minority group, had a dual identity and dual relationship with white society" (127). Early articulations of this argument—as well as its inherent contradictions—can be found in the war-era work of Ruth Muskrat Bronson and Ella Cara Deloria. Each worked for the betterment of her particular community and for the advancement of Indian peoples generally, and each used her considerable writing and public-speaking abilities to promote a better understanding of the contemporary Indian situation among the White public and the federal government. Both women were politically and socially "progressive," and each was aligned with Christian, activist, governmental, and/or academic institutions dedicated to preserving (at least some) Indian traditions and to promoting Indian equality.[13] As Collier had discovered in the previous decade, these goals often were viewed as being at odds; to develop a persuasive argument for balancing tradition with the contemporary "privileges" and "responsibilities" of civil equality was no easy task. Given this context, as well as the context of the war, which had diverted both resources and public interest away from Indian Affairs, it is no surprise that Bronson's and Deloria's major works from this period invoke aspects of the Indian past in order to promote a limited or directed self-determination for Indian individuals and communities in the present. Much like Erik Schwimmer, the first editor of New Zealand's Department of Maori Affairs journal *Te Ao Hou*, Bronson and Deloria each advocated a benevolent but nonetheless top-down approach to managing contemporary indigenous identity.

Bronson's *Indians Are People, Too* and Deloria's *Speaking of Indians,* both published in 1944, argue that, like other Americans, Indians should have the right to determine the way of life that works best for them—within certain bounds. The boundaries are wide but clear: Indians must build contemporary lives within the ideals of Christian morality and unselfish American citizenship. Only those aspects from the indigenous past that represent the "seeds" of these modern ideals need be saved. Deloria also represents this overdetermined relationship in her fiction. Key passages of her historical novel *Waterlily,* however, resist connections between the indigenous past and the Christian present.[14] The scenes in question raise the possibility that non- or pre-Christian aspects of indigenous culture might endure into the present and even into the future. And they suggest the possibility of reading Deloria's narrative as a more disruptive, activist text than either her own or Bronson's nonfiction efforts.

Bronson's work reflects her allegiances to the Christian missions, the Indian Rights Association (IRA), and the NCAI.[15] *Indians Are People, Too* was published by the Friendship Press, then associated with the National Council of Churches; like the IRA's *Indian Truth* and other "friends of the Indian" publications, it is targeted at a progressive White Christian audience. From the first page, Bronson launches her thesis of Indian equality by mobilizing three discourses sure to arouse the sympathies of progressive White Christians. She juxtaposes arguments for civic and political equality in order to ask how a nation that believes "all men are created equal" can allow one group of those men, who have done no less than defend the "homeland," to remain "wards" of the government. Bronson then reminds readers of the Protestant value of equality before the eyes of God that is supposed to be the foundation for their "civilizing" work. Throughout the text, Bronson's tripartite rhetorical strategy juxtaposes the discourses of civic, political, and Christian equality to argue that Indians deserve to be treated as "people"—to assert, that is, that Indians deserve to be treated as progressive White Christian Americans.

One of Bronson's tactics is to write in the inclusive plural, aligning her readers' sense of civic and Christian duty with her own. Another is to engage the blood/land/memory complex, but she revises her mobilizations of "blood," "land," and "memory" by filtering them through the discourses of civic, political, and Christian equality. Bronson mobilizes a discourse on "blood," for instance, when she counts as one group all Indian peoples of North and South America "scattered across the two continents from Alaska to Cape Horn," arriving at a total indigenous population of "thirty million." "Here is a *race* of people powerful enough in numbers alone," she writes, "to wield profound influence on the future of the world" (2, emphasis added). She then states in a section titled "From Many Tribes, One People" that all Indians are united "by a strong feeling of *racial* kinship" (31, emphasis added). A few lines later, however, she reframes these statements in terms of Christian equality: like "all people," Indians are "children of one Father" (32). The revision undercuts the activist potential of her "blood" talk, reassuring her readers that, despite a racial fellow feeling, these thirty million are indeed "people" as well as Indians, and thus subject to (White) Christian authority.

Other sections launch and revise discourses on indigenous "land" and "memory." In chapter 2 of her book, "Our Mother, the Land," Bronson asserts that the past is wedded to the present and that "for the Indian, past history is living history" (34). To support her point, Bronson mobilizes a generalized discourse of indigenous spirituality, in which "for life-giving and for the sacred memories of their dead, the Indian's homeland was reverently loved" (36). She argues that for Indians "to lose that cherished relationship [with their lands] and to be torn from the land where their fathers slept, was to be lost indeed, for this was to be spiritually cast adrift and the life-pulse of the race to be broken" (36). The argument appears ambivalent; it can be read either as an assertion of indigenous land rights or as an account of the unfortunate but inevitable sundering of Indians from the basis of their "pagan" beliefs. Loss of land opens the way for the light of Christianity. Indeed, in chapter 3, "Strong Is the Indian Spirit," Bronson revises the assertions of her second chapter by contending that "the Indian has shown his ability to integrate his own ideals and spiritual satisfactions with the higher concepts of Christianity" (84). She now refers to Indian spiritual ideals as "germs of spiritual truth" that Christianity can nourish and enrich (86). What becomes clear in this revision is that while Bronson advocates self-determination as the civic and political right of all U.S. citizens, she also believes, in step with her sense of Christian equality, that "Some of these [Indian] ways cannot fit into a modern world, and so will have to be discarded" (64). As a general principle, her position is extremely practical, especially for the 1940s, when Indians began leaving the reservations in record numbers. Her examples, however, give one pause. Bronson lists no specific Indian lifeways that ought to be retained. The only "values" she lists are "reverence and humility" (65). Indian Christians ought to behave very much like their White counterparts, and their spiritual syncretism, such as it is, ought to offer their White brethren little challenge.

Toward the end of the book, Bronson celebrates Indian service in World War II in order to revise the pan-continental racial identity she describes in her first chapter. She evokes the ideal of an unselfish and racially homogenized American citizenship, based on Christian fellowship and removed from "the prison house of self-interest" brought on by "segregation" (125). Bronson brings her book to closure by restating her title in a context appropriate to her audience: "Indian welfare and happiness, Indian needs and perils, are interdependent with your life and mine—for *Indians are people, too*" (181). By revising her assertions of the blood/land/memory complex with the discourses of civic, political, and Christian equality, Bronson effectively evacuates native indigeneity of its implications of radical difference and separatism that might disturb White Christians.

Deloria's work too reflects a long association with Christian organizations, educational institutions, and government agencies.[16] *Speaking of Indians* was published by the same Friendship Press that published Bronson's *Indians Are People, Too,* and it was written for the same predominantly White Christian audience.[17] As in her own life, in *Speaking of Indians* Deloria attempts to synthesize the goals of missionary work with the goals of the emerging science of anthropology for the purpose of promoting Indian rights and welfare. When *Speaking of Indians* was reprinted in 1979, Agnes Picotte and Paul Pavich felt compelled in their introduction to point out that while "At times [Deloria's] ideas on Indian progress may seem assimilative . . . she is constantly aware of the importance of her traditions" (xviii). They remark that "there are indications that [Deloria] planned to revise the work during the 1960s, and it may be that she had changed her views somewhat after seeing the resurgence of interest and pride in the traditional Indian ways" (xviii). However she saw the work of the missions or of anthropologists in the 1960s, Deloria's goal in the 1940s was to employ the discourses of both, whether or not they could be fully reconciled, in her own revisions of the blood/land/memory complex.

Deloria advances current anthropological theories of Indian cultures and their origins in part 1 of her book, "This Man Called Indian." But her scientific account of prehistoric migrations from Asia, cultural isolation in the Americas, and the development of linguistic and cultural diversity over long spans of time is countered by a discourse on the role "spirit" plays in cultural diversity, a discourse that confirms assimilationist goals. Having established the authority of archeological evidence, for example, Deloria states, "The vital concern is not where a people came from, physically, but where they are going, spiritually" (1). She fleshes out her account of land-bridge migrations by employing personal imagination and a transgenerational identification with Indian ancestors, creating history for which there is no material record; in other words, she engages the blood/land/memory complex. Her specific maneuvers, however, offer a subtle apology for Christian missions:

> I can picture that dog, pulling a small travois on which are piled his master's few belongings. I can picture a line of early men, women, and children, struggling along on foot, and among them, those burdened dogs. Snow and winds harshly whip across their primitive faces. All are heading for America, to become unwittingly the First Americans. If one stops to muse on them coming thus, one must feel a little sorry for them, for they were walking deliberately into a trap. With each step they were cutting themselves off for thousands of years from the rest of mankind. (2)[18]

Deloria's account brings the distant past to life in the present, a goal of Boasian descriptive anthropology. But her "musing" reframes the early migrations as a loss of kinship. Christianity becomes the means for restoring the kinship of "the great human family" (6).

Deloria fuses Christian and anthropological discourses in the final section of part 1, titled "Spiritual Culture Areas." Because of its centrality to her intentions, I quote the definition of spiritual culture areas in full:

> I mean such ethical values and moral principles as a people discovers to live by and that make it a group distinct from its neighbors. I mean all those unseen elements that make up the mass sentiment, disposition, and character—elements that completely blend there, producing in an integrated pattern a powerful inner force that is in habitual operation, dictating behavior and controlling the thought of all who live within its sphere.

It's an elusive area, without any location that we can visit bodily. Like heaven, it is hard to define, delimit, and describe. And yet it is the "realist" part of a people, just as is the inner life of an individual. (12)

Throughout her career, these intangible elements were Deloria's particular interest; she develops her account of the Dakotan "spiritual culture area" most fully in her historical novel *Waterlily*, in which she imagines the precontact life of a virtuous Sioux woman. In *Speaking of Indians*, the focus on spiritual culture areas is an effective strategy that allows her to combine the secular objectivity of science with the Christian idea of a split between body and spirit. By asserting that the "inner life" is more important than the material, Deloria sets up an argument almost identical to Bronson's: American Indian "values" with Christian cognates should be retained, while "traditions" unfamiliar to White Christians can be replaced with little or no ill effect. Deloria's description of the Dakota as "understand[ing] the meaning of self-sacrifice" and as having "made almost a fetish of giving" links Dakotan identity to the ideals of Christianity (14).

Deloria emphasizes the intangible over the material and connects Dakota camp life, religion, education, and economics to Christian ideals throughout part 2 of *Speaking of Indians*, titled "A Scheme of Life That Worked." In part 3, "The Reservation Picture," she again foregrounds anthropological interpretations of the Dakota, a return signaled by an epigraph from Boas's *Anthropology and Modern Life* (1932). Deloria builds on Boas's idea that "under undisturbed conditions the processes of changes of culture are slow" (49). Rapid change in Dakota culture after the arrival of first Europeans and then Americans, Deloria argues, was not only inevitable but also "necessary." "A relatively small group of mankind could not rightly refuse to share their vast rich domain with others," she writes, again revising her "objective" anthropological discourse with an appeal to Christian morality. "They could not rightly prevent its exploitation for the good of the many" (51). Furthermore, Deloria asserts that "I do not think there is a Dakota who would doubt the rightness of that, if only he understood. But the way in which it happened was cruel" (51). In the remainder of part 3, she develops her condemnation of the means by which the Dakota were forced onto the reservations and forced to assimilate American lifestyles, while praising the resultant ends of Western education and Christianity. As part 3 concludes, anthropological discourse has been superseded completely by the discourse of Christian missions. "The call for strong church work in the Indian country increases," Deloria writes. "The Dakotas and indeed all Indians need the churches, now as never before. May we never forget that" (87).

Deloria's title for part 4, "The Present Crisis," is intended to have a double meaning: the crisis in Indian affairs, along with the crisis of World War II. She attributes the high level of Indian participation in the war to the old kinship obligations she has detailed in previous sections. Like Bronson, she argues that the war has changed the perspectives of all Indians, especially those of the young. The restrictions of tribal life will no longer seem tolerable. "Tribal life is only a phase in human development anyway," she writes with anthropological certainty. "The next step, for every people, is national life. Usually that is a slow process; but in the case of the Indians it needn't be, since national life pervades the very atmosphere they breathe" (97). Deloria calls for government and the churches to work together to help reeducate Indians out of reservation paternalism and out of "those elements surviving from the past that hinder growth" into full citizenship (99, 104). Without question, the church should take the leading role. Deloria's concluding sentence, meant to stir her audience into action, sounds as if it had been lifted from a sermon: "And only a people motivated by spiritual power and committed to the teachings of the Master can bring the right thing to pass" (105).

On the whole, Bronson's and Deloria's nonfiction manages to disrupt dominant discourses by engaging the blood/land/memory complex, insisting on the inclusion of Indian perspectives on history and even prehistory. At the same time, these texts bolster dominant discourses on the superiority of Christian morality and American citizenship. How, then, are we to read them? Both women's dedication to advancing the spiritual *and* material welfare of Indians should caution against reading their works as little more than apologetic tracts advocating assimilation. As noted in the introduction to part 1 of the present study, Gerald Vizenor has challenged readers to consider specific historical and tribal contexts when deciding whether or not particular texts qualify as "resistance" literature, posing the question "What were tribal identities at the turn of the century?" Bronson's and Deloria's nonfiction engages, at least in part, Vizenor's question, modified, however, for their own era: what are tribal identities at the end of World War II? They answer that those identities are syncretic, moving in a dialectic between indigenous traditions and contemporary American lifestyles. Tribal identities can never be again as they had been in the past. Christianity, they assert, is the binding force between tradition and modernity that liberates contemporary American Indians from the potential destructiveness of both.

Deloria's work of fiction more directly addresses Vizenor's specific question. In *Waterlily* Deloria couples her extensive knowledge of the Dakota with the power of her imagination to produce a fictional account of a Sioux woman's life during the transition from the precontact to the contact era. When she was writing *Waterlily* in the 1940s, Deloria was uniquely situated to answer Vizenor's question for a wide audience. She was an educated Indian woman who had indeed "heard the stories of the past" in her native tongue both as a tribal member and as a working ethnographer. Hers was what James Clifford has called the "ironic stance of participant observation": "the condition of off-centeredness in a world of distinct meaning systems, a state of being in culture while looking at culture."[19] Although she wrote *Waterlily* in the mid- 1940s, encouraged by Boas himself and by his student Ruth Benedict, the novel was not published until 1988.[20] Thus far, critics have focused primarily on its wealth of ethnographic information, particularly its details about the everyday lives of Sioux women.[21] Deloria is praised foremost as a valuable native informant. But that characterization underestimates the novel's constructedness as a work of literature and ignores its activist potential in either its original or contemporary contexts. Clifford draws a crucial distinction between ethnographic experience, which he describes as inevitably "ambivalent and unruly," and ethnographic writing, which works to produce a coherent "cultural fiction" through processes of selection, combination, and revision.[22] Meaning is produced in the suppression of incoherence and contradiction. The effects of this process are readily observed in *Speaking of Indians,* a work of nonfiction that fails to hide all of the unruliness and ambivalence of Deloria's experience as a contemporary Indian. In fact, we can chart Deloria's movements between the competing and at points contradictory discourses of anthropological science and Christian missions work as she attempts to present a coherent and compelling portrait of Indians for her White Christian audience. *Waterlily* presents a more seamless surface, but it is no less constructed out of competing discourses. Although the novel is often subtle in its literary and activist effects, it is not a simple collection of raw data.

Waterlily's potential for multiple readings is evident in passages that overtly engage the blood/land/memory complex. For instance, in recounting part of Waterlily's adolescence, the narrator links the development of human memory to the feeling of pride in one's kin: "Incidents now stood out more distinctly, and lingered, in Waterlily's memory so that she could recall them with nearly the same immediacy as when they actually happened and could feel the same sensation they had first aroused. Three of these were events that had to do with her brother Little Chief. . . . These were deeds that made her very proud of him, as a sister should be" (83). The first event Waterlily remembers is a family hunting expedition. During the trip, her father discovers and kills an enemy. Although it is his right to receive honor for the kill, he allows Waterlily's brother, Little Chief, to count first coup. It is the boy's initiation into a warrior's life and thus marks an auspicious honor for him—but also for Waterlily:

> It was indeed something to cheer about. Of course the entire matter was formal, a vicarious honor for a vicarious deed. Yet it was no less meaningful for the boy's record. Blue Bird [Waterlily's mother] took Little Chief to one side and whispered to him, "Do not forget this, son. Do no forget that you have a father who is so unselfish as to transfer the honor he has earned to his son. It is because he wants you to get top glory. Such a deed is praiseworthy. You are fortunate to have such a father." (85)

The episode is rich with ethnographic details about the workings of the Dakota kinship system and the rearing of Dakota children into responsible adulthood. But it is rich in other ways as well. Waterlily's reflection demonstrates that the active memory of significant events of the past can produce pride in self and community in the present. It also offers a potential strategy for reading the entire novel.

For American Indian readers, *Waterlily* can function not only as a source of accurate "ethnographic data," but also as a store of collective "memory" of the indigenous past presented as an accessible text written primarily in English. Conceived as memory, the novel can function as a catalyst for pride both in a specific indigenous culture and, potentially, in a larger, pan-tribal indigenous identity. For Indians cut off from personal memories, family stories, or their nation's oral traditions because of changed demographics or loss of indigenous languages—a situation increasingly common for young people after World War II—

such a reading strategy might prove personally and culturally invaluable. Moreover, Deloria uses Waterlily's memory to introduce the concept of "vicarious honor" and to detail its procedures among Dakota kin. Vicarious honor has both synchronic and diachronic functions within the kinship system, transferring honor both within and across generations. Although the implications of transferring honor across the generations is left implicit, the next generation of Indian writers and activists, led by N. Scott Momaday, made this process of "blood memory" a key tactic for asserting contemporary indigenous identities.[23]

Deloria develops the strategy of engaging her novel as indigenous memory when Waterlily's family honors the memory of her grandmother Gloku by performing the yearlong rite of ghost-keeping. The narrator points out that despite the demands of the protracted ritual, "life did not stand still in the *tiyospaye* [a group of related families]; the daily life did not differ from the normal. That would be both unnecessary and impossible" (147). A "ghost lodge" is set up to house Gloku's spirit. One of Waterlily's cousins watches over the lodge and the ghost bundle it houses, making sure courtesy food is always available for visitors who wish to pay their respects. "Only the ghost lodge remained set apart," the narrator informs readers. "Secular life went on around it still" (147). These passages are suggestive of the potential to maintain aspects of traditional culture in the midst of contemporary society. At the end of the year, a ceremony is performed to release the grandmother's spirit, to effect "a second dying" (157). In a symbolic feast, four of Gloku's granddaughters partake of her last courtesy food (155). The narrator explains that "like a parting admonition from the dead grandmother's ghost, [the girls] felt that nothing on earth could be more important than the continuance of her spirit of hospitality. And now the responsibility would fall on them. Should her good deeds die with her? Never—if they could help it" (158). For at least part of its potential audience, *Waterlily* can function as this kind of "parting admonition" from the indigenous past. Reading the novel can cause the "ghosts" to "linger . . . some seasons longer amid honor and reverence" (160), and this remembrance of the past can become an instruction in kinship responsibility. The younger generation learns to revere and emulate its ancestors. The more forceful the ritual account of the ancestor's deeds, the episode suggests, the more likely it will impress itself on the young. In this reading, at stake in the writing of historical fiction is nothing less than the continuance of essential markers of indigenous identity. As Schwimmer asserts with regard to *Te Ao Hou*'s "marae on paper," reading can keep indigenous traditions "alive" through a type of "use."

Deloria extends the implications of "vicarious honor" and "ghost-keeping" when Waterlily delivers her first child. Auspiciously, the boy enters this world at the moment an elder leaves: "[Waterlily's] grand-father lay dying in one tipi while she gave birth in the one next to it. Simultaneously and with perfect timing the baby came and the old man went, at dawn" (219). A "wise man" interprets the remarkable event thus:

> "Life never ends; it slows down but to pick up and go on again. . . . The boy is the old man; he is privileged, for he has acquired the qualities ready-made for him from the old one. He is strangely blessed. His grandfather has left him these traits he made for himself through a long life—gentleness, kindness, fortitude, patience. The boy should carry his name." (219)

This intimate relationship of "blood" and "memory" figures an on-going spiritual relationship, despite change, between indigenous ancestors and contemporary American Indians. In this way Deloria's scene of simultaneous death and birth anticipates the emblematic figure of the grandparent-grandchild bond developed for asserting indigenous identity during the renaissance experienced by both American Indians and New Zealand Maori.[24]

Only the Blackjacks Remain: The End of Indigenous Memory

When Bronson and Deloria posit forms of memory that can link desirable American and Christian qualities to their indigenous seeds, they argue for the possibility of transition for Indians into full American and Christian citizenships. Their contemporary John Joseph Mathews also believed Indians would necessarily assimilate into the mainstream. But in contrast to Bronson and Deloria, he focuses less on the possible links to the past and more on the effective loss of indigenous memory, and with it the loss of indigenous cultures "as they were." If Mathews's work from this period shares with Bronson's and

Deloria's a certain nostalgia, it also offers a sobering refusal to revise the blood/land/memory complex. It counterpoises Bronson's and Deloria's pragmatic sketches of Indians as universalized "people" adjusting to necessary change with glimpses of his specific nation, the Osage, losing literal and psychic ground to the disruptive forces of U.S. colonialism.

Mathews is best known today for his works published before World War II, *Wah'Kon-Tah: The Osage and the White Man's Road* (1932), the first Book-of-the-Month Club selection written by an American Indian (or published by a university press), and his semi-autobiographical novel of a mixed blood torn between tradition and modernity, *Sundown* (1934). In the 1950s and 1960s, he published two lesser-known works of biography and history, *Life and Death of an Oilman: The Career of E. W. Marland* (1951) and *The Osages: Children of the Middle Waters* (1961). In between, in 1945, Mathews published *Talking to the Moon*, a book that has been described as a natural history, a literary autobiography, a work of philosophical reflection, and "a kind of Osage *Walden*."[25] Beautifully rendered, this book offers an often subtle and sometimes highly romantic account of the ten years Mathews spent living alone among his beloved blackjack oaks in northern Oklahoma. Mathews writes that he wanted "to learn something of the moods of the little corner of the earth which had given me being" (2). Organized around the seasons, with chapters named for the Osage months or "moons," the book focuses on the intricate balance of nature Mathews witnessed on his secluded sandstone ridge. He describes Osage elders and their traditions, conversations with his neighbors, hunting partners, and occasional visitors from the East, and his philosophical musings on the importance of humankind's role in the natural balance, especially its unmatched potential for destruction.

Robert Allen Warrior (Osage) notes that *Talking to the Moon* anticipates Momaday's now famous admonition that "Once in his life a man ought to concentrate his mind upon the remembered earth."[26] In his work on how Mathews fits into a twentieth-century American Indian intellectual tradition, Warrior investigates how *Talking to the Moon* might offer "a vision of how the act of writing functions in the struggle for self-determination" (101). I focus instead on an aspect of this text scholars largely have avoided, namely, Mathews's unshakable sense that he had witnessed the demise of distinctly Osage people and lifeways. He did not share Bronson's or Deloria's confidence in national movements—whether they were Christian missions or Indian rights organizations—to ameliorate such radical change or to help retain a sense of indigeneity.[27] Nor did he share Deloria's confidence in the power of writing to maintain vital links with the past. In Mathews's "organic" formulation, indigenous survival is possible only at the level of the local and only at a significant remove from U.S. "civilization": that is, only with Osage land intact and flourishing and only with the Osage memory fully operative across the generations. At the end of World War II, he considered the prospects for such survival at best grim.

Ironically, it is in the vibrant "Summer" section of *Talking to the Moon* that Mathews records his most poignant portraits of indigenous decline. The first, an essay titled "Moccasin Prints," describes the collective "consciousness" of the last of the Osage "old men" as they contemplate their own and their culture's impending deaths. Mathews opens the essay by bluntly listing those features of "traditional" identity that the old men see as vanishing with them when they die: "The confusion into which Christianity and mechanism has thrown the Osage Indian, the man who was a part of the balance of my blackjacks and prairie, is only a part of the tragedy. The old men lament the destruction of their social structure, but they are more concerned over the consequent end of the tribe as a unit, the sudden rupture of their record, and the loss of their individual immortality" (86). The latter features, signifying "memory," become the focus of the essay. The old men see the loss of their community's oral tradition and its memorialization of earlier generations as by far the clearest sign of their demise as a distinct people: "But now their consciousness points out to [the Osage elders] the end of their race, the end of their god, the complete assimilation of their children, and the end of their immortality. It is the sheet-water of oblivion that washes their moccasin prints from the ridges and agitates their last thoughts" (86). Mathews eventually narrows his focus to a specific elder, Eagle-That-Gets-What-He-Wants, who has asked Mathews to record his stories in a book "so that his words will live" beyond him (89). Mathews writes that this elder "knows that his passing, and the passing of the other older men of the tribe, will be the symbolic passing of the tribe in so far as the old order is concerned, and he feels that he will be cheated of that very precious immortality which is the tribal memory" (89). Much of the essay is presented as the quoted dialogue of the elder or his wife, who tells her own stories of the significant past. Thus it is the older Osage themselves who predict that "Soon [the young people] will be white men and women . . . and they will not remember very long what the old people have said" (89). Although he records the elders' words, there is no sense in Mathews's telling that the recording of this indigenous "memory" will have any effect on today's youth or on future generations.

In a second essay, titled "For Posterity," Mathews describes his attempts to have portraits of the older Osage painted for the new tribal museum. "This was real conservation," he writes, "since these old men would soon pass away and with them the Osage as he was, the era and the type passing with the individuals" (126). Mathews depicts the uncooperativeness of the old men, their tendency to miss appointments, their unwillingness to sit for the White artist unless Mathews himself is also present, and their occasionally short temper. There is humor in this portrayal, but there is also melancholy. Mathews writes, "I had to rekindle their interest when time came for the sitting by assuring them that their portraits would hang in the museum; that people would come many hundreds of years later to look at them and know that the Osage once lived here and were great people" (127). During a third attempt to secure one elder's portrait, that of Claremore, Mathews cajoles him by saying, "People's memory is short. If they do not see that picture there, they will say that there is no Claremore. We will not be there a hundred years from now to tell these people that there was a Claremore" (128). The old man's pride gets the best of him, and he not only submits to the artist's gaze but also insists on dressing in his finery, despite the intense summer heat. Mathews ends the essay with a description of the opening of the new museum. Although the four clans of the Osage celebrate by "coming together for the first time in many years to dance to the earth rhythm of the drums like befeathered and gorgeously painted gods," Mathews's tone is mournful. He laments all the possible scenes of camp and ceremonial life that the White artist has not been able to capture "for posterity" (136). Without such a record, he implies, there will be no lasting memory of the Osage, since the next generations will be altered so radically.

Despite Mathews's faith in the cycles of nature, he does not mobilize the blood/land/memory complex to articulate a vision of indigenous continuity or renewal; nor does he offer revisions of "blood," "land," or "memory" filtered through dominant discourses. In the final pages of *Talking to the Moon* he remarks that he really does not know about the old religion because "I have only seen [the Osage] in the transition period" (239).[28] Throughout the book, when he refers to his people as distinctly Osage he consistently uses the past tense. And his few references to the possibility of continuity or renewal are embedded within long lists of evidence to the contrary, where they can have little effect. In the "Summer" section, for instance, Mathews undercuts his hopeful statement that the dance he witnesses "is still a prayer to Wah-Kon-Tah of the old religion" by situating it between a negative description of the dancers' "fat bellies and fat, flabby arms and [overly] gorgeous costumes" and a limiting adverbial clause, "notwithstanding the symbols of Peyotism with which [the dancers] adorn themselves" (83). After Mathews writes that he has only seen the Osage in transition, he offers the possibility of renewal by describing this era as "the period between bluestem [a native grass] and *perhaps* the return of bluestem" (239, emphasis added). The hope of this ecological metaphor is immediately undercut: "Perhaps the bluestem of Wah-Kon-Tah will be replaced by the man-nurtured flowers of Christianity in the ultimate assimilation" (239). Only the blackjacks will remain as they have been in the past, and the best Mathews hopes for in his refusal to revise the blood/land/ memory complex is "to make more comfortable the assimilation of the Osage" (14).

A Humanly Acceptable
Landscape: The Discourse of Transformation

The work of D'Arcy McNickle contrasts Mathews's focus on contemporary Osage decline by reimagining the distant indigenous past as both vibrant in itself and sustaining of the present and future. No other individual had a greater impact on American Indian literature and activism in the mid-twentieth century. McNickle published three novels in 1936, 1954, and (posthumously) in 1978; sixteen short stories (collected together for the first time in 1992); four nonfiction works of anthropology, history, and biography, spanning the years 1949 to 1973;

and numerous nonfiction articles published in a wide range of popular, government, "friends of the Indian," and academic journals over the long course of his working life. Scholars are drawn to McNickle because of his role in the development of public policy and community-based activism.[29] There is particular interest in McNickle's work from 1955 to 1967, after he left Indian Affairs, running summer leadership training workshops for Indian college students, as these proved to be a catalyst for an emerging American Indian youth movement.[30] Furthermore, as a founding member of the NCAI and a primary architect of the "Declaration of Indian Purpose" produced during the 1961 American Indian Chicago Conference, McNickle is recognized as a significant force in Indian activism.

McNickle produced two major texts in the first decades after World War II, *They Came Here First: An Epic of the American Indian*, a work of anthropology and history published in 1949, and *Runner in the Sun: A Story of Indian Maize*, his second novel, published for a juvenile audience in 1954. Critics have argued that the latter is a "fictional equivalent" of the former and that it expresses McNickle's contemporary concerns over federal termination policies, even though it is set in the precontact Southwest.[31] Little in the texts themselves support these conclusions. What they do have in common is a focus on the least-known and most contested era in Indian history, those years and centuries and even millennia before European or American "contact." Both *They Came Here First* and *Runner in the Sun*, like Deloria's *Water-lily*, engage the blood/land/memory complex by inventing compelling—if idealized—narratives of precontact Indian history, culture, and personality. But even more directly than Deloria's novel, McNickle's (pre)historical narratives insinuate themselves into the dynamics of change that characterized the postwar present. They do so not by creating specific analogies to the perceived evils of termination but rather by demonstrating that, from the beginnings of their history on the American continents, Indians have initiated and actively responded to dramatic transformations. Tenaciously, like the maize they cultivated into one of the world's staple foods, the Indians in McNickle's accounts survive, improve, and thrive over time.

They Came Here First is divided into three parts that correspond to a standard academic division of Indian history, excluding the contemporary era.[32] Part 1, "Unsealing a Continent," covers the period of "prehistory"; part 2, "New World Rediscovered," covers early contacts with Europeans; and part 3, "Supplanting a People," covers treaty making, the so-called Indian wars, and confinement to the reservations. What is not standard is the length of part 1, the largely speculative period of prehistory, to which McNickle devotes almost a third of his book. In these ninety-one pages, he supports his title's claim that his book will serve as an Indian epic. McNickle transforms archeological speculation into a powerful narrative—memory—of Indian migrations into the Americas, full of drama and triumph and rivaling the legends of Columbus and Cortez. In this way part 1 begins the argument about precontact transformations that McNickle develops more fully in *Runner in the Sun:* the roots of a celebrated "American" spirit of change and ingenuity are planted deep in "Indian" history.

Part 1's opening paragraphs are dynamic and ambiguous. They employ unattributed dialogue, collective nouns and plural pronouns, and a limited omniscient point of view to invite readers to speculate about the identity of early migrants to a "new land":

> "There is a new land over there. Across the water. Somebody has been there, and come back again. So we hear. They had all the meat they could eat. It is a plentiful land. Life is easy."
>
> The world was full of rumors just then. A marvelous thing had happened. A new land had been discovered, just when it was needed too. The people had wandered to the end of the world, in quest of food and safety.
>
> Somewhere in their rear, in their dim racial memory, were scenes of mortal struggle, in which they had been vanquished and driven away. Somewhere back there was a fearful dream they wanted to escape from and forget. So they had worked their way northward, into the outer darkness. Life got thinner as they went along. Forests thinned, then disappeared. Game animals were found less easily. The people had to keep moving, and they had to divide their camps into even smaller numbers. Yet they could never turn back, but must move ahead, hoping to come upon a kindlier country. This wandering had continued, now, for generations so numerous the old people could not count them. It seemed to have lasted from the beginning of time.
>
> Now, there were these rumors. A new land. A plentiful land. . . . (15)

The protagonist in McNickle's legend is collective rather than individual. At first it is unclear where "the people" come from, but the dialogue establishes them as having aspirations similar to those attributed to European explorers and settlers. McNickle is careful to suggest that "the people" are of ancient descent, possessing a "racial memory" that extends into an even mistier past. Their movement into what emerges as the Americas is cast as one of a series of migrations; this is part of an ongoing story of a people moving to "new land" rather than a fatal moment in their history. Unlike Deloria's brief account of migration from Asia, McNickle's extended narrative contains no note of loss or despair, no sense of crippling isolation from a larger humanity. The migrants' recognition of their new status as "a people apart" is triumphant: "Finally they were there. They knew the place at once, from the way it had been described. . . . After that first long look, they turned their eyes back upon each other. Perhaps then and there they saw each other for the first time and realized that they were a people apart. They had survived together and the knowledge of that would never leave them. . . . A handful of people standing in a new world!" (16). McNickle's migrants do not participate in a moment of pristine first contact with "new" land: there is no absolute point of American origins. McNickle's early travelers, unlike Deloria's, discover that others have been to the new continent before them: "It seemed at first that they had stumbled upon an entirely empty land. . . . But wait! Here was an old campfire! And here, a rock shelter. Someone had been there before them! The land was less lonely then" (16–17). The people's ability to see and to celebrate evidence of prior inhabitants is an implicit critique of the blind eye of European and American imperialism and of the importance of first arrival in European and American legends of discovery. McNickle situates Indians in alternative processes of transformation and narrative accounting whose authenticity does not depend on a myth of "virgin" land.

McNickle advances his argument that Indians were never a "static" people by recounting the story of maize. The cultivation of this "noble grass," he argues, is a "transcendent symbol" of humankind's quest to "transform the natural into a humanly acceptable landscape" (74). Maize and its many representations in Indian art are reminders of humankind's purposeful transformations of and in the Americas. However appealing the stereotypical image, Indian communities have never been simply "natural." Moreover, McNickle demonstrates that while corn has been improved over its generations, it remains recognizably and fundamentally maize. He concludes part I by extending the idea of

transformation without loss of essential identity to contemporary Indians. He engages the trope of "memory," in other words, to connect
his arguments about indigenous "land" to indigenous "blood." In a
direct contrast to Mathews's sobering ecological metaphors, McNickle
compares the retention of Indian conceptions of language and thought
—vital but elusive "inner" qualities of indigenous identity—to a plant's
ability to retain and replicate its essential qualities over time, despite
attempts to kill it. "Indians who are no longer hunters," he writes, "who
no longer even inhabit the hunting ground which was once theirs, still
think and talk as their grandfathers thought and talked before them.
Theirs is the secret of the twig that emerges ever green from the severed
stump" (98–99). Despite expropriations of land and despite drastic
changes in lifeways, McNickle asserts that a distinctively "Indian" identity is renewed across generations. The processes of transformation
continue, but so too do the essential characteristics of Indian "blood."

Runner in the Sun refashions the arguments advanced in part 1 of
They Came Here First so that they are more inclusive of contemporary
audiences and more obviously linked to contemporary times. That
said, it is important to caution against reading *Runner in the Sun* as the
"fictional equivalent" of McNickle's earlier work, as some scholars have
suggested. Parts 2 and 3 of *They Came Here First* detail the history of
how Indians were exploited first by Europeans and then by Americans,
a history *Runner in the Sun* never directly engages. Whether or not it
alludes more obliquely to some of the issues involved in that history is
up for debate. Consider McNickle's dramatic—yet oddly agentless—
summary of the history of Indian-White relations at the end of *They
Came Here First*:

> What has been told follows the broad outline of the story of Indian-
> white relations in the New World.
> First, there was wonder and delight, on both sides.
> Then uncontrolled exploitation, resulting in practices of enslavement
> and wastage of human life.
> Following that began the long and devious record of attempts to
> control exploitation, to govern the rights of ownership, and to work out
> a final adjustment between peoples of two widely different heritages.
> Results would not have been easy to bring about under the best of
> circumstances. In man's ignorance of man—not as of a century ago but as
> of today as well—it is astonishing that solutions ever rose above the level
> of murder and armed robbery. (286–87)

The tone is clearly pessimistic. But, in his attempt to write an even-handed account that will appeal to a White audience, McNickle refuses to blame or condemn anyone. Although he describes Indian-White relations as violent, he recounts the history of that violence in the passive voice, as though it were a sequence of unavoidable natural occurrences rather than a narrative of actions designed and committed by specific actors. Now compare this passage to the opening paragraph of Mc-Nickle's foreword to *Runner in the Sun*. Here the tone is upbeat, and the passage's focus emphasizes rather than suppresses the idea of agency in U.S. history. In fact, McNickle offers his intended audience of young people a vision of U.S. history as a multifaceted story in which both Indians and settlers are equally actors: "Most of us grow up believing that the history of America begins with the men who came across from Europe and settled in New World wilderness. The real story of our country is much older, much richer, than this usual history book account" (vii). In effect, McNickle refashions part 1 of *They Came Here First* instead of simply repeating its account of prehistory. Whereas the nonfiction text describes "the people" as an exotic Other, *Runner in the Sun* presents its protagonist and his people as heretofore unknown kin (in a symbolic sense if not in terms of blood): they are unknown elements of the readers' own history as Americans. McNickle's subtle use of inclusive pronouns, like Bronson's direct plea in the final sentences of *Indians Are People, Too*, invites White readers to connect their own lives to the lives of Indians. And, unlike *They Came Here First*, *Runner in the Sun* presents the connections in a completely positive light. In the remainder of his foreword, McNickle briefly describes Indian contributions to the world, which include the domestication of corn and "the gift of peace on earth." He concludes by stating that Indians "belong to the great tradition we call American" (x).

McNickle maintains his focus on these gifts throughout the novel. Set in the pre-Columbian Southwest, *Runner in the Sun* follows the adventures of its young protagonist, Salt, as he undertakes a journey from the Valley of the White Rocks to the Fabled Land of Mexico in order to save his cliff-dwelling community from dilemmas that threaten the viability of its agriculture and its political institutions. McNickle writes, "This is the story of a town that refused to die. It is the story of the angry men who tried to destroy, and of the Indian boy called Salt, in the language of his people, who stood against them" (1). It is tempting to connect the novel's opening description of Salt's village to the context of the Indian termination debate of the early 1950s. Alfonso Ortiz (San Juan), for instance, argues that the "town" may refer to "the Indian world in general," and that the "angry men" "would fit a description of the behavior of white colonists from Jamestown onward, as well as proponents of the policies D'Arcy McNickle and other Indian leaders were fighting in the years just preceding and just after publication of *Runner*" (242). But the analogy between Salt's pre-Columbian world and the termination era is at best strained, and no scholar offers textual evidence in support of this reading beyond McNickle's opening description. If indeed McNickle's story has a contemporary analogue, it seems more likely to be the general postwar context of strife between the generations, strife, that is, between governing elders and younger Indian men (and women) whose experiences during the war years prompted them to disregard or openly challenge traditional authority. Details throughout the text support this reading. No alien culture threatens the village. The "angry men" who wish to seize political control from the elders are from the village's own Spider Clan; they are led by Dark Dealer, a man who has assumed a position of power that is inappropriate for someone his age. "Dark Dealer was not an old man," the narrator tells us, "yet he occupied a place of leadership which normally fell to only the oldest men in the clan" (40). Moreover, Dark Dealer incites dissension even among members of the ruling Turquoise Clan by suggesting that the old form of government and its aging leaders are no longer useful in contemporary times.

Salt, the adolescent protagonist, is positioned in the generation behind Dark Dealer's; he is on the cusp of becoming a man. Early in the novel, when his life is endangered, the male and female elders of the village, who represent the grandparent generation, place Salt under their protection. Eldest Woman orders the kiva to reverse the ceremony that has recently made Salt a man, and she immediately removes from Salt's neck the turquoise pendant that is the sign of his adulthood (36). Salt is demoted to the social status of a child, which serves to emphasize that the novel's conflict is between generations. The village's elderly chief, called the Holy One, becomes Salt's mentor and grandfather figure. The Holy One makes Salt his apprentice and proxy, and he names Salt as his "successor" (58). *Runner in the Sun* thus becomes a story about the blood/land/memory complex, about the difficulties of maintaining traditional forms of leadership, especially hereditary leadership, during a period of uncontrollable changes in the environment (the climate is becoming drier, and the fields are producing weaker and weaker yields of corn) and political dissension within the human community (some in the middle generation seek to overthrow the old order). Salt's connection to the elder generation is made complete in a final act before he begins his journey to the south: the Holy One replaces Salt's turquoise pendant with his own. "The giving of the turquoise," McNickle writes, "was the most shattering experience of all that long day. Salt felt as if the image in which he had been born had been broken, and he had been born a new person" (166). In order to meet the challenges of the present and to ensure success in the future, Salt is reborn in the image of the ancestral. When Salt successfully returns from his long journey, he succeeds the Holy One as village chief. Traditional leadership is maintained. Dark Dealer is a ruined man and submits himself to Salt's judgment.

McNickle situates Salt's story within an ongoing narrative of Indian transformations and accommodations. The story is focused primarily on the village's ability to survive in the face of internal strife and environmental difficulty—but it is not concerned, as Ortiz and others contend, with the village's right to survive. Salt's people are not threatened with the kind of "termination" of corporate status that some Indian nations faced in the 1950s and 1960s. Rather, the people of Salt's village are faced with the question of where they will live, who will govern them, and how political power will be passed on to the next generation; in other words, it is a question of how to sustain continuity in the face of change. Like many of the stories published in *Te Ao Hou* in Aotearoa/New Zealand in the 1950s and 1960s, McNickle's novel is focused inward and on galvanizing the community, rather than outward and on demanding reform.

It is no surprise that *Runner in the Sun* argues for the kind of modified traditional leadership that McNickle's mentor John Collier advocated in the 1930s. Less obvious, perhaps, is the point that McNickle was also following Collier's lead in looking toward Mexico as a positive inspiration for change in North American Indian communities. In the journal *Indians at Work*, Collier advocated, among other things, that North American Indians should follow the positive examples of their racial relatives across the southern border. In the issue dated 1 November 1933, for example, Collier wrote in his editorial that through the

Indian Conservation Corps, which he had initiated, "we are trying to help release the Indians' own powers and ambitions, that they may go on to conquer their own future—like Mexico's Indians 'with practical armament and with flying mystical banners'" (3). And, in the issue dated 1 May 1934, Collier reprinted a talk he gave to Indian students at Bacone College in Oklahoma, in which he argued:

> But looking with a wider sweep, you will find twenty million Indians in the hemisphere, an advancing population which, in our next-door re- public, Mexico, has become dominant in government, in society and in economic life, and which is seizing for its use the most forward-reaching of the modern techniques, even while it goes on feeding a rich complex stream of tradition into the future Mexican civilization. You are not apart from this wider sweep of your race and of world-affairs but rather, here at a place like Bacone, you are made one with it. (31)

McNickle gestures toward Collier when Salt travels to the Land of Fable. While in Mexico he meets a young slave slated for ritual sacri- fice. Salt rescues Quail and she travels with him to his village in the north. It is she who carries the seed corn that will rejuvenate the vil- lage's agriculture. When the villagers see the mark of Quail's slavery, they reinterpret the tattoo on her forehead as "the mark of the sun," as a sign of her power to help them (226, 231).[33] The villagers adopt Quail and give her a new name, Red Corn Woman, making her one of their own (231–32). Thus through her personal transformation Quail brings not only new agricultural stock into the village community but also new "blood" and a new "memory." In the end, under Salt's leader- ship the people abandon their traditional home in the cliffs and move south "into the valley of the big fields" (233), where the new strains of corn produce "such harvests as had never been known" (233). To mark their relationship to their new land, the people develop a new cere- mony, which they call the Red Corn Dance (234). McNickle's vision of the distant past argues that continuities are indeed possible in the face of major change and, significantly, that Indians themselves are capable of determining and implementing the specific courses of action nec- essary for their material and spiritual survival. It was an argument McNickle would make again, explicitly for the contemporary era, in the early 1960s.

A Declaration of Accommodation

From 13 through 20 June 1961, 460 American Indians representing ninety tribes gathered on the University of Chicago campus to participate in an unprecedented event, the American Indian Chicago Conference (AICC). Although the conference was coordinated by University of Chicago anthropologists Sol Tax and Nancy Lurie, almost all of the participants were Indians. The NCAI played a significant supporting role, and D'Arcy McNickle served as chairman of the Steering Committee. To prepare for the national conference, delegates first attended regional meetings, where they drafted preliminary statements on federal policies. After consensus was reached in Chicago, the revised statements were collected into a single document, titled *The Voice of the American Indian: Declaration of Indian Purpose.*[34] In August 1961, a specially bound edition of the *Declaration* was presented to President Kennedy.

The AICC and the document it produced mark the end of the immediate post–World War II era of Indian activism and writing—rather than the early beginnings of the so-called American Indian renaissance that became fully evident in the mid- and late 1960s. The *Declaration,* although written twenty years after U.S. entry into the war, exhibits many of the discursive habits of Indian activists and writers working in the 1940s and 1950s, who were more closely aligned with the BIA, the "friends of the Indian" organizations, and/or the Christian missions than would be their counterparts in the 1960s and 1970s. Nevertheless, several of the *Declaration*'s specific points do embrace the ideals of the American Indian renaissance: the rejection of federal termination policies, the assertion of the continuing importance of traditional land bases to indigenous identity, and the argument for some level of Indian self-determination. In general, however, the *Declaration* looks to federal policies developed before World War II to provide solutions for contemporary and future problems. Throughout the document, one can sense the NCAI's pro-government timidity; and in specific passages, one can feel McNickle's hand in shaping a narrative of Indian survival through accommodation. Most telling is the *Declaration*'s endorsement of the ideals of the 1934 Indian Reorganization Act.[35] To introduce its list of legislative and regulatory proposals, the delegates state that "it is proposed that recommendations be adopted to strengthen the principles of the Indian Reorganization Act and to accomplish other purposes" (5). Furthermore, even though the document's statement of purpose argues that "our Indian culture is threatened by presumption of being absorbed by the American society," it offers as solution a New Deal–style policy of accommodation, concluding that "the Indians must provide the adjustment and thus freely advance with dignity to a better life" (4).

As in the other major nonfiction works produced in the immediate postwar era, the overall structure and language of the *Declaration* is strikingly ambivalent. Parts of the document are clearly directed at BIA personnel and other federal bureaucrats, appropriating the discourse of federal policy making and providing detailed recommendations for policy changes. Indeed, the document aligns itself with specific pieces of legislation.[36] These maneuvers attempt to balance separation and supervision, marking the delegates' desire to influence the federal legislative process through the subtle engagement of treaty discourse.

Other parts of the document, however, are directed at "the American people" more generally. These sections reframe the legal issues raised in specific policy recommendations as matters concerning the national conscience. "We pose a moral problem which cannot be left unanswered," warns the formal concluding statement. "For the problem we raise affects the standing which our nation sustains before world opinion" (19). Throughout these sections, the document works to establish American Indians' moral footing by emphasizing the common ideology that Indians and other Americans supposedly share as members of a single nation. The American Indian Pledge, printed inside the *Declaration*'s front cover, begins this process. It states that, like "all other true Americans," Indians declare their "absolute faith in the wisdom and justice of our American form of Government" and "join with all other loyal citizens of our beloved country in offering our lives, our property and our sacred honor in the defense of this country and of its institutions." The pledge further states that Indians "denounce in emphatic terms" the promotion of "any alien form of government" that might deny freedom to Americans or threaten "the peace and safety of mankind." And the pledge reassures readers that diverse American Indians are united in a common loyalty to country, that they "arise as one in pledging to the President of the United States and to our fellow citizens our assurance that upon these principles we and our children shall forever stand." Put simply, the pledge begins the document's more general work of moral suasion by offering non-Indian readers assurances of a common nationalism. As hard evidence of loyalty to country, readers are reminded of the heroic sacrifices of Indians during World War II, a common strategy in the postwar period.[37] The pledge also echoes both Bronson's work and McNickle's foreword to *Runner in the Sun* in its use of inclusive plural pronouns. Much of the pledge's language, however, suggests a strategy specific to the early years of the Cold War, exhibiting thinly disguised, McCarthy-era fears that conference delegates will be branded as political subversives.[38] Even before listing their document's table of contents, delegates to the AICC offer a preemptory pledge of American allegiance.

McNickle's influence is evident in the anthropological tone of the AICC Creed and the *Declaration*'s concluding statement. Structured as three general beliefs, the creed advocates the kind of cultural pluralism inherent in the Indian Reorganization Act. It justifies cultural pluralism on the basis of archeological evidence, restating McNickle's argument that Indian cultures are capable of accommodating change and developing their own lifeways according to their own ideals. Moreover, the creed argues that Indian success rests on the American public's willingness to remove such "destroying factors" as federal policies that have "produced uncertainty, frustration, and despair" in Indian communities (5). The creed ends by focusing on the necessity of future Indian-White cooperation. Like the American Indian Pledge, the AICC Creed works to quell Cold War fears that angry "Red" Indians might prove unfaithful to dominant ideals. The concluding statement falls into two parts. The first offers readers a highly condensed version of McNickle's account of Indian history; the second argues the complexity of solving the "moral problem" now posed by the AICC. The delegates compare their determination to hold on to the "scraps and parcels" of their land base and their indigenous cultures to the tenacity of "any small nation or ethnic group [that] ever determined to hold to identity and survival" (19). But the comparison does not embolden the delegates to offer radical solutions. In the final paragraph, like other Indian writers of the period, they restate their commitment to a "weak" treaty discourse: "In short, the Indians ask for assistance, technical and financial, for the time needed . . . to regain in the America of the space age some measure of the adjustment they enjoyed as the original possessors of their native land" (20). Led by McNickle and the NCAI, delegates to the AICC quietly ask to receive "some measure" of self-determination supervised by the federal government.

Among the names listed in the *Declaration*'s "AICC Indian Registration" are Mel Thom (Northern Paiute) and Clyde Warrior (Ponca). Unlike most of the older attendees, who were connected to the NCAI or the tribal councils, Thom and Warrior arrived at the AICC by way of the summer leadership training workshops that McNickle was running at the University of Colorado. In 1960 Warrior had been elected president of the Southwest Regional Indian Youth Council; Thom had served as president of the Southwestern Youth Conferences.[39] Like many other young, educated Indians, Thom and Warrior grew increasingly dissatisfied with the NCAI's tactics of accommodation. They left Chicago feeling that it was time to begin a new Indian organization, run on new principles. With the help of other young Indians, later in the summer of 1961 they founded the National Indian Youth Council (NIYC). Over the next decade, calls for both emancipation and accommodation were drowned out by demands for a "new tribalism." The desire for tribal "memory" that Mathews had found lacking among the young Osage in the 1940s would emerge as a national force in the 1960s and 1970s. The NCAI's argument that Indians possessed a "dual identity" as tribal Indians and individual Americans would become more pointed and more complex as younger activists began to argue that they were tribal members first, Indians second, and Americans only third.

PART II

AN INDIGENOUS RENAISSANCE

Te Roopu o te Matakite, the group organizing the [land] march, see the unity of the Maori people as the greatest tool they have in fighting for the retention of their lands.—Publicity brochure for the 1975 Land March

At first, we found ourselves parroting the words of Indian experts. This didn't do anyone much good. We spoke from our mouths only—not from our hearts. We received encouraging words from tribal leaders, but many of them were part of a tribal faction and did not have ambitions of real unity. The strongest unity seems to lie with the younger people. So, it is here that we must build that unity.—Mel Thom, "The New Indian Wars"

FOR THE NEXT GENERATION of indigenous minority activists and writers in the United States and Aotearoa/New Zealand, the national pride generated by achievements in World War II was no longer powerful enough to sustain a politics—or an aesthetics—of accommodation. In the United States, the policies of the termination and relocation era, plus a new international conflict, the war in Vietnam, worked to alienate American Indians from the ideals and goals of the dominant culture and the federal government. In fact, as I detail below, in many cases Indian participation in an ugly war in Vietnam spurred ex-servicemen into indigenous activism back home. In Aotearoa/New Zealand, the national government's renewed attempts to force Maori into the Pakeha mainstream by expropriating remaining Maori land holdings triggered a series of indigenous land and cultural rights movements. In short, the 1960s and 1970s proved to be a period of increased political and social turmoil for indigenous minorities in both the United States and Aotearoa/New Zealand. In this climate, one of the greatest challenges for both Indian and Maori activists turned out to be the need to effect and maintain indigenous unity. Internal factionalism proved as much of an impediment to indigenous progress as outside pressures to lower activist voices and to play by the rules of the dominant culture's protracted legislative and judicial processes. The dominant culture and the dominant media also looked for unity in indigenous minority activist movements, and contemporary indigenous minority writing was inevitably regarded as one possible source for the expression of that unity. Unlike their predecessors in the previous generation, Indian and Maori writers in this period tended not to be aligned with either tribal or national governments or with national religious or political watchdog organizations—that is, they were less likely to potentially "represent" a defined constituency—yet they found their works increasingly designated by nonindigenous audiences, including scholars, as "representative" of the diverse voices of the indigenous minority community.

Part 2 of this study investigates the construction of indigenous identity in New Zealand Maori and American Indian literary and activist texts during the second half of the early contemporary period. It should surprise no one familiar with the history of the 1960s and 1970s that these years of ferment among indigenous peoples resist easy or neat summary. In the early decades after the beginning of World War II, the number of texts produced by indigenous minorities that became "public" was relatively small, and many of the indigenous minority activists and writers who garnered the public spotlight operated in similar if not always exactly the same contexts. In the 1960s and 1970s, by contrast, the production of tribal, activist, and commercial texts by indigenous minority authors skyrocketed, and, especially in the United States with its more diffuse indigenous population, activists and creative writers were less clearly aligned than in the earlier period. With a larger and even more diverse range of public texts, the latter period is in many ways more complicated than the former, making a generalized assessment all the more difficult. The comparative frame used to examine events in the United States and Aotearoa/New Zealand is one way to help organize this abundance of material; it enables one to highlight the narrative tactics developed to assert an increasingly strident indigenous minority voice in First World settler nations. Some readers may be disappointed that, guided by this comparative frame, I do not perform extended readings of texts that are typically showcased as paradigmatic of indigenous minority writing in the 1970s, such as Witi Ihimaera's *Tangi* in the case of Aotearoa/New Zealand or Leslie Marmon Silko's *Ceremony* in the case of the United States. Similarly, some may wish I had prioritized themes typically emphasized in studies of contemporary indigenous literatures from a single nation, such as the role of oral traditions in shaping the aesthetics of written texts. The chapters that follow do address Ihimaera's and Silko's celebrated first novels and the influence of Maori and American Indian oral traditions on specific written works. But my primary focus, in line with my comparative analyses in part 1, is on the transition from an indirect to a more direct indigenous minority opposition to continuing colonialism and on how that transition can be understood through the lens of the blood/land/memory complex and treaty discourse.

Indigeneity, Biculturalism, Multiculturalism, Citizenship

One of the complications of the 1960s and especially the 1970s is the rise of multiculturalism, both as a template for how national settler governments in countries like the United States and Aotearoa/New Zealand intervened in the lives of various racial and ethnic minorities and as an evolving analytic category for the social sciences and for literary scholarship. Early in the contemporary period it became clear to American Indian and Maori activists and scholars that the dominant culture's efforts to define an indigenous minority as one of many similarly distinct and similarly disadvantaged "cultural groups" in the contemporary "multicultural" settler nation were inadequate and misguided. It is true that the African-American civil rights and Black Power movements in the United States, as well as other U.S. minority rights struggles, provided inspiration and models for Maori and American Indian activism in the 1960s and 1970s. But it is not true that models for understanding the historical or contemporary relationships of African Americans and other nonindigenous U.S. minorities to the dominant culture and its institutions—known collectively today as "multiculturalism"—necessarily apply to indigenous minorities. As early as 1970, at the First Convocation of American Indian Scholars held at Princeton University, Rupert Costo (Cahuilla), then president of the Indian Historical Society and a recognized spokesman for the Cahuilla Indian Tribe of southern California, lamented that "We are continually confronted with ready-made programs that are carbon copies of programs for blacks, Chicanos and other ethnic groups. These programs have no relationship to our history and culture, nor to our situation today, and they are absolutely worthless, either for teaching about Indians, or for teaching Indians themselves."[1] A quarter century later, American Indian activist and scholar M. Annette Jaimes Guerrero (Juaneño/Yaqui; previously M. Annette Jaimes) argued similarly in 1996 that "Multiculturalism favors treating American Indians as ethnic minorities, rather than as descendants of indigenous peoples and members of tribal nations, whether the latter have federal recognition or not. But the history of indigenous peoples in the United States is . . . one of colonization."[2] Dakota activist, writer, and scholar Elizabeth Cook-Lynn added in 1998 that "Indian Nations are dispossessed of sovereignty in much of the intellectual discourse in literary studies, and there as elsewhere their natural and legal autonomy is described as simply another American cultural or ethnic minority."[3] In Aotearoa/ New Zealand, Maori activist and scholar Ranginui Walker wrote in 1982 that "The Pakeha in-word 'multiculturalism' has negative connotations for Maori because it denies the basic reality of biculturalism. . . . Biculturalism is predicated on the basis that there are tangata whenua, indigenous people of the land, and non-indigenous colonisers."[4] Efforts to redefine Aotearoa/New Zealand as multicultural, in other words, work to invalidate the biculturalism established under the British-Maori Treaty of Waitangi. As these statements suggest, multiculturalist paradigms have tended to suffer not only from reductionism (or, put another way, from a desire to create "consensus" out of diverse minority experiences) but also from historical amnesia.[5]

Debates over multiculturalism typically have been predicated on traditional studies of North American immigrant ethnicity and more recent studies of postcoloniality, both of which emphasize the phenomena of migration, exile, and diaspora over that of indigeneity.[6] Indigenous minorities who assert an ongoing cultural distinctiveness and/or collective political rights to specific lands and other resources, often with explicit reference to treaties and other binding agreements they negotiated with colonizing powers on a nation-to-nation basis, do not fit easily within these dominant paradigms.[7] Unfortunately, historical amnesia enables members of dominant European-derived cultures, including well-meaning academics, to continue colonial practices of reframing indigenous collective political identities as individual political interests, performing a conversion, as Wendy Brown points out, that "recasts politicized identity's substantive (and often deconstructive) cultural claims and critiques as generic claims of particularism endemic to universalist political culture."[8] Such reframing constitutes what Stuart Hall describes as a "peculiar form of homogenization" that does not seek to obliterate difference but rather to absorb it within a dominating conception of the world.[9] Movements to describe the United States or Aotearoa/New Zealand as "multiracial," "multicultural," or "multiethnic," despite their positive contributions to liberal democracy, obscure indigenous claims to a status *different from* that of other minority populations. Furthermore, these "multi-" labels potentially can be used by the majority culture to attempt the invalidation of treaties and other binding agreements negotiated in past eras between imperial or national governments and indigenous nations. In the typical multicultural universe, indigenous claims to priority are construed as either incomprehensible or anachronistic. Despite invoking the ideals of antiracism and anti-Eurocentrism, settler multiculturalism has produced its own casualties.

Until quite recently, most theorists of multiculturalism expressed antagonism toward government support for any particular minority group's cultural survival within a liberal democracy, and this was the context within which Maori and American Indian activists had to work not only during the 1960s and 1970s but also into the 1990s, as statements by Guerrero and Cook-Lynn suggest. So-called radical or critical multiculturalists in the academy may have developed new formulations that are less hostile toward support for indigenous nations, but a pluralistic multiculturalism, which typically turns a blind eye toward international comparisons, continues to prevail in dominant discourses in both the United States and Aotearoa/New Zealand. Government support for a minority group's cultural survival, based on the recognition of collective identities and rights, still is viewed as being in conflict with liberal democracies' ideal of individual autonomy and authenticity. Pluralistic multiculturalist paradigms thus typically promote the visibility and acceptance of "minorities" in terms of individuals and their civil rights, not of groups and their collective rights—and certainly not of nations and their full, partial, or limited sovereignty.[10] Interpellated as oppressed minority *individuals*, indigenous minorities are invited to join pluralist coalitions of struggle against dominant power, but they are simultaneously disinvited to assert the priority of their specific rights as members of indigenous nations. The particular difference of indigenous peoples is inextricably connected, however, to their ongoing histories not only as groups of individuals but also as recognized political entities in the lands they still inhabit and/or claim. Acknowledgment of this fact by some scholars has led to the idea of a "differentiated citizenship," which would recognize "indigenous peoples' rights to a distinct, permanent, and differentiated status that attaches to collectivities of distinct peoples. These supplement the traditional political, civil, and social rights attaching to indigenous people as individual citizens."[11] For many non-indigenous citizens of settler nations, whether or not they identify themselves as multiculturalists, such ideas will seem too radical, too divisive, or simply too difficult to implement. Nonetheless, the persistent calls of indigenous minorities for self-determination alongside national civil rights will mean that the case for differentiated citizenships will be argued with increasing frequency. The foundations for such arguments were laid in the 1960s and 1970s, when indigenous minority activists worked to reverse the dominant culture's conversion of their nations' political identities into generic political interests and to expose the dominant culture's attempts to homogenize their distinctiveness out of existence.

Maori Activism: A Critique from Within

In the 1950s and early 1960s Maori activism had worked steadily but quietly for the recognition and promotion of Maori language, for health and justice reforms, and for the return of Crown-controlled Maori land. In the mid- and late 1960s, Maori activism became more politically focused and more publicly visible. Parliament's Maori Affairs Amendment Act 1967, which continued and strengthened the colonial project of commodifying and alienating Maori land, triggered a series of Maori land rights movements that would dominate Maori affairs and the national media over the next decades.[12] In addition, the continuing concentration of the Maori population in major urban centers like Auckland and Wellington, coupled with a steady increase in the Maori population, created an urban underclass of Maori youth, who began organizing as "gangs." In 1970, concerned about escalating incidents of crime and violence among urban Maori youth, the national Maori Council organized a Young Maori Leaders Conference at Auckland University. Out of this conference emerged one of the first contemporary Maori activist organizations, Nga Tamatoa, or the Young Warriors. By the mid-1970s, a decade that Ranginui Walker has characterized as "nga tau tohetohe," the years of anger, these and other urban Maori activists had taken on the difficult task of critiquing from within a First World nation that prided itself on its political, economic, and social successes, including purportedly the best race relations in the world. Nga Tamatoa, for instance, worked throughout the early 1970s for better Maori language instruction in primary and secondary schools. In 1973 Nga Tamatoa initiated a protest of New Zealand's national celebration of Waitangi Day (which commemorates the sign-ing of the Treaty of Waitangi in 1840), converting the holiday into "a day of mourning for the loss of 25.2 million hectares of Maori land."[13]

This "new" style of protest was actually a return to earlier attempts to assert Maori rights under the Treaty.[14] Activism in the 1970s culmi-nated in major protest demonstrations, most notably in large-scale occupations of confiscated lands. Protestors occupied the Raglan golf course near Hamilton in 1972 and the prime real estate of Auckland's Bastion Point in 1977–78. In 1975 a pan-tribal national Land March traversed over three hundred miles down the length of the North Island to protest the continuing loss of Maori land. Widely reported in the national press, such activism made it impossible for Pakeha New Zealanders to continue to ignore Maori grievances. As I argue in the Introduction, in this respect it is useful to think of this politics of embarrassment as performances of ethno-drama. Designed to high-light enduring differences between Pakeha and Maori, the continuing importance of the land base to contemporary Maori identity, and the failure of the dominant settler society to live up to its own ideals of justice, the dramatic structure of these events staged the "facts" of Maori presence and Maori indigeneity and a version of contemporary Maori "reality." The particular circumstances and charismatic leaders of individual protest events were able to bring together a wide range of tribal groups, rural and urban individuals, and diverse radical and moderate protest factions, but only for a limited period of time. No single activist group or protest event was able to sustain itself or its membership beyond the circumstances of narrowly defined griev-ances. After a particular event, such as the 1975 Land March, some members lost interest; factions split; new groups formed. In this sense Maori activism in the 1970s was a series of discrete though related performances staged by activist groups whose memberships were con-tinuously renewed and reformed, rather than a single, steady "move-ment." And in this sense the performance of Maori activism resembles the production of Maori renaissance literature, which also produced a series of discrete though related performances of contemporary Maori indigeneity.

The late 1960s and the 1970s saw the publication of powerful Maori political writing in grassroots journals like the *Republican*, MOOHR (Maori Organization on Human Rights), and *Te Hokioi* (mysterious night bird), which took its name from the first independent Maori newspaper, out of Waikato, established in 1862. *Te Hokioi*'s first issue in August 1968 proclaimed that the journal would serve as "A Taiaha [traditional weapon] of Truth for the Spirit of Kotahitanga [unity] within the Maori Nation." Maori activists also began to publish articles in mainstream magazines, such as the "Korero" (news) series in the *New Zealand Listener*. Departments of Maori studies were established in New Zealand's major universities, making available to urban Maori of all ages the study of Maori language and history, on Maori rather than on Pakeha terms, as well as providing centers for Maori political activism. Tribal, pan-tribal, and church-based groups began to build Maori community centers and urban marae complexes in order to facilitate Maori community building, promote Maori cultural activities, and meet particular Maori ceremonial needs in urban areas. In response to Maori challenges, in 1975 Parliament created the Waitangi Tribunal, which allowed Maori to grieve claims against the Crown for violations of the Maori language version of the Treaty of Waitangi.[15]

In this context of increased political activism, there developed a number of government-sponsored and independent national Maori news and literary journals that followed *Te Ao Hou*'s example of Maori authorship but also enabled Maori oppositional politics to find its way more easily into print. Maori writers began to publish more regularly and in greater numbers. The first anthology of contemporary Maori writing, published in 1970 and edited by Margaret Orbell, consists largely of stories and poems culled from the pages of *Te Ao Hou*. More than a decade would pass before the next anthology of contemporary Maori writing appeared; edited by Witi Ihimaera and D. S. Long, *Into the World of Light* (1982) made available to a wide reading audience both established and new Maori voices.[16]

Maori writers achieved a number of important publishing breakthroughs in the decade between 1964 and 1975. Hone Tuwhare's *No Ordinary Sun* (1964) was the first published collection of poems by a Maori poet; six subsequent volumes of Tuwhare's poetry were to appear between 1970 and 1987. Witi Ihimaera's *Pounamu, Pounamu* ("greenstone," nephrite jade), the first published collection of short stories by a Maori author, appeared in 1972. The first play published by a Maori playwright, Harry Dansey's *Te Raukura/The Feathers of the Albatross*, followed in 1974. The next year, 1975, marked the publication of the first book of stories written by a Maori woman, Patricia Grace's *Waiariki* (hot springs; the Maori name for the Rotorua area), and the publication of the first Maori novel set during the precontact and early contact periods, Heretaunga Pat Baker's *Behind the Tattooed Face.* Both Ihimaera and Grace soon followed their story collection debuts with first novels. Ihimaera published his novels *Tangi* (noun: funeral ceremonies; verb: to cry in mourning) in 1973 and *Whanau* (noun: family; verb: to be born or to give birth) in 1974. He followed these with a second story collection, *The New Net Goes Fishing,* in 1977, and a third novel, *The Matriarch,* in 1986, which won New Zealand's Wattie Book of the Year Award. In 1986 his first collection of stories, *Pounamu, Pounamu,* was published in a Maori-language edition, translated into Maori by Jean Wikiriwhi, and his fourth novel, *The Whale Rider,* appeared in 1987. Grace's first novel, *Mutuwhenua: The Moon Sleeps,* was published in 1978, followed by her second collection of stories, *The Dream Sleepers and Other Stories,* in 1980, and her second novel, *Potiki* (youngest child), in 1986.

In 1973 these and other emerging Maori writers, along with contemporary Maori artists, formed the Maori Artists and Writers' Association and began holding annual meetings on different marae to discuss their artistic, cultural, and political concerns. The Maori Artists and Writers' Association also published its own journal, *Koru* (curling fern frond shape; a common motif in Maori carving and scroll painting). These events marked the beginnings of a Maori literary renaissance that promoted a pan-iwi, national Maori identity. In the 1980s a growing number of Maori authors, writing primarily in English, became prominent in New Zealand literature. In addition to Tuwhare, Ihimaera, Grace, and Baker, these writers include Apirana Taylor, whose first collection of poems, *Eyes of the Ruru* (owl), was published in 1979, followed by the publication of his first collection of stories, *He Rau Aroha: A Hundred Leaves of Love* in 1986; Keri Hulme, whose first collection of poems, *The Silences Between (Moeraki Conversations)* was published in 1982, followed by her first novel, *The Bone People,* published in 1984, which won the Booker Prize, the New Zealand Book Award, and the American Pegasus Prize for Literature; and Bruce Stewart, whose stories were collected in 1989 as *Tama and Other Stories.* All continued to write and publish in the 1990s.

Chapter 3 argues that these writers of the Maori renaissance, like their activist counterparts, revised the narrative tactics developed in the earlier period so that they more openly voiced Maori claims to native indigeneity and more forcefully challenged dominant power in Aotearoa/New Zealand. Deploying emblematic manifestations of the blood/land/memory complex that figure the successful passing down of tradition from ancestors to contemporary Maori, the continuing relevance of the Treaty of Waitangi and its guarantees of Maori control over Maori possessions, and the vital, empowering connection between individual and communal Maori identities, these writers assert the renewal of the indigenous past in the Fourth World present.

Indian Activism: Re-recognizing Broken Treaties, Rebuilding Broken Lives

The year 1964, when the federal government prepared to send U.S. combat troops to fight in Vietnam, can be considered an early watershed in the so-called American Indian literary and political renaissance. Before the U.S. war in Vietnam was declared officially ended, an estimated 42,000 American Indian soldiers would be stationed in Southeast Asia between 1965 and 1973.[17] Placed in its demographic context, this figure is startling. The total Indian population during the Vietnam War era—men, women, and children—is estimated at less than one million. As Tom Holm (Cherokee/Creek) points out in his study of Indian Vietnam veterans, even though American Indians made up nearly 1.4 percent of all the troops sent to Southeast Asia, Indians in general never constituted more than 0.6 percent of the total population of the United States in the same period. Approximately one out of four eligible Native Americans served in the U.S. military forces in Vietnam, compared to one out of twelve in the general population (*Strong Hearts, Wounded Souls*, 123).

Of those 42,000 Indian soldiers, 230 died in action overseas (11). Holm's work chronicles the often devastating impact that involvement in Vietnam combat has had on returning Indian veterans. But his study also argues convincingly that many Indians were able to reinterpret their Vietnam experiences in terms of their tribe's warrior traditions, thus converting one of that generation's most compelling "American" experiences into an experience distinctively Native. Many American

Indian communities were able to help their veterans cope with Vietnam War trauma by successfully mobilizing traditional ceremonials designed to integrate the warrior who has seen battle back into active community life. Furthermore, Holm's work demonstrates that significant numbers of Indian Vietnam veterans used the military, organizational, and cross-cultural skills they acquired during their national service to become effective tribal and pan-tribal warriors in ongoing battles against the U.S. government that had been escalating while they were away. Most notably, Holm shows, Indian Vietnam veterans participated in the armed occupation at Wounded Knee, South Dakota, in 1973 (176–79).[18]

American Indian political activism in the 1970s, epitomized by the occupation at Wounded Knee, also had its roots firmly planted in 1964, when the American Indian vote drew national attention for the first time. Vine Deloria Jr., who would become a significant voice in American Indian political and cultural critiques before the end of the decade, was elected executive director of the National Congress of American Indians (NCAI). In California, a group of Sioux men living in the San Francisco Bay area briefly occupied Alcatraz Island and claimed it as Indian land under the 1868 Treaty of Fort Laramie, a prelude to the signal occupation of Alcatraz by the activist group Indians of All Tribes in 1969.[19] Of perhaps greatest importance, the National Indian Youth Council (NIYC), formed in 1961, initiated what was arguably the twentieth century's first nationally significant American Indian political protest by actively supporting the fishing rights demonstrations of the Puyallup-Nisqually peoples and other Indian nations in the Pacific Northwest. Organized to protest state violations of federal treaty guarantees of Indian fishing rights negotiated in the mid-nineteenth century, these "fish-ins" were soon followed by local acts of political protest around the country, organized by Indian groups large and small, tribal and pan-tribal. Angered by the legacy of U.S. treaty violations and inspired by the successes of the ongoing civil rights and Black Power movements, Indians soon coined the phrase "Red Power."[20] The relationship between the U.S. government, the dominant American culture, and American Indian nations would never be the same.

In addition, in 1964 the newly formed American Indian Historical Society launched its journal, the *Indian Historian*, in order "to correct the record, to write the history [of American Indians] as it should be written, [and] to interpret correctly the aboriginal past."[21] The Society chose its name "because of Indian traditional meanings: the tribal historians were the honored people of each tribe," the editors noted, "preserving the tribal traditions and history. A Society was part of the life of all the tribes, being either ritualistic, warrior, or honor societies."[22] In the first issue of the journal, the editors pointed out that it was produced "entirely by American Indians." Moreover, the editors linked the survival of American Indians as culturally distinct individuals and communities to the preservation of their memory of the past: "[The American Indian] doesn't forget. And this tugging at the soul, this urging of the spirit, makes it almost impossible to exterminate his independent mind, just as it was not possible to exterminate him as a human being."[23] As I describe below, one of the Society's first significant actions on behalf of American Indians exemplified its stated mission of preserving Indian history and, along with the Pacific Northwest "fish-ins" that had gained the attention of the national media, marked the emergence of contemporary Indian activism.

In January 1965 the American Indian Historical Society acquired title to the Ohlone Indian Cemetery, located in Fremont, California. Members of the Miwuk nation, the Ohlone people had built the Mission of San Jose for the Spanish friars; in the early 1960s, the cemetery and the remains of more than four thousand Indians buried there were still owned by the Oakland Catholic Diocese. After the transfer of title, the Society restored the two-and-a-half-acre site as the Ohlone Indian Memorial Park, opened it to the public, and hired a family of Ohlone Indians as caretakers. Over the next several years, the *Indian Historian* published a number of articles that described Ohlone culture and chronicled their long history. The Society's efforts at preserving and publicizing the Ohlone site can be read as significant acts of ethnodrama. Its actions held up sacred lands and ancestors as important links to the Indian past and as important components of contemporary Indian identity. The creation of the Ohlone Indian Memorial Park visibly reinserted Indian historical memory into the landscape of contemporary America.

Most commentaries on the American Indian renaissance understandably point to the year 1968 as the significant watershed. That year President Johnson brought Indian issues to national attention when he delivered his special message to Congress on "The Forgotten American" and established the National Council on Indian Opportunity (NCIO). Congress passed the Indian Civil Rights Act, unilaterally extending to all Indian nations and individuals—and imposing on them —the guarantees of the U.S. Constitution. The Navajo nation founded Navajo Community College, the first tribally controlled institution of higher education in the country.[24] In June 1968 a National Aborigine Conference was held in Oklahoma. In July the urban-based, pan-tribal American Indian Movement (AIM) was begun in Minnesota, and it soon developed into a national protest organization. That same summer the activist group United Native Americans (UNA) formed in San Francisco. In 1968 Stan Steiner published his important study, *The New Indians,* which, for the first time, documented in compelling detail twentieth-century Indians' frustrations with federal policies, as well as the growing number of Indian cultural revitalization and activist movements. *Akwesasne Notes,* published by the Mohawk nation, emerged in 1968 and quickly developed into the first national indigenous newspaper. With an estimated circulation of 50,000 in the early 1970s, *Akwesasne Notes* made political reporting and commentary from an Indian perspective more widely available to Indian people than ever before.[25] And in 1968 N. Scott Momaday (Kiowa) published his first novel, *House Made of Dawn,* which would win the Pulitzer Prize in 1969 and usher in a new generation of American Indian writing that, by 1980, would irreversibly alter the landscape of American literary and ethnic studies.

The Pacific Northwest "fish-ins" begun in 1964 also gained momentum through the late 1960s. In 1969, a decorated Vietnam combat veteran of Yakima and Cherokee descent, Private Sidney Mills, dramatized the potential role Indians returning from Southeast Asia might play in events of political activism. While on leave in Washington State, Mills publicly resigned from the Army and committed himself to his people's struggle over fishing rights. In his published statement, Mills declared that he owed "first allegiance to Indian people in the sovereign rights of our many Tribes" and that he had "served the United States in a less compelling struggle in Vietnam and [would] not be restricted from doing less for [his] people within the United States."[26] Holm's survey of Indian Vietnam veterans suggests that Private Mills was not alone in realigning his national commitment, and

other published Indian texts from the Vietnam era are similarly suggestive.[27] The National Indian Youth Council published a cartoon in
the December 1969–January 1970 issue of its journal, *Americans Before
Columbus,* captioned "From Wounded Knee to Mi Lai / Only the
uniform has changed." A cigar-smoking, contemporary White U.S.
soldier runs his bayonet through the stomach of a "traditional" American Indian. As he is murdered, the unarmed Indian holds out, perhaps
as a shield, a document marked "TREATY," signed by the U.S. government and prominently displaying its promises for Indian education,
health, and land rights.[28] *Akwesasne Notes* created a similar effect in its
April 1972 issue when it reprinted a widely circulated photograph of
Vietnamese war victims with the following caption: "This is Vietnam,
1972. It could be Cheyenne, Lakota, or Pomo country, a century or less
ago. . . . The area where these [Vietnamese] children live is known to
the U.S. troops as 'Indian Country'." In her poem "The Long Root"
(1972), Wendy Rose (Hopi/Miwok) also emphasizes the parallels
many American Indians saw between the contemporary Asian conflict
in which they were being asked (or compelled) to participate and the
"Indian wars" fought against their own nations in the nineteenth century. "And no matter how I try," Rose writes, "there is no way to shake /
Cambodia from my Wounded Knee."[29]

Beginning in 1969 and inspired as much by years of antiwar protest
as by the civil rights movement begun in the previous decade, Indian
activism exploded onto the national scene in hard-hitting political
writing and in large-scale protest demonstrations designed to capture
media attention. A pan-tribal group calling itself Indians of All Tribes
successfully occupied Alcatraz Island from 20 November 1969 until 11
June 1971, when the remaining protestors were physically removed by
federal agents. During the occupation, Indians of All Tribes issued a
"Proclamation to the Great White Father and His People," in which
they reclaimed Alcatraz Island as Indian land "by right of discovery"
and offered "the Caucasian inhabitants" of the island a parodic "treaty."
This and other documents issued by the protestors at Alcatraz appropriated and parodied dominant discourses—including proclamations,
declarations, and treaties—as part of the interpretive ideological frames
of indigenous minority ethnopolitical conflict and as part of the emblematic figures of indigenous minority ethno-drama. The Indians of
All Tribes received support from AIM, and the experience at Alcatraz

paved the way in 1972 for a pan-tribal, cross-country American Indian caravan and subsequent occupation of the Bureau of Indian Affairs in Washington, D.C., which would become known as the Trail of Broken Treaties. Next, in 1973, came the armed occupation at Wounded Knee, South Dakota, by Oglala Sioux, other Indian protestors, and non-Indian supporters.

In addition to these major events of political activism, American Indian groups staged a number of smaller protests. In 1970, for instance, AIM's participation in the capture of a replica of the *Mayflower* and the attempted seizure of Ellis Island by Indian students in New York struck at two icons of European immigration to the United States. Around the country, Indians held sit-ins at various BIA offices, and AIM declared Thanksgiving, as Nga Tamatoa would declare Waitangi Day in Aotearoa/New Zealand, a national day of mourning.[30] In 1971 AIM targeted an important icon of U.S. political legitimacy, the Mount Rushmore National Memorial. In a dramatic demonstration, protestors reclaimed the granite heads of the four U.S. presidents as sacred Indian land. Each of these events was designed to draw attention to centuries-old American Indian struggles for treaty, cultural, and land rights. As the work of Peter Matthiessen, Joane Nagel, Stephen Cornell, Paul Chaat Smith and Robert Allen Warrior, and others has documented, Indian activism in the late 1960s and early 1970s was also a direct response to termination and relocation policies enacted by Congress in the early 1950s as part of the federal government's attempt to end its services to Indian nations and Indian individuals. In addition, protestors were responding to War on Poverty programs initiated in the 1960s that were targeted at a wide range of minority and economically disadvantaged groups, including both reservation and urban Indians. These programs, which were expanded in the early 1970s with the establishment of the BIA's Indian Business Development Fund (1971) and the passage of the Indian Education Act (1972) and the Indian Self-Determination and Education Assistance Act (1975), provided activists with models of access to economic and political power. Often these models favored pan-tribal organization as well as the grieving of specific tribal claims.[31] There were in fact notable—if limited—American Indian victories during the early 1970s that offered hope that national sentiment and federal policy could be changed. Taos Pueblo, for instance, rejected a cash settlement and successfully lobbied to have their sacred Blue Lake returned to their control in 1970. In 1972 federal termination policies begun in 1953 were finally overturned. And in 1973 the Menominees, who had been terminated in 1954, were restored to federally recognized tribal status.

Like the major events of civil rights protest in the 1950s and early 1960s, the major incidents of Indian activism in the late 1960s and early 1970s were widely reported locally, nationally, and even internationally. During demonstrations, media presence helped keep in check local and federal attempts to suppress protestors, and, perhaps unwittingly, the media helped disseminate Indian-generated images of contemporary Natives. These television, radio, and newspaper images offered U.S. and international audiences sharp contrasts to the popular images of nineteenth-century Plains Indian cultures and personalities that were celebrated (and sometimes fabricated) by the dominant American culture in books like Dee Brown's account of the 1860s wars between western Indian nations and the U.S. cavalry, *Bury My Heart at Wounded Knee*, published in 1970, and the disingenuous "autobiography" of a hundred-year-old Sioux Indian, *The Memoirs of Chief Red Fox*, published in 1971.[32] In addition to media attention, each of the major protest demonstrations mentioned above was followed by the publication of at least one commemorative or apologetic text written or edited by Indian participants or observers: *Alcatraz Is Not an Island*, edited by Peter Blue Cloud (Mohawk), appeared in 1972; Vine Deloria Jr.'s (Sioux) *Behind the Trail of Broken Treaties: An Indian Declaration of Independence* was published in 1974; and *Voices of Wounded Knee, 1973, in the Words of the Participants*, a publication of Akwesasne Notes, also appeared in 1974. These and other texts offered contemporary Indian perspectives to balance accounts generated by the dominant media and by local, state, and federal governments.[33] They also ensured that the political, racial, and social complexity of Indian protest events would not be forgotten by future generations. "As with Viet Nam," the editorial collective of Akwesasne Notes states in its introduction to *Voices From Wounded Knee, 1973*, "we felt that our Government should not be permitted to secretly conduct an undeclared war" (3).

With the publication of *Custer Died for Your Sins: An Indian Manifesto* in 1969, Vine Deloria Jr., who had served as the executive director of the NCAI from 1964 to 1967, emerged as the most important voice of American Indian political and cultural critique. He followed *Custer*

Died for Your Sins with *We Talk, You Listen: New Tribes, New Turf* in 1970, *God Is Red* in 1973, and, as noted above, *Behind the Trail of Broken Treaties* in 1974. In these works Deloria reminded readers of American Indians' long history of resistance and activism since Europeans first arrived on the continent. And he introduced into an evolving discourse of Indian protest systematic and comprehensive critiques of historical and more recent U.S. federal Indian policies, of academic anthropological practices, of Christian doctrine and mission activities, and of the civil rights movement—all from an Indian perspective. In addition, in 1971 Deloria edited *Of Utmost Good Faith,* a collection of documents vital to contemporary Indian political and legal battles. Throughout his work, Deloria has been most concerned with living American Indian individuals and communities, in all their complex contemporary diversity, and with the question of how they are to construct viable futures as indigenous peoples.[34]

In 1969 Momaday published his second book, *The Way to Rainy Mountain,* a mixed-genre text that weaves together traditional Kiowa storytelling, Western-style history, and personal narrative. At the First Convocation of American Indian Scholars in 1970, Momaday delivered his influential address concerning contemporary Indian identity, "The Man Made of Words." A collection of his poetry, *Angle of Geese and Other Poems,* appeared in 1974, and in 1976, against the backdrop of the U.S. Bicentennial celebrations, he published his personal memoir, *The Names,* and a second collection of poetry, *The Gourd Dancer.* Other Indian writers were producing books during the mid- and late 1960s that were giving some visibility to an indigenous minority literature: Gerald Vizenor (Chippewa) published volumes of poetry in 1964, 1965, and 1967; a historical novel by Dallas Chief Eagle (Sioux), *Winter Count,* appeared in 1967; also in 1967, Emerson Blackhorse Mitchell (Navajo) published an autobiographical novel, *Miracle Hill: The Story of a Navaho Boy*; and a volume of poetry by Duane Niatum (Klallam), *Ascending Red Cedar Moon,* was issued in 1969. After Momaday's success, however, many more Indian writers began to publish with greater regularity, and they began to receive wider critical attention.

Besides producing works of nonfiction in 1972 and 1978, Vizenor published in 1978 his first novel, *Darkness in Saint Louis Bearheart* (reissued in 1990 under the title *Bearheart: The Heirship Chronicles*). In addition to publishing more volumes of poetry in 1970, 1973, and 1977,

Niatum edited an important anthology of contemporary Indian poetry, *Carriers of the Dream Wheel*, in 1975. A book of poetry by James Welch (Blackfeet/Gros Ventre), *Riding the Earthboy 40*, appeared in 1971 and was followed three years later by his critically acclaimed first novel, *Winter in the Blood*; his second novel, *The Death of Jim Loney* (1979), was also a critical success. In 1972 Hyemeyohsts Storm (Cheyenne) published his popular but controversial novel *Seven Arrows*. The year 1972 also saw the publication of the historical novel *Tsali* by Denton R. Bedford (Munsee), which gained less attention.

Two contemporary American Indian women launched their writing careers in 1974: Janet Campbell Hale (Coeur d'Alene/Kootenai) with *Owl's Song*, a novel, and Leslie Marmon Silko (Laguna) with *Laguna Woman*, a volume of poetry. Hale was to publish in 1978 a poetry chapbook, *Custer Lives in Humboldt County*. Meanwhile, Silko, whose literary influence has come to rival Momaday's, won wide acclaim in 1977 with her novel *Ceremony*.

Other writers who made a mark in the later 1970s include Simon Ortiz (Acoma), who published his first book of poetry in 1976, *Going for the Rain*, and a second in 1977, *A Good Journey*, as well as in 1978 a book of stories, *The Howbah Indians*; Martin Cruz Smith (Seneca del Sur/Yaqui), whose popular first novel, *Nightwing*, appeared in 1977; D'Arcy McNickle, whose third novel, *Wind from an Enemy Sky*, was published posthumously in 1978; Linda Hogan (Chickasaw), whose first volume of poetry, *Calling Myself Home*, appeared in 1978; Joy Harjo (Creek), another Indian writer from Oklahoma, who published in 1979 her first poetry volume, *What Moon Drove Me to This?*; and Barney Bush (Shawnee/Cayuga), whose first volume of poetry, *My Horse and a Jukebox*, came out in 1979. Four additional American Indian poets published first books in 1980: Ray A. Youngbear (Mesquakie) with *Winter of the Salamander*; Wendy Rose (Hopi/Miwok) with *Lost Copper*; Jim Barnes (Choctaw) with *This Crazy Land*; and Carter Revard (Osage) with *Ponca War Dancers*. That year, Hanay Geiogamah (Kiowa/Delaware) gathered several of his dramatic works in *New Native American Drama: Three Plays*.

During these years a large number of anthologies of American Indian traditional and contemporary poetry, short stories, essays, and oratory also were published. In addition to Niatum's important contribution, notable among these are Jerome Rothenberg's anthology of traditional poetry, *Shaking the Pumpkin* (1972); Kenneth Rosen's anthology of stories, *The Man to Send Rain Clouds* (1974), and his anthology of poetry, *Voices of the Rainbow* (1975); Dick Lourie's anthology of poetry, *Come to Power* (1974); Shirley Hill Witt (Mohawk) and Stan Steiner's *The Way: An Anthology of American Indian Literature* (1974); Frederick W. Turner's *The Portable American Indian Reader* (1974); Abraham Chapman's *Literature of the American Indians: Views and Interpretations: A Gathering of Indian Memories, Symbolic Contexts, and Literary Criticism* (1975); Alan R. Velie's *American Indian Literature: An Anthology* (1979); and Geary Hobson's *The Remembered Earth: An Anthology of Contemporary Native American Literature* (1979). A growing number of specifically American Indian publications and newspapers provided forums for Indian writers of poetry, fiction, and nonfiction. In 1967 the American Indian Historical Society transformed its mimeographed journal, the *Indian Historian,* into a substantial quarterly. In 1971 the Society added a juvenile magazine, the *Weewish Tree,* to its publications, and the Indian Historian Press began a national newspaper, *Wassaja,* in 1973. And between 1964 and 1980 more than eight hundred newspapers, newsletters, and journals were begun by tribal councils, community centers, student groups, and activist organizations around the country.[35] During this renaissance the work of American Indian writers also began to appear widely in mainstream American magazines and journals.

Chapter 4 chronicles how American Indian activists and writers pushed beyond the accommodations and largely indirect opposition of the preceding generation to develop a range of narrative tactics that more openly challenged conventional settler representations of "reality." Like their Maori counterparts, they engaged the blood/land/ memory complex in order to represent indigenous minority intellectual, emotional, spiritual, and political perspectives in their works and in order to code these perspectives in emblematic forms marked as distinctively indigenous. Beginning in the mid-1970s, Maori and American Indian activists and writers, working at opposite ends of the globe, together helped set the stage for experiments in organizing international indigenous coalitions and in defining indigenous identity on a global scale.

3

REBUILDING THE ANCESTOR

Constructing Self and Community in

the Maori Renaissance

On a genealogical time-scale extending to the mythological time of
the gods, historic events in Maori thought are as fresh in the memory as if they happened only yesterday.
—Ranginui Walker, "Indigenous Counter-Culture"

Tell me poet, what happens to my chips
after I have adzed our ancestors
out of wood?
—Hone Tuwhare, "On a Theme by Hone Taiapa"

Hone Tuwhare compares the writing of contemporary Maori identities through the textual representation of ancestors to the releasing
of carved figures from their houses of wood.[1] The comparison is compelling, for it suggests a plausible whakapapa (genealogy) for bringing
writing, in both Maori and English, into the larger whanau (family) of
Maori expressive arts.[2] Moreover, writing, through its comparison to
carving, becomes an assertion not only of artistic excellence but also
of continuing spiritual practice and indigeneity. Carving releases ancestors from wood, from native trees grown in a soil imbued with
the ancestors' bones. When the carving of a figure is completed, the
chips are set on fire to ritually dispose of dangerous tapu (spiritual
power). The writer's question—"what happens to my chips . . . ?"—
acknowledges excess in the practice of representation, whatever its
medium, the rough cuts and rough drafts, the words and figures discarded or whittled away. All representation must be conducted with
the care of carving, the poem suggests, its spiritually dangerous ex-
cesses handled in accordance with Maori tradition.

I have argued in chapter 1 that between 1952 and the late 1960s Maori
texts invited potentially counterhegemonic readings even within the

context of the government-sponsored journal *Te Ao Hou*. Specific narrative tactics developed over this period include the representation of the rural land base, the juxtaposition of Maori and Pakeha discourses, the use of prophetic dreams, the deployment of Maori language, the production of dual-language texts, and the representation of communion with ancestors. Chapter 1 ends with a discussion of J. H. Moffatt's "The Homecoming," in which the protagonist reconnects to his Maoritanga through communion with the carved images of ancestors in the whare tipuna on his home marae. Such communion, I suggest, becomes a pervasive figure for indigeneity because it conveys a vital connection between contemporary Maori and ancestral traditions, including connection to specific lands. I now will focus on the narrative tactics of texts produced during the so-called Maori renaissance. Rather than follow a chronology, the present chapter is organized around three emblematic figures developed in Maori literary and activist texts produced between 1970 and the mid-1980s, spanning what Maori commentators have designated the years of anger and the decade of protest. Each figure represents a related but distinct manifestation of the blood/land/memory complex: first, the emblematic bond between grandparent and grandchild, which foregrounds "blood" in order to figure the passing of tradition from ancestors to contemporary Maori; second, the emblematic return of taonga (prized possessions), which foregrounds "land" in order to figure the continuing relevance of the Treaty of Waitangi and its promise of tino rangatiratanga (quintessential chieftainship); and, third, the emblematic rebuilding of the whare tipuna (ancestral house), which foregrounds "memory" in order to figure the potent act of rebuilding a viable self as well as a viable community.

These highly charged figures assert ongoing relationships between contemporary Maori, indigenous ancestors, and specific lands. Part of their significance lies in their deployment across genres, media, and personal, social, and political contexts. The figure of the grandparent-grandchild bond, for instance, has been mobilized as a symbol of pan-tribal unity and political protest. During the 1975 Land March, an image of this intergenerational bond was captured in what has become a famous photograph, originally printed in the *New Zealand Herald*. Activist and kaumatua (elder) Whina Cooper, wearing a headscarf and leaning on a cane, holds the hand of her young grandchild as they lead the Land March down the length of the North Island from Te Hapua in the far north to the Parliament buildings in Wellington in the far south.[3] Cooper organized the march as leader of Te Roopu o te Matakite (the group of the prophetic visionaries) to protest the continuing loss of Maori land to Pakeha settlers. After six months of planning, the march began on 14 September under the slogan "Not one more acre!" It crossed Auckland's harbor bridge on 23 September and reached Wellington on 13 October. As they approached towns and cities along the way, the core ranks of activists swelled with hundreds and even thousands of supporters. Cooper's grainy black-and-white image is emblematic of the connection between Maori generations and Maori land and of their role, together, in the creation of a future *as Maori*. Photographed from behind, the figures walk a gravel road cut through a deforested landscape that extends to an overcast horizon. In the foreground, Cooper's and her grandchild's hands clasp together above the center line of the road. Attention is drawn to their link. Beneath their clasped hands, extending to the left, Cooper's and her grandchild's shadows converge. The intergenerational solidarity represented in this confluence connects Cooper and her grandchild back to ancestors and forward to generations unborn. The figure of the conjoined shadow mobilizes for contemporary land rights protest the full force of the community as understood in Maori terms—those members living, those passed on, and those yet to arrive. This genealogical underpinning links the long road of land rights struggle to the very continuation of the Maori community.

The figure of the return of taonga (prized possessions) was staged both as a series of events and as an impressive text during the well-publicized traveling art exhibit *Te Maori*. After more than a decade of planning, *Te Maori* opened at New York City's Metropolitan Museum of Art in 1984. The exhibit featured 174 objects from the Maori "classic" period (900–1850), including architectural sculptures, canoe carvings, fishing implements, carved figures, weapons, tools, musical instruments, and personal adornments. After being shown in New York, the exhibit traveled to museums in Saint Louis, San Francisco, and Chicago. *Te Maori* was the first international exhibit devoted exclusively to Maori art, and all of its pieces originated in New Zealand collections. Elders accompanied *Te Maori* on its long journey overseas, ensuring the observance of proper ritual protocol and providing an unprecedented living context for an indigenous art exhibition. In 1986 *Te Maori* made its triumphant return to Aotearoa/New Zealand. The overwhelming success of the exhibit bolstered both Maori and Pakeha pride in the Maori artistic heritage and generated interest in subsequent exhibitions of both classic and contemporary Maori art at home and abroad. *Te Maori* also initiated broad-based debate about who "owns" ancestral art objects and other taonga, including natural resources, widely considered "national treasures." The handsome exhibition catalog, which includes a large number of color plates and a range of contextualizing and interpretive essays written by prominent scholars of both Maori and Pakeha descent, has become a model of bicultural scholarship.

The figure of rebuilding the whare tipuna (ancestral house) was captured as an image in the documentary "Bastion Point Day 507" produced by Merata Mita and first aired on New Zealand's TVNZ "Contact" program in 1981. On 25 May 1978, the final day of the 1977–78 occupation of Bastion Point in Auckland, six hundred police, army personnel, and state union workers were deployed to remove the activists, whose ranks included elders and children, and to tear down the wharenui (meeting house) that the activists had constructed to assert their claim to Bastion Point as members of Ngati Whatua, the site's iwi (tribal) owners at the time of first significant contact with Europeans. Police and government officials attempted to force reporters to leave, but Mita managed to film illegally. In her documentary, Ngati Whatua elders defiantly hold on to the front posts of the meeting house. One hundred fifty protestors then are shown being led or carried away by police. In the climactic image, a line of uniformed police separates the removed protestors from their house. Behind them, a large earthmoving machine pushes against the whare, which the activists have named Arohanui (great love). The machine begins its destruction at the back end. In the final image of the house, its porch and bargeboards, representing the ancestor's brains and his arms outstretched in welcome, crash to the ground. Mita overdubs a Maori lament. The image of the New Zealand government attacking and demolishing Arohanui, an embodiment of ancestral tradition and a symbol of contemporary Maoritanga, situates the house and all it stands for firmly at the center of the land rights struggle and the battle over the representation of Maori identity. Like the bond between generations and traditional lands, and like the return of taonga, the ancestral house is figured as central to Maori individual and communal identities, asserting a future-oriented "native" indigeneity in contemporary Aotearoa/New Zealand.

E Kui Ma, E Koro Ma, Mokopuna Ma:
A Maori Literary/Genealogical Calculus

Whakapapa, or genealogy, is "the preeminent object of Maori scholarship."[4] Its literal meaning is "to lay one thing upon another" or "to recite in proper order," and the term covers "the genealogical descent of all living things from the gods to the present time."[5] Thus everything in the universe has a whakapapa, including the gods and humankind, birds and fish, trees, rocks, and mountains. Whakapapa is the laying of one generation upon another; in the human community, it is proper to speak of "ancestors upon our shoulders." Descent is traced through either the mother's or the father's lines, depending on which provide the descendant the most vitality and power: "The greater the success of one's ancestors in war, magic, oratory, and feasting, the greater the mana (prestige) that they [pass] down the descent line to their descendants."[6] Ideally, all members of the community should be able to recite the names of their immediate ancestors. But in each whanau (extended family) or hapu (sub-tribe), certain members will be selected when they are children to be trained as experts in the genealogy of the iwi (tribe) and in the genealogies of the cosmos and the gods, the primal genealogies of humankind, and the genealogy of the waka (vessels) that carried the ancestors to Aotearoa/New Zealand.

As the basis of kinship, social organization, and economic systems, the relationships encoded in whakapapa serve as a primary terminology—a system of names and a set of coordinates—for the analysis of one's rightful place in the universe. In the decades following World War II, however, urbanization threatened the continued transmission of this vital cultural knowledge. In the cities, the survival of the Maori language was increasingly at risk because of the dominant educational policy, which punished children for speaking Maori at school, and from lack of use; iwi and hapu affiliations active in the rural social networks were similarly endangered by urban housing, employment, and social arrangements.[7] Sustained relationships between grandparents and grandchildren often broke down, and oral traditions of passing Maori knowledge on to the next generation were disrupted.[8] As a consequence, non-oral texts became important media for disseminating a wide range of knowledge, including whakapapa. Maori texts produced after 1970 represent both the learning and the continuation of whakapapa in the figure of the bond between grandparent —kuia (female elder) or koro (male elder)—and grandchild (mokopuna). In fact, the figure of the idealized grandparent-grandchild relationship often is emblematic of a Maori "scene of instruction" in the operation of the blood/land/memory complex. The photograph of Whina Cooper and her grandchild dramatizes this instructional scene: an elder walks the land with her grandchild, pointing out its features, speaking its names, reciting its history, and thereby placing the newest generation within the local community's significant landscape and within the larger Maori universe. Often this instruction is conducted in the whare tipuna on the marae. Here the grandparent serves as a living conduit between the grandchild and his or her tribal tipuna (ancestors) embodied in the house. By entering whakapapa's narrative system of names and significant actions, the younger generation assumes its rightful place in Maori society, enabling its members to move forward and to "build anew the world."

The need for this type of supervised world building became only more pressing during the "years of anger." Harry Dansey's two-act play *Te Raukura: The Feathers of the Albatross*, first performed in Auckland in 1972, employs a scene of instruction as an ideological interpretive frame in order to recount the history of nineteenth-century Maori resistance to Pakeha encroachment and domination in a manner that will prove meaningful to an audience of contemporary Maori young people. The play's prologue stages a formal dialogue between the emblematic characters Koroheke (Elder Man) and Tamatane (Young Man), who figure the grandparent-grandchild bond in broad, pantribal terms. Koroheke's opening lines establish the elder's role in instruction: "I am Koroheke. As an elder mine's the task to set the scene of this examination of our people's past that we may see how this extends into the present, how the deeds of those long since departed on the spirit path reach back to us to warn and teach and guide us in our day and age." Tamatane responds: "I am Tamatane; Youth, they call me. Mine the role to query, question, break if need be, build anew the world. I listen for a space at least to Koreheke until complacency and cant shall goad me in disgust to toss aside the cloak of courtesy I wear with such unease" (1). Dansey's prologue evokes specifically its late 1960s–early 1970s context, when Maori young people began to question the attempts of their grandparents' generation to live peaceably with the Pakeha at all costs. More generally, it also evokes a context in which every generation is expected to question its elders' teachings and to experiment with the world in which it must live. In both instances, the elder sets the contemporary situation within the broader context of tradition. Koroheke counters Tamatane's "passion" for quarrel with the Pakeha with the "fact" of Maori history (2). Throughout the play, Koroheke invites an impatient Tamatane to "watch" the history of Maori resistance as it unfolds in all of its complexity. Tamatane continues to question his elder's interpretation of key events and, at times, openly challenges it with interpretations of his own. Tamatane is the one who speaks the final lines of contemporary narration, and he articulates his activist generation's incorporation of Maori history into its sense of self:

Across the years I hear the voices call; . . .
The [Pakeha] who broke, and bent, and turned the law
Have done great evil, not alone to those
Of that far time, but also to our own.
And so I hold their sons to answer for
The fathers' sins, and thus I justify
What I may do in this my day and age. (56)

The grandparent-grandchild bond also figures prominently in the stories gathered in Witi Ihimaera's first collection, *Pounamu, Pounamu* (1972), although often with less obvious political valence. The first-person narrator in many of these stories is a child or an adult remembering his childhood in the rural east coast village of Waituhi. The whare tipuna occupies a central place in the landscape of these stories, and both the narrator's grandparents and their private home are linked to the ancestral house and the safekeeping of this and other taonga, including books that record whakapapa. When his grandparents' homestead burns down in "Fire on Greenstone," it is as if the meeting house itself has burned. The narrator explains, "The homestead wasn't just four walls and rooms. It was the manawa, the heart of the whanau, the heart of the family" (38). Though seemingly nostalgic, these remarks contain positive political statements. They place at their center the scene of instruction through which young Maori may lay claim to their cultural inheritance and indigeneity. In later works and particularly in his 1986 novel *The Matriarch,* Ihimaera explicitly describes actions of affiliation with taonga as a teaching technique whereby elders instruct the young in their Maoritanga. Here is the process through which children, especially those chosen specifically for this task, learn their place in Maori culture.

"The Whale," perhaps the most strikingly ambivalent story in *Pounamu, Pounamu,* appears on one level to be a sad allegory on the death of Maori traditions, but it too invites a future-oriented reading. An "old kaumatua," the last of his generation, is ready to die. The elder is linked to the community's whare tipuna, "the only thing remaining in his dying world," but he feels "stranded," out of place in contemporary times. He bids the ancestral house farewell: "So still he stands, this kaumatua, that he seems to merge into the meeting house and become a carved figure himself" (121). The distressed elder wanders down to the shore, where he discovers a beached whale "threshing in the sand, already stripped of flesh by the falling gulls" (122). The whale is an obvious symbol for the dying old man and for a debilitated Maori culture. Ihimaera complicates the obvious reading, however, by embedding an oral narrative in the story. In remembered scenes of instruction, the kaumatua explains to his granddaughter that the meeting house is "also the body of a tipuna, an ancestor" and that the house "lives" (116). During these teaching sessions, the elder describes the house as a "book": "All the carvings, they are the pages telling the story of this whanau" (117). When he recounts the stories carved into the walls of the house, "page by page, [carved] panel by [carved] panel" (117), he describes in detail the story of the mythical ancestor Paikea: "This is Paikea, riding a whale across the sea to Aotearoa. He was told not to let the whale touch the land. But he was tired after the long journey, and he made the whale come to shore. It touched the sand, and became an island. You can still see it, near Whangara . . ." (117). The story of Paikea suggests an alternative—though no less disturbing—reading for the story's ending. Contemporary Maori have violated ancestral instructions, and the result has been a significant transformation. But Paikea's whale, though changed, remains present. Transformed into an island, it is isolated, like the kaumatua and the ancestral house with which he becomes identified, yet Paikea's whale also remains close to shore, still visible and within reach, a reminder of the vitality of the past. Maoritanga may be in jeopardy at the time of Ihimaera's writing, but it has not yet fully succumbed.

Can the knowledge passed from grandparent to grandchild guarantee Maoritanga's survival and renewal? Ihimaera's ending in "The Whale" is ambivalent but not completely pessimistic, especially if, as in the case of Dansey's play, the Maori audience becomes identified with the Maori young person involved in the scene of instruction. For those readers, the story itself can become such a scene. It is not until Ihimaera's fourth novel, *The Whale Rider*, published in 1987 after the successes of the Maori renaissance, that he fully recuperates the figure of Paikea's whale—along with the grandparent-grandchild bond—as emblematic of the vitality of contemporary Maori culture and its unbroken links to the ancestral past. But even in "The Whale" Ihimaera argues that the whare tipuna is more than a symbolic object. The carved house serves as the whanau's "book," the key text of who they are; elders serve as the whanau's key interpreters of their text. Hirini Melbourne argues similarly that carved houses constitute a "literary" tradition, pointing out that "To define a boundary for contemporary Maori writing is difficult, as the term 'contemporary,' according to Maori perceptions of time and place, is not confined to the present. So long as the living connection between past and present remains unbroken, the oral and written forms in which Maori expressed their sense of the world a thousand years ago will be as much part of the present as a haka [chant] composed [today]."[9] It is the maintenance of this connection that compels Ihimaera's kaumatua to pass on the keys for interpreting the text of the whare tipuna to his grandchildren's generation.

In her early work Patricia Grace was more obviously optimistic than Ihimaera about Maori survival and renewal. Although the young protagonist of Grace's first novel, *Mutuwhenua: The Moon Sleeps* (1978), marries a Pakeha and moves to the city, she is linked to her grandmother, with whom she shares a name, as well as to other Maori ancestresses. Significantly, Linda's own child, who is part Pakeha, is linked to his Maori grandparents by ties that are even stronger. In a scene of simultaneous death and birth (reminiscent of the similar scene at the end of Ella Deloria's novel *Waterlily*), Linda's mixed-blood child is born at the moment of her full-blood father's death; this child is given the name of his grandfather and then left at the rural homestead to be raised by his grandmother.[10] Linda suggests the possibility of indigenous renewal across generations when she addresses her father's body during his tangi (funeral): "You breathed out as he breathed in so that now your breathing is his breathing. He stands where you have stood, and so he must walk where you have walked, and must know the things you would have wanted him to know. I wouldn't take him from you, or [his grandmother]" (150). Like Ihimaera's old kaumatua, Grace's young Maori woman understands the vital necessity of the grandparent-grandchild bond for the continuation of Maori indigeneity into the future.

The figure of the grandparent-grandchild bond is all the more striking as a manifestation of the blood/land/memory complex when considered in the context of Maori demographics. According to 1991 census figures, men and women over the age of sixty make up 4 percent of the Maori population, compared to 15 percent of the total population of New Zealand.[11] For too many young Maori, the scene of instruction is an unlikely real-life scenario. When the kaumatua Eruera Stirling decided in the mid-1970s to create a book about his life and his understanding of Maori traditions (told to anthropologist Anne Salmond and published in 1980 as *Eruera: The Teachings of a Maori Elder*), he hoped to give an important "gift to a new generation" (8). Divided into three parts—"The Book of the Ancestors," "The Book of My Lifetime," and "The Book of the Rising Generation"—Stirling and Salmond's text stages an extended scene of instruction. "When I remember that old man Matiu teaching the children of Raukokore how to respect the customary ways of their forefathers," says Stirling, "it comes into my mind to help the children of Te Ao Hou [the new world] in exactly the same way, by saying to them, 'Listen, tamariki ma [children], and I will explain to you this custom, and that . . .'" (227). Salmond writes that Stirling and his wife Amiria (with whom she produced a book in 1976) "have been friends and grandparents to me, teachers and guides in the Maori world" (245). She notes that "our meetings were not interviews, but more like formal classes. I asked questions sometimes but mostly Eruera talked, explaining customs, telling traditions, and recounting main events of his life" (247). Salmond goes on to describe how Stirling placed her in the role of the grandchild chosen to receive esoteric knowledge: "He told me that when I first came to his house in 1964, he had looked to see if I had the 'right spirit,' and he wove a metaphor of kinship and apprenticeship between us that made our work together peaceful and unworried. For all that, he always kept this book in mind, and it seemed to me that our conversations were a deliberate and serious passing-on of knowledge, into the tape recorder and out to future generations" (247). The scene of instruction is the proper context for future generations to receive valued taonga from the past.

Me O Ratou Taonga Katoa:
"Prized Possessions" and Treaty Allegory

Maori activist newsletters produced in the 1960s and 1970s focused specifically on the controversy over the Treaty of Waitangi's second article, which in the Maori version guarantees the chiefs, the sub-tribes, and all Maori people the "unqualified exercise of chieftainship over" "o ratou taonga katoa," all their prized possessions. In Maori literary texts, taonga appear as part of the New Zealand and specifically Maori setting, and often a particular text's conflict involves competition over taonga of high economic or spiritual value. But the deployment of taonga in texts produced after 1970, and particularly after 1975 when the government created the Waitangi Tribunal, also can be read more specifically as allegories of the Treaty and of conflicting traditions of Treaty interpretation.

Specific analyses will be clearer if we first attempt to translate *taonga*'s wide array of meanings into English. In both nineteenth- and twentieth-century Maori discourses, *taonga* specifies an inexhaustible and thus controversial range of tangible and intangible phenomena. Bruce Biggs, a prominent linguist, defines the basic meaning of *taonga* as "valuable material possession" and cites early nineteenth-century examples of taonga as including material assets (such as greenstone, woven articles, weapons, pieces of land), social and cultural features (such as carving, dance, warfare), and personal attributes (such as attractive eyebrows).[12] In the Treaty, Biggs argues, the phrase "o ratou taonga katoa" "can be taken, in strict accordance with language usage, to include all material and cultural possessions" (308). In the context of cultural heritage, Maori scholar I. H. Kawharu argues that in the Treaty *taonga* "refers to all dimensions of a tribal group's estate, material and non-material—heirlooms and wahi tapu [sacred spaces], ancestral lore and whakapapa [genealogy], etc."[13] Maori scholar Mason Durie adds that the idea of *taonga* includes the notion of "guardianship." Durie cites Maori submissions to the 1988 Royal Commission on Social Policy that describe "people, especially children and the elderly," as taonga. "Guardianship on their behalf," Durie paraphrases, "is to be considered in the same light as guardianship over land, forests, and fisheries."[14] In the specific context of "art" objects, Maori artist and art historian Sidney Moko Mead, who was instrumental in organizing the *Te Maori* exhibit, focuses on the spiritual significance of taonga, defining them as a bridge between the living and the dead. Mead emphasizes the ideas of "taonga tuku iho" (taonga handed down from the ancestors) and "he kupu kei runga" (objects invested with interesting talk); the korero (discourse) associated with taonga during their production and use gives them imminent power.[15] In the legal context, lawyer and legal scholar David Williams notes that during the Te Atiawa claim (1983) the Waitangi Tribunal found that *taonga* has a "metaphorical sense" in the Treaty that covers "a variety of possibilities rather than itemised specifics."[16] The tribunal's finding is supported by linguists such as Biggs, who confirms that "Maori nouns with concrete referents are commonly, even usually, used for abstractions that can be seen as metaphorical extensions of the basic meaning."[17] Taonga have been interpreted as having this "metaphorical sense" in a number of claims heard by the Waitangi Tribunal. In the Manukau claim (1985), for instance, the Tribunal found that the inclusion of taonga creates a "metaphysical dimension" in the Treaty, which "gives Maori [spiritual] values an equal place with British values, and a priority when the Maori interest in their taonga is adversely affected."[18] And, perhaps most significantly, in the Te Reo Maori (Maori language) claim (1986) and in the Radio Frequencies claim (1990), "taonga came to acquire a range of meaning wide enough to include, in the former, a treasure which no one could have thought to mention in 1840 and, in the latter, a resource which no one then knew to exist."[19]

The central place of taonga in the Maori version of the Treaty, coupled with taonga's wide array of context-dependent meanings, has guaranteed controversy over its legal definition and over the extent of the Crown's obligations to secure Maori control over taonga that range from land and fisheries to personal items and spiritual values. The precise definition of *taonga* has become a site of conflict between Maori and Pakeha, between Maori and Maori, and between individuals or groups and New Zealand institutions. Specific taonga have become embroiled in controversies over who should control natural resources, their use in academic research, their marketing for tourism, their placement in museums, and their designation by Maori spiritual experts as tapu (invested with power, restricted) or by the government as national reserves, both of which restrict public access. In Maori activism, the moral authority of scarce, endangered, or vulnerable taonga has been mobilized to help make Maori grievances comprehensible to Pakeha and the international community. Conversely, specific taonga also have served as focal points for local and national attempts at inclusive biculturalism. Perhaps most impressively in this capacity, specific taonga have served as part of public relations efforts for the promotion of international investment and tourism. In literary texts, taonga resonate with several types of value, each of which adds to both the specific taonga's and the text's larger meaning. First, taonga can possess economic or sentimental value for the narrator or characters. Second, often related to the first, taonga can possess a social and/or spiritual value in a Maori cultural context. Third, taonga also can possess a Western legal value after 1840—and especially after 1975—as part of the Treaty of Waitangi's guarantee of quintessential chieftainship. Fourth, and related to the third, taonga can possess a political value as part of contemporary Aotearoa/New Zealand's public and private discourses on the Treaty, individual and communal rights, race relations, and so forth. The last value, in particular, invites an allegorical reading.

The text that best exemplifies the mobilization of treaty allegory through the employment of taonga is Witi Ihimaera's "The Greenstone Patu," included in his second collection, *The New Net Goes Fishing* (1977), published two years after the national Land March and the creation of the Waitangi Tribunal. A patu is a hand weapon, often misdescribed in English as a "club." It has a sharp, flat blade; in close hand-to-hand combat, it can deliver a fatal blow. Patu were and are carved from wood, whalebone, or stone. Patu carved from pounamu, or greenstone (nephrite jade), were and are considered the most valuable. In addition to its use in actual combat, a beautifully carved patu pounamu is valued as an item of personal regalia and often brandished during formal oratory to emphasize a speaker's important points.[20] Like other greenstone carvings, patu pounamu are passed down in families as treasured heirlooms. For all these reasons a patu pounamu is considered a taonga, a prized possession. Particularly old, beautiful, or important patu can possess their own names; such is the case in Ihimaera's story.

The plot of "The Greenstone Patu" can be summarized briefly: Many years ago the Mahana family lost a prized patu pounamu, one of a set. Cut from a single piece of greenstone, one of these "twins" is "an emblem of peace, the other a symbol of battle" (118). The missing twin has been passed down in another family, who mistakenly think it belongs to them. But the patu seeks out the Mahana family in dreams, swimming toward them in shafts of light, calling out its name; they become convinced the patu wants to come home. Responsibility for its location passes from the family's elder, Nanny Tama, to his son Rongo, and then to Rongo's sister, Auntie Hiraina. Aided by prophetic dreams, she discovers that the patu is held by a young woman living in Wellington. Auntie Hiraina enlists the assistance of her nephew, Tama (Rongo's son and Nanny Tama's namesake, and also the story's first-person narrator), who has left Waituhi on the remote east coast and now also lives in Wellington. Together Tama and Auntie Hiraina confront the young woman, who has married a Pakeha and, at first, does not understand the authority of the Mahana family's claim. She refuses to return their taonga. In the climactic scene, Auntie Hiraina announces that if the young woman must be convinced of the rightful owner, "then let the patu pounamu choose between us" (116). At that moment the patu, hidden in a mirrored cabinet in the young woman's home, reveals itself in a vision. The cabinet's panels begin to buckle, and Auntie Hiraina smashes the breaking glass to retrieve the patu. Later, the young woman formally asks Auntie Hiraina to accept the patu on behalf of the Mahana family. When Auntie Hiraina leaves, she asks Tama to return with her to Waituhi. He refuses, but the story ends with Tama wondering how long it will be before he too returns to where he belongs.

This is not a dispute over the "ownership" of the patu as ownership

is understood in European-derived cultures, but rather a taonga's assertion of its relationship to a particular family and its insistence on the
responsibilities entailed by that relationship. The patu asserts its claim,
however, within a colonial context of capitalism. Though the claim is
based in precontact and pre-Treaty cultural systems, Auntie Hiraina is
forced to acknowledge the power of the dominant culture: in an effort
to secure the patu through the Pakeha legal system she engages a
barrister, but this effort proves ineffective. Treaty allegory is mobilized
in the conflict between a Maori understanding of one's relationship to
taonga, which carries the weight of reciprocal obligations and ancestral
precedence, and a Pakeha understanding of the ownership of treasures,
which is based in the idea of property as commodity and backed by the
force of law. Ihimaera's patu pounamu is emblematic of taonga: part of
the earth but also part of the kinship system (the patu possesses a name
and a place within a family line), it functions as a metonym for both
Aotearoa (Maori land) and te iwi Maori (the Maori people or nation).
This dual role of carved greenstone—originating in the earth's marrow
but brought into the human community through artistic endeavor
(whakairo), significant talk (korero), and acts of naming (hua)—allows
the patu pounamu to figure the reciprocal relationship between Maori
and their land and resources, to serve as a manifestation of the blood/
land/memory complex. The patu asserts its ongoing relationship with
the Mahana family despite expropriation. Dis- or misplacement, even
over several generations, has not meant enduring loss; rules of affiliation and obligation still hold. In prophetic visions the patu swims
through "water shafted with sunlight," invoking the journeys of Polynesian ancestors from Hawaiki, the ancestral homeland, across the
waters of the Pacific to Aotearoa.[21] The patu thus announces its continued presence and asserts its desire to return by reenacting the Maori
claim to Aotearoa/New Zealand as its indigenous inhabitants. In mid-
nineteenth-century British legal systems, such status made the Maori
appropriate partners for a binding treaty.

Ihimaera's story is driven by obligations of whakapapa (kinship)
rather than by desires for personal gain. The recovery of the patu is an
opportunity for the younger generation to learn more about their
heritage and the obligations it continues to require of them. In a scene
of instruction, both Tama and the young woman are asked to contemplate who they are and where their allegiances lie. The narrative's

climax rehearses the conflict between Maori and Pakeha understandings of ownership, history, and memory. It is here that the taonga's significance as *patu* is revealed: "Forget about it? Auntie had yelled [when told to give up her search]. Never. And how can you say it doesn't mean anything? The world hasn't changed that much that we forget about ourselves, has it? Even if it has, then perhaps we need our patu pounamu more than we think. To fight back with, to use as a weapon. To remind us of who we are" (114). An emblematic figure for the link between Maori and their land, the patu also signifies an enduring warrior tradition, upheld as much by women as by men.

Strikingly, the climactic scene, when the patu "chooses" where it belongs, is staged as a struggle between two Maori *women*: Auntie Hiraina from the village of Waituhi and the young woman who has married a Pakeha and lives in Wellington. The patu is held in a cabinet, "imprisoned behind the glass" (116), suggesting the display of taonga in museums. It glows with "a terrible fire," suggesting ahi kaa roa, the "long burning homefires" that signify continued occupation of a specific land base, a traditional claim to land rights. This reading is strengthened, first, by the fact that the family name Mahana translates into English as "warm," and second, by an earlier passage in which Tama laments the death of so many elders: "The hearth fires were fading and needed to be stoked to flame again" (110). The patu thus privileges its Maori value as a "living" member of the community over its contemporary Pakeha relegation as an artifact to be displayed behind glass. Women can be referred to in Maori as te whare tangata, "the house of mankind, because all humans are conceived and develop in the womb."[22] The struggle between these particular women can be read as a struggle over the future direction of Maori society, between the continuance of relevant ancestral traditions and the movement toward greater assimilation of Pakeha values. At the story's end, Auntie Hiraina explains, "But you forget why your Nanny and your father wanted [the patu] returned to us. For the future, Tama. For the future generation . . ." (118). A mature and knowledgeable Maori woman, Auntie Hiraina successfully passes the patu pounamu and its values to the next generation.

That the climactic scene is staged in the capital city of Wellington, where Parliament sits and where the Treaty of Waitangi is displayed at the National Archives, invites an allegorical reading.[23] The absent text of the Maori version of the Treaty arbitrates the outcome of the struggle between Maori and Pakeha understandings of ownership, confirming the rights of Maori to exercise their "quintessential chieftainship" over taonga even if they become enmeshed in Pakeha economic and legal systems. When Auntie Hiraina and Tama arrive at the house in Wellington, they are met at the door by the young woman's Pakeha husband. During their brief conversation, the Maori elder and the young Pakeha have the following exchange:

> —We have no quarrel with you, Auntie answered him. All we want is what is rightfully ours.
> —But all this business happened so long ago, the husband continued. As far as my wife is concerned, she inherited the greenstone from her father. Can't you understand how she feels?
> Auntie Hiraina smiled sadly.
> —It was not his right to give, she whispered. The patu pounamu does not belong to any one person.
> —Well, the man answered. You seem to have very long memories. All I can say is that the sooner you forget about the past the better. (115)

The husband rehearses typical Pakeha complaints over Maori grievances based on the Treaty: it all happened so long ago, outside Pakeha memory. Auntie Hiraina counters by repeatedly shifting the argument to the issue of "rights." The debate continues when the young woman arrives home. She questions the legitimacy of Auntie Hiraina's "evidence" of ownership and tells Auntie Hiraina that she has "talked with my lawyer and he says you haven't got a claim to [the patu] at all" (115). She then orders Tama and Auntie Hiraina out of the house and threatens to call the police. At this point Auntie Hiraina declares that the patu itself will "choose between us."

Auntie Hiraina's rhetorical moves—as well as Ihimaera's staging of this scene as a negotiation of rights to property, complete with presentations of evidence and deference to outside authorities—are clear if subtle signals of treaty allegory. As in other public and private discourses, representatives for Maori and Pakeha interpret the Treaty's second article to their own advantage. Representatives for the Pakeha emphasize that the English versions of the Treaty enshrine Western conceptions of ownership and governmental authority in overseeing economic transactions. Representatives for the Maori emphasize the Maori version's guarantee of quintessential chieftainship and the provision that Maori will sell land (or any possession) only when they want to and only at a price to which they agree. Auntie Hiraina and the young woman could be delivering depositions before the Waitangi Tribunal. Auntie Hiraina's reasoning about why Tama should leave Wellington makes the distinctions between Maori and Pakeha understandings clear: "This place is no good for you. The heart cannot survive here. It loses its warmth and forgets to stir the blood. . . . Nothing down here except the dollar" (117). Ihimaera's allegorical ending suggests that, as many activists maintain, a Maori interpretation of the Treaty of Waitangi can serve as a basis for the peaceful resolution of conflicts between Maori and Pakeha.

Other texts written after 1970 also employ taonga to signal treaty allegory. Grace's *Mutuwhenua* similarly allegorizes the disparity between versions of the Treaty by staging recitations of conflicting Maori and Pakeha understandings of ownership and responsibility toward taonga "discovered" by Pakeha on Maori land. Grace's Maori protagonist, Linda, remembers when a Pakeha from the local council visited her family. The man is accompanied by his son, and the boy joins the Maori children in their outdoor play. While exploring a creek bed, the children discover a piece of greenstone "about a foot in length, tongue-shaped at one end and tapered towards the other" (6). The description suggests that the stone is an ancestral taonga, that it has been brought into the human community. The Maori cousins treat the stone like any of "the special stones or shells we found" (7), but the Pakeha asserts a superior knowledge and, by right of that knowledge, ownership: "And, suddenly, the boy, who was older than any of us, said, 'It came in the floods from the hills and it took years and years to get here. It's hundreds of years old.' He picked it up and walked towards the house and we followed with our eyes popping" (7). Back at the house, the boy claims he "found" the greenstone. His father, a government official, immediately responds that the stone "Must be worth a coin or two" (7). To his surprise, Linda's grandfather, Toki, insists that the stone, which may have been washed out of an ancient grave site and is undoubtedly spiritually dangerous, must be returned to the hills.[24] The Pakeha tries to reason with the old man that "It was my boy who found it. . . . But it's your land. There's something in it for everyone" (7). Toki, however, refuses to comply with the Pakeha's assumptions of the right of discovery, ownership, and profit. While the men argue about "value," Linda's cousin, also named Toki, removes the greenstone from the Pakeha's car. When the angry man and his son leave, Linda's grandfather and father take the taonga "far back into the hills," where they cover it with rock and earth (8).

Throughout the novel, Linda recalls the stone and what her family chose to do with it whenever she experiences a crisis of identity. She feels that "part of myself is buried in that gully" and that "the stone was my inheritance" (8, 121). The greenstone and its tie to the land represent Linda's enduring Maori identity as she chooses to marry a Pakeha and to follow her husband to the city. Grace does not reveal the Maori reasoning behind burying the greenstone or Linda's full understanding of the event until the novel's final pages. After her father's death, Linda and her mother recall that day and its implications:

> ". . . You remember that day, don't you? You were all frightened—you and Dad, Nanny, and Grandpa Toki, and the others. Scared of what the boy brought in and showed you."
> "You can't steal from the dead without harming the living. It wasn't ours, or his, to have."
> "But there was nothing you could have said to the man that would have helped him to know what you knew. And nothing he could have told you that would have persuaded you he was right."
> "One of us would have suffered, if not all."
> "And I knew. That's what I'm trying to say . . ."
> "That it should be returned and we could suffer because of it."
> "Yes, I knew that too, most surely, and I still do. But I'm speaking of something else as well. I knew about differences . . . that could never be resolved. It was all there in Nanny's kitchen that afternoon. People standing not an arm's length from each other, yet being so far apart." (151–52)

Grace alludes to the Treaty by tying Maori understandings of responsibility toward taonga associated with the dead—and the dangers of not meeting those responsibilities—to the negotiation of entrenched differences between Maori and Pakeha values.

In light of Linda's interpretation at the end of the novel, we can reread the scene in her grandfather's kitchen in terms of how it stages competing values in relation to taonga. When the Pakeha government official "weighs" the material value of the greenstone in his hands, Grace describes the Maori adults as "they too had become stone in the leaping silence of the room" (7), explicitly drawing an affective and spiritual—rather than a merely economic—link between Maori and taonga. When Toki says that the stone must be returned to the hills, the Pakeha insists on his counter-interpretation: "'Come off it,' the man said. 'Can't you see?'" When the Maori adults again do not respond, he attempts to explain the greenstone's "use value": "Well, look, think of it this way. What use is it to anyone back there in the hills. Who can see it there?" Furthermore, the Pakeha seeks to negotiate a means for everyone to "share" expected profits, saying, "There's something in it for everyone" (7). Grace's narration makes it clear that the Pakeha understandings of value and sharing asserted here are irreconcilable with Maori understandings of responsibility. The dispute over the greenstone is a conflict between texts. Interpreting the meanings of the versions of the Treaty, Maori and Pakeha representatives state conflicting versions of the appropriate power relations between indigenous Maori and the Pakeha settlers who "discovered" Maori resources.

In both Ihimaera's and Grace's narratives, the Maori interpretation of the Maori language version of the Treaty's second article prevails—although not without the assistance of either ancestral forces, which invest the secular and too often impotent discourse of the Treaty with spiritual power, or contemporary tactics of diversion and stealth. Although Maori account for roughly 15 percent of New Zealand's population and have a more prominent voice in national politics than American Indians do in the United States, the indigenous re-recognition of treaty discourse, as in the United States, is rarely powerful enough, on its own, to effect real change.

Hanga E Te Iwi Tetahi Whare Tipuna Hou/ The People Build a New Ancestral House

Ka pu te ruha, ka hao te rangatahi: the old net lies in a heap, the new net goes fishing. Maori proverbs create metaphors from central traditions of fishing, carving, and food gathering to represent the necessity of new generations fulfilling the vital roles of the old—of new generations becoming, in effect, ancestors. One of the primary issues addressed by authors writing during the Maori renaissance is how contemporary rangatahi ("new nets") are to become future ancestors in the post–World War II context of urbanization and loss of Maori language and cultural traditions. Novels written in the 1970s and 1980s by Witi Ihimaera, Keri Hulme, and Patricia Grace present strategies for reclaiming a Maori self that necessarily involve re-creating or reforming, in a sense redefining, the Maori community. This end is achieved by the physical act of rebuilding the whare tipuna, the ancestral house, on the protagonists' home marae. As was discussed in chapter 1, the whare tipuna is itself a manifestation of the blood/land/memory complex: it both incarnates the body of the community's principal ancestor in its architectural design and, in its ceremonial functions, gathers together and symbolically stands for the body of the contemporary community. To rebuild the ancestral house means literally to rebuild the community's ancestor—its significant past—and the community's self—its significant present and possible future, and to do so at the very source of the community's primary material and spiritual resources, its historical land base.

Grace's 1986 novel *Potiki,* although not the first inscription of the rebuilding of the ancestor, best exemplifies the full development of this emblematic figure and manifestation of the blood/land/memory complex. It makes central to its plot what is only implied in Ihimaera's first two novels, *Tangi* (1973) and *Whanau* (1974), and what is described only peripherally in Hulme's internationally acclaimed novel, *The Bone People* (1984). In other words, Grace builds her house on foundations laid by Ihimaera and Hulme. *Potiki* narrates a Maori community's battles to save its coastal homeland from Pakeha developers who want to build a resort there. Hemi and Roimata Tamihana "come home" to the coast to raise a family and to develop a modified "traditional" life that requires gardens, access to the sea, and spiritual unity within the community.[25] They are soon harassed by commercial developers, driven by capitalism's definitions of commodity and profit, who attack each component of the community's subsistence economy: flooding the gardens and the cemetery, polluting the sea, and finally setting fire to the whare tipuna.

Grace develops the whare tipuna's significance for the community by retelling myth and by relating the Tamihana family's experiences with the house in a variety of voices. Its destruction is thus clearly characterized for non-Maori readers as the emotional and spiritual catastrophe it represents for Maori. The novel opens, for example, with a meditation on the relationship between the master carver and the wood from which he "seek[s] out and expos[es] . . . figures" of the ancestors. These figures depend "on the master with his karakia [chanting] and his tools, his mind and his heart, his breath and his strangeness to bring them to other birth" (7). The relationship between the carver and the wood he works into ancestors sets up the novel's central metaphor of a child giving "other" birth to its parent: "It is as though a child brings about the birth of a parent because that which comes from under the master's hand is older than he is, is already ancient" (8). The narrative incarnates this metaphor when Hemi's adult sister Mary, who is described as mentally childlike, unexpectedly gives birth to a physically handicapped son, Toko, a mysterious and prophetic "ancient" boy. Though he is Mary's firstborn, Hemi and Roimata raise Toko as their own; he becomes their youngest child, the potiki, or the final born. Grace links Toko both to the Christian story of a prophetic savior's mysterious birth to an innocent virgin and to the traditional stories of Maui Potiki, the central cultural hero in Maori myth.

Not only is Maui a potiki, a final born, he is also an aborted child.[26] In the stories, Maui's mother wraps him in the hair of her topknot and discards him in the sea, returning the unborn child to the gods.[27] Unbeknown to her, however, Maui is revived. Similarly, Mary gives birth to Toko alone on the stony beach and carries his small, crooked body to the water. Toko's "sister," Hemi and Roimata's daughter Tangimoana (crying of the sea), rescues the baby from drowning. Roimata and the rest of the family then revive Toko, who is not only "crooked" but has been born with a caul. Grace's narrative links Toko not only to mythical and family ancestors (he is named after Granny's brother) but also explicitly to the whare tipuna. Granny calls Toko "Little Father" (57), and Toko says of himself that he has a "special oldness" (155). Like the ancestral house, which is periodically rebuilt, Toko represents the ancient embodied in the present.

Grace stresses the whare tipuna's guiding role as ancestor, describing it as the community's "parent" (84), its "jumping off place" (94) and "main book" (104). But the fire and the community's response to its burnt house illuminates another, more deeply spiritual aspect of the whare tipuna. Immediately, before any decision is made to rebuild, the community literally becomes the house, physically standing in place of its walls: "We could only stand silent in the night's silence and in the night's darkness. It was as if we were the new tekoteko [carvings] figured about the edges of the gutted house, unhoused, standing in the place of those that had gone to ash" (136). It is not the old whare tipuna that they become but rather a new ancestral house. In their first response to this act of Pakeha aggression, the community already looks ahead to its future, when a new whare tipuna with new carvings will stand on the same site. This scene strongly suggests that the members of the community will rebuild, for it is themselves they must house. Rather than haul the charred debris away, they bury the remains on the site, "so that the new could spring from the old which is the natural way of things" (141). So long as the community remains, the house and the ancestor it incarnates never cease to exist.

The destruction of the whare tipuna actually brings about good for the community. Grace sets up the larger significance of rebuilding the whare tipuna by first telling the story of the people of Te Ope, whose land was appropriated by the government during World War II but was never returned to them as promised. Te Ope's whare tipuna was torn down as part of New Zealand's war effort. After long legal struggles and public protest, initiated not by Te Ope's elders but by its young people, and after unfortunate compromises, Te Ope finally reclaims a part of its traditional land and rebuilds its whare tipuna: "At last they had a place to put their feet, and it was their own place, their own ancestral place, after all the years and all the trouble" (84). This is what is important, the narrative stresses, and what is required to define oneself as indigenous: one's own ancestral place. Building the new whare tipuna after the fire requires that the community's young people learn the carving, weaving, and building skills of their ancestors (143). And in the process of rebuilding the house, the young people build themselves, creating their own identities by integrating recent history into the carvings and by breaking some traditions to meet the needs of the present situation. Most significant is the addition of Toko's likeness to the carved figures. Toko has always been physically weak, and he dies during the carving of the new whare tipuna. By adding Toko's likeness to the house, the community reforges itself in his image—as ancient children, new ancestors of future Maori generations.

The centrality of the destruction and rebuilding of the ancestral house in *Potiki* illuminates the presence of this figure in Ihimaera's early works. His first two novels present an inverted "before and after" look at a rural Maori community, with the "after" published first. *Tangi* (noun: funeral ceremonies; verb: to cry in mourning) presents an idyllic vision of Maori village life. Waituhi's painted whare tipuna, Rongopai (good news), is in good repair and the community functions well, meeting its obligations during funeral ceremonies for the narrator's father.[28] The narrative's central conflict is whether or not the narrator, who has been living in Wellington, will adjust to his father's death and his new role as the man of the family.[29] But, in this process of coming home and redefining himself, Tama does not have to rebuild the whare tipuna. That work has already been done for him. Ihimaera's second novel, *Whanau* (noun: extended family; verb: to give birth or to be born), is set chronologically before the events of *Tangi*. Rongopai is in disrepair and sits unused by the village. A central story line explains how the community comes to the decision to restore its house. The community's kaumatua, its eldest member, attempts to run away with his young grandson when the family suggests putting the old man in a nursing home located far from the village. The community, which has been depicted as dysfunctional and alarmingly alcoholic, mobilizes to search for the elder. The search for the "ancestor" provokes Waituhi's citizens into behaving as a family. Their search ends at Rongopai, the neglected whare tipuna, where the kaumatua wishes to die.[30] It is the renewed sense of family, along with witnessing the elder's spiritual relationship to the whare tipuna, that prompts the community's resolve to restore its house. Ihimaera does not describe the actual restoration of Rongopai; that event occurs in the unwritten but essential interim between *Tangi* and *Whanau*.

Unlike *Potiki*, *Tangi* and *Whanau* avoid making overt racism an issue central to their plots. *Potiki* was published some ten years into the openly political struggle of the Maori renaissance, whereas Ihimaera's early novels were published at the very beginning of contemporary Maori activism. In *Tangi*, the central conflict is between the narrator and himself; in *Whanau*, between the community and itself. Though the Pakeha world looms at the edges of both novels as temptation and as a potentially destructive force, in neither does it openly encroach on the details of the unfolding story.[31] *Whanau* relates how an art gallery wanted to transport Rongopai to Auckland to have it restored and put on display. The gallery's interest in the whare tipuna as a "historical monument" prompts the members of the community to see their house in a new light, as important and meaningful. They respond, "No, although we have been embarrassed by our house, it must remain here. And even though some of us have felt ashamed of Rongopai, it is ours. We will restore it ourselves and perhaps it will forgive us" (121). The gallery is disappointed, but it does not pester the community further. In *Potiki,* Pakeha seek to destroy Maori artifacts for material gain. In *Whanau,* although Pakeha seek to co-opt a sacred artifact, the effect of their actions is to provoke preservation. Pakeha may not understand the importance of the artifact to the life of the Maori community, but in Ihimaera's early novels the whare tipuna and what it represents do not become the open battlefield in a war between conflicting Maori and Pakeha values. Rather, the house and the blood/land/ memory complex it manifests are re-recognized as important focal points for Maori introspection and renewal.

Hulme describes rebuilding the ancestral house in *The Bone People,* but she describes the event peripherally and after the fact. The whare tipuna appears only briefly and late in this novel, and yet its rebuilding is of paramount spiritual significance to the protagonist, Kerewin, and to the resolution of the novel's central conflicts. It is only after Kerewin rebuilds the whare tipuna on her home marae that she can reclaim her Maoritanga, rebuild her own house, and reunite with her family. From the first pages, Hulme links houses with identity. Estranged from her family, "self-fulfilling," and made wealthy through a lottery, Kerewin builds the Tower, a house that embodies Pakeha individualism. But her "pinnacle" of individuality soon transforms into an "abyss," a "prison" she cannot tear down (7). Here lies Kerewin's and the novel's central conflict: though only an eighth Maori by blood, she has always felt "all" Maori by "heart, spirit, and inclination"—until now, shut away in her Tower. Its isolation cuts her off from a Maori identity rooted in community.

The Bone People's complex narrative is fundamentally a chronicle of Kerewin's steps toward regaining her Maoritanga. In the first step, she learns about family through her relationship with Joe, a Maori man who also feels "that the Maoritanga has got lost in the way I live" (62), and Joe's adopted son Simon.[32] Joe helps Kerewin tear down her Tower. During the process of destruction, Kerewin fashions a clay tricephalos, a three-headed bust; through her art, she links herself to Joe and Simon, her new family, just as earlier, through her house-building, she cut herself off from her old family. When she sets the Tower's debris on fire, she creates both kiln and pyre for the tricephalos, associating Kerewin with the figure of the phoenix, the tricephalos with the phoenix's egg (320). Though Kerewin sees herself as dying (she has developed a mysterious "disease"), the figure of the phoenix sets up Kerewin as the one who will rise from her own flames refashioned.

In the second step, Kerewin embarks on a journey that takes her farther away from family and Maoritanga, to the point that she laments she has "No marae for beginning or ending. No family to help and salve and save. No-one no-one no-one at all" (411). Her identity again is associated with a type of house. She travels to her family's holiday place, a small hut that looks as impoverished as Kerewin feels, to face death. Confined to bed and delirious, she "discovers" what the tricephalos has already made manifest, that "Life is lonely. / Foe we all are, / one apart from the other" (424). At this point a strange "small dark person" visits the hut and seems to effect Kerewin's healing. Although the "person" vanishes without telling its name, the narrative suggests that, whether human or spirit, the "small dark person" is Maori (424–25). Following this event, Kerewin dreams that chanting Maori voices call her to a beautiful land, where "a wrecked rusting building" stands. Dream and vision are important narrative strategies throughout the novel, often serving as the vehicles through which characters connect with their Maori spirituality. In this dream Kerewin "touched the threshold, and the building sprang straight up and rebuilt, and other buildings flowed out of it in a bewildering colonisation" (428). Hulme ironically contrasts harmful British colonization with beneficial Maori colonization. She also suggests that rebuilding will have a continuing effect, that rebuilding one Maori house will lead to subsequent rebuildings. The only wrecked buildings Kerewin can think of are her Tower and "the old Maori hall at Moerangi," her home marae. She realizes she must go to her home marae and rebuild the whare tipuna before she can rebuild her own house; she must rebuild the ancestor in order to rebuild her own identity. Kerewin travels to Moerangi; and when she enters the whare tipuna, "a great warmth flows into her. Up from the earth under her feet into the pit of her belly, coursing up like benevolent fire through her breast to the crown of her head" (430). Alluding to the earlier phoenix imagery, destructive fire is transformed into benevolent fire.[33] Surprisingly, though, in this long, richly complex novel, little space is devoted to the actual rebuilding of the whare tipuna. Instead, it is related primarily through a journal entry. Kerewin writes: "I started rebuilding the Maori hall because it seemed, in my spiral fashion, the straight-forward thing to do. It didn't take long for curious locals [to become interested in the project and help] . . . it might have been building itself" (431). The spiral—or koru, a curling fern-frond shape—is one of the most widely used motifs in Maori carving. Early in the novel, double spirals are associated, like the phoenix and the tricephalos, with "rebirth" and the "outward-inward nature of things" (45). Here the narrative contrasts spiral (Maori) thinking with linear (Pakeha) thinking. Rebuilding the ancestral house has a transpersonal (Maori) rather than an individual (Pakeha) effect: as in Ihimaera's *Whanau,* it revives the community by providing a common purpose. When the whare tipuna is repaired, Kerewin writes that it has "got a heart of people once more" (432). Kerewin is ready to go home.

In the third step, Kerewin rebuilds the dismantled Tower. This event reunites Kerewin with both her estranged traditional family and with Joe and Simon, her nontraditional family. It also suggests hope for a Maori future. In marked contrast with her original Tower, Kerewin decides to build a new house with a "shell-shape, a regular spiral of rooms expanding around the decapitated Tower . . . privacy, apartness, but all connected and all part of the whole . . . studio and hall and church and guesthouse, whatever I choose, but above all else HOME. Home in a larger sense than I've used the term before" (434). This is the contemporary indigenous identity Kerewin has reforged through the course of the narrative. It is traditional in the sense that family and community remain the focus, but it is modified to meet contemporary needs. When all are gathered in the new spiral, when Kerewin is re-united with family and with Joe and Simon, Maori and initiated Pakeha, the narrative suggests that there will be Maori descendants in some form or another for the future. *The Bone People* opens with a prologue titled "The End at the Beginning" and closes with the phrase "te mutunga—ranei te take" (the end—or the beginning). Beginnings are linked to ends, ends to beginnings, pointing up the novel's plot of reforging identity: what has come before is remade into what is to come and will continue to be remade. These links reinforce the Maori pun from which the novel's title is taken: e nga iwi o nga iwi. Playing on the word *iwi,* which means both "people" and "bones," the pun translates into English as "the bones of the people" or "the people of the bones." In other words, the people who create other people—that is, ancestors. Contemporary Maori become ancestors not by trading Maori identities for Pakeha ones but rather by continuously reforging their Maori identities to fit contemporary situations. By the end, Kerewin, Joe, and Simon, who at the novel's beginning are for various reasons cut off from their Maoritanga, all successfully reconstruct a contemporary Maori identity. Like a spiral, the narrative suggests, Maoritanga moves forward by looking backward, by keeping its eye on the center, which is the necessity of staying together. Simon "doesn't know the words for what they are. Not family, not whanau. . . . But we have to stay together. If we are not, we are nothing. We are broken. We are nothing" (395). By redefining themselves as together, they become new ancestors.

While *The Bone People* does not foreground issues of overt racism to the degree that *Potiki* does, Hulme's novel does raise these issues to a greater degree than *Tangi* or *Whanau*. Here the central conflict is over how individuals are to negotiate tensions between self and community. Rebuilding the whare tipuna—rebuilding the ancestor and thus the community—is of utmost importance to Kerewin's spiritual development. However, rebuilding her own house—rebuilding her individual self—is of utmost importance to the resolution of the novel's primary conflicts, which take into account the reality that many Maori now live away from their home marae. Emphasis is shifted from the whare tipuna to Kerewin's house, and the two are linked through Kerewin's dream and the double rebuilding. Kerewin puts her own house in order by rebuilding it as a spiral; she puts her "self" in order by reforging it as a modified traditional structure. In this way she successfully mediates between Pakeha and Maori values and constructs a viable contemporary Maori self.

The figure of rebuilding the ancestor on the protagonist's home marae provides a material as well as a spiritual link between the (post)-colonial present and the indigenous past. One narrative tactic these authors engage to represent that link is to deploy Maori language in predominantly English texts. Grace, for example, includes untranslated Maori throughout *Potiki*. These are usually common words or terms for which there are no ready English equivalents, although, occasionally, she includes untranslated dialogue that requires readers to glean meaning from the narrative context. For the attentive bilingual reader, Grace also signals the presence of Maori punning in English language passages.³⁴ The novel's final moment, however, stands out as an extended passage of untranslated Maori, arranged into lines like a poem. In the penultimate section, written in English, the voice of the whare tipuna speaks through the voice of the deceased potiki, whose likeness has been carved into the whare tipuna's wall. The poetic language here echoes the opening meditation on carving, and its images of people and bones evoke the pun on the word *iwi*. Readers limited to English may assume that the novel's final lines continue this theme:

> Ko wai ma nga tekoteko
> Ka haere mai?
> Ko nga tipuna
> O te iwi e.
> Ko wai ma nga tangata
> Ka whakarongo atu?
> Ko te iwi
> O tenei whenua.
> Ko wai te tamaiti
> E noho ai i tera?
> Ko ia
> Te potiki e.
> Ko ia
> Te potiki e.
> No reira, e kui ma, e koro ma, e hoa ma. Tamariki ma,
> mokopuna ma—Tena koutou. Tena koutou, tena koutou
> katoa.
> Ka huri.

The passage can be translated into English thus:

> Who are the carved figures / coming here? / They are the ancestors / of the people. / Who are the people / listening to them? / They are the people / of this land. / Who is the child / residing (sitting) there? / He is / the potiki. / He is / the potiki. / Therefore, elder women, elder men, friends. Children, / grandchildren—greetings to you, greetings, greetings to you all. / It turns [meaning that the narrative has finished].

Potiki's final passage raises several issues. The presence of untranslated Maori, as in the dual-language texts in *Te Ao Hou*, is metonymic of an alternative discourse and an alternative culture. For readers limited to English, the passage is an inscrutable and exclusive sign of persistent Maori difference. For bilingual readers, the passage locates that difference in Maori spirituality and ceremonial practice—more precisely, in the whare tipuna. The series of questions and answers play on the relationships between carvings, ancestors, tangata whenua (people of the land), and the "ancient child" represented in the figure of the potiki. The final lines follow the protocol of whaikorero, formal speech-making on the marae, extending greetings to all the generations gathered before the ancestor. The greeting *Tena koutou* translates literally as "You all are there." *Potiki* argues that the living Maori community gathered on its land *is* the ancestor. The community's success in rebuilding its whare tipuna is the measure of the community's success at staying alive.

Ihimaera and Hulme provide different degrees of contrast to Grace's linguistic tactic, which align with their different levels of overt activist engagement. Ihimaera typically translates Maori words and phrases in his texts immediately. When in *Tangi,* for example, a young Tama asks, "What is a Maori?" his father lists the names of the seven ancestral canoes in which the Maori migrated to Aotearoa. He then says, "—To manawa, a ratou manawa. / Your heart is also their heart" (49). All readers of English, whether or not they understand Maori, are included. Ihimaera couples Maori language with its immediate translation in order to create a type of Maori "vernacular" English that invites the linguistic outsider into the discourse.[35] Hulme also mediates between English and Maori languages, providing a formal glossary for the untranslated words, phrases, and dialogue she deploys in her novel. Her tactic maintains the integrity of Maori within the narrative, but also ensures greater access for readers limited to English. In effect, she excludes and includes simultaneously.

Whakahoua E Te Tipuna Te Wairua O Te Iwi/ The Ancestor Renews the Spirit of the People

The emblematic figures of the grandparent-grandchild bond, the return of taonga, and the rebuilding of the whare tipuna often are deployed in combination. For example, Apirana Taylor's poem "Sad Joke on a Marae," from his collection *Eyes of the Ruru* (1979), stages a scene of instruction in which the ancestral house itself returns vital taonga to a disinherited youth. The poem's speaker, Tu (to be wounded; to stand; to fight), is a young man alienated from his Maoritanga, the poem's "Sad Joke." Standing upon an unnamed marae, he encounters the ancestral house, carved with the figures of famous adventurers, warriors, and prophets. The only Maori he can offer the ancestors is the formulaic opening for whaikorero (speech making): "Tihei Mauriora," which recalls a newborn child's first breath and celebrates new life.[36] Enraged by the situation of the contemporary Maori, in the moment of genealogical recognition the tekoteko (carved figure) offers the alienated and silenced Tu an ancestral taonga, his own tongue:

> Tihei Mauriora I called
> Kupe Paikea Te Kooti
> Rewi and Te Rauparaha
> I saw them
> grim death and wooden ghosts
> carved on the meeting house wall.
> In the only Maori I knew
> I called
> Tihei Mauriora.
> Above me the tekoteko raged.
> He ripped his tongue from his mouth
> and threw it at my feet.
> Then I spoke.
> My name is Tu the freezing worker.
> Ngati D. B. is my tribe.
> The pub is my Marae.
> My fist is my taiaha.
> Jail is my home.
> Tihei Mauriora I cried.
> They understood
> the tekoteko and the ghosts
> though I said nothing but
> Tihei Mauriora
> for that's all I knew. (15)

The tongue (arero) of a human figure is often enlarged and highly stylized in Maori carvings. It represents voice and speech, especially if incised with spirals to indicate mobility, but it also represents defiance and the claim of victory in battle. A warrior's out-thrust tongue (wha-atero) instills awe and defies enemies; a carved figure's protruding tongue also can be a symbol of protective magic.[37] When the tekoteko offers his tongue, he offers his voice and the warrior tradition—the power of defiance—as protection in contemporary times. When Tu speaks with this ancestral tongue he follows Maori protocol for formal introduction, listing his name, his tribal affiliation, his home marae, and his residence. Tu's designations—slaughterhouse worker, a brand of beer, the pub, jail—describe his alienation from Maori traditions and his substatus in Aotearoa/New Zealand's dominant Pakeha culture. At this point only the line "My fist is my taiaha" suggests defiance, and it is neither appropriate nor effective. A taiaha is a weapon, a long staff of which the lethal fighting end is carved into the shape of the war god's tongue.[38] Alienated from society, Tu has been "speaking" with his fists. His formulaic introduction is a "sad joke," a narrative cycle of numbing work, hard drinking, inevitable fighting, and incarceration. Given contemporary statistics on Maori conviction and prison rates, Tu's is a cycle all too common for young Maori men.[39] Answering his cries of "Tihei Mauriora"—new life—the ancestral house offers Tu an alternative voice, replacing his inarticulate fists with an equally defiant but more effective tongue. The speaking of the poem manifests the blood/land/memory complex in a declaration of a contemporary indigenous identity connected to the ancestral past.

Contemporary Maori writers renew the indigenous past by refiguring it as a necessary part of the present.[40] Read within the context of Maori rather than Western aesthetics, as taonga the emblematic figures discussed above effect a narrative alchemy that connects the present to the significant past while looking ahead to the future. Anne Salmond describes this "alchemy of taonga" as the capacity to cause a "collapse of distance in space-time" and thus "a fusion of men and ancestors."[41] Bruce Stewart, like Patricia Grace and Apirana Taylor, evokes this collapse in his fiction. When the mixed-blood protagonist of Stewart's *Tama and Other Stories* (1989) leaves the Pakeha world, he discovers living in the secluded mountains an "old Maori man" who appears to be "from another age" (137). The elder instructs Tama in Maori language and culture, and trains him in traditional martial arts. When Tama returns to the Wellington suburb Porirua (two peoples) to fight on behalf of his Maori relatives besieged by government officials and police who have come to tear down the community's meeting house, Tama too, though a young man, appears as if he were "someone [who] had come back from another age" (149).[42] This fusion, in fact, is one of the functions of Maori art. Sidney Moko Mead writes that art objects— taonga—provide "the bridge between the living and the dead."[43] Similarly, historian Judith Binney demonstrates that in the Maori oral tradition the telling of history involves "a continuous dialectic between the past and the present."[44] Structured around kin, the telling of history is concerned not with mimetic or historic accuracy as understood in the literate West but rather "with the holding and the transference of mana (power, prestige) by successive generations." History is seen, in other words, as "an extension of mythology" into contemporary times (18). Like an encounter with taonga, in the Maori oral tradition the telling of history "rests on the perceived conjunction between the past and the present, and between the ancestors and the living" (26). One's right to speak in the present often derives from the mana of specific ancestors, and the contemporary narrator may tell history as though he or she participated in significant past events (19, 24). In each effective telling, the contemporary generation engages the blood/land/memory complex and rebuilds the ancestor as itself.

4

BLOOD/LAND/MEMORY

Narrating Indigenous Identity in the

American Indian Renaissance

This is a call for Indian scholars to come together and take the lead
in formulating clear-cut stands and goals on the issues. This is a call
for Indian scholars . . . to demonstrate that we are not the inarticulate masses about whom so much benevolent concern has been
voiced in the past.—Steering Committee, First Convocation of
American Indian Scholars, 1970

Reservation—To the white racist, land and water as yet uncon-
quered; to the white liberal, a concentration camp; to an Indian, a
homeland to be defended at all costs.
—"NIYC Dictionary," *Americans Before Columbus*

On the first page of his groundbreaking political and cultural critique,
Custer Died for Your Sins: An Indian Manifesto (1969), Vine Deloria Jr.
announces that "Our foremost plight [as contemporary American In-
dians] is our transparency." "To be an Indian in modern American
society," Deloria continues, "is in a very real sense to be unreal and
ahistorical" (2). Like the conveners of the First Convocation of American Indian Scholars, Deloria confronts Indian invisibility in his critique of the federal government's "disastrous" Indian policies and his
analysis of the current conditions under which American Indians must
work to better their tribal and individual lives. And like the National
Indian Youth Council in the biting humor of its "Dictionary of Indian
Terms . . . unabridged and undaunted," Deloria challenges the Indian stereotypes promoted by White conservatives and White liberals
alike.[1] Whether romanticized as nineteenth-century Plains Indian
warriors (distinctly Other but characteristically "American" in their
fighting spirit) or pitied as members of a contemporary underclass

hampered by poverty and racism (their problems easily solved through recourse to programs designed for "minorities"), Indians are represented as vanquished and ultimately as vanished. By 1969, Deloria demonstrates, White Americans and the U.S. government were unable to see American Indians as indigenous peoples living in the twentieth century, fighting a number of distinctly indigenous twentieth-century wars.

In this chapter I analyze activist and literary tactics developed to increase Indian visibility during the so-called American Indian renaissance of the late 1960s and 1970s. Comprehensive studies of renaissance literature have emphasized the overwhelming concern of this body of work with themes of personal identity and sense of place, articulation and inarticulateness, and commitment to community, as well as its concern with the influence of Native oral traditions on the form, aesthetics, and specific content of written texts.[2] The many manifestations of the blood/land/memory complex can be situated within this thematic and stylistic matrix as examples of the narrative tactics American Indian writers and activists employ to represent the recovery of self, place, voice, and community—specifically, to represent the rearticulation of individuals as indigenous and indigenous nations as sovereign. Given my comparative framework, I focus on those tactics that engage the blood/land/memory complex in ways that are highlighted by the emblematic figures developed by activists and writers during the concurrent Maori renaissance. A number of correspondences are readily apparent. The grandparent-grandchild bond and the scene of indigenous instruction—or their devastating absence—play significant roles, for instance, in Dallas Chief Eagle's *Winter Count,* N. Scott Momaday's *House Made of Dawn, The Way to Rainy Mountain,* and *The Names,* James Welch's *Winter in the Blood,* Leslie Marmon Silko's *Ceremony,* Gerald Vizenor's *Bearheart,* and D'Arcy McNickle's *Wind from an Enemy Sky.* The return of taonga (prized possessions) is explicit in *Wind from an Enemy Sky* and implicit in other works in which activists or fictional characters seek the return of land, resources, or aspects of culture, which often links the return of prized possessions, as in Maori renaissance texts, to the discourse of treaties. Rebuilding the ancestor and becoming ancestors for future indigenous generations is also a major theme in these works. Chief Eagle redeploys and innovates Plains Indian pictographic traditions so that they bear the weight of narrative history; Silko revises south-western ceremonial traditions to meet the changing needs of contemporary times; and Momaday develops "blood memory" as a trope for continuity across indigenous generations and as a process for contemporary indigenous textual production. Space does not permit a detailed analysis of each of these correspondences. In the sections below, I investigate two sets of related narrative tactics made especially visible by the comparison with New Zealand Maori texts, the re-recognition of the artifacts of indigenous memory and the development of the controversial trope "memory in the blood."

The Discourse of Hides and Treaties: Re-recognizing the Artifacts of Indigenous Memory

During their nineteen-month occupation of Alcatraz Island in 1969–71, American Indian activists calling themselves Indians of All Tribes published a document in their protest newsletter titled "'We Hold the Rock': Alcatraz Proclamation to the Great White Father and His People."[3] The Indian activists announce that they "reclaim" Alcatraz Island "by right of discovery" and then present "the Caucasian inhabitants of this land" a parodic "treaty" in order "to be fair and honorable in our dealings with all white men." In mock treaty provisions, the activists offer to purchase Alcatraz Island for twenty-four dollars "in glass beads and red cloth" and vow to establish a "Bureau of Caucasian Affairs." The treaty promises that this agency will set aside a portion of land for the benefit of Caucasians, "to be held in trust . . . in perpetuity —for as long as the sun shall rise and the rivers go down to the sea." In further provisions, the activists offer their Caucasian treaty partners "our religion, our education, our life-ways in order to help them achieve our level of civilization and thus raise them and all their white brothers up from their savage and unhappy state."

The parameters for a viable American Indian activist discourse had changed dramatically since 1961, when the American Indian Chicago Conference (AICC) adopted the *Declaration of Indian Purpose*. The AICC document begins with "The American Indian Pledge," a four-point statement of "absolute faith in the wisdom and justice of our American form of Government" designed to assure "all other loyal citizens of our beloved country" that Red Power need not arouse a 1950s-style red scare. By the end of the decade, the newly formed and contingent activist group Indians of All Tribes eschews assurances of a common nationalism and offers their "fellow citizens" instead the culmination of their worst fears of a separatism motivated by indigenous memory. In its specific language use, the Alcatraz Proclamation conflates the Dutch purchase of Manhattan Island in 1626 with the creation of the U.S. Bureau of Indian Affairs in 1832 and with the preambles and specific articles of nearly four hundred treaties negotiated between the United States and various Indian nations between 1788 and 1868.[4] The proclamation thus aligns the activist occupation of Alcatraz Island with a larger project of Indian historical reclamation and reimagination, demonstrating an indigenous sensibility that past events and the written and oral traditions that record them possess ongoing, "living" relevance in the present. Furthermore, the rhetorical effectiveness of their effort is accomplished, in part, by anchoring the activists' contemporary demands and "radical" interpretations of American history to corroborating evidence already inscribed in discourses that the federal government and most non-Indian U.S. citizens recognize as dominant, in particular, to evidence inscribed in the discourse of treaties. The evocation of the literally hundreds of texts in which the federal government recognizes and affirms indigenous sovereignty enables Indians of All Tribes to enlarge the political scope of their action, to convert the "tiny island" of Alcatraz into "a symbol of the great lands once ruled by free and noble Indians."

The Alcatraz Proclamation exemplifies literary and activist redeployments of treaty discourse in its evocation of generalized treaty contents and its foregrounding of the surface features of treaties—the literary style, figures of speech, and narrative devices in and associated with their preambles and specific articles. Given this fact, it is useful to think of the discourse of nineteenth-century U.S.-Indian treaties as having two related components.[5] First, this discourse includes the particular language use, rhetorical constructions, and tropes employed in actual treaty documents and verbal agreements. Specific features include the exclusive use of English language on paper and the detailed negotiation of what legal scholar Charles F. Wilkinson calls a "measured separatism." In *American Indians, Time, and the Law* (1987), he argues that the explicit goal of treaties, "as viewed both by Indian tribes and by the United States, was [not only] to limit tribes to significantly smaller domains but also to preserve substantially intact a set of societal conditions and tribal prerogatives that existed" at the time of signing (18). "The reservation system," Wilkinson explains, "was intended to establish homelands for the tribes, islands of tribalism largely free from interference by non-Indians or future state governments. This separation is measured, rather than absolute, because it contemplates supervision and support by the United States" (14). In other words, in the complex rhetorical situation of treaty making, if in few others, White Americans and American Indians agree on, and the U.S. government promises to uphold, the essential—albeit supervised—sovereignty of Indian nations.[6] As the Alcatraz Proclamation suggests in its provision for Caucasian reservations overseen by Indian bureaucrats, tension between separation and supervision remains at the heart of ongoing treaty disputes and, in many ways, defines the discourse of treaty documents.

This tension is especially acute in the discourse of those nearly two hundred treaties negotiated in the years spanning the large-scale removals of southeastern Indian nations to the Indian Territory west of the Mississippi River and the final large-scale "Indian wars" fought on the central, southern, and northern Plains. Typically, these mid-nineteenth-century treaties open with a declaration of peace between the U.S. government and the specific Indian nation (if they have been involved in a declared war) or with a vow that both the United States and the Indians desire "perpetual peace and friendship" and wish to "bind themselves to remain firm allies and friends."[7] The government then agrees to the reservation of specified lands "set apart for the absolute and undisturbed use and occupation of the Indians,"[8] guarantees protection from "bad men among the whites,"[9] and promises the steady supply of annuities and necessary provisions—including expert personnel such as teachers, physicians, carpenters, farmers, blacksmiths, millers, and engineers—either for a specified number of years or in perpetuity. For their part, the Indian nations "relinquish all right to occupy permanently the territory outside their reservation,"[10] promise local submission to the institutions of American "civilization"—schools, churches, trading posts, military posts, and government agencies—and give right of way through their remaining territories for "the emigrant trains, the mail and telegraph lines"[11] and for "all the necessary roads and highways . . . which may be constructed as the country improves."[12] Wilkinson details how "the structure and words of the treaties" resulted in the idea among both Indians and the U.S. government that these documents "guaranteed a substantial separatism as well as federal protection and provision of services" and that this idea "has been embodied in the case law from the beginning" (15, 16).[13] As related statements, these documents remain of interest to Indians because they were produced within particular, historically and geographically determined relations of power between the United States and specific indigenous nations, and because they were immediately imbued by both parties with the supralocal power of federal law, whether or not they were eventually ratified by the Senate. Furthermore, as in Aotearoa/New Zealand, treaties remain of interest because they were the site of articulation and codification for future relations of power between these entities. Despite an often violent history of broken treaties, both the spirit and the specific provisions of these documents continue to provide an important basis for federal Indian policy and a powerful inspiration for indigenous minority cultural and political activism.

The second component of treaty discourse is the ongoing tradition of language use, rhetorical constructions, and tropes that have become associated with treaties and with treaty making in both Indian and dominant American discourses, as well as in the mass media. Specific features here include stilted metaphors—"the Great White Father"— and the depiction of an idealized treaty moment.[14] Often such a moment is constructed as a brief, rational pause between what is seen as the ignoble past of conquest and the present disaster of Indian policy. Despite vague references to treaties in popular accounts of American frontiers or in contemporary land rights and resources disputes, the sheer number of individual Indian treaties and their lack of representation in history textbooks and literature anthologies has meant that the majority of U.S. citizens—Indian and non-Indian alike—have read very few of these documents.[15] What most non-Indian Americans think they "know" about the discourse habits of treaties they have learned from several popular but misleading traditions, including textbooks regularly assigned in the public schools but also dime novels and literary westerns, pulp journals devoted to the "True West," and western dramas performed on radio, television, or film.[16]

For many American Indian individuals and communities, treaties had, by the late 1960s, come to be regarded as a significant public record and the clearest hard evidence of the sovereign nature of indigenous nations; as such, they were seen as valid before the international community.[17] Moreover, like Maori in Aotearoa/New Zealand, many Indians—though certainly not all—had long regarded treaties as sacred covenants, solemn pledges between their ancestors and the U.S. government made before the eyes of the Creator.[18] And increasingly—but especially during and after attempts in the 1950s to terminate several tribes' federally protected status—treaties became important symbols of Indians' continuing distinctiveness as nations and peoples.[19] By the late 1960s, therefore, local, ongoing histories of treaty violations acquired political and moral connotations that resonated far beyond the reservation boundaries established in specific documents. During the Alcatraz occupation, for example, the Treaty of 1868, signed at Fort Laramie by representatives of various Sioux bands and their allies the Arapaho, was held up as symbolic of the sovereignty of *all* Indian nations and of the continuing responsibilities of the federal government toward its treaty partners.[20] This same treaty was evoked again in 1973, during the armed occupation at Wounded Knee, South Dakota, to declare an independent Oglala nation.[21]

The Alcatraz Proclamation makes clear how Indian appropriations of treaty discourse can conflate a popularized version of treaties and treaty making—in which the government pledges to uphold promises "for as long as the sun shall rise and the rivers go down to the sea"—with the less colorful provisions of specific documents. Though deployed as a parody, the treaty sections of the proclamation appropriate a colonial discourse in order to foreground Indian memories of their own sovereign nations, and to invite their audiences to re-recognize the discourse through which the United States both recognizes their nations as sovereign and solemnly pledges to uphold that sovereignty. The century-old Treaty of Fort Laramie could serve as a powerful marker of indigeneity for Indians of All Tribes because it memorializes a significant "victory" for independent American Indians on the northern Plains. The document signed by representatives for the Sioux and the Arapaho in 1868 "recognized hunting rights of the Indians in the Powder River area, closed the Bozeman Trail [to immigrating settlers] and withdrew the military posts built to protect it, and established a Sioux reservation west of the Missouri [River] in what became the state of South Dakota."[22] Although representatives for the United States may have intended these provisions "to turn the nomadic warriors into peaceful farmers," twentieth-century activists, relying more on popular sentiment than on a close reading of the text, interpreted the very existence of the treaty to mean that all Indians were guaranteed a permanent land base.[23] By mobilizing the discourse of the Treaty of 1868 as a metaphor for this blanket guarantee, the activists publicly lamented a century of decline in the sovereignty and land rights of American Indians, and they demanded restitution.[24]

During the year preceding the takeover of Alcatraz, another century-old treaty had been memorialized in a contemporary text produced by American Indians, although for different purposes than those expressed at Alcatraz and with far less attention from the media. In 1968, the Navajo nation self-published a handsome commemorative history, *Navajo: A Century of Progress, 1868–1968.*[25] As the title indicates, the 1868 treaty negotiated between the United States and the Navajo nation is employed not as a marker of decline but rather as a marker of progress. This 1868 treaty ended the devastating four-year internment of the Navajo at Fort Sumner, New Mexico Territory, that followed the infamous Navajo Long Walk in 1864, and it established a permanent reservation to which survivors could return "home."[26] The book reprints the complete text of the treaty, without commentary, as its second chapter; it serves as a transition between the first chapter, "A Time for Suffering," and the third, "Exodus." Though it consists of only four pages, the second chapter is visually striking and rhetorically loaded in its deployment of the treaty document as a metonym for U.S. recognition of Navajo sovereignty. It opens with a photographic reproduction of the worn first page of the treaty document, which asserts the authority of the U.S. president to enter into this contract, and it closes with photographic reproductions of the document's final pages, which record the treaty's "confirmation" by the U.S. Senate and prominently display an embossed U.S. seal. Although it serves a different immediate purpose, the chapter is designed, like the Alcatraz Proclamation, to re-recognize the binding authority of the 1868 treaty.[27]

Like the activists who occupied Alcatraz and Wounded Knee, and like the Navajo who celebrated the return of their homeland, American Indian writers also have appropriated the discourse of treaties in their representations of contemporary identities as indigenous and Indian nations as sovereign. One example is the little-known historical novel *Winter Count* by Dallas Chief Eagle, first published in 1967, two years before the Alcatraz occupation and a year before the publication of Momaday's celebrated *House Made of Dawn*.[28] Chief Eagle tells the story of the dispossession and subjugation of the Teton Sioux, chronicling the fifteen difficult years that preceded the infamous massacre of more than two hundred Sioux men, women, and children at Wounded Knee, South Dakota, on 29 December 1890. The novel centers on the adventures and eventual destruction of the fictional warrior Turtleheart and his wife Evensigh, a White woman raised by the Sioux from infancy.[29] Turtleheart and Evensigh survive the depredations of Indian enemies, White gold miners, and the U.S. cavalry; and they adjust to a life confined to the reservation, only to die tragically at Wounded Knee. Their infant child, Little Sun, survives the massacre unharmed, and the novel suggests that its author and his generation are descendants (figuratively if not literally) of this survivor. In its narrative tactics, *Winter Count* anticipates not only the Alcatraz Proclamation but also James Welch's highly regarded 1986 historical novel *Fools Crow*. Like *Winter Count*, *Fools Crow* recreates the years leading up to an Indian massacre and dramatizes the violent subjugation of a powerful Plains Indian people—in Welch's novel, the cavalry's surprise morning raid on Pikuni Blackfeet camped on the Marias River in the hard winter of 1870. Mistaking the peaceful camp for one led by a Blackfeet "renegade," the cavalry killed 173 Blackfeet at the Marias, including significant numbers of women, children, and the elderly. A direct descendant of one of the few survivors, Welch grew up hearing his father retell his great-grandmother's eyewitness accounts of the morning raid and of the Blackfeet's subsequent confinement to the reservation.

In their re-creations of Indian history, *Fools Crow* and *Winter Count* foreground textual artifacts of Indian historical memory, including oral and pictographic traditions as well as written records. To bring these often conflicting versions of events into meaningful contact, both writers feature prominently in their narratives treaty documents and the intricate processes of treaty making. In *Fools Crow*, Welch creates dramatic tension and powerful emotional effect by freighting the physical characteristics of treaty documents with the power of a historical witness. A survivor of the massacre on the Marias, for instance, relates that "Curlew Woman says [Chief] Heavy Runner was among the first to fall. He had a piece of paper that was signed by a seizer chief. It said that he and his people were friends to the Napik-wans. But they shot him many times" (383–84). In Welch's retelling of this scene, itself a retelling, the detail of "a piece of paper that was signed by a seizer chief" resonates as irrefutable hard evidence of U.S. perfidy. The chief attempts to shield his community behind this writ-ten guarantee of "perpetual peace and friendship," but the cavalry guns down Heavy Runner and his people and then burns their village to ash.[30] The metonymic power of Welch's "piece of paper" becomes part of a Blackfeet tradition of remembering the specific treachery at the Marias River as well as part of a wider tradition of remembering every Indian massacre's relationship to an ongoing history of U.S. hypocrisy, deceit, and violence.[31]

In *Winter Count*, Chief Eagle establishes the treaty context for his story in a formal introduction. He reviews the history of the "peace" treaties that the Sioux signed in 1825, 1851, and 1868, only to find each successively violated. Chief Eagle ends by quoting Chief Red Cloud, who refused to join other Sioux in their 1876 declaration of war against the United States: "[Red Cloud's] words were, 'I have signed the treaty of 1868, and I intend to keep it.' In point of honor," Chief Eagle reminds readers, "[Red Cloud] towered far above the five generals who signed the treaty with him" (iv). Throughout *Winter Count*, U.S. repre-sentatives are portrayed as deceptive in treaty negotiations. At one point, federal agents ply the Sioux men who are already corralled on the reservation with whiskey in order to get them to sign away their rights to the Black Hills (191–94). Chief Eagle opens the chapter following this scene by writing that "Civilization, which was to be brought to the Indians by the 'Great White Father,' in exchange for the land and freedom of the people, now appeared to be merely *courtship promises* which never were intended to be kept" (200, emphasis added). The image of treaties as "courtship promises" encourages readers to view the love relationship between Turtleheart and Evensigh as a contrast to Indian-White treaty relations. These lovers are able to uphold their promises despite racial difference and despite difficult circumstances beyond their control because they share cultural convictions, especially their high regard for honor. Their positive example of Indian-White relations, made possible by Evensigh's Sioux adoption and education, is echoed in the character Hidetrader, a White man who marries an Indian woman and successfully integrates into Sioux society while remaining a cultural go-between. When his wife and child are killed and scalped by Whites after the battle of the Little Bighorn, Hidetrader declares White society "evil" and rejects it completely (127).[32] Chief Eagle ends his novel with the massacre at Wounded Knee. Although an elder marks Turtleheart and Evensigh's wagon with a piece of white cloth, a metonym for the various treaties signed by Sioux leaders as well as a makeshift flag of peace, they are both shot by the cavalry. As a treaty metaphor, the couple's unprovoked murder signals the larger significance of the Wounded Knee massacre for all American Indian peoples.

In addition to the dominant discourse of treaties, both Welch and Chief Eagle appropriate and redeploy an indigenous discourse tradition that evokes the textual artifacts of Indian historical memory: the pictographic writing system of the Plains Indian "winter count." Before and well into the reservation period, Plains Indian cultures employed a variety of pictographic writing systems as memory aids, personal communications, biographical and tabulary records, geographical charts, chronologies, and records of exploits, as well as for decoration on tipis and shields. A winter count is a pictographic calendar in which each year or "winter" is recorded as a pictograph that represents a significant event in the life of the tribe or, more commonly, a particular band. Band historians recorded their symbols for each year on tanned buffalo, elk, or deer hides until White encroachment and overhunting made hides less available; winter counts then were drawn or painted on cloth and paper. Pictographs typically are arranged either in a spiral formation, which begins in the center and moves out and around either clockwise or counterclockwise, or in a series of rows back and forth across the hide, cloth, or paper canvas. Some Sioux winter counts are known to have depicted more than three hundred years of history.

Several features distinguish the discourse of pictographic winter counts from Western-style historical records. First, the year symbols are ideographic rather than illustrative; typically, a single image portrays an entire year. Individual pictures may be highly schematic and stylized or more idiosyncratic to the particular historian, but each represents a complete idea. Second, winter counts can appear "incoherent" to Western sensibilities, because "in no sense do they aim at narrative; their chief concern is the erection of calendric milestones," "a trustworthy supplement to the memory."[33] The pictographs collected on a given winter count show no continuity of emphasis from year to year. And, third, historians choose to represent events that are outstanding or facts that are of significance to their particular community rather than to the tribe or the larger confederation of tribes. In other words, "they are not bodies of general history but are, rather, individual records of an individual group."[34] This feature in particular marks winter counts as providing an Indian point of view on contact with intruding Whites.[35] When, during the Alcatraz occupation, Indians of All Tribes inscribed their May 1970 "Declaration of the Return of Indian Land" on a stretched hide, they mobilized the force of the winter count tradition to assert a distinctly indigenous perspective on American Indian history.[36]

In *Fools Crow*, Welch also appropriates and redeploys the conventions of the winter count to meet his specific dramatic purposes. During his protagonist's extended dream/vision, Welch uses the painted designs on a yellow skin to foreshadow tragic events that lie in the future for his nineteenth-century characters—but lie in the past for his contemporary readers (see 353–59). In the dream/vision, the painted designs begin to move across the skin as though alive; later, they also produce sound. Fools Crow tries to flee the frightening vision, but he finds he cannot move. Welch writes that "He [is] powerless to keep from seeing" (354). Fools Crow's ability to interpret the skin increases as he watches the designs change and he becomes attuned to their method, and thus readers receive increasingly detailed—and increasingly recognizable—descriptions. As in literary deployments of treaty discourse, the skin becomes a readable, multiperspectivist text targeted at multiple audiences inside and outside the narrative. For readers, the skin bears historical witness to Indian memories outside the scope of the novel's plot. Thus the redeployed winter count allows Welch to embed his narrative of 1867–70, the final years of a fully independent Blackfeet cultural system, within the larger scope of Indian history. Like the novel's protagonist, readers exposed to the decorated skin are "powerless to keep from seeing" the larger significance of Welch's unfolding story.

In a similar way, Leslie Marmon Silko appropriates and redeploys southwestern pictographic traditions of sand painting and shield painting in her widely acclaimed 1977 novel *Ceremony*. Silko repeats the motif of a "star map of the overhead sky in late September" (214) in the medicine man Betonie's ceremonial sand painting, in the design painted on an old war shield (constructed, like a winter count, from an animal hide), and finally in the sky itself during the novel's climax. As in *Fools Crow*, in *Ceremony* the significance of these textual traditions lies in the "convergence of patterns" (254) and in the protagonist's ability to interpret the patterns within changing cultural and historical contexts. When Silko's mixed-blood Laguna protagonist sees the star pattern in the sky itself, he realizes that "The stars had always been with them, existing beyond memory, and they were all held together there. . . . Accordingly, the story goes on with these stars on the old war shield" (254). In both *Fools Crow* and *Ceremony*, representations of pictographic traditions serve as metonyms for indigenous memory in the contemporary written text. They evoke the continuity of that memory across generations and the endurance of indigenous historical memory despite cultural change.[37]

Chief Eagle employs two types of pictographic calendars in *Winter Count*, although, in order to meet the novel's particular dramatic and activist purposes, he presents the second type, a personal "exploit skin," as an innovation of the winter count concept rather than as an established tradition. Turtleheart inherits the responsibility for keeping his band's calendar upon the death of his grandfather. In addition to the band winter count, however, his grandfather leaves him a "smaller winter count . . . [his] own personal calendar" (75). No other Sioux in the novel possesses a personal calendar. Blue Thunder, an elder, finds the small winter count "interesting" and "different," explaining that "It does not tell of the band, but of Turtleheart. It is his personal history" (138). Turtleheart's good friend, the White-educated warrior Strong Echo, remarks, "Hah. It is a crude way to keep a history, but I can see where it can be favored by an individual" (138). Though Chief Eagle suggests that the personal winter count is an innovation, in fact "picture autobiographies" or "brag skins" were common among the Sioux. Usually they were created by the warriors themselves, in order "to make heroes of the autobiographers."[38] Chief Eagle's innovation is that Turtleheart's grandfather has kept a personal winter count for his grandson since his infancy, a biography that Turtleheart will continue as an autobiography.

As the plot develops, the personal winter count plays a crucial symbolic role, and its strategic placement suggests Chief Eagle's attempt to authenticate his novel as Indian memory. Turtleheart carries his personal winter count with him at all times. At Wounded Knee, already shot and bleeding to death, he reaches beneath his shirt and "t[akes] out his winter count and form[s] a shield for Little Sun's face" before beginning his desperate journey away from the massacre site to the reservation mission. As he walks through the winter storm, Turtleheart's mind replays the events recorded on his personal history (229). He reaches the mission and is able to hand over his son, wrapped in the personal winter count, to the priest. The novel ends with Turtleheart's death outside the mission. The priest interprets the warrior's offering of his child as a conversion to Christianity, but the emblematic action of wrapping Little Sun in the winter count suggests that, despite tragic loss, Turtleheart's Sioux memory has been preserved and passed on to the next generation.

Chief Eagle's novel was published in 1967. Coincidentally, 1967 also saw the delayed publication of *A Pictographic History of the Oglala Sioux,* drawn and annotated by Amos Bad Heart Bull, an Oglala of the Hunkpatila band. Bad Heart Bull's pictographic record of the Oglala includes over four hundred pictures recorded in a ledger book. Drawn between 1890 and Bad Heart Bull's death in 1913, the pictures cover the period beginning about 1856, through the turbulent years of wars with the U.S. cavalry, the Wounded Knee massacre, and the transition to reservation life. Bad Heart Bull's manuscript was well known to people living on the Pine Ridge Reservation, but it was not revealed to the outside world until 1926, when Helen Blish, a graduate student in anthropology at the University of Nebraska, learned of its existence from officials at the Pine Ridge Agency. After securing permission from Bad Heart Bull's family, Blish worked at interpreting the manuscript until her untimely death in 1941. In 1927, the first year Blish "rented" the ledger book, the entire manuscript was photographed.[39] It would take more than two decades for the University of Nebraska Press to publish the photographed manuscript of Bad Heart Bull's pictures with Blish's interpretive text and an introduction by Mari Sandoz.

Beyond the coincidence of its publication date, the Bad Heart Bull manuscript is suggestive of how Chief Eagle's novel translates Sioux pictographic traditions into the conventions of Western history and literature. Blish's interpretation stresses that the Bad Heart Bull manuscript is not a traditional winter count, that is, "ideographic and purely chronological in character" (18). Rather, Bad Heart Bull's pictures are "illustrative, detailed and realistic," giving "the full action of the story in illustrative style. . . . The whole scene is suggested . . . something is actually *taking place*" (22, 27). Most remarkably, the manuscript as a whole has a high narrative content. As Blish explains:

> In purpose and character, the Bad Heart Bull document is quite different from the winter counts. In the first place, it gives full historical and cultural detail; and in the second place, that detail is given in generally chronological and coherent sequence, with interruptions only to allow for a complete "discussion" of some phase of tribal life or organization— social, religious, political—and then only as that "discussion" belongs integrally to the action. The design . . . is narrative rather than calendric. The record is intended to give a full and authentic account of the tribal life of the Oglala Dakotas during that period of stress and strife and rebellious readjustment which falls within the sixty or seventy years covered by the record. (27)

What Blish says here can serve equally well as an account of the method of Chief Eagle's historical novel.

Furthermore, Blish's account of Bad Heart Bull's influences and purposes in putting together his pictographic record is suggestive of the particular dynamics of the hybridity at work in Chief Eagle's text. Blish recounts that "According to the uncle, the boy [Amos] for some time had been interested in treaties and other official documents concerning Indian-federal government relations and had been collecting them; as a result, he possessed a considerable number of books and published reports, which, incidentally, he could not read himself" (8). Bad Heart Bull was interested also in Sioux histories, and Blish reports that sometime before 1891 he "had drawn a complete winter count . . . of the Oglala Dakotas, which covered some three hundred years" (8). According to Blish, it was during the completion of this project that Bad Heart Bull realized the limitations of the pictographic method of winter counts. "Prompted by a real historical and sociological sense," Blish writes, "he decided that it was most desirable to make a more complete record" (8). With no formal schooling, he taught himself to draw and later to write fluently in Lakota; after contact with Whites while enlisted as a scout for the U.S. Army, he was able to write at least a little in English. His detailed illustrations of Oglala life often include annotations in Lakota and occasional brief notations in English—a multiply hybrid and polyvocal text.[40]

In addition to treaties and other documents, Bad Heart Bull may have consulted older winter counts for information about events in Sioux history before his own lifetime. He relied on his own memory for those years and events in which he had himself participated. But much of his historical narrative, Blish argues, was based on the recited memories of his father and uncles and other older Sioux. And many of his detailed, dynamic pictures of Sioux exploits, Blish argues further, were the result of *"the constructive powers of his own imagination"* (59, emphasis added). Bad Heart Bull's accomplishment, in other words, like Ella Deloria's accomplishment in the 1940s, represents not only the recording and passing on of indigenous history, traditions, and specific family memories but also the active construction of literature. A hybrid work of imaginative literature rooted in indigenous historical memory, Bad Heart Bull's pictographic record anticipates Chief Eagle's and Welch's historical novels, which also are based in both historical documents and tribal and family memories. Both textual forms—pictographic and literary—are made to evoke the blood/land/memory complex; they maintain and assert indigenous distinctiveness through linguistic, stylistic, and content markers of indigenous identity. And both forms are made to insist on remembering the cross-cultural and cross-national agreements forged between Indian leaders and the U.S. government. In all of these texts, contemporary indigenous identity becomes wedded to the government's solemn pledges of continued Indian sovereignty. That identity is expressed in the confluence of personal memory, oral tradition, and official records written in complementary traditions of ink on paper and paint on skins.

Quantum Fitness: Repoliticizing Blood, Imagination, Memory

In Chief Eagle's and Welch's historical novels set in the nineteenth century, American Indian racial identity and racial distinctiveness remains intact and unquestioned for the majority of the characters. Both novels do, however, raise issues of cultural and racial mixing. *Winter Count* features two White characters who, along with their mixed-blood children, live as Indians. *Fools Crow* includes the historically based character Joe Kipp, the mixed-blood son of a Blackfeet woman and a White trader. Kipp finds his position "between" worlds difficult to navigate, and he makes a place for himself in the Montana Territory's turbulent 1860s by serving as a scout and interpreter for the cavalry. By contrast, in most other Indian novels, short stories, poems, and essays produced during the American Indian renaissance—and especially in those set in contemporary times—issues of racial mixing and Indian authenticity are central. A crisis around these issues often is linked specifically to the federal government's official system and the White American public's (typically vague) understanding of quantifying Indian "blood."

Local, state, and federal policies have subjected African American citizens of the United States to an exclusionary "one drop" rule of racial identification that emphasizes their non-European heritage; but local, state, and federal policies have subjected American Indian citizens to an inclusive standard of "blood quantum" or "degree of Indian blood" that emphasizes instead the admixture of European and other bloodlines. A standard of racial identification, blood quantum originally served as a device for documenting "Indian" status for the federal government's purposes of dividing and subsequently alienating collectively held Indian lands. Blood quantum enshrines racial purity as the ideal for authentic Indian identity; tabulations of blood quantum thus highlight the genetic hybridity of most contemporary U.S. citizens who claim Indian status. In effect, mixed-blood Indians are considered genetically estranged from their full-blood indigenous ancestors once a certain "degree" of mixing with Europeans, White Americans, African Americans, or others has been passed.

Indian activist and scholar M. Annette Jaimes (Juaneño/Yaqui) has traced the federal government's standard of blood quantum to 1887 and the passage of the General Allotment Act, also known as the Dawes Act. Indians were required to prove that they had one-half or more Indian blood in order to receive preset allotments of their tribal estate; "surplus" lands were then made available to non-Indian settlers. As Jaimes documents, following the so-called success of allotment policies—between 1887 and 1934 the already shrunken Indian land base was "legally" reduced by another staggering ninety million acres—the standard of blood quantum was developed into a taxonomy of variable Indian identity that came to control Indian access to all federal services, including commodity rations, annuity payments, and health care.[41] Indian identity became subject to a genetic burden of proof. Indians who did not "look" Indian enough were—and are today—particularly suspected of falsifying indigenous identity. Indians of mixed tribal descent can find themselves "full-bloods" who do not qualify for Indian services because they do not meet specific half- or quarter-blood requirements for inclusion in a particular tribe or nation. Indians who were "adopted out" as infants often do not know their tribal affiliations, and Indians whose ancestors did not enter their names on the allotment rolls in the nineteenth century often do not qualify for official tribal membership. Any of these reasons can be used to disqualify individual Indians from federal Indian status. And from around 1975 onward, during a period marked by literary and political "renaissance," it has been not only federal government agencies or White Americans who have pointedly asked, "How much Indian blood do you have?"[42] As competition for limited federal monies and services has increased, Jaimes notes with obvious despair, "Indians themselves have increasingly begun to enforce the race codes excluding the genetically marginalized from both identification as Indian citizens and consequent entitlements" (129).

For Jaimes and many other Indian activists, standards of blood quantum represent a fundamental attack on the sovereignty of American Indian nations. Federal degree of blood criteria prevent Indian nations from determining their own criteria for tribal membership.[43] In the works of many Indian writers produced during the contemporary American Indian renaissance, the issue of blood quantum or degree of Indian blood is a site of perpetual conflict, opening on their pages as painful wounds that are inextricably personal—"Are you a real Indian?"—and political—"How much Indian blood do you have?" Perhaps paradoxically, in many of these works blood quantum is also a source of potential power. Whether addressed directly or hidden in elaborate metaphors, blood quantum stands as a metonym for the "problem" of defining contemporary American Indian personal and communal identities. "Mixed" blood can mean denigrated status in both Indian and White communities, a sense of belonging nowhere and to no one. But once identified, knowledge of specific indigenous bloodlines—ties to specific nations, bands, families, and individuals, particularly to living elders or illustrious ancestors—can serve as a catalyst for the recuperation of an integrated and successful contemporary American Indian identity.

Arguably, the most recognizable trope deployed in American Indian literary texts published after 1968 is *memory in the blood* or *blood memory*. Coined by N. Scott Momaday in his Pulitzer Prize–winning first novel, *House Made of Dawn,* and developed in his subsequent works, blood memory achieves tropic power by blurring distinctions between racial identity and narrative. Momaday's trope seems an obvious appropriation and redeployment of the U.S. government's attempt to systematize and regulate Indian identities through tabulations of blood quantum. The trope's provocative juxtaposition of *blood* and *memory* transforms that taxonomy of delegitimization through genetic mixing into an authenticating genealogy of stories and storytelling. Blood memory redefines Indian authenticity in terms of imaginative re-collecting and re-membering.[44] The connotative possibilities of Momaday's trope have been developed by other contemporary writers as well, most notably by Gerald Vizenor in his comic novel *The Heirs of Columbus* (1991). Unlike redeployments of the discourses of Plains Indian pictographic writing or U.S.-Indian treaty documents, however, blood memory has generated significant controversy.[45] For unlike redeployments of the discourses of winter counts and treaties, which are grounded in the materiality of artifacts and in verifiable events of indigenous contact with settler-invaders, the deployment of blood memory relies on a series of contemporary assertions rooted in indigenous worldviews and personal experience. These include the assertion of an unmediated relationship to indigenous land bases (whether or not those lands remain under indigenous control), the continuation of oral traditions (whether or not those traditions continue in Native languages), and the power of the indigenous writer's imagination to establish communion with ancestors. The analysis of blood memory thus forces us to confront emotionally charged issues of racial identification and indigenous spirituality and to contemplate the roles these can play in indigenous minority activism.

Blood memory appears in all of Momaday's significant work to date, and in many ways the trope has become his literary and imaginative signature. To read and reread the body of Momaday's literary production, both in and out of the order of its publication, is thus to encounter not only a palimpsest but also a unified whole. The novels, essays, traditional Kiowa stories, personal reflections, and poems all return to a set of familiar images, characters, and narratives, often reworking the same material in several forms and various combinations. Momaday's explicit references to blood memory form an unfolding and self-reflexive discourse on the complex potential meanings of contemporary American Indian identities based on indigenous memory. Like ceremonial formulas repeated with slight but significant variation, this palimpsestic, unfolding discourse presents a building theme and a persistent argument that narrative, geography, and transformative spiritual power interact in multiple relationships. Blood memory also renders as a trope the synthesis of these relationships, their contemplation in the human imagination, and their subsequent recollection in human memory. In his 1970 address, "The Man Made of Words," Momaday states to an audience of other educated American Indians that "An Indian is an idea a given man has of himself." Based in blood memory, such an idea liberates Momaday's own and other Indians' identities from imposed definitions of indigenous authenticity, including standards of blood quantum and/or standards that demand the uninterrupted and uncontaminated inheritance of indigenous languages, lifeways, or habits of art.[46]

Momaday's short poem "Carnegie, Oklahoma, 1919," part of his 1992 collection of selected and new poems, *In the Presence of the Sun,* exemplifies his argument and method. The poem mobilizes the trope blood memory, and it illustrates Momaday's process for rendering his contemporary indigenous identity as text:

> This afternoon is older
> than the giving of gifts
> and the rhythmic scraping of the red earth.
> My father's father's name is called,
> and the gift horse stutters out, whole,
> the whole horizon in its eyes.
> In the giveaway is beaded
> the blood memories of fathers and sons.
> Oh, there is nothing like this afternoon
> in all the miles and years around,
> and I am not here,
> but, grandfather, father, I am here. (136)

The poem is a condensed and companion version of a story Momaday tells more elaborately in his 1976 memoir, *The Names* (see 93–97).[47] In

that version Momaday remembers himself as a young boy visiting his
Kiowa grandmother in Oklahoma. He imagines himself as that boy,
who begins to wonder about his dead grandfather, whom he never
met; the boy then imagines himself alive in 1919, when his grandfather,
Mammedaty, was given a horse. The boy Momaday has imagined
knows the details of the ritual giveaway because his father has told him
the story of how his grandfather was honored and because his father
has pointed out the places in the Oklahoma landscape where this
auspicious event occurred. In order to imagine himself as part of that
ritual, the boy first imagines himself as part of a vision experienced
by his grandfather, the story of which Momaday's father also has recounted to him. Momaday retells a fuller version of the story of his
grandfather's vision as part of *The Way to Rainy Mountain.* In that text
from 1969, Mammedaty looks out at the high summer grass, listening
to the meadowlarks "calling all around": "There was nothing but the
early morning and the land around. Then Mammedaty heard something. Someone whistled to him. He looked up and saw the head of a
little boy nearby above the grass. He stopped the horses and got down
from the wagon and went to see who was there. There was no one;
there was nothing there. He looked for a long time, but there was
nothing there" (72).

In *The Names,* the boy Momaday has imagined stands outside his
grandmother's house in Oklahoma and experiences Mammedaty's vision himself: "I see a boy standing still in the distance, only his head
and shoulders visible above the long, luminous grass, and from the
place where he stands there comes the clear call of a meadowlark" (94).
The boy Momaday has imagined becomes the boy in his grandfather's
vision. Momaday then describes the Oklahoma landscape in further
detail, using it as a transition to the next phase in the boy's imagined
experience: ". . . and there in the roiling dust a knoll, a gourd dance and
give-away, and Mammedaty moves among his people, answers to his
name; low thunder rolls upon the drum. A boy leads a horse into the
circle" (94). Finally, the boy imagines himself as the boy leading the
horse, as a vital part of the ceremony honoring his grandfather: "It
is good and honorable to be made such a gift—the gift of this horse,
this hunting horse—and honorable to be the boy, the intermediary in
whose hands the gift is passed. My fingers are crisped, my fingertips
bear hard upon the life of this black horse. *Oh my grandfather, take hold*

of this horse" (94–96). A photograph of Mammedaty wearing modified traditional dress and holding a feather fan is inserted as page 95 of *The Names*. As Momaday describes himself as a boy imagining himself as part of the traditional giveaway that honored his grandfather, the reader literally confronts Mammedaty's—and, by extension, Momaday's—image as a traditional Kiowa. We are invited to read Momaday's inscription of his imaginative experience not as a reenactment of history but rather as a repetition that suggests a continuation. It represents an assertion, as does Ella Deloria's *Waterlily,* of "vicarious honor."

The poem "Carnegie, Oklahoma, 1919" compresses significant landscape, storytelling, and memory into the representation of a single "afternoon." Momaday's father had told him the stories of his grandfather's life and pointed out the places in the Oklahoma landscape where these events occurred. Momaday situates himself—physically and imaginatively—in this landscape, remembers the stories, and in the remembering imagines himself as playing a part in them. In the poem, he makes these stories his own, part of *his* memory, part of *his* "blood"; imaginatively re-collected and re-membered, they articulate his identity in an ongoing genealogical sequence as a member of the Mammedaty/Momaday family, as a Kiowa son and grandson. Blood memory thus tropes the conflating of storytelling, imagination, memory, and genealogy into the representation of a single, multifaceted moment in a particular landscape. Blood memory also names the process through which Momaday "beads" the "memories of fathers and sons" into a single, integrated text. The contemporary Indian writer renders himself coincident with indigenous ancestors and with indigenous history—and makes available to readers both that indigenous past and his contemporary identity *as indigenous*—through tactics of narrative re-membering and transgenerational address. In a maneuver similar to the "alchemy of taonga" at work in much of Maori renaissance literature, Momaday's deployment of "blood memory" allows him to effect a collapse of distance in space-time. "And I am not here," Momaday is enabled to write, "but, grandfather, father, I am here."

Other works detail more fully Momaday's development of the process of blood memory as a method for re-collecting and re-membering as text his indigenous identity. The whole of *The Way to Rainy Mountain,* for instance, can be read as an exercise in blood memory. In the introduction, Momaday focuses attention on the role of his grand-mother, Aho, as his direct "blood" link to the Kiowa past and to the Kiowa oral tradition. Through a series of associations, Momaday projects himself back in time through Aho's lifespan and beyond to the golden age of Kiowa history:

> She had lived to be very old and at last infirm. Her only living daughter was with her when she died, and I was told that in death her face was that of a child.
>
> I like to think of her as a child. When she was born, the Kiowas were living the last great moment of their history. For more than a hundred years they had controlled the open range. (5–6)

Momaday associates Aho's old age with the look of childhood; in turn, he associates Aho's childhood with the final moments of precontact Kiowa history; the second association allows Momaday to evoke the full flowering of precontact Kiowa culture. Repeating almost verbatim a passage in *House Made of Dawn*, Momaday then refers explicitly to Aho's "memory in the blood": "Although my grandmother lived out her long life in the shadow of Rainy Mountain, the immense landscape of the continental interior lay like memory in her blood. She could tell of the Crows, whom she had never seen, and of the Black Hills, where she had never been. I wanted to see in reality what she had seen more perfectly in the mind's eye" (7). Part of the project of *The Way to Rainy Mountain* is for Momaday to recount the physical pilgrimage he made across the Kiowa's ancestral landscape and to couple his account of this journey with his knowledge of extant Kiowa oral narratives and the written historical and anthropological records of the Kiowa in order to develop in his own memory what the Kiowa oral tradition, still fully operative in his grandmother's lifetime, had developed as Aho's "memory in the blood."

The book's three chapters are organized to reflect both the Kiowa's ancestral journey and Momaday's contemporary physical and imaginative pilgrimage. In each section, Momaday juxtaposes Kiowa oral traditions with historical or anthropological accounts and with personal reflections. In each set, the oral tradition stands alone on the left-hand page of the open book. The historical account and personal reflection stand on the facing page; together, they balance and respond to the transcribed oral narrative. Perhaps the best known of the Kiowa oral narratives is the story of the arrowmaker (46). A Kiowa arrow-maker and his wife sit alone one night when the man realizes that someone is watching them through a small opening where the hides of the tipi are sewn together. The arrowmaker pretends to speak to his wife but actually addresses the unknown person outside, asking him to speak his name if he understands what is being said to him in Kiowa. All the while the arrowmaker points his arrow in various directions as though testing its aim. When he realizes the man outside does not understand Kiowa—and is thus an enemy—the arrowmaker aims for the opening between the hides and kills the intruder. Momaday him-self retells and interprets the story of the arrowmaker in his address "The Man Made of Words" (59–62). Literary scholars often note the story for the connections it draws between language and identity: the arrowmaker identifies his enemy through language use, and he and his wife then defeat this enemy through a ruse of language. On its own, the story of the arrowmaker is compelling; read alongside its companion historical and personal texts, it becomes part of a demonstration of the process of blood memory. The historical passage establishes the role of arrowmakers in the Kiowa community and notes the traffic in arrows between the older generation of arrowmakers and the younger genera-tion of warriors. The personal reflection then recounts a story told to Momaday by his father about an old Kiowa arrowmaker who visited the family when Momaday's father was a boy. Momaday writes, "In my mind I can see that man as if he were there now. I like to watch him as he makes his prayer. I know where he stands and where his voice goes on the rolling grasses and where the sun comes up on the land" (47). Together, the three accounts link Momaday to Kiowa ancestors and Kiowa traditions of language use, warfare, and exchange through genealogy, storytelling, and imagination—all grounded in a specific landscape.

In the epilogue to *The Way to Rainy Mountain,* Momaday evokes one of the tangible artifacts of Kiowa historical memory, their pictographic calendars. He notes that one of the earliest events recorded on the Kiowa calendars is the great meteor shower that was observable across the United States in 1833 (85).[48] Momaday then asserts that the event is "within the reach of memory still, though tenuously now, and more-over it is even defined in a remarkably rich and living verbal tradition which demands to be preserved for its own sake. The living memory and the verbal tradition which transcends it were brought together for me once and for all in the person of Ko-sahn" (86). Momaday ends *The Way to Rainy Mountain* by remembering Ko-sahn, the hundred-year-old Kiowa woman whom he knew as a child. In a scene of indigenous instruction, Ko-sahn had told him a story from her own childhood, an account of the Kiowa Sun Dance. Preparing for the ceremony, an old woman carries a bag of sandy earth to sprinkle across the dance arena. After recounting Ko-sahn's story, Momaday wonders if she ever imagined herself as the ancient woman of her own youth, and he speculates, "in her mind, at times, did she see the falling stars?" (88). As in his introduction, in his epilogue Momaday imagines Kiowa elders in order to project himself back through their lifespans—through their "blood" —and beyond to even older Kiowa memories.

Momaday returns to the imagined figure of Ko-sahn in "The Man Made of Words." Here, her evocation is emblematic of the process of blood memory and, in many respects, of the project of much of American Indian literature written in this period: Momaday uses English language and contemporary writing practices to conjure an indigenous ancestor into present reality. Most startlingly, Momaday describes his encounter with the conjured ancestor as occurring through and on the written page of his own literary work. This scene draws clear connections between an emerging American Indian written literature and the recovery—or reemergence—of indigenous identities.

After a brief introduction about "the relationship between language and being," in "The Man Made of Words" Momaday tells his Indian audience the "story" of how he finished writing *The Way to Rainy Mountain*: "I had projected myself—imagined myself—out of the room and out of time. I was there with Ko-sahn in the Oklahoma July" (51). He then describes how, after he had imagined the old Kiowa woman and imagined himself as part of her story, Ko-sahn literally emerged from his written text:

> My eyes fell upon the name Ko-sahn. And all at once everything seemed suddenly to refer to that name. The name seemed to humanize the whole complexity of language. All at once, absolutely, I had the sense of the magic of words and of names. Ko-sahn, I said, and I said again KO-SAHN.
>
> Then it was that that ancient, one-eyed woman Ko-sahn stepped out of the language and stood before me on the page. I was amazed. Yet it seemed to me entirely appropriate that this should happen. (51)

Momaday's provocative scene offers an explanation of its own workings: the writer conjures the ancestor through the magic of words and names. He ritually repeats Ko-sahn's name, and she appears. But Momaday's "magic" also lies in the scene's careful construction and subtle rhetorical devices. He plays with the pun in English linking "eye," the subject of seeing, with "I," the subject of being. Momaday focuses his "eye"—and thus concentrates the reader's attention—on the inscription of the ancient Kiowa name, Ko-sahn. He then states that "everything seemed suddenly to refer to that name"—not that the name seemed suddenly to refer to everything. In other words, with his "eye" focused thus, the whole of his mixed-genre text seems to refer to the name of the indigenous ancestor. In that moment, the name Ko-sahn becomes a metonym for Momaday's meditation on the relationships between landscape, imagination, memory, and blood, a metonym for "the whole complexity of language." Distinctions between perception and being collapse in Momaday's concentration on the name, and Ko-sahn, that "one-eyed" woman, steps "out of the language" to stand before Momaday "on the page." There she articulates the genetic and social implications of Momaday's magic by hailing him as "grandson."

Having conjured up Ko-sahn through the power of language, Momaday reports that their short verbal exchange explores the nature of imagination. When Momaday protests that "this has taken place—is taking place in my mind," Ko-sahn responds, "You imagine that I am here in this room, do you not? That is worth something. You see, I have existence, whole being, in your imagination. It is but one kind of being, to be sure," Ko-sahn continues, "but it is perhaps the best of all kinds. If I am not here in this room, grandson, then surely neither are you" (51). Momaday has imagined Ko-sahn as sly, the moment of their encounter as humorous. But the moment also evokes a profound statement about the relationship between generations of American Indians.[49] As in New Zealand Maori writing from this period, the bond between grandparent and grandchild figures the relationship of contemporary indigeneity to the ancestors. Before receding back into Momaday's text, Ko-sahn relates her own experiences of imagining the Kiowa past beyond her lifetime and personal memory: "There are times," she remarks, "when I think that I am the oldest woman on earth. You know, the Kiowas came into the world through a hollow log. In my mind's *eye I* have seen them emerge . . ." (52, emphasis added).

Momaday explains Ko-sahn's process of imagining herself in the ancient past as a process of appropriation: "For it remained to be imagined. She must at last deal with it in words; she must appropriate it to her understanding of the whole universe" (55). This is also an explanation of Momaday's own process of blood memory, and thus Ko-sahn provides an indigenous precedent for Momaday's contemporary practice. He follows this explanation with a passage in which he projects himself into the Kiowa past through a first-person recitation of Ko-sahn's own imagined memories, assuming an oral storytelling persona that some anthropologists have termed the "kinship I" (55).[50] Momaday's careful prose stages an authenticating communion with the indigenous ancestor and allows him to speak a version of the Kiowa past into the present.

Momaday expands his project of constructing a viable indigenous identity in *The Names*. He begins the story of his own Kiowa name, Tsoai-talee, with a significant juxtaposition. First, he reprints "a notarized document issued by the United States Department of the Interior, Office of Indian Affairs, Anadarko [Oklahoma] Area Office." This brief document records Momaday's connection to his grandfather's name, Mammedaty, notes the date and place of Momaday's birth, and establishes his official blood quantum: "Novarro Scott Mammedaty was born February 27, 1934 at Lawton, Oklahoma and is of ⅞ degree Indian blood, as shown on the Kiowa Indian Census roll opposite Number 2035" (42).[51] Immediately following the reprinted document, Momaday writes: "The first notable event in my life was a journey to the Black Hills. When I was six months old my parents took me to Devil's Tower, Wyoming, which is called in Kiowa Tsoai, 'rock tree.' Here are stories within stories; I want to imagine a day in the life of a man, Pohd-lohk, who gave me a name" (42). The juxtaposed government document and the "stories within stories" of how Momaday received his Kiowa name represent culturally divergent ways of defining his "authentic" American Indian identity. The stories within stories, in which knowledgeable elders situate the young child within the coordinates of tribal narrative, parallel the emblematic "scenes of instruction" prominent in Maori renaissance literature.

Momaday is silent on the issue of his official status "opposite Number 2035," but his narrative strongly suggests that he considers blood memory a marker of his Kiowa identity that is superior to blood quantum. When Momaday imagines that the old man Pohd-lohk visits Momaday's great-grandmother, the blind Keahdinekeah, on his way to confer the auspicious name, Momaday writes that Keahdinekeah "thought of Tsoai and of her great-grandson. Neither had she ever seen, but of Tsoai she knew an old story" (55). Momaday then retells the story of the monolith Tsoai, the "Rock Tree," which he had recounted in his grandmother's voice in the introduction to *The Way to Rainy Mountain.* After this retelling, through Keahdinekeah's imagined thoughts Momaday reveals the significance of his parents' decision to take him to visit Tsoai: "And her grandson Huan-toa [Momaday's father] had taken his child to be in Tsoai's presence even before the child could understand what it was, so that by means of the child the memory of Tsoai should be renewed in the blood of the coming-out people [the Kiowa]" (55). Momaday's name, Tsoai-talee, "Rock-Tree Boy," binds him to a significant landscape in the Kiowa memory and to the stories associated with that landscape. In giving the name, Momaday imagines that Pohd-lohk's storytelling also binds Momaday to Kiowa origins and to historical events that are important to the Kiowa's sense of themselves and their destiny, since Pohd-lohk tells "how it was that everything began, of Tsoai, and of the stars falling or holding fast in strange patterns on the sky." Finally, "Pohd-lohk affirmed the whole life of the child in a name, saying: Now you are, Tsoai-talee" (57). It is not Momaday's blood quantum, inscribed by the U.S. government in official documents, that confers his Kiowa identity; rather, it is his blood memory, the story of his being situated within ongoing Kiowa narratives of their identity as a people in the North American landscape.

In the epilogue to *The Names,* Momaday tells part of the story of his journey retracing the Kiowa migration left out of the account given in *The Way to Rainy Mountain,* his return to Tsoai as an adult. "This strange thing," he writes, "this Tsoai, I saw with my own eyes and with the eyes of my own mind" (167). This statement is perhaps the clearest description of the process of blood memory, the overlay and interpenetration of experience and imagination in language and in memory. In a 1987 interview, Momaday told his friend Charles Woodard, a professor of English at South Dakota State University, "There are times, Chuck, when I think about people walking on ice with dogs, pulling travois, and I don't know whether it's something that I'm imagining or something that I remember. But it comes down to the same thing" (Woodard, *Ancestral Voice*, 22). What is at issue in these passages is the relevance of particular experience, recently or distantly past, lived physically or imaginatively, to personal and communal identity. In other words, Momaday emphasizes the processes of imagination and memory in the expression of a successful and meaningful idea of the self: collapsing distance in space-time through tactics of re-collecting and re-membering, transgenerational address, assuming the story-telling persona of the "kinship I," and so forth. As Momaday states succinctly in "The Man Made of Words," to an audience of other con-temporary Indians, "The greatest tragedy that can befall us is to go unimagined" (55).

American Indian writers following Momaday have explored and developed the possible meanings of the trope blood memory in their own works. In their readings of James Welch's novel *Winter in the Blood* (1974), for example, critics generally focus on the anonymous narra-tor's quest to remember or to find his Blackfeet identity.[52] The narrator begins to find such an identity when he discovers—and/or imagines—that the blind elder, Yellow Calf, is actually his grandfather. The narra-tor visits Yellow Calf on the occasion of his hundred-year-old grand-mother's death; he wants to know if Yellow Calf knew her. The old man is able to tell her story: as the grandmother's story unfolds, her life takes on new significance for the narrator, and Yellow Calf becomes increasingly implicated in the old woman's and now the young narra-tor's life. As in Momaday's *The Way to Rainy Mountain,* the grand-mother's death prompts an investigation of the narrator's connection to his indigenous past. In Yellow Calf's "distant" blind eyes, Welch's narrator begins to see "a world as clean as the rustling willows, the bark of a fox or the odor of musk during mating season" (151)—that is, the Blackfeet world before the corruptions brought on by White invasion. As Yellow Calf recounts his story of how he and the narrator's grand-mother survived the hard winters and the cavalry attacks of their youth, the narrator slowly pieces together his connection to the old man. In the course of the narrator's realization of whom and what he is hearing, the winter landscape suddenly comes to life with the Blackfeet past: "And so we shared this secret in the presence of ghosts, in wind that called forth the muttering tepees, the blowing snow, the white air of the horses' nostrils. The cottonwoods behind us, their dead white branches angling to the threatening clouds, sheltered these ghosts as they had sheltered the camp that winter. But there were others, so many others" (159). The narrator realizes that when his father took him to visit Yellow Calf when he was a boy, "he had taken me that snowy day to see my grandfather" (162). Significantly, he attributes his realization to the power of Yellow Calf's "blood" to speak to him across the generations: "The answer had come to me as if by instinct . . . as though it was his blood in my veins that had told me" (160). Other characters in the novel have assumed that Yellow Calf is dead, but Yellow Calf and his world have become very much alive for the narrator—so much so, in fact, that for a moment the narrator forgets that his grandmother has passed on (162). In the final, comic scene of the funeral, the narrator acknowledges the Blackfeet world to which he has become newly reconnected by gesturing toward the Blackfeet practice of burying significant possessions with the dead. He tosses the grandmother's tobacco pouch into the grave he has helped to dig, offering readers hope that the hapless narrator has found a means for building an integrated Blackfeet identity for himself.

In *Ceremony,* during her protagonist Tayo's significant journey into the mountains, Silko attributes blood memory to animals as well as to humans: "Maybe the dawn woke the [horse's] instinct in the dim memory of the blood when horses had been as wild as deer and at sunrise went into the trees and thickets to hide" (182–83). While in the mountains, Tayo experiences a Laguna sense of time strikingly reminiscent of Momaday's collapsing of present, past, and future in the process of blood memory: "The ride into the mountain had branched into all directions of time. He knew then why the oldtimers could only speak of yesterday and tomorrow in terms of the present moment: the only certainty" (192). After he has successfully completed his ceremonial journey of healing and fought the witchery, Tayo realizes that nothing has been lost because the landscape remains, not only as a physical entity but also as an integral part of the people's sense of themselves, their past, and their future destiny: "The mountain outdistanced their destruction, just as love had outdistanced death. The mountain could not be lost to them, because it was in their bones" (219). Tayo realizes that the Laguna community's "vitality" is "locked deep in *blood memory,* and the people were strong, and the fifth world endured, and nothing was ever lost as long as the love remained" (220, emphasis added). Silko makes clear that her mixed-blood protagonist's success becomes possible because he is able to tap into this blood memory, because he is able to finally see "the pattern, the way all the stories fit together—the old stories, the war stories, their stories—to become the story that was still being told. He was not crazy; he had never been crazy. He had only seen and heard the world as it always was: no boundaries, only transitions through all distances and time" (246).

Journeys through ancestral landscape also evoke blood memory in Joy Harjo's poems collected in *She Had Some Horses* (1983). In the poem "New Orleans," for instance, Harjo's Creek narrator searches the deep South "for evidence / of other Creeks, for remnants of voices" (42). Mid-poem, the narrator confesses,

> I have a memory.
> It swims deep in blood,
> a delta in the skin. It swims out of Oklahoma,
> deep the Mississippi River. It carries my
> feet to these places. . . .
> My spirit comes here to drink.
> My spirit comes here to drink.
> Blood is the undercurrent. (42)

Harjo's narrator finds "voices buried in the Mississippi / mud" and "stories here made of memory" (43). Having journeyed from Oklahoma, where the Creeks were forcibly removed in the 1830s, to the Creek's ancestral southern landscape, Harjo's narrator is able to recover pieces of the indigenous past and to "remember [the invader] DeSoto" (43). Similarly, in the poetry of Barney Bush (Shawnee/Cayuga), the midwestern landscape of the Ohio River valley evokes blood memory in poems titled "Directions in Our Blood" and "The Memory Sire." In the poem "Taking a Captive/1984," Bush's turns of language summarize blood memory's tropic power for recuperating an integrated contemporary American Indian identity. Following Momaday, Bush's narrator imagines an indigenous past for his young son as "continuous / memory absorbed into blood."[53]

Gerald Vizenor's celebrated "trickster discourse" has pushed the potential meanings of Momaday's trope the furthest.[54] Although Vizenor has critiqued the potential for blood memory to become a form of debilitating essentialism, he has also advanced the project of indigenous recovery and reimagination begun by Momaday. Vizenor's novel *Darkness in St. Louis Bearheart* (1978), for instance, cautions against romanticizing Momaday's trope into yet another rigid category for static "Indian" identity, no different from the ossified definitions imposed first by Europeans and then by White Americans. "Who is this *romancioso momaday?*" a character asks during a critical scene when Vizenor's post-apocalyptic, mixed-blood pilgrims must gamble for their lives, "Is he the one who loves wheeling horses?" (114). The latter question refers to Momaday's early poem "Plainview: 2," originally published in 1973 and included in his collection *The Gourd Dancer* (1976). The speaker of the poem sees "an old Indian / At Saddle Mountain": "He drank and dreamed of drinking / And a blue-black horse / . . . Remember my horse wheeling / Remember my horse / . . . Remember / Remember" (21–23). In the context of Vizenor's novel, and in the context of the pilgrims' fight with the evil gambler, the reference to "Plainview: 2" is an oblique but precise critique of the potential for Momaday's deployment of Indian "memory" to be read as a racialist nostalgia for a past golden age, especially when it is bolstered by a narrative tactics that simulates ritual (here, Momaday's invocation of ceremonial discourse in his repetition of formulaic lines, each beginning with the word "Remember"). Nostalgia of this sort can serve no purpose in the present except to lock contemporary Indians into stereotypical self-images rooted in the past and prevent them from reimagining viable identities for the present and future. Vizenor's character Proude Cedarfair, who comes closest to an individual protagonist in *Darkness in St. Louis Bearheart*'s communal narrative, warns his fellow mixed bloods that "We become our memories and what we believe. . . . We become the terminal creeds we speak" (147). Such befalls one of Vizenor's many conflicted characters, Belladonna Darwin-Winter Catcher, the mixed-blood daughter of a tribal shaman and a White anthropologist, who claims she was conceived during the activist occupation at Wounded Knee: she becomes a victim of her romance with a static Indian identity based on an idealized Indian past. At the same time, however—as Vizenor stresses in its revised 1990 title, *Bearheart: The Heirship Chronicles*—*the novel* is a comic exploration of the processes for imagining contemporary narratives of indigenous descent and, in this sense, it is an extension of Momaday's project of exploring the power of oral traditions to create an imagined order out of contemporary chaos.[55] Vizenor explores this transgenerational and healing power most fully in his comic novel *The Heirs of Columbus* (1991), where he pushes the implications of Momaday's blood memory trope to one of its logical extremes: the development of a genetic research center dedicated to harnessing the power of American Indians' "stories in the blood" and to decoding American Indians' "genes of survivance." Vizenor's mixed-blood characters learn to harness the "story energy" that "somehow influences the genetic codes" and has the power to heal deformed and abused tribal children (164). On the eve of the Columbus quincentenary, Vizenor deploys blood memory to trope the restoration of viable indigeneity in contemporary times.[56]

Destruction into Survival, Fabrication into Truth: Indigenous Identity as Public Memory

When the American Indian political and literary renaissance began, Indian activists and writers worked in a frustrating context of transparency and misrepresentation. The dominant U.S. culture had fallen in love with a powerfully romantic vision, "objectively" told by outside experts, that all the real Indians had perished at the end of the nineteenth century. And the dominant culture preferred the fabricated tales of a supposedly hundred-year-old living Indian relic, Chief Red Fox, a last Noble Red Man, to realistic accounts of contemporary reservation life, urban poverty, or events of indigenous activism.[57] In a climate of willful ignorance and selective amnesia—in a climate of imperialist nostalgia in which the dominant culture seemed to enjoy mourning that which it had itself destroyed—Indian activists and writers worked to reinstate the indigenous into America's performance of a triumphantly settler present.

Like their Maori counterparts in Aotearoa/New Zealand, Indian activists and writers devised during this period of "renaissance" narrative tactics that create both metonymic and metaphoric connections to the indigenous past. The preceding sections demonstrate how Indian activists and writers re-recognized and/or revalued existing indigenous and non-indigenous discourses so that they might become appropriate for representing mostly private American Indian memories—of struggle, of perseverance, of survival—as public memory. Activist proclamations, essays, memoirs, novels, and poems render public both the painfully and the joyfully intimate dimensions of contemporary indigenous life in North America. Overwhelmingly self-reflexive, these works foreground the moral implications of literature and politics. They commemorate significant events in the lives of American Indian individuals and communities, and they consciously bear historical witness to present and future generations. Against the odds, they invest contemporary texts with ancestral power and indigenous presence.

In June 1974 the first International Indian Treaty Council met on the Standing Rock Reservation in South Dakota to add its part to a growing American Indian public memory. The council's official public document, the *Declaration of Continuing Independence*, situates the plight of contemporary American Indian nations within a history of international and ongoing colonialism. The United States is identified as a breakaway settler colony, and its federal government is named as an overseer of an oppressive internal colonialism. In their declaration, delegates to the council, representing some ninety-seven American Indian nations, engage the blood/land/memory complex by linking their demands that the federal government protect American Indians' rights to aboriginal lands, to religious freedoms, and to basic human rights to the re-recognition of treaties. They demand nothing less than that the federal government uphold "the sacred treaties solemnly entered into between the Native Nations and the government of the United States of America," "interpreted according to the traditional and spiritual ways of the signatory Native Nations." Part of the declaration's narrative tactics is to expand the scope of their demands—and the range of their support—from the domestic to the international arena. Delegates shame the U.S. government for not signing the Treaty on Genocide drafted by the United Nations in 1948; they then shame the UN for excluding "the indigenous Redman of the Western Hemisphere" from its roster of world representatives. Further, delegates align their struggles as American Indians with the struggles of other "aboriginal" peoples. Such alignment marks the beginnings of the international indigenous rights movement—the invention of the Fourth World—which is the subject of the concluding chapter.

CONCLUSION

Declaring a Fourth World

I am suggesting to you that there has to be a Fourth World in order for mankind to survive. I am suggesting to you that we have to develop a political mechanism, an economic mechanism and perhaps a cultural mechanism to establish for ourselves as people, world people[,] a framework of survival and equality, dignity and pride for all our people and I suggest this is the principal purpose, reason, objective of why we decided to try to form, and I want to put a lot of emphasis on trying, to form a relationship between all indigenous minorities of the world. This is our principal objective. —George Manuel (Shuswap), World Council of Indigenous Peoples, Copenhagen, 1975

The thing that link[s] the aboriginal people of the world, as I believe it, are the family ties, the tribal ties, and the kinship ties, [the] most important links of our people. The second thing that links us together is our devotion to the land, and so I believe that we have certain thing[s] in common.—Neil A. Watene (Maori), World Council of Indigenous Peoples, Copenhagen, 1975

The formation of the World Council of Indigenous Peoples (WCIP) and its attempts to articulate a global definition of indigenous minority identity is a useful marker, although not an exact marker, of a shift that occurred in the tenor of indigenous activism and writing in both Aotearoa/New Zealand and the United States. In the first decades after the beginning of World War II, a small number of indigenous minority activists and emerging indigenous minority writers struggled to produce and disseminate works of nonfiction, fiction, and poetry, and to stage events of ethno-drama, largely from within the structures of dominant institutions and dominant discourses. By the mid- and late

1960s, indigenous minority activism and writing proliferated both within and outside dominant cultural formations, and growing numbers of indigenous minority activists and writers began to form politically viable institutions and discourses of their own. The WCIP was conceived during the upswing of that indigenous minority "renaissance"; it was one of the newly formed institutions that were supposed to change the lives of indigenous minorities for the better. That the WCIP was unable to effect such change in a tangible way will surprise no one familiar with the history of coalition movements, particularly those organized by groups that were both politically and financially dependent on the very sources of power they sought to critique and persuade. One of the ironies of the formation of the WCIP, although it was perhaps unavoidable, is that its funding came largely from First World settler governments and a number of Christian organizations. Its primary delegates came not from the growing ranks of young radicals but rather from the leadership of established national indigenous organizations such as the National Congress of American Indians, the New Zealand Maori Council, and the National (Australian) Aboriginal Consultative Committee.[1] In this sense, the WCIP resembled the American Indian Chicago Conference of 1961 more than it did the International Treaty Council of 1974.

Whether or not the WCIP made a positive contribution to the evolving discourse of indigenous minority activism, however, is a related but ultimately separate issue, one that requires a more subtle analysis. This is because, despite its delegates' connections to dominant powers, the WCIP's international vision of indigeneity was a genuinely new step, and its early leaders were genuinely "committed to the principle that indigenous people must themselves organize and control the conference."[2] Both in their private deliberations and in their production of public documents, delegates attempted to translate the efforts of specific indigenous minorities to the international arena, to seize control of the symbolic and metaphoric meanings of indigenous "blood," "land," and "memory" at the level of the global. A focus on the WCIP is thus a fitting conclusion to the arguments advanced in part 1 and part 2. As will become clear in the analyses below, the WCIP's narrative tactics testify to the broad discursive appeal and the perceived symbolic power of the blood/land/memory complex, as well as to the perceived necessity of building an activist indigenous minority politics within the paradigm of nation-to-nation status encoded in the discourse of treaties. My concern in this chapter, therefore, is threefold: first, to chronicle the development of the WCIP's 1975 definition of the Fourth World as a particular episode in ongoing negotiations over the meanings of native indigeneity; second, to examine the narrative tactics deployed by the WCIP, especially as those tactics engage the blood/ land/memory complex and treaty discourse; and, finally, to link the WCIP's endeavor in the early 1970s to subsequent efforts by indigenous minority activists and writers in the United States and Aotearoa/New Zealand to develop a body of "indigenous theory." This emerging theory, I want to argue, represents a legacy of the WCIP's attempts to construct a discursive "framework of survival and equality, dignity and pride" for indigenous minority peoples living in the contemporary era.

The most striking feature of the WCIP's 1975 definition of "Indigenous Peoples"—with its emphasis on a globalizing capital *I*, capital *P*— is that it is forged not as a list of "objective" criteria but rather as a narrative. By eschewing the trappings of political "science" for the conventions of literature, the WCIP created a (post)colonial auto-ethnography that attempts to counter—through a tactics of engagement and activist occupation—the First World's dominant discourses of master narrative and ethnic taxonomy.[3] The WCIP's narrative definition thus can be read as a symbolic attempt at collective repossession. Delegates representing diverse indigenous minority peoples erected communal signs of their individual cultural and political sovereignties, asserted the legitimacy of their versions of history and law, declared title to their lands and to themselves, and created a public record of these significant actions in a form and through a forum, though highly syncretic, that could be recognized not only by themselves and their home communities but also by the contemporary "concert of nations," whose attention they sought to direct and whose judgment they endeavored to persuade. In the forum of the WCIP, delegates imitated the deliberative practices and infiltrated the moral space of the dominant internationalist discourse of the United Nations. There they invented a collective and collaborative subject, "Indigenous Peoples," and a narrative of this invented subject's history. Like the goals of the member states of the UN, moreover, the goals of the delegates to the WCIP were in the end not exclusively global in their scope but significantly local as well. The formation of an international coalition and the creation of a narrative of international identity were tactical maneuvers designed to redirect power relations in the delegates' local, regional, and national contexts and to rewrite local and national narratives of power.

Inevitably, in assessing the effectiveness of these tactics, my analysis of the WCIP's founding documents leads to a consideration of the complicated and politically charged distinction that typically is drawn between a strategically collectivist vision of the Fourth World and a limiting and ultimately debilitating essentialist vision of diverse indigenous peoples. Postcolonial critics have directed our attention to the political and theoretical ramifications of activists creating openly politicized ethnicities like the WCIP's global "Indigenous Peoples." Stuart Hall, for instance, describes such maneuvers as the "first form of identity politics," in which activists constitute "a defensive collective identity against the practices of racist society." Hall further writes that "This is an enormous act of what I want to call imaginary political re-identification, re-identification and re-territorialization, without which a counter-politics could not have been constructed."[4] The WCIP's tactics may remind some readers of Gayatri Spivak's celebrated, somewhat abused notion of a "strategic essentialism" deployed consciously as a "situational practice" in order to fight against oppression. Those tactics may also bring to mind Frantz Fanon's insistence two decades earlier "that the construction of essentialist forms of 'native' identity is a legitimate, indeed necessary stage in the emergence from the process of 'assimilation' imposed by colonial regimes to a fully decolonized national culture."[5] These and other scholars characterize the development of essentialist markers of ethnopolitical identity as an often necessary early stage in the struggle to achieve some form of postcolonial liberation that is ultimately anti-essentialist. But the assumption of an inevitable shift in tactics that will fall in line with radical politics and theoretical purity—in this case, in line with the anti-essentialism typically espoused by postcolonial and multicultural critics alike—may be of limited use for understanding the development and, in particular, the endurance of essentialist markers of identity within the particular dynamics of Fourth World (post)coloniality. What has struck me, contrary to the models put forward by Hall, Spivak, or Fanon, is how closely aligned indigenous minority ethnopolitical struggle remained, throughout the early contemporary period, with the supposedly "first" form of identity politics. Whether or not anti-essentialism was among the ultimate goals of indigenous minority activists in the 1960s and 1970s—or is today—the demands, possibilities, and limitations of the specific occasions of their activism appear to require essentialist markers of indigenous minority identity. Without clear lines drawn, literally, in the sand, indigenous minorities risk their total engulfment by powerful settler nations.

Differentiating Between First and Fourth Worlds

The individual most responsible for the initial development and dissemination of the idea of the Fourth World as an international phenomenon is George Manuel, the Shuswap Indian leader from Canada who was elected president of Canada's National Indian Brotherhood (NIB) in 1970. In his capacity as NIB president, he not only traveled extensively in North America and established a strong working relationship with the NCAI in the United States; he also went to Australia and New Zealand to meet with Aboriginal and Maori leaders in 1971, and the next year he visited Copenhagen, London, and Geneva to meet with the International Work Group on Indigenous Affairs (IWGIA), Survival International (SI), and the World Council of Churches, respectively. In 1974, as he was organizing the formation of the WCIP, Manuel published in Canada and the United States his personal memoir and political manifesto, *The Fourth World: An Indian Reality*, written with Michael Posluns and introduced by U.S. American Indian scholar Vine Deloria Jr.[6] In *The Fourth World*, Manuel designates the Shuswap's relatively recent experiences of "the forces of conquest and colonial rule" in British Columbia following World War I as "a microcosm of the whole Aboriginal World," given the attacks on indigenous land and languages, along with restrictions on indigenous cultural, political, and economic freedoms (1, 2). Manuel's extrapolation from the disrupted Shuswap world to a much larger "Aboriginal World" inscribes a tactics of moral critique that, by 1974, was common to indigenous minority activist writing. His dense local knowledge of material and discursive violence authorizes a global critique of ongoing colonialism in First World settler nations. Though Manuel states that he is writing primarily "to my own grandchildren" (261), casting his book as an extended scene of indigenous instruction, he draws heavily not only from his personal and tribal experiences but also from his extensive Canadian and more recent international experiences in Indian and indigenous affairs. He develops a definition of the Fourth World that attends to the specific details of Canadian politics while attempting, as Deloria notes in the foreword to Manuel's book, "to illustrate the relationship between the various aboriginal peoples of the globe" (ix).[7]

Manuel's book-length definition of the Fourth World stresses cultural attributes over political organization or racial descent. Like other spokespersons in Native North America, Manuel describes the global Aboriginal World as having in common four general characteristics. These engage the blood/land/memory complex in recognizable ways, defining indigenous racial identity ("blood") largely in terms of "land" and "memory." The elements of that definition are, first, a "common understanding of the universe" (5); second, a "common attachment to the land" (6); third, a history of persistent resistance to "colonial conquest" and the "destructive forces" of the West (69);[8] and, fourth, the fact that indigenous peoples have survived as distinct communities into contemporary times (214). Manuel does not develop his idea of what a "common understanding of the universe" might mean in international indigenous terms. In his discussion of a "common attachment to the land," however, he sets forth an equation that seems to formulate a foundation for that common understanding: indigenous cultures exist in and at the conjunction of specific geography and specific history (6, 191). The loss of either element threatens the survival of particular indigenous cultures. Manuel also argues the familiar idea that the crux of the colonial struggle is a clash between radically different "ideas of land," underlying which is a basic "conflict over the nature of man himself" in the worldviews of aboriginal and invading peoples (6). Deloria develops similar ideas in his book *God Is Red* (1973).[9] Resistance to domination and endurance over time, in Manuel's definition, reveal the "strength" and assertiveness of both indigenous ancestors and future indigenous generations, countering Western stereotypes of indigenous passivity (261).

In developing his definition, Manuel seems to take his cue not only from Deloria but also from N. Scott Momaday. Like Momaday in his "The Man Made of Words" address to the First Convocation of American Indian Scholars in 1970, Manuel stresses the role of the "imagina-tion" in the recognition of "aboriginal rights." What is needed most, Manuel argues, is "the re-evaluation of assumptions" and the develop-ment of "a new language in which the truth can be spoken easily, quietly, and comfortably" (224). Underlying this call is a strong belief that nonindigenous peoples lack an adequate language in which to conceive or articulate indigenous experience. Moreover, in Manuel's formulation this type of discursive innovation is indicative of the Fourth World condition. "We do not need to re-create the exact forms by which our grandfathers lived their lives—the clothes, the houses, the political systems, or the means of travel," he writes. "We do need to create new forms that will allow the future generations to inherit the values, the strengths, and the basic spiritual beliefs—the way of under-standing the world—that is the fruit of a thousand generations' cultiva-tion of North American soil by Indian people" (4). Articulated as a manifestation of the blood/land/memory complex, the Fourth World does not refer to fossilized cultures desperately clinging to their pasts but rather to "a vision of the future history" of indigenous peoples (12). Like D'Arcy McNickle in the first decades after World War II or Keri Hulme in the 1980s, Manuel emphasizes enduring "values, strengths, and the basic spiritual beliefs" that can be refashioned locally to meet the changing needs of future generations; specific cultural technologies or artifacts are secondary. To become museum curators should not be the present generation's aim, he argues. Their chief role is to forge, as in the emblematic figure of the grandparent-grandchild bond, a vital link "to the ways of our grandfathers," which will ensure that future generations are "strong" enough to become indigenous ancestors themselves (47).

Alongside his discussion of Fourth World innovation is Manuel's critique of the so-called Third World. Here he seems to follow the lead of the National Indian Youth Council. In their biting 1971 "Dictionary of Indian Terms," the NIYC defines "Third World Movement" as "A coalition of non-white peoples using white men's money, white men's ideology so as to be like white men."[10] Likewise, Manuel characterizes the formerly colonized peoples of the Third World as imitating the First, "rapidly learning to adapt [their] life-style[s] to Western technol-ogy" (5), whereas he sees the Fourth World as seeking ultimately to develop a "new society" (261) in which indigenous peoples will be allowed "to design our own model" rather than be forced to imitate Western forms (220). Although Manuel's characterization of the Third World may seem naive today, especially in light of the sources of funding for both the NIB and the WCIP, his critique raises an important conceptual distinction between "technology," which he characterizes as belonging equally to all the world's peoples, and "values and beliefs," which he characterizes as belonging to specific peoples or nations inhabiting specific soils over time (181–82). Manuel's essentialism, such as it is, locates the definition of indigenous identity ("blood") at the intersection of indigenous "land" and "memory." This is an essentialism that is likely to endure so long as indigenous minorities assert that they possess distinct identities at the level of the communal; ultimately, it is the assertion of communal longevity in the land that authorizes the Fourth World's moral and political claims. Finally, Manuel stresses that the demands of the Fourth World are not for "special status," as nonindigenous critics often assert, but rather for the same rights "enjoyed by those who are already masters of their own house" (213).[11]

In 1974 Manuel organized a preparatory meeting of the International Conference of Indigenous People, held in Georgetown, Guyana. Delegates represented New Zealand Maori, Australian Aborigines, Scandinavian Sami, Inuit from Greenland, American Indians from the United States, First Nations peoples from Canada, and South American Indians.[12] The committee responsible for defining "Indigenous People" reported that "The term . . . refers to people living in countries which have a population composed of different ethnic or racial groups who are descendants of the earliest populations living in the area, and who do not, as a group, control the national government of the countries within which they live."[13] Notable for its brevity and its obvious attempt to create a list of "objective" criteria, this definition differs from Manuel's more elaborate version in tenor as well as in specific content. Juxtaposed, the two definitions point up a basic tension between what James Clifford has called competing metanarratives of homogenization and emergence, loss and invention.[14] Both definitions locate indigenous identity in its difference from other ethnic or racial groups rather than in its particular essence.[15] Manuel's definition, however, emphasizes those things minority indigenous peoples claim to possess in contemporary times: distinct worldviews, an attachment to specific land bases despite large-scale expropriation, a history of resistance to domination, and the fact of survival as distinct communities despite often overwhelming odds against them. Above all, Manuel's definition orients indigenous difference toward the future. The preparatory meeting's definition emphasizes the things that minority indigenous peoples have lost since the coming of Europeans and their descendants: majority population status and supra-local political power in their own lands. In this sense the preparatory meeting's definition mimics the discourse of First World taxonomies of ethnicity, which typically orient difference toward the past and which typically predict inevitable assimilation over time.

The First General Assembly of the WCIP was held the following year (27–31 October 1975), hosted by the Sheshaht Band of Nootka on their reserve in Port Alberni, British Columbia.[16] Fifty-two delegates divided into groups to reach consensus on a "Solemn Declaration" of collective indigenous identity. Initially, the draft declaration read as follows:

> We are the Indigenous Peoples of the Earth,
>> We are proud of our Past,
>> Our lives were one with the Earth,
>> Our hearts were one with the Land,
>> We walked in Beauty [and Strength and Humbleness][17]
> We shared our path thru life with all that was on the Earth
>> and most of all with each other[,]
> We developed the inside of our lives, and our relationship
>> with the world around us,
> Then other people came to our lands,
> These others did not know our ways,
> They took from us our lands, our lives, and our children,
> But they could not take from us our Memory of what we had been,
>> Now we know that many of us remain,
> Together we can help each other regain our dignity and pride,
> We are coming together to form one group,
> So that the others can hear us as we speak in one voice,
> So that we can in some measure control again our own destiny,
> So we can once again walk in Beauty [and Strength].[18]

In contrast to the preparatory meeting's "objective" criteria, the draft Solemn Declaration invents a Fourth World that rivals the magnitude of the First.[19] It translates the local significance of delegates' individual understandings of their people's particular pre- and post-contact histories into a single narrative of common experience: an unprovoked attack on innocent Indigenous Peoples, their resilience against their enemies, and their contemporary desire, now that they are armed with an international consciousness, to regain their lost "dignity and pride."

This translation is achieved, in part, through the narrative's use of a generic "committee speak" that is meant to render decipherable the formidably indecipherable junctures among distinct indigenous cultural and historic realities. Despite this bland language, however, key phrases ground the draft Solemn Declaration in specific indigenous experience. Those lines that assert a strong spiritual relationship between indigenous peoples and the earth, for instance, bear the mark of North American Indian traditions. "We walked in Beauty" evokes the distinctive language of the Navajo Night Chant: throughout this nine-day ceremony, the chanter repeats variations of the formulaic phrase "In beauty [*hozho*] may I walk"; at the ceremony's close, the patient is told, "Thus will it be beautiful, / Thus walk in beauty, my grandchild."[20] In the draft Solemn Declaration, attention is drawn to Beauty (and Strength and Humbleness) as an important indigenous concept through its repetition, placement at key points in the text, and capitalization; this use of capitalization is the closest the narrative comes to inscribing indigenous cultural and linguistic difference metonymically. Furthermore, in a general way, the dramatic structure of the narrative reflects the method of the Navajo revitalization rite. The first nine lines assert positive Indigenous—with a capital *I*—values, implying the possibility of Indigenous healing. These are immediately followed by four lines describing the "evil" of the "others." Dramatic tension is created in their opposition. Finally, as in the nine-day Night Chant, the narrative ends in a rejuvenation of its "patient"—Indigenous Peoples—relieving its dramatic tension by repulsing "evil" (loss of "our lands, our lives, and our children") and attracting "holiness" (again controlling "our own destiny").[21]

Other lines describing Indigenous Peoples suggest additional, sometimes composite influences. These images may have sources outside as well as within specific indigenous cultures, but here they are mobilized to figure indigenous status and to do so in a manner that will resonate with nonindigenous as well as indigenous audiences. "Our hearts were one with the land" may read as Western nostalgia for some agricultural golden age, but it may also evoke the traditional Sami story that the Great Creator placed a reindeer cow's beating heart deep within the earth, "so that when the Sami people are in trouble, they can put an ear to the ground and listen for the heartbeats from below. If the heart is still beating, this means there is still a future for the Sami people."[22] Similarly, "Our lives were one with the Earth" may evoke a composite of Aboriginal, Maori, and American Indian traditions that strongly link the livelihood of the human community to that of the earth and its nonhuman inhabitants. In *The Fourth World*, George Manuel states a Shuswap understanding of this idea simply and powerfully: "Our culture is every inch of our land" (6).[23]

The Fourth World is made visible as a distinct corporate entity in the evocation of a history of Indigenous encounters with "other people." These "others" are not named as Europeans or their descendants, but they are cast as ignorant of the knowledge of Indigenous Peoples and covetous not only of indigenous peoples' traditional land holdings but also of their very lives and the lives of their children. Thus the narrative's climax is marked by the image of stolen futures, indigenous "destiny" controlled by "others." The draft Solemn Declaration makes no attempt to explain the motivations of "these others." Having served for generations as the objects of First World political administration and anthropological study, in telling their common history from their particular point of view *for the first time,* delegates to the WCIP counter-invent a generalized, corporate First World as simply the "other people."

It is here—in the echo of Manuel's insistence that the Fourth World is "a vision of the future" rooted in "the values, the strengths, and the basic spiritual beliefs" of indigenous ancestors—that we can locate the narrative's specific tactics. The narrative states explicitly that indigenous peoples are coming together for the purpose of coalition, to form a new group in order to grieve claims on a global scale and to assert greater political influence through greater numbers. "Memory"—with a capital *M*—is invoked as the last bastion of indigenous resistance to the "others'" possessive colonization and assimilative policies. Echoing Momaday, the narrative asserts that this same "Memory"—rather than pure bloodlines or the uninterrupted continuance of indigenous languages or specific lifeways—has ensured the survival of distinct, indigenous peoples into contemporary times. In the global context of the WCIP, indigenous "blood" in all its local variety is brought together and converted into "Memory," a master narrative that generalizes the diverse experiences of indigenous peoples. In turn, this master narrative enables the collection of diverse indigenous individuals and communities under the single rubric Indigenous Peoples, the assertion of a meta-bloodline that enables WCIP delegates to speak "in one voice" and to fight for their common "destiny" as peoples and nations. In other words, the draft Solemn Declaration collects diverse bloodlines into a common story; simultaneously, the declaration's single narrative legitimizes the assertion of a collective bloodline. Blood is rendered as narrative, narrative as blood.

Like Manuel's extrapolation from a specifically Shuswap world to a global Aboriginal World, the evocation of a shared indigenous Memory inscribes a tactics of moral critique that privileges the asserted values of the Fourth World over the assumed values of the First. Unlike Manuel's earlier text, however, here a constellation of dense local memories is condensed into an all-inclusive indigenous Memory. The sacrifice of specificity is obviously "strategic," although not exactly in the manner described by postcolonial critics. By collapsing delegates' diverse local memories under a single rubric, the draft Solemn Declaration attempts to negotiate not only a collective Fourth World identity, but also a collective Fourth World strategy for resistance. Indigenous Memory—singular and marked by a capital letter—asserts a powerful and powerfully ambiguous counter to the First World's master narratives of Manifest Destiny, providential accident, the inevitability of Western "progress," and the inevitable vanishing of indigenous peoples. Enlisted as part of a politics of embarrassment, this Memory attempts to reconvert the First World's master narratives from catalogs of merely symbolic acts (the "taming" of various frontiers) back into a record of real actions taken upon human bodies and human cultures with enduring real-world effects ("They took from us our lands, our lives, and our children"). The narrative's final lines declare an international indigenous solidarity—a collective identity—made possible in contemporary times by this same shared Memory.

The narrative ends with assertions of WCIP objectives: for indigenous peoples again to control their futures—"in some measure"—and for indigenous peoples to regain spiritual harmony with their environments. In the first assertion, the phrase "in some measure" can be read as a subtle engagement with the "measured separatism" of U.S.-Indian treaty discourse, a signal of the maintenance or reassertion of the Fourth World's insistence on a nation-to-nation treaty paradigm that can arbitrate peaceful coexistence for settlers and indigenous peoples. It also can be read, however, as a deflation of the narrative's otherwise boldly defiant language. Either reading suggests that delegates wanted to assure nonindigenous audiences that their communities had no intention of seceding from First World nations. In the second assertion of objectives, the powerful imagery of "walk[ing] in Beauty" concludes the narrative with a high level of indigenous cultural specificity, but it also leaves much room for interpretation for non-Navajo audiences. A potential problem with each assertion, then, is that its language can be interpreted as equivocal and therefore be dismissed by dominant powers either as merely symbolic or as politically immature. Exactly what this international coalition of indigenous peoples is demanding from First World settler nations remains unclear.

By the end of the First General Assembly, delegates reached consensus on an amended Solemn Declaration, which the wcip adopted by formal resolution. The narrative of Indigenous experience is fleshed out in greater detail and organized more purposefully into stanzas. The two main actors in this drama are more fully characterized, raising the stakes of the narrative's moral critique by heightening the asserted differences between Fourth and First World values and by assigning specific motivations for the violent actions of the "others." At the same time, however, the final version amends the draft's bold marks of specific indigeneity into less distinctive evocations of pan-indigenous identity:

> We, the Indigenous Peoples of the World, united in this corner of our Mother the Earth in a great assembly of men of wisdom, declare to all nations:
> We glory in our proud past:
>> when the earth was our nurturing mother,
>> when the night sky formed our common roof,
>> when Sun and Moon were our parents,
>> when all were brothers and sisters,
>> when our great civilizations grew under the sun,
>> when our chiefs and elders were great leaders,
>> when justice ruled the Law and its execution.

Then other peoples arrived:
> thirsting for blood, for gold, for land and all its wealth,
> carrying the cross and the sword, one in each hand,
> without knowing or waiting to learn the ways of our worlds,
> they considered us to be lower than the animals,
> they stole our lands from us and took us from our lands,
> they made slaves of the Sons of the Sun.

However, they have never been able to eliminate us,
> nor to erase our memories of what we were,
> because we are the culture of the earth and the sky,
> we are of ancient descent and we are millions,
> and although our whole universe may be ravaged,
> our people will live on
> for longer than even the kingdom of death.

Now, we come from the four corners of the earth,
> we protest before the concert of nations that,
> "we are Indigenous peoples, we who have a
> consciousness of culture and peoplehood on the
> edge of each country's borders and marginal to
> each country's citizenship."

And rising up after centuries of oppression,
> evoking the greatness of our ancestors,
> in the memory of our Indigenous martyrs,
> and in homage to the counsel of our wise elders:

We vow to control again our own destiny and
> recover our complete humanity and
> pride in being Indigenous People.[24]

The rhetorical force of the Solemn Declaration, in its original context of coalition building, cannot be overstated. The WCIP's narrative definition of global indigenous identity constructs a set of analogies that translate specific indigenous realities into a comprehensive and comprehensible generalization. In order to satisfy delegates representing diverse indigenous peoples and to reach its target audience, "the concert of nations," the Solemn Declaration participates in a number of distinct meaning systems simultaneously—those of the First Nations, the American Indians, the Maori, the Sami, the Aboriginal peoples, *and* Western culture.[25] It is in this sense that the declaration is autoethnographic: it negotiates a single narrative out of the worldviews, memories, and aspirations of disparate indigenous cultures while also constructing a dialogue between indigenous and nonindigenous understandings of indigenous minority experience. Stanza two foregrounds powerful indigenous signifiers—nurturing mother, common roof, Sun and Moon, the Law—that strongly suggest a collective Indigenous identity without privileging any particular indigenous signified. Local differences are transcended by generalizing a time in the past before contact with "others," and through references to widely applicable natural phenomena, non-Western categories of relationship/kinship, and generalized past "glories." Stanza three then generalizes the motivations behind the brutal attacks of the "others" against specific indigenous nations, and it reinforces stanza two's declaration of Indigenous Peoples' significant spiritual relationships with the earth and cosmos. Indigenous identity with a capital *I* is thus evoked rather than specifically characterized: it is asserted as a way of being *in* the world (stanza two) and a particular experience *of* the world (stanza three), rather than as a set of easily observed or easily measured criteria. This evocation allows for multiple contradictions and inconsistencies (such as the inclusion of "White" Sami living in Europe). As in Manuel's *The Fourth World,* the Solemn Declaration's moral critique on behalf of the Indigenous community as well as its communal political claims are grounded in an essentialist definition of indigenous "blood" that is expressed in terms of "land" and "memory."

In addition to joining together diverse indigenous peoples, the narrative attempts to construct a bridge by means of which the First World might gain access to a Fourth World reality. The Solemn Declaration meets this goal by assembling a composite of various indigenous narrative traditions: a syncretic story of the Fourth World performed as if it were part of an idealized tradition of Indigenous storytelling, an "authorless," communal narrative of global significance in which the earth is "our nurturing mother" and Sun and Moon are "our parents." This composite narrative counters the First World's master narratives that justify or rationalize the European conquest, colonization, and settlement of "new" worlds and that traditionally posit an "allegory of man" in which indigenous peoples are constructed as an earlier stage in the more advanced cultural evolution of the West. In its declaration of a distinct Fourth World identity, the narrative also appropriates an idiom of opposition typical of First World settler nations, especially the United States. As a formal declaration of independence, the

Solemn Declaration works to disincorporate the Fourth World from the First, to disengage indigenous minorities from the West's self-invention as the most advanced, most fully human people on earth.[26] By making Indigenous history visible on a global scale, the Solemn Declaration asserts the Fourth World as an analogue to the whole of the First World (rather than to Europe or England or the United States)—a distinct reality, a counter example of a globally significant cultural system.

This process of disincorporation is signaled by stanza four's rhetorically loaded conjunction "However" and by its subsequent shifts in verb tense from past to present to future. Moreover, stanza four asserts that in the future the world's indigenous minorities, whose populations make up small or tiny percentages of First World nations, will be counted together as politically significant "millions."[27] The precariousness of survival for particular indigenous peoples is recast as the inevitability of future endurance through sheer "Indigenous" numbers. The fifth and sixth stanzas then define the context for contemporary indigenous protest. As in Manuel's 1974 definition, the centerpiece of the Solemn Declaration's narrative is not particular technologies or sociocultural artifacts designated "indigenous" but rather a particular "consciousness of culture and peoplehood" rooted in indigenous "memories of what we were." And while the singular Indigenous Memory of the draft version has been amended to plural "memories" in stanza four, it is this consciousness, conspicuously singular, that is now held up in stanza five as the rallying point for contemporary indigenous protest, set off by quotation marks to indicate the expressed collective voice of Indigenous Peoples. Stanza five positions this consciousness at the borders of specific First World nations and at the margins of specific national citizenships, mobilizing spatial metaphors that evoke both indigenous political substatus and all too common indigenous substandard living conditions. In stanza six this consciousness then links contemporary indigenous peoples to "ancestors" and invokes a persistent history of indigenous resistance to colonial oppression. The "vow" made in the final stanza amends the potential equivocation in the draft version to assert that the WCIP will pursue neither equal nor civil rights as defined by the First World's nonindigenous majority or minority populations; the aim will be, instead, to seek self-determination and the recovery of indigenous peoples' "complete humanity."

At its best, the narrative harnesses the forces of both contradiction and opposition as creative ambiguity, allowing for a high level of inclusion under the rubric Indigenous Peoples without giving over authority for making claims of inclusivity to nonindigenous outsiders. The narrative also resists First World pretensions to absolute objectivity in systems of human taxonomy (such as tables of blood quantum or elaborate nomenclatures of miscegenation) by exploiting contradiction and opposition against a common ground of humanity ("we who have a / consciousness of culture and peoplehood"). At its most basic, the Solemn Declaration reiterates the long-standing argument that the First World must recognize its indigenous minorities as fully human but different and that it must allow indigenous individuals and communities to define themselves. The basis for such self-definition, the narrative asserts, will be indigenous "memories" and "consciousness," a sense of belonging to the narrative's protagonist "We." In other words, an identity constructed through self-reflexive "emblems of differentiation" rather than "objective" criteria.[28] The Solemn Declaration's protagonist "We" asserts a collective identity constructed as a global interest group, an international base for alliances through which to combat *at the local level* the First World's dominant ideologies and the First World's dominant national and international political structures. The Solemn Declaration's critical thrust is thus moral rather than taxonomic. It forcefully resists imitation of dominant, "scientific" First World discourses, and it hopes to transform the situation of indigenous minorities. The Solemn Declaration draws its authority from the significance indigenous cultures attach to narrative and the significance First World nations attach to formal declarations of independence as sanctioned modes of oppositional discourse. This latter aspect links the WCIP's project to those of New Zealand Maori and American Indian activists and writers who appropriate and redeploy the discourse of treaties.

It is tempting to end my analysis here and pronounce the WCIP's development of essentialist markers of indigeneity in terms of "land" and "memory" a "strategic" success. By foregrounding an elaborate representation of a singular Indigenous past—necessarily vague, overly simplified, and idealized—and by avoiding representation of any specific indigenous present, through its omissions the Solemn Declaration attempts to make room for the complex diversity of contemporary indigenous minority communities and individuals. More so than the draft, the more elaborate final version embraces a narrowly defined "authentic" Indigenous experience as a counter to the First World's own narrow definitions. But, as I stated at the beginning of this chapter, the wcIP was in fact not successful in 1975 at producing tangible change. It did not launch a global program for indigenous minority liberation and empowerment. Its founding document has not become an enduring manifesto for indigenous activism. The "success" of the wcIP's development of essentialist markers of Indigenous identity must be measured, therefore, in tactical and occasional terms. The draft and final versions of the Solemn Declaration reveal a concern with discourse and an attempt to locate the appropriate genres of discourse for discussing indigenous identity among various international audiences. While "the concert of nations" ostensibly refers to the member states of the UN, it also refers to indigenous minority peoples themselves. These texts draw our attention to how indigenous minority activists render habitable the discursive space of the settler Other through tactics of repossession and appropriation. The wcIP documents also draw our attention to the complex set of negotiations required in order to devise a syncretic narrative of collective identity. In the use of language that will not unduly offend settler governments (unlike the International Treaty Council's 1974 *Declaration of Continuing Independence*, there is no mention here of settler "colonialism" per se), the declarations inscribe a tactics of indirect opposition whereby politically and militarily weak indigenous minorities attempt to galvanize their potential international community without counterproductively threatening dominant powers.

An occasional or episodic approach draws our attention to the fact that the wcIP's 1975 Solemn Declaration was out of date before it could be adequately disseminated—and to the fact that dissemination was not the wcIP's primary aim. Its greatest "victories" occurred during the moments of negotiation and formal articulation of its founding documents among indigenous delegates. In these performances the Solemn Declaration met the wcIP's immediate, tactical goal of articulating a coalition among diverse indigenous peoples. Once it was prepared as a text for wider circulation, however, the Solemn Declaration's narrative definition of collective identity—vibrantly multiperspectivist in delegates' negotiations of relationships among distinct indigenous peoples—was no longer a process of Fourth World invention. No longer part of an exclusively local, highly flexible, and effectively closed rhetorical situation, the Solemn Declaration as a fixed text is open to antagonistic interpretations that can expose and misrepresent its alignment with the politics of a specific occasion. Settler governments—in particular, First World nations—could (and can) easily dismiss the Solemn Declaration's claims as irrelevant for indigenous communities within their jurisdictions, since these communities neither define their identities nor grieve their claims from a global perspective, which is the only real basis for the Solemn Declaration's or any similar document's potential power. The Solemn Declaration thus displays how the strength of local political tactics is precisely their inherent disability: they rarely transfer to other localities, even when the originating locality is an international forum.

At the Second General Assembly of the wcip, held in Kiruna, Sweden, in 1977, delegates formally declared yet another definition of "indigenous peoples," now without the globalizing capital *I* and capital *P*:

> Indigenous peoples are such population groups as we are, who from age-old time have inhabited the lands where we live, who are aware of having a character of our own, with social traditions and means of expression that are linked to the country inherited from our ancestors, with a language of our own, and having certain essential and unique characteristics which confer upon us the strong conviction of belonging to a people, who have an identity in ourselves and should thus be regarded by others.[29]

At first glance, the wcip appears to have returned to a set of "objective" criteria. In the wake of the Solemn Declaration's narrative definition, however, these new criteria are assertively self-reflexive rather than narrowly objective: we are who we are because we know and publicly declare we are. Although less dramatic and less politically demanding in its substitution of "population groups" for "Peoples," this definition is another version of blood as narrative/narrative as blood. And it points up how central the blood/land/memory complex had become to the way indigenous minorities imagined themselves as distinct peoples and constructed a politics of identity and positive change.

The assertive self-reflexivity of the wcip's brief 1977 definition may have had additional motivations as well. The year the WCIP met in Sweden, the United Nations began efforts to formally recognize the world's indigenous peoples. In 1977 the UN sponsored an International Non-Governmental Organizations Conference on Indigenous Peoples in the Americas, which became a first step toward forming its Working Group on Indigenous Populations in 1982.[30] While the WCIP would continue to meet, in the 1980s and 1990s the Working Group effectively replaced the older organization as the central forum for the articulation of international indigenous identity.[31] The Working Group's mandate to produce a comprehensive Declaration on the Rights of Indigenous Peoples and to establish a Permanent Forum for Indigenous Peoples by 2004 has dominated the focus of international scholarship. Thus far, the Working Group's draft declarations have organized their definitions of indigenous peoples around primarily "objective" criteria.[32] In its 1982 draft definition, for instance, emphasis is placed on such criteria as (1) overcome by outsiders, (2) politically subordinate, *but* (3) identifiably nonconformist in arenas the First World considers significant but relatively unthreatening in small populations—"social, economic and cultural traditions."[33]

The UN's criteria, unlike the WCIP's 1975 narrative definition, thus creates a number of potential problems for members of the Fourth World. First, the UN definition reduces indigenous peoples and nations to mere remnant "populations" (as does the WCIP's own 1977 definition). Indigenous minorities are compared not to politically significant First World corporate entities—peoples, nations, or states—but rather to less politically significant subgroups of First World individuals. The key term opening the UN definition is "existing descendants" rather than "existing nations." This individuation of the Fourth World promotes the incorporation of indigenous individuals and groups into existing First World social, political, and economic structures. By failing to challenge the claims to national unity made by the UN's powerful cohort of First World settler nations, the term "indigenous populations" potentially undermines all levels of Fourth World self-determination. Furthermore, under the UN's criteria it is difficult to classify as indigenous most individuals and groups who have identified themselves as indigenous minorities in the post–World War II era. For example, it is unclear under the UN's definition exactly what it might mean for the majority of contemporary American Indians or New Zealand Maori, who live, work, and study in major urban centers among majority European-descended and other minority populations, to "live more in conformity with their [own] particular social, economic and cultural customs and traditions than with the institutions of the [First World] country of which they now form a part." It is also unclear whether American Indian or Maori business owners, writers, university professors, or government officials qualify as "indigenous" under the UN's definition, or whether tribal groups or indigenous nations that have developed successful tourist operations, gaming institutions, and other "Western" economic ventures still count as part of the UN's global "indigenous" peoples.

The Working Group's institutionalization within the UN has produced certain advantages for indigenous peoples who wish to make their voices heard by the international community, but it also has produced disadvantages. The UN organization and its individual member states, including ones hostile to the demands of indigenous minority peoples, not only determine the time, location, and format for the "occasions" when indigenous activists are allowed to assert their identities and voice their concerns; they also mandate the specific shape and the specific duration of that indigenous activist discourse.[34] Moreover, the UN's attempt to create a single, all-encompassing definition for the world's diverse indigenous peoples, whether they are majority or minority populations, threatens the specificity of the Fourth World and thus undermines the potential legacy of the wcip's Solemn Declaration.

Reading Indigeneity

Although it is difficult to construct direct links between the wcip's attempt to define an international indigenous identity and the subsequent development of "indigenous theory" by individual New Zealand Maori and American Indian activists and writers, I want to suggest that such links do exist.[35] One link is the Solemn Declaration's insistence that indigenous peoples themselves must determine the ground rules and set the standards for how and in what terms it is appropriate to discuss contemporary indigenous identities and the construction of indigenous futures. Indigenous theory typically takes this insistence as a basic assumption. But because this assumption continues to be contested by dominant settlers and their institutions, indigenous theory also typically elaborates a version of the argument that, given the context of their ongoing colonization, it is time for indigenous peoples themselves to define the terms of the discourses used to describe them as individuals and communities, as well as the terms of the discourses used to circumscribe their efforts to assert themselves as distinct social, economic, and political entities.

Another link is the failure of the Solemn Declaration's essentialism—its attempt at defining a globally significant Indigenous Peoples —to provide an effective model for Fourth World political and personal identity. The movement from the draft to the final version of the Solemn Declaration is suggestive of the types of negotiations required for a narrative tactics that includes an essentialist definition of indigenous identity, but it is suggestive also of the problems that result when such negotiations are in fact successful. The final version amends the draft's bold marks of specific indigeneity ("We walked in Beauty") into less distinctive evocations of a pan-indigenous identity ("the earth was our nurturing mother"), indicating a vertical movement between levels of abstraction.[36] Stated plainly, the final version lacks grounding in a specific indigenous land base and thus in a specific indigenous political entity, a people or nation defined by their connection(s) with specific lands. The loss of such specificity is the loss of a clear marker of indigenous difference—really, the loss of the indigenous trump card, physical and spiritual longevity in the land—making it easier for settler governments, multicultural or Third World coalitions, and other entities either to ignore the Solemn Declaration's narrative definition or to absorb it into their own agendas. Without the claim to specific lands and independent nation rights, Indigenous Peoples become indistinguishable from the long list of the world's oppressed. Indigenous theory has focused precisely on articulating indigenous minority survivals within contexts of forceful colonial inclusions. In other words, it has focused on moving down rather than up between levels of abstraction. Whatever its immediate field of focus—politics, aesthetics, history, literature, semiotics, education or health care policy, anthropological or sociological research methodologies—an indigenous theory declares its independence from dominating discourses by localizing its theoretical position.[37]

In the United States, the critical work of Jack Forbes, Gerald Vizenor, and Elizabeth Cook-Lynn stands out for its commitment to making theory local for indigenous peoples. All three direct us, in different ways, toward analyses of the meanings that contemporary indigenous minority literary and activist texts potentially hold for indigenous minority individuals and nations themselves rather than for readers from the dominant culture or another minority culture. Forbes, for instance, focuses our attention on the issue of an indigenous minority text's primary audience and its potential practical purposes of "problem-solving, political agitation, political theory, philosophy, strategy and tactics" in the interests of specific indigenous communities. Forbes alerts us to pay attention to indigenous minority literature's role as a "social transaction . . . involving the process of dissemination as well as reception by a specific audience" and to distinguish between texts produced independently by and for indigenous minority consumption and those produced through the dominant culture's media industries largely for a dominant or cosmopolitan audience.[38] Vizenor focuses our attention on the more specifically literary issue of defining imaginative tactics through which contemporary indigenous minority writers combat the dominant culture's inventions of tribal identities. He urges us to look for the possibilities of the "postindian," that is, for the possibilities of a self-representation of indigenous minority identity that pushes beyond the dominant culture's inventions of "the" Indian and his or her demise in the nineteenth century.[39] And Cook-Lynn focuses on the directly political issues of an indigenous minority nationalism and the ongoing importance of the treaty status paradigm for reading and assessing contemporary indigenous minority texts. More aggressively than her colleagues, Cook-Lynn insists on emphasizing the connection between native indigeneity and the ongoing connection to specific lands and specific nations.[40] "A people's national history cannot simply be stamped out or ignored or relegated to obscurity," she writes in defiance of totalizing discourses that would subsume the specific and ongoing history of her Lakota/Dakota nation—whether those discourses are labeled U.S. national, pan-Indian, pan-indigenous, multicultural, or postcolonial. "A nation does not cease to exist simply because another nation [or political movement] wishes it to."[41] Moreover, Cook-Lynn writes, characterizing her own work and the work of other emerging indigenous theorists, "What distinguishes Native American intellectualism from other scholarship is its interest in tribal indigenousness."[42]

Cook-Lynn's articulation of indigenous nationalism as a vantage point for literary theory not only links her work to the efforts of the WCIP in the early 1970s but also across the globe to the work of her indigenous peers in Aotearoa/New Zealand. The critical work of Hirini Melbourne, Merata Mita, Sidney Moko Mead, Ngahuia Te Awekotuku, and other Maori scholars takes as its starting point the assumption of a treaty paradigm based on specific land rights and on nation-to-nation status. Melbourne enlists the carved meeting house (whare whakairo), which is situated at the intersection of a specific indigenous land base and a specific indigenous history ("memory"), as a central metaphor for Maori literary production. Melbourne also focuses on the issue of language, arguing that "So long as Maori can only assert the values and attitudes of their culture in English, they necessarily remain victims of the colonial legacy."[43] Merata Mita makes the similar argument that "If we revitalize our oral story-telling and use this as the basis to create our own literature, we will . . . regain ourselves and our identity."[44] Timoti Karetu complicates the argument about indigenous language, however, by pointing out that Maori oral traditions continue to thrive in specific forms, especially waiata (song) and haka (chant with movements) compositions, which are featured at regional and national Maori cultural competitions. "It is unfortunate that much of what the Maori world has to say in Maori is available for Maori consumption only—that is, for speakers of Maori," Karetu writes. "Therefore much of what is said in the dance arena is available to only a limited audience, an elitist group, those who speak and understand Maori."[45] There is sad irony in the fact that speakers of Maori can be described as an "elitist" group. The question of such elitism in public texts has become largely moot in the United States, where the loss of indigenous languages has been severe, although there are notable exceptions among the larger American Indian nations. In the Southwest, for instance, contemporary Navajo poets Rex Lee Jim and Luci Tapahonso compose in both English and Navajo; Tohono O'odham (Papago) poet and linguist Ofelia Zepeda writes in English and O'odham. What is critical in these debates, however, especially in Aotearoa/New Zealand, is that they center on the issue of the contemporary needs of the local indigenous audience, independent of considerations of the desires or standards of the dominant culture. Even Karetu's position on the exclusive use of Maori language in the dance arena is a response to the needs of Maori audiences who have been dispossessed of their indigenous language but who nonetheless wish to participate in the ongoing development of their indigenous culture.

The emphasis on localizing theory responds directly to critical methodologies that have stressed instead the idea of indigenous "mediation" or "translation"; such methodologies assume that the narrative tactics developed by indigenous minority writers are directed primarily at nonindigenous audiences.[46] In the United States, the literary-critical work of Greg Sarris (Pomo/Miwok) responds by attempting to "collapse the dichotomy between [indigenous] personal narrative and scholarly argument" in order "to show how criticism can move closer to that which it studies."[47] The more recent work of Craig Womack (Creek) responds by attempting to create a "tribally specific" literary criticism.[48] In Aotearoa/New Zealand, Maori filmmaker Barry Barclay demands the right and asserts the responsibility of Maori to produce representations of themselves that are accessible to Maori audiences and that employ Maori rather than dominant forms, while activist scholar Linda Tuhiwai Smith argues for the necessity of bringing Maori concepts to the center of academic research paradigms. Smith echoes Barclay's passionate call when she argues that "We [Maori] have a different epistemological tradition which frames the way we see the world, the way we organize ourselves in it, the questions we ask and the solutions which we seek."[49] Indigenous theory's most radical move in the fight for self-determination has been and will continue to be its demand to set the terms of indigenous representation in *every* arena.

One of the particular dynamics of Fourth World (post)coloniality is that the "occasion" for Fourth World self-definition is the demand for the re-recognition of nation-to-nation status inscribed in treaty documents and other binding agreements produced in past eras, along with the demand for the self-determination attendant on that re-recognition, including the right to "rebuild the ancestor" as the self. As yet, these occasions cannot be organized into a postcolonial trajectory that begins with a "first stage" of essentialist markers of indigenous identity and progresses toward some version of anti-essentialism. That trajectory will not exist so long as indigenous minorities insist on fighting not only for "civil" or "equal" rights within multicultural First

World settler nations but also for the re-recognition of political identities based on a treaty paradigm of nation-to-nation status. Despite the elaborate theorizing of postcolonialists and multiculturalists, the treaty paradigm requires a level of essentialism, a clear border between one nation and its treaty partner. It is the idea of that clear border, described in the shifting emphases of the blood/land/memory complex, that has made it both compelling and possible for politically, economically, and militarily weak indigenous minorities, however "objectively" assimilated into the dominant settler population's language, genetic pool, and/or culture, to continue to claim their distinct identities in the contemporary era.

I began this book by defining the blood/land/memory complex of interrelated tropes and emblematic figures that were developed by American Indian and New Zealand Maori writers and activists to counter and, potentially, to subvert those dominating discourses that either predicted or simply described as fact the imminent demise of indigenous minority communities as distinct and viable nations. As the intervening chapters have demonstrated, indigenous minority writers and activists in the early contemporary period developed a range of narrative tactics that enabled them to define an enduring indigenous identity ("blood") in terms of narratives of connection to specific lands ("memory"), and to use narratives of connection to specific lands ("memory") to assert an enduring identity ("blood"). There is a circular logic here that may make some readers uncomfortable. My purpose has been neither to applaud nor to denounce such tactics but, instead, to analyze the operation and effects of their specific maneuvers. Indigenous minority activists and writers have created an interdependent and essentially inseparable triad out of "blood," "land," and "memory," and this triad has come to define minority indigeneity, its celebrated past, its contested present, and its imagined futures. In the Fourth World context of (post)colonial competition between "native" and "settler" forms of indigenous identity, the blood/land/memory complex asserts criteria for what ought to count as truth and truth's close cousin, authenticity: not in terms of the West's sense of an increasingly homogenized global order, but rather in terms of an indigenous minority sense of a persistently heterogenous local ground.

APPENDIX

Integrated Time Line, World War II to 1980

National and International Government Actions, Political
Activism, and Publications Relevant to American Indians,
New Zealand Maori, and Other Fourth World Peoples

1939

N.Z. establishes volunteer Maori unit, subsequently known as 28th Maori
Battalion

Over 17,000 Maori enlist during WWII and 11,500 Maori work in essential industries (Maori population estimated to be 82,000 in 1936)

First Young Maori Conference

1940

American Indian population estimated to be 345,252; Bureau of Indian
Affairs (BIA) claims a "legal" American Indian population of 360,500
under its jurisdiction

U.S. Congress enacts America's first peacetime draft

Four Arizona Indian tribes ritually forswear the use of swastika designs

1941

U.S. Congress declares war on 8 December

1942

U.S. Marine Corps organizes an all-Navajo signal unit of "Code Talkers"

War Relocation Authority leases American Indian lands for Japanese internment camps

Publication of Felix S. Cohen, *Handbook of Federal Indian Law*

1943

18,000 American Indians reported to be in U.S. military service

Publication of the *American Indian* (quarterly), American Association on Indian Affairs

1944

25,000 American Indians reported serving in U.S. fighting forces

First meeting of National Congress of American Indians (NCAI)

Publication of Ella Cara Deloria (Sioux), *Speaking of Indians* (nonfiction)

Publication of Ruth Muskrat Bronson (Cherokee), *Indians Are People, Too* (nonfiction)

1945

U.S. Office of Indian Affairs (OIA) reports more than 40,000 Indians have left reservations for war work

John Collier resigns as commissioner of Indian affairs

Publication of OIA pamphlet, *Indians in the War*

Publication of John Joseph Matthews (Osage), *Talking to the Moon* (autobiography)

Publication of NCAI *Newsletter*

N.Z. Maori population estimated to be 100,000

Passage of Maori Social and Economic Act leads to formation of the Maori Council

Signing and ratification of United Nations Charter; UN founding members include U.S. and N.Z.

1946

U.S. Congress passses Indian Claims Commission Act

U.S. Congress passes legislation requiring compulsory school attendance for American Indian children

Publication of Pei Te Hurinui Jones (Waikato/Tuwharetoa/Maniopoto), *Te Tangata Whai-rawa o Weniti* (Maori translation of *The Merchant of Venice*)

First UN General Assembly

Creation of UN Commission on Human Rights

1947

H.R. 1113, the so-called "Indian Emancipation Bill," is narrowly defeated in U.S. Congress

Publication of *NCAI Washington Bulletin* (newsletter)

N.Z. Department of Native Affairs replaced by Department of Maori Affairs

Creation of UN Sub-Commission on Prevention of Discrimination and Protection of Minorities

1948

BIA initiates off-reservation job placement program for single Navajo men

Arizona and New Mexico grant Indians voting rights

Completion of Ella Cara Deloria's manuscript of *Waterlily* (novel); published in 1988

Founding of Maori Community Center, Auckland

UN Decolonization Mandate

UN Universal Declaration of Human Rights

1949

Publication of D'Arcy McNickle (Cree/Salish), *They Came Here First* (nonfiction)

Publication of *Indian Affairs* (newsletter), Association on American Indian Affairs

Publication of *Smoke Signals* (journal), Indian Association of America

Founding of Kauhanganui (Maori Independence Movement)

Publication of Te Rangi Hiroa/Peter Buck (Taranaki/Ngati Mutunga), *The Coming of the Maori* (nonfiction)

1950

American Indian population estimated to be 357,499

BIA extends off-reservation placement services to other Indians

1951

U.S. Indian Claims Commission reports 370 petitions, representing 852 separate claims

BIA establishes Field Relocation Offices in Denver, Salt Lake City, Los Angeles, Chicago; offices subsequently added in Oakland, San Jose, Dallas, Cleveland

N.Z. Maori population estimated 115,000

Founding of Maori Women's Welfare League, first national Maori organization

Teaching of Maori language begins at Auckland University

Publication of Reweti Kohere (Ngati Porou), *The Autobiography of a Maori*

Ratification of the Convention on the Prevention and Punishment of the Crime of Genocide

1952

BIA provides transportation, placement, and subsistence help under Indian Voluntary Relocation Program; 868 Indians placed

Publication of *Te Ao Hou/The New World* (national Maori journal, 76 issues, 1952–75), Department of Maori Affairs

1953

U.S. Indian Termination Policy begins with passage of House Concurrent Resolution 108 and Public Law 280

U.S. Congress repeals liquor laws that discriminate against Indians

Passage of Town and Country Planning Act, Maori Affairs Act, Maori Trustee Act

1954

Termination of Menominee Nation

NCAI organizes emergency conference in Washington, D.C.

Publication of D'Arcy McNickle, *Runner in the Sun* (juvenile novel)

Queen's visit to N.Z. inspires celebration of Waitangi Day, 6 February, as a national pageant

1955

Indian health services transferred from BIA to Department of Health, Education, and Welfare

Establishment of American Indian Center, Chicago

Publication of Dan M. Madrano (Caddo), *Heap Big Laugh* (humor)

1956

U.S. Congress passes Indian Vocational Training Act

BIA reports that over 5,000 Indians are participating in Voluntary Relocation Program

N.Z. Maori population estimated to be 137,000

Formation of Nordic Sami Council

1957

Publication of Chief Joe Shunatona (Pawnee/Otoe), *Skookum's Laugh Medicine* (humor)

Ratification of UN Supplementary Convention on the Abolition of Slavery, the Slave Trade and Institutions and Practices Similar to Slavery

International Labour Organization (ILO) adopts Convention 107, Protection and Integration of Indigenous and Other Tribal and Semi-Tribal Populations in Independent Countries

1958

Publication of A. T. Ngata (Ngati Porou), ed., *Nga Moteatea I* (traditional)

1959

Publication of D'Arcy McNickle, *Indians and Other Americans* (nonfiction)

Publication of *Navajo Times* (newspaper), Navajo Nation

Founding of Federal Council for the Advancement of (Australian) Aboriginals and Torres Strait Islanders

1960

American Indian population estimated to be 532,591

Publication of *Indian Times* (newsletter), White Buffalo Council of American Indians, Denver

Department of Maori Affairs issues "Hunn Report" on contemporary Maori land, housing, education, arts, and policy (published 1961)

Department of Maori Affairs institutes an urban relocation program

UN Declaration on the Granting of Independence to Colonial Countries and Peoples; U.S. abstains from voting

1961

U.S. Secretary of Interior Stewart Udall appoints Task Force on Indian Affairs

"Declaration of Indian Purpose" prepared during American Indian Chicago Conference

Founding of National Indian Youth Council (NIYC)

N.Z. Maori population estimated to be 167,000

1962

BIA founds Institute of American Indian Arts, Sante Fe, New Mexico

Publication of D'Arcy McNickle, *Indian Tribes of the United States* (nonfiction)

Publication of John Waititi (Whanau-a-Apanui), *Te Rangatahi I* (Maori language textbook)

1963

Publication of *Americans Before Columbus* (newspaper), NIYC

Publication of *Indian Voices* (newsletter), University of Chicago

Founding of N.Z. Maori Arts and Crafts Institute, Rotorua

Publication of *Te Kaunihera Maori* (quarterly), N.Z. Maori Council

1964

American Indian vote emerges on a national scale

Vine Deloria Jr. (Sioux) elected executive director of NCAI

NIYC supports fishing rights demonstrations ("fish-ins") in the Pacific Northwest

First American Indian invasion of Alcatraz Island

Publication of Gerald Vizenor (Chippewa), *Raising the Moon Vines* (poetry)

Publication of *Indian Historian* (quarterly), American Indian Historical Society

Publication of Hone Tuwhare (Ngapuhi/Ngati Tautahi/Te Popoto), *No Ordinary Sun* (poetry)

Publication of Joan Metge, *A New Maori Migration* (nonfiction)

Publication of John Waititi, *Te Rangatahi II* (Maori language textbook)

1965

Taos Pueblo rejects Indian Claims Commission's cash settlement for sacred Blue Lake

Publication of Gerald Vizenor, *Seventeen Chirps* (poetry)

Opening of first urban marae, Te Puea, Auckland suburb of Mangere

The Cook Islands, a former N.Z. Trust, becomes self-governing

1966

N.Z. Maori population estimated to be 201,000

Opening of Te Unga Waka, a Catholic-initiated Maori community center

1967

U.S. Congress passes Indian Resources Development Act

BIA reports that 5,800 Indians are participating in the Voluntary Relocation Program

Publication of Dallas Chief Eagle (Sioux), *Winter Count* (novel)

Publication of Emerson Blackhorse Mitchell (Navajo), *Miracle Hill* (novel)

Publication of Gerald Vizenor, *Empty Swings* (poetry)

Passage of Maori Affairs Amendment Act

Founding of Maori Organization on Human Rights (MOOHR)

Publication of Joan Metge, *The Maoris of New Zealand* (nonfiction, rev. 1976)

Founding meeting of National Indian Brotherhood (NIB), Canada

1968

President Johnson delivers special message, "The Forgotten American," to U.S. Congress

Establishment of National Council on Indian Opportunity (NCIO)

Passage of the Indian Civil Rights Act

Founding of the American Indian Movement (AIM)

Founding of United Native Americans (UNA)

National Aborigine Conference, Oklahoma

Founding of Navajo Community College, first tribally controlled institution of higher learning (opens in January 1969)

Publication of N. Scott Momaday (Kiowa), *House Made of Dawn* (novel)

Publication of Stan Steiner, *The New Indians* (nonfiction)

Publication of *The Warpath* (newspaper), United Native Americans, San Francisco

Publication of *Te Hokioi* (underground Maori newsletter)

Publication of *MOOHR* (underground newsletter), MOOHR

Publication of Erik Schwimmer, ed., *The Maori People in the Nineteen-Sixties* (nonfiction)

Founding of International Work Group on Indigenous Affairs (IWGIA), Denmark

1969

Indians of All Tribes occupy Alcatraz Island (20 November 1969–11 June 1971)

Founding of Americans for Indian Opportunity

Founding of National Indian Education Association

N. Scott Momaday wins Pulitzer Prize for *House Made of Dawn*

Publication of N. Scott Momaday, *The Way to Rainy Mountain* (mixed-genre)

Publication of Vine Deloria Jr. (Sioux), *Custer Died for Your Sins* (non-fiction)

Publicaton of Duane Niatum (Klallam), *Ascending Red Cedar Moon* (poetry)

Publication of *Akwesasne Notes* (national newspaper), Mohawk Nation

Cook Bicentennial Celebrations

Publication of *Te Maori* (quarterly, formerly *Te Kaunihera Maori*), N.Z. Maori Council

Ratification of UN International Convention on the Elimination of All Forms of Racial Discrimination

Founding of Survival International (SI), Britain

Founding of *Gesellschaft für bedrohte Völker* (Organization for Endangered Peoples), Germany

Founding of Committee for Original People's Entitlement (COPE)

1970

American Indian population estimated to be 792,730

President Nixon calls for Indian policy of "Self-Determination without Termination"

Restoration of Blue Lake to Taos Pueblo

AIM participates in capture of replica of the *Mayflower*

American Indian students in New York attempt to seize Ellis Island

Sit-ins held in several BIA offices

Pit River Indians occupy Lassen National Forest, Burney, California

Founding of Native American Rights Fund (NARF)

Formation of North American Indian Women's Association (NAIWA)

First Convocation of American Indian Scholars, Princeton University

N. Scott Momaday delivers address, "The Man Made of Words"

Publication of Martin Cruz Smith (Senecu del Sur/Yaqui), *The Indians Won* (novel)

Publication of Duane Niatum, *After the Death of the Elder Klallam* (poetry)

Publication of Dee Brown, *Bury My Heart at Wounded Knee* (nonfiction)

Publication of Vine Deloria Jr., *We Talk, You Listen* (nonfiction)

Publication of D'Arcy McNickle and Harold Fey, *Indians and Other Americans* (nonfiction)

Publication of Angie Debo, *A History of the Indians of the United States*

Publication of *A.I.M. News* (Newsletter), AIM

Ranginui Walker (Whakatohea) organizes Young Maori Leadership Hui, Auckland University

Emergence of activist group Nga Tamatoa (The Young Warriors)

Maori "gangs" begin to draw national attention

Nga Pitiroirangi/Rowley Habib (Ngati Tuwharetoa) becomes first Maori to win New Zealand Literary Fund award

Publication of Hone Tuwhare, *Come Rain, Hail* (poetry)

Publication of Margaret Orbell, ed., *Contemporary Maori Writing* (anthology)

Ratification of UN Convention on the Non-Applicability of Statutory Limitations to War Crimes and Crimes against Humanity

George Manuel (Shuswap) elected president of NIB, Canada

1971

U.S. Congress passes Alaska Native Claims Settlement Act

Founding of National Tribal Chairman's Association

Formation of American Indian Press Association (AIPA)

National Conference on Indian Self-Determination, Kansas City

Second Convocation of American Indian Scholars, Aspen, Colorado

AIM demonstrates at Mount Rushmore

Publication of James Welch (Blackfeet/Gros Ventre), *Riding the Earthboy 40* (poetry)

Publication of Alvin M. Josephy Jr., ed., *Red Power* (collected articles)

Publication of Joseph H. Cash and Herbert T. Hoover, eds., *To Be an Indian: An Oral History* (collected interviews)

Publication of Vine Deloria Jr., ed., *Of Utmost Good Faith* (collected documents)

Publication of D'Arcy McNickle, *Indian Man: A Biography of Oliver La Farge*

Publication of Ruth Roessel (Navajo), editor, *Navajo Studies at Navajo Community College* (nonfiction)

Publication of Hazel Hertzberg, *The Search for an American Indian Identity* (nonfiction)

Publication of Earl Shorris, *The Death of the Great Spirit: An Elegy for the American Indian* (nonfiction)

Publication of *Weewish Tree* (juvenile magazine), American Indian Historical Society

Publication of *Sun Tracks* (annual), University of Arizona Amerind Club

Publication of *Indian Education* (journal), National Indian Education Association

N.Z. Maori population estimated to be 227,000

Passage of Race Relations Act, New Zealand

Nga Tamatoa protest Treaty of Waitangi celebrations, calling for day of mourning

Formation of Te Reo Society, Victoria University, Wellington

George Manuel meets with indigenous leaders and activists in N.Z. and Australia

1972

U.S. Congress passes Indian Education Act

Final overturning of U.S. termination policy

Trail of Broken Treaties caravan and occupation of BIA headquarters, Washington, D.C.

American Indian activism at Plymouth Rock on Thanksgiving Day

Akwesasne Notes wins Robert F. Kennedy Memorial Foundation Journalism Award Citation

Publication of John (Fire) Lame Deer (Sioux) and Richard Erdoes, *Lame Deer, Seeker of Visions* (life history)

Publication of Peter Blue Cloud (Mohawk), ed., *Alcatraz Is Not an Island* (mixed-genre)

Publication of Hyemeyohsts Storm (Cheyenne), *Seven Arrows* (novel)

Publication of Denton R. Bedford (Munsee), *Tsali* (novel)

Publication of Jerome Rothenberg, ed., *Shaking the Pumpkin* (poetry anthology)

Publication of Gerald Vizenor, *The Everlasting Sky* (nonfiction)

Publication of Marion Gridley, *Contemporary American Indian Leaders* (nonfiction)

Establishment of Race Relations Office, Auckland

Nga Tamatoa sets up "Maori Embassy," Te Whare o Te Iwi (The House of the People), on steps of the Parliament House

Maori activists protest at Raglan Golf Course

Publication of Witi Ihimaera (Aitanga-a-Mahaki/Rongowhakaata/Ngati Porou), *Pounamu, Pounamu* (stories)

Publication of Hone Tuwhare, *Sapwood and Milk* (poetry)

Founding of Cultural Survival, Cambridge, Massachusetts

George Manuel meets with IWGIA in Copenhagen, SI and Anti-Slavery Society in London, and World Council of Churches in Geneva

Australian Aboriginal peoples erect Tent Embassy on Parliament grounds in Canberra

1973

Occupation at Wounded Knee, South Dakota (71 days)

U.S. Congress passes Menominee Restoration Act

Publication of Duane Niatum, *Taos Pueblo* (poetry)

Publication of Thomas E. Sanders (Nippawanock/Cherokee) and Walter W. Peek (Metacomet/Narragansett), eds., *Literature of the American Indian*

Publication of Vine Deloria Jr., *God Is Red* (nonfiction)

Publication of D'Arcy McNickle, *Native American Tribalism* (nonfiction)

Publication of Kirke Kickingbird (Kiowa) and Karen Ducheneaux (Sioux), *One Hundred Million Acres* (nonfiction)

Publication of *Wassaja* (national newspaper), Indian Historian Press

First Maori Artists and Writers Conference, Te Kaha marae

Publication of Witi Ihimaera, *Tangi* (novel)

UN declares decade against racism

1974

U.S. Congress passes Indian Financing Act and Hopi Land Settlement Act (also known as Navajo Relocation Act)

First Boldt decision on American Indian fishing rights

Founding of Women of All Red Nations (WARN) in affiliation with AIM

AIM sponsors first large-scale meeting of Indian representatives, leading to formation of International Indian Treaty Council

Publication of James Welch, *Winter in the Blood* (novel)

Publication of Janet Campbell Hale (Coeur d'Alene/Kootenai), *Owl's Song* (novel)

Publication of Leslie Marmon Silko (Laguna), *Laguna Woman* (poetry)

Publication of N. Scott Momaday, *Angle of Geese and Other Poems*

Publication of Kenneth Rosen, ed., *The Man to Send Rain Clouds* (story collection)

Publication of Frederick W. Turner III, ed., *The Portable North American Indian Reader* (collection)

Publication of Shirley Hill Witt (Mohawk) and Stan Steiner, eds., *The Way: An Anthology of Indian Literature*

Publication of Robert K. Dodge and Joseph B. McCullough, eds., *Voices From Wah'kon-tah: Contemporary Poetry of Native Americans*

Publication of Vine Deloria Jr., *Behind the Trail of Broken Treaties* (nonfiction) and *The Indian Affair* (nonfiction)

Publication of *Voices from Wounded Knee, 1973, in the Words of the Participants* (nonfiction)

Publication of *Studies in American Indian Literatures* (newsletter), Association for the Study of American Indian Literatures (ASAIL)

Publication of *American Indian Culture and Research Journal* (academic journal), University of California, Los Angeles

Publication of *American Indian Quarterly* (academic journal), Southwestern American Indian Society

Publication of *Indian Law Reporter* (monthly), American Indian Lawyer Training Program

Publication of *Indian Family Defense* (quarterly), Association on American Indian Affairs

Maori youth groups initiate Maori Language Day

Second Maori Writers and Artists Conference, Wairoa marae

Publication of Witi Ihimaera, *Whanau* (novel)

Publication of Harry Dansey (Ngati Tuwharetoa/Te Arawa), *Te Raukura/The Feathers of the Albatross* (drama)

Publication of Hone Tuwhare, *Something Nothing* (poetry)

Publication of MOOHR, *Te Karanga a Te Kotuku* (mixed-genre)

Publication of *Marae Magazine* (3 issues)

Publication of *Rongo* (newspaper), Te Huinga Rangatahi o Aotearoa (N.Z. Maori Students' Federation)

UN Economic and Social Council grants NIB Non-Governmental Organization (NGO) observer status

Preparatory meeting for World Council of Indigenous Peoples (WCIP), Guyana

Publication of George Manuel, *The Fourth World* (nonfiction)

1975

U.S. Congress passes Indian Self-Determination and Education Assistance Act

Founding of Council of Energy Resource Tribes

Publication of Duane Niatum, ed., *Carriers of the Dream Wheel* (poetry anthology)

Publication of Kenneth Rosen, ed., *Voices of the Rainbow* (poetry anthology)

Publication of *American Indian Journal* (monthly), Institute for the Development of Indian Law

N.Z. Parliament passes Treaty of Waitangi Act 1975, establishing Waitangi Tribunal

Te Roopu o te Matakite sponsors National Maori Land March and Tent Embassy on Parliament grounds

Third Maori Writers and Artists Conference, Waitara marae

Publication of Patricia Grace (Ngati Raukawa/Ngati Toa/Te Ati Awa), *Waiariki* (stories)

Publication of Heretaunga Pat Baker (Whakatohea/Ngati Kahungunu), *Behind the Tattooed Face* (novel)

Publication of Pei Te Hurinui Jones, *Nga Rupai'aha a Oma Kai'ama* (Maori translation of *The Rubaiyat of Omar Khayyam*)

Publication of Witi Ihimaera, *Maori* (nonfiction)

Publication of Michael King, ed., *Te Ao Hurihuri/The World Moves On: Aspects of Maoritanga* (nonfiction)

Publication of Anne Salmond, *Hui* (nonfiction)

First General Assembly of the wcip, Nootka Reserve, Port Alberni, Vancouver, Canada

UN grants International Indian Treaty Council ngo observer status

First conference for nuclear-free Pacific held in Fiji

1976

Celebration of U.S. Bicentennial

U.S. Congress passes Indian Crimes Act and Indian Health Care Improvement Act

Publication of N. Scott Momaday, *The Names* (memoir) and *The Gourd Dancer* (poetry)

Publication of Simon Ortiz (Acoma), *Going for the Rain* (poetry)

Publication of Peter Blue Cloud (Mohawk), *Turtle, Bear, and Wolf* (poetry)

Publication of James L. White, ed., *The First Skin around Me: Contemporary American Tribal Poetry* (anthology)

Publication of *Highlights* (monthly), National Tribal Chairman's Association

Publication of *Koru: The New Zealand Maori Artists and Writers Annual Magazine*, vol. 1

UN passes International Covenant on Civil and Political Rights and Covenant on Economic, Social and Cultural Rights

Publication of *Cultural Survival* (quarterly)

1977

Publication of Leslie Marmon Silko, *Ceremony* (novel)

Publication of Martin Cruz Smith, *Nightwing* (novel)

Publication of Simon Ortiz, *A Good Journey* (poetry)

Publication of Duane Niatum, *Digging Out the Roots* (poetry)

Publication of Peter Blue Cloud, *White Corn Sister* (poetry)

Publication of Mary Tall Mountain (Athabascan), *Nine Poems*

Publication of Elizabeth Cook-Lynn (Sioux), *Then Badger Said This* (poetry)

Publication of Joseph Bruchac (Abenaki), *This Earth Is a Drum* (poetry)

Publication of *Indian Natural Resources* (quarterly), Association on American Indian Affairs

Orakei Maori Action Group sponsors occupation of Bastion Point (506 days)

Founding of Te Ika a Maui Players, Maori theater group

Second General Assembly of the WCIP, Kiruna, Sweden

George Manuel nominated for Nobel Peace Prize

First Inuit Circumpolar Conference, Barrow, Alaska

NGO Conference on Discrimination against Indigenous Peoples of the Americas, Geneva

Establishment of Documentation Centre for Indigenous Peoples (DOCIP), Geneva

Formation of Indigenous Peoples' Network (IPN)

UN grants International Indian Treaty Council NGO status

1978

"Longest Walk" march to Washington, D.C.

U.S. Congress passes American Indian Religious Freedom Act and Indian Child Welfare Act

U.S. Congress passes Tribally Controlled Community College Assistance Act

Disbandment of Indian Claims Commission

U.S. Supreme Court rules in favor of limited Indian sovereignty in *United States v. Wheeler*

Formation of Indian Law Resource Center (ILRC), Helena, Montana

Posthumous publication of D'Arcy McNickle, *Wind from an Enemy Sky* (novel)

Publication of Gerald Vizenor, *Darkness in Saint Louis Bearheart* (novel) and *Wordarrows* (nonfiction)

Publication of Simon Ortiz, *The Howbah Indians* (stories)

Publication of Linda Hogan (Chickasaw), *Calling Myself Home* (poetry)

Publication of Tim A. Giago Jr. (Sioux), *The Aboriginal Sin: Reflections on the Holy Rosary Indian Mission School* (poetry)

Publication of Janet Campbell Hale, *Custer Lives in Humbolt County* (poetry)

Publication of Joseph Bruchac, *There Are No Trees inside the Prison* (poetry)

Publication of Akwesasne Notes, *Basic Call to Consciousness* (nonfiction)

N.Z. national government creates new Maori policy entitled Tu Tangata ("Stand Tall")

Maori gangs reemerge on national scene

Publication of Patricia Grace, *Mutuwhenua: The Moon Sleeps* (novel)

Publication of Hone Tuwhare, *Making a Fist of It* (poetry)

Publication of *Koru*, vol. 2

World Conference to Combat Racism and Racial Discrimination, Geneva

1979

U.S. Congress passes Archaeological Resources Protection Act

Publication of James Welch, *The Death of Jim Loney* (novel)

Publication of Joy Harjo (Creek), *What Moon Drove Me to This?* (poetry)

Publication of Barney Bush (Shawnee/Cayuga), *My Horse and a Jukebox* (poetry)

Publication of Alan R. Velie, *American Indian Literature: An Anthology*

Publication of Vine Deloria Jr., *Metaphysics of Modern Existence* (non-fiction)

N.Z. Maori population estimated to be 280,000

He Taua activists disrupt University of Auckland engineering students' "haka party"; New Zealand's "first race riot"

Publication of Apirana Taylor (Te Whanau-a-Apanui/Ngati Porou/Taranaki), *Eyes of the Ruru* (poetry)

Publication of *Te Kaea* (national journal, formerly *Te Ao Hou*, 5 issues, 1979–81), Department of Maori Affairs

Emergence of Sami Action Group (SAG), Norway

1980

American Indian population estimated to be 1,361,869

U.S. Congress passes Maine Indian Claims Settlement Act

Publication of Simon Ortiz, *Fight Back* (poetry)

Publication of Joseph Bruchac, *Translator's Son* (poetry)

Publication of Ray A. Young Bear (Mesquakie), *Winter of the Salamander* (poetry)

Publication of Wendy Rose (Hopi/Miwok), *Lost Copper* (poetry)

Publication of Jim Barnes (Choctaw), *This Crazy Land* (poetry)

Publication of Carter Revard (Osage), *Ponca War Dancers* (poetry)

Publication of Hanay Geiogamah (Kiowa/Delaware), *New Native American Drama: Three Plays*

Formation of Maori Peoples Liberation Movement of Aotearoa

Emergence of Mana Motuhake Party

Opening of Hoani Waititi Marae, Auckland

Publication of Patricia Grace, *The Dream Sleepers and Other Stories*

Publication of Hone Tuwhare, *Selected Poems*

Publication of Anne Salmond, *Eruera: The Teachings of a Maori Elder* (nonfiction)

Russell Tribunal meets in the Netherlands on the Rights of the Indians of the Americas

Second Inuit Circumpolar Conference, Nuuk, Greenland

Founding of Workgroup on Indigenous Peoples (wip), Netherlands

NOTES

Introduction

1 Momaday coined the phrase in his Pulitzer Prize–winning first novel, *House Made of Dawn.* A character uses blood memory to describe the intensity of his Kiowa grandmother's knowledge of her people's oral tradition: "Though she lived out her long life in the shadow of Rainy Mountain [in Oklahoma], the immense landscape of the continental interior— all of its seasons and its sounds—lay like memory in her blood" (129).

2 Ngahuia Te Awekotuku, *Mana Wahine Maori: Selected Writings on Maori Women's Art, Culture and Politics,* 111; Gerald Vizenor, "Crows Written on the Poplars: Autocritical Autobiographies," 103.

3 Michel de Certeau, *The Practice of Everyday Life.*

4 Aotearoa is the contemporary Maori name for the whole of New Zealand.

5 Postcolonial theory has manipulated its key term into a variety of forms. Most common is the hyphenated "post-colonial," which indicates an attention to historical periodization (that is, "after" the colonial period), or the run-together "postcolonial," which suggests an emphasis on ideological continuity (that is, both "during" and "after" the historical period of active colonial encounter). The alternative "colonial/postcolonial" binds its ostensible Others together across an ambiguous diagonal slash, while additional prefixed forms forgo the pretense of "post" altogether in order to designate conditions of "neocolonialism," "internal colonialism," and "paracolonialism." As I explain below, throughout the book I describe the situation of indigenous minorities with the ironic term "(post)colonial," which employs parentheses to raise the specter of an asserted "post" that is not quite one.

6 Because identification as Maori is typically self-selective in the contemporary period, the Maori percentage of the total New Zealand population varies depending on the terms by which people are queried about their identity and on who does the counting. Numbers reported in the New Zealand media and in New Zealand scholarship generally vary between 12 and 15 percent. The official 1996 census lists Maori as 14.5 percent of the total New Zealand population (*New Zealand in Profile 1998*).

7 Amy Gutmann, Introduction to *Multiculturalism: Examining the Politics of Recognition,* 11.

8 Literally, tangata whenua translates into English as "land people" or "people of the land"; in certain contexts, tangata whenua also translates as "hosts."

9   Pete Bossley, *Te Papa: An Architectural Adventure.*

10 Notable exceptions include Denmark's granting self-government to Greenland and the creation of an Inuit territory, Nunavut, in Canada's Arctic region.

11 See Ashcroft, Griffiths, and Tiffin, *The Empire Writes Back: Theory and Practice in Post-colonial Literatures,* 135–40. For specific contemporary examples of the struggle over defining indigeneity, see the essay collection *Pakeha: The Quest for Identity in New Zealand,* edited by Michael King. Obviously, the European settler paradigm I am sketching here does not apply to indigenous minorities like the Ainu in Japan. However, there are striking similarities: Until 1986, the government of Japan denied Ainu existence and its own colonial history and claimed that Japan was a "mono-ethnic" nation. See United Nations, *Seeds of a New Partnership: Indigenous Peoples and the United Nations,* 20.

12 United Nations, *Seeds of a New Partnership,* 42.

13 Notions of cultural performance and national invention are explored, as well, in Eric Hobsbawm and Terence Ranger's *The Invention of Tradition* and in Benedict Anderson's *Imagined Communities: Reflections on the Origins and Spread of Nationalism.*

14 Homi K. Bhabha, *The Location of Culture,* 2; Mary Louise Pratt, "Arts of the Contact Zone," 34.

15 For an analysis of a particular instance of ethnopolitical conflict, see Linda Pertusati, *In Defense of Mohawk Land: Ethnopolitical Conflict in Native North America;* for a definition of ethnodrama, see Robert Paine, "Ethnodrama and the 'Fourth World': The Sami Action Group in Norway, 1979–81."

16 Pertusati, *In Defense of Mohawk Land,* x.

17 See Joane Nagel, "The Political Mobilization of Native Americans."

18 See Luci Tapahonso, *Sáanii Dahataal/The Women Are Singing,* xii, and *Blue Horses Rush In: Poems and Stories,* xiv. I also have heard American Indian poet Wendy Rose (Hopi/Miwok), who recounts the painful difficulties of her particular mixed-blood and dislocated experience in a powerful essay titled "Neon Scars," describe her writing as her experience of indigenous land.

19 Maori concerts have a long history in Aotearoa/New Zealand, beginning in the nineteenth century.

20 For a more detailed discussion of colonial territorialization, see Robert J. C. Young, *Colonial Desire: Hybridity in Theory, Culture, and Race,* 170–74.

21 For analyses of specific contemporary examples, see Winona LaDuke, *All Our Relations: Native Struggles for Land and Life.*

22 For a discussion of Momaday's trope and the controversy it has generated, see Chadwick Allen, "Blood (and) Memory."

23 Throughout his works, Momaday employs the term "racial memory" to refer to the collective memories of a people passed down from generation to generation through the oral tradition.

24 Leela Gandhi, in *Postcolonial Theory: A Critical Introduction,* critiques Ashcroft, Griffith, and Tiffin's analysis by pointing to their "striking resistance to the possible heterogeneity of postcolonial experience and literary production" (162; see also 136, 163). Drawing on the work of Elleke Boehmer, Gandhi also critiques these and other orthodox postcolonial critics' "generalising assumption that all colonial texts are repressive" (154).

25 Among others, Young articulates this potential in his *Colonial Desire.*

26 The U.S. government ceased contracting new treaties with indigenous nations in 1871, but it continued to negotiate official "agreements" into the next century. For a history of U.S.-Indian treaty making and a complete list of ratified treaties, see Francis Paul Prucha, *American Indian Treaties: The History of a Political Anomaly.* Vine Deloria Jr. points out in his review of Prucha that, although it is an excellent source of information, this account is not sympathetic to Indian points of view on the contemporary relevance of treaties (see Deloria, "The Subject Nobody Knows"). For a historical overview of New Zealand's founding charter, see Claudia Orange, *The Treaty of Waitangi.* For an analysis of Maori levels of literacy at the time of the treaty's negotiation and the ability of Maori rangatira to "sign" the document, see D. F. McKenzie, *Oral Culture, Literacy and Print in Early New Zealand: The Treaty of Waitangi.*

27 Manuka Henare argues that in 1840 "The Treaty of Waitangi was seen as a covenant, he kawenata hou, by people like Hone Heke and Patuone. Their understanding of covenant came from their knowledge of Old Testament theology, as writings by both men indicate" ("Colonials at the Helm," 38). Also see E. T. J. Durie, "The Treaty in Maori History."

28 Henry Louis Gates Jr. employs the phrase "silent second text" to name the unspoken knowledge that is shared between speaker and listener in a number of African-American rhetorical traditions. "Signifyin(g)," Gates argues, "depends on the success of the signifier at invoking an absent meaning ambiguously 'present' in a carefully wrought statement" (*The Signifying Monkey: A Theory of African-American Literary Criticism,* 86). Treaty allegories in contemporary Maori written texts operate similarly, though often with far less ambiguity than the speech acts Gates describes.

29 For a discussion of "the context of consumption" and "historical production," see Michel-Rolph Trouillot, *Silencing the Past: Power and the Production of History,* esp. chap. 5, "The Presence in the Past."

30 See Bruce Biggs, *Let's Learn Maori: A Guide to the Study of the Maori Language.*

A Directed Self-Determination

1   Anne Salmond, *Hui: A Study of Maori Ceremonial Gatherings*, 28. Ranginui Walker, in *Ka Whawhai Tonu Matou*, describes how in 1939 the Maori members of Parliament "persuaded the Government to establish a volunteer Maori unit, subsequently known as the 28th Maori Battalion" (195). Unlike the segregated African-American units in the United States, which were led by White officers, New Zealand's Maori Battalion was led by Maori officers. Most American Indians were integrated into White U.S. units.

2   See Michael King, "Between Two Worlds," 303.

3   Alison Bernstein, *American Indians and World War II: Toward a New Era in Indian Affairs*, 40, 73.

4   Office of Indian Affairs, *Indians in the War*, 49.

5   Bernstein, in *American Indians and World War II*, quotes articles that appeared in the *New York Times* and the Buffalo, New York, *Evening News* on 14 October 1940, which reported that three member tribes of the Iroquois Confederacy claimed separate-nation status and therefore exemption from the draft (28–29). Bernstein also notes that "one and one-half times as many [Indian] men enlisted as were drafted" (42).

6   Ibid., 67–71.

7   Gerald Vizenor, *Manifest Manners: Postindian Warriors of Survivance*, 51.

8   For a detailed discussion of direct and indirect forms of opposition among indigenous communities, see Noel Dyck, "Aboriginal Peoples and Nation-States: An Introduction to the Analytical Issues." For a discussion of indigenous "rights talk" and an indigenous "politics of confrontation, embarrassment, and shame in liberal democracies," see Paul Havemann, ed., *Indigenous Peoples' Rights in Australia, Canada, and New Zealand.*

9   Glenn T. Morris notes, in "International Law and Politics: Toward a Right to Self-Determination for Indigenous Peoples," that "Of the current members of the United Nations, over 100 were previously colonies, and have achieved their independence since the end of World War II" (73). These circumstances would seem to bode well for Fourth World peoples seeking self-determination. However, the UN's resolutions extend the right of self-determination almost exclusively to "colonies," and colonies are defined by criteria that include "geographical separation from the colonizing power" (74). Despite attempts to extend the UN's decolonization mandates to Fourth World peoples, the so-called salt-water thesis, which requires that "colonies be separated from the colonial power by a substantial body of water, preferably an ocean," "has predominated in international debate" (74).

10   In the United States, see, for example, Jack Forbes, "Colonialism and Native American Literature: Analysis"; Arnold Krupat, "Postcoloniality

and Native American Literature," and "Postcolonialism, Ideology, and Native Literature"; Louis Owens, *Other Destinies: Understanding the American Indian Novel*; Elizabeth Cook-Lynn, *Why I Can't Read Wallace Stegner and Other Essays: A Tribal Voice* and "Introduction" to *The Politics of Hallowed Ground*; Jace Weaver, "From I-Hermeneutics to We-Hermeneutics: Native Americans and the Post-Colonial"; and Russell Thornton, "Introduction and Overview."

11 Exceptions include Gerald Vizenor, who employs "paracolonial" to describe the situation of the United States, although without a clear definition of this term, and Chidi Okonkwo, who employs "paracolonial" to describe the various countries of the "European Diaspora" ("Australia, Canada, New Zealand, the United States of America and the Latin American countries"): "Such a paracolonial country comprises two different societies, with the conquered population existing as the Third World underbelly of the dominant European society" (*Decolonization Agonistics in Postcolonial Fiction*, x). Okonkwo's use of "Three Worlds" theory is meant to enable him to align what I have designated Fourth World literatures with the so-called Third World literatures of Africa and the Caribbean. Many of his comparisons are illuminating; nevertheless, they elide crucial historical, demographic, and cultural differences in both the production and reception of what he designates "paracolonial" and "excolonial" literatures. Scholars in American studies also have begun to situate the United States within contexts of ongoing colonialism and imperialism, whether or not they directly engage orthodox postcolonial theories, most notably in the collection edited by Amy Kaplan and Donald Pease, *Cultures of United States Imperialism*.

12 Owens, *Other Destinies*, 6.

13 Ibid., 7. Although Ashcroft, Griffiths, and Tiffin's assertion of a single three-stage model is itself problematic, it is unclear why Owens places contemporary American Indian literature in their second stage ("literature produced 'under imperial license'") rather than in their third ("the development of independent literatures").

14 Krupat, "Postcolonialism, Ideology, and Native American Literature," 30. On 39–50, Krupat employs Appiah's *In My Father's House: Africa in the Philosophy of Culture* (New York: Oxford University Press, 1992).

15 For relevant critiques of Ashcroft, Griffiths, and Tiffin, see E. San Juan Jr., *Beyond Postcolonial Theory;* Leela Gandhi, *Postcolonial Theory: A Critical Introduction;* and Okonkwo, *Decolonization Agonistics in Postcolonial Fiction.*

16 See, for example, San Juan, *Beyond Postcolonial Theory.*

17 For a related discussion that focuses on supposed essentialism in "classic" postcolonial texts, see Benita Parry, "Resistance Theory/Theorising Resistance: or Two Cheers for Nativism."

18   Anne McClintock, "The Angel of Progress: Pitfalls of the Term 'Postcolonialism,' " 257–58.

19   Eric Cheyfitz, *The Poetics of Imperialism: Translation and Colonization from The Tempest to Tarzan,* xii–xiii, emphasis added.

20   Walker, *Ka Whawhai Tonu Matou,* 98–99.

21   Weaver, "From I-Hermeneutics to We-Hermeneutics," 12–13.

22   San Juan, *Beyond Postcolonial Theory,* 22. San Juan's critique follows the lead of Aijaz Ahmad, who has been extremely critical of orthodox postcolonial theory's "denial of history" and displacement of "an activist culture with a textual culture"; see Ahmad's *In Theory: Classes, Nations, Literatures.*

23   Okonkwo, *Decolonization Agonistics in Postcolonial Fiction,* 3.

24   Walker, *Ka Whawhai Tonu Matou,* 197.

25   Bernstein, *American Indians and World War II,* 86, 150.

26   See Joan Metge, *A New Maori Migration: Rural and Urban Relations in Northern New Zealand* and *The Maoris of New Zealand: Ruatahi;* Erik Schwimmer, ed., *The Maori People in the Nineteen-Sixties: A Symposium;* Salmond, *Hui;* and Walker, *Ka Whawhai Tonu Matou.*

27   Walker, *Ka Whawhai Tonu Matou,* 197.

28   *Indians at Work* was issued from 1933 to 1945.

29   Unless otherwise indicated, all references to Department of Maori Affairs documents—letters, memoranda, reports, press releases, advertising sheets, and so forth—are to materials held in the New Zealand National Archives/Te Whare Tohu Tuhituhinga O Aotearoa in Wellington.

30   An exception to this was Collier's publication over the years of occasional articles written by various tribal chairmen and several articles written by D'Arcy McNickle (Cree/Salish). Collier hired McNickle to work with him in Indian Affairs in 1936. See my discussion of McNickle's career in chapter 2.

31   I. L. G. Sutherland, "Some Aims For Te Ao Hou," n.d., New Zealand National Archives.

32   December 1945: "An Act to make provision for the social and economic advancement and the promotion and maintenance of the health and general well-being of the Maori community." The act came into force on 1 April 1946; its provisions were later consolidated under the 1962 Maori Welfare Act.

33   In addition to the U.S. journal *Indians At Work,* the Department of Maori Affairs appears to have been aware of a South African journal, the *African Drum,* produced for Africans by the South African Native Welfare project in Capetown. On 14 April 1951 the New Zealand *Herald* ran an article advocating the creation of "A Maori Journal" that referred to the *African Drum* as a possible model. A copy of the *Herald* article is included in the *Te Ao Hou* files held in the New Zealand National Archives. The first issue

of *The African Drum: A Magazine of Africa for Africa* was published in
March 1951.

34 Summarized in H. D. B. Dansey, "Te Ao Hou: Report To The Minister Of
Maori Affairs," 13 March 1974, New Zealand National Archives.

35 Bernstein, *American Indians and World War II*, 110.

36 Ibid., 168.

37 Robert K. Thomas, "Pan-Indianism," 80.

38 Kenneth R. Philp, *Termination Revisited: American Indians on the Trail to
Self-Determination, 1933–1953*, 171.

39 Donald Fixico, *Termination and Relocation: Federal Indian Policy, 1945–
1960*, 183.

40 See Havemann, *Indigenous Peoples' Rights in Australia, Canada, and New
Zealand*, 474.

41 No comprehensive study of Maori writing from this period has been
attempted since Bill Pearson included a twelve-page section on "Writing
by Maori" in his chapter-length survey of "The Maori and Literature
1938–65," published in 1968 as part of Schwimmer's symposium *The
Maori People in the Nineteen-Sixties*. To date there has been no individual
study of the journal *Te Ao Hou*. For a more recent assessment of Maori
writing, see, for example, Ken Arvidson, "Aspects of Contemporary Maori
Writing in English."

1 A Marae on Paper

1 There is evidence of Maori use of writing beginning in the late 1820s. In
1862 the Maori King Movement set up the first independent Maori press
and created the first Maori newspaper, *Te Hokioi* (the mysterious night-
bird). See Michael D. Jackson, "Literacy, Communications and Social
Change."

2 *Te Ao Hou*'s editors were Erik Schwimmer (1952–1961), Margaret Orbell
(1962–1966), and Joy Stevenson (1966–1975). Bruce Mason, a well-known
playwright, filled in for Schwimmer during a leave of absence, overseeing
the six issues produced between June 1960 and June 1961.

3 The National Film Unit was established in 1941 and was originally part
of the Prime Minister's Department. It produced a news magazine, the
Weekly Review, as well as documentaries and tourist films. When a new
government took over in 1950, the Film Unit became part of the Tourist
and Publicity Department (see Robert Allender, "Disordered Cinema").
Weekly Review #324, dated 17 November 1947, for example, is titled
"Maori School." Featured in this eight-and-a-half-minute, black-and-
white installment is a Native school of 300 predominantly Maori pupils
located on the remote East Coast. The film emphasizes that the school

provides "training for living . . . not a specialist training." For Maori girls, this training includes access to a "model home," which is a "special classroom for cleaning, cooking, and making beds"; for Maori boys, "the whole land is a classroom."

4 Quoted on the box containing "Aroha" in the New Zealand National Archives. The film is dated 10 July 1951 and was directed by Michael Forlong; Professor Ernest Beaglehole served as "Anthropological Advisor." *Aroha* translates into English as "love" or "empathy." The character is played by Moana Kahui.

5 Schwimmer was neither a native New Zealander nor a more typical British immigrant. Originally from Amsterdam, he arrived in Aotearoa/New Zealand in 1940 by way of Indonesia. He joined the Department of Maori Affairs after completing a degree in classics at Victoria University in Wellington. Memoranda indicate that he put forward the idea for *Te Ao Hou* in 1949, when he was still a basic grade officer. Schwimmer is not listed as editor until issue 6 (Royal Tour Number, 1953).

6 I am working under the assumption that Schwimmer either wrote or supervised the Maori version of his editorials, since they are not attributed to a translator either in the magazine itself or in any of the official memoranda or editorial correspondence I have read.

7 Unless indicated otherwise, all translations of Maori into English are my own.

8 In the public record, officials from Maori Affairs, the Information Service, and the Department of Tourism and Publicity, all of whom had a hand in *Te Ao Hou*'s early production, asserted that they did not wish the magazine to be used as "propaganda" or to have a "political character." But in a 1952 memo to Schwimmer, Maori Affairs states in no uncertain terms that "in subject matter ours [that is, the government's] is the only voice." After publication of the first several issues, Maori Affairs, the Information Service, and Tourism and Publicity attempted to discipline Schwimmer because of his Maori-centered editorial slant. In Maori Affairs memoranda there are rumors of attempts to block Schwimmer's promotion and other disciplinary actions. In memoranda dated 1955 and 1956, the director of Information Services argues that the publication of *Te Ao Hou* cannot be justified for any reason other than that it is a "publicity medium" designed to "lead the readers towards the Government's objectives." References to Department of Maori Affairs documents, unless otherwise indicated, are to materials held in the New Zealand National Archives/Te Whare Tohu Tuhituhinga O Aotearoa.

9 Anne Salmond, *Hui*, 31.

10 Hiwi Tauroa, *Te Kawa o te Marae/A Guide to Marae*, 5.

11 Ranginui Walker, *Ka Whawhai Tonu Matou*, 70.

12 *Te Ao Hou*'s third editor, Joy Stevenson, created a separate Young Readers' Section beginning in issue 57 (December 1966).

13   In what appears to be an early draft of Schwimmer's first editorial, these ideas are expressed even more pointedly: "Life on the marae, sports, haka, arts and crafts . . . can, in fact, be the basis for *an entirely new and significant Maori culture*" (emphasis added).

14   Form letter from the Editor to potential advertisers in *Te Ao Hou,* 3 October 1952. From the early stages of planning the magazine, Department of Maori Affairs memoranda indicate that there was tension between Schwimmer's personal goals for *Te Ao Hou* and the goals of higher officials. Nevertheless, even though Schwimmer is highly supportive of the Maori people throughout his editorials, he constantly weighs Maori "cultural" desires against "essential" needs for living in a predominantly Pakeha society. Furthermore, although he states in his final editorial that his role as editor has been to "give the Maori people the opportunity to hear their own voice," elsewhere Schwimmer describes his role in far more directive terms and in close alignment with government edicts. In a memorandum Schwimmer wrote to Maori Affairs while under attack in 1957, he details how he chose which material to publish in *Te Ao Hou:* "Inevitably my selection of material followed some educational programme, which could not help being based on a definite view of the most desirable type of society for the Maori people. This view was composed of three elements: the ideals of the dominant European group, the aspirations of the Maori leaders[,] and the editor's conception of a 'sane society' satisfying human needs. The material in the magazine represents the area of agreement between the three conceptions." Clearly, Schwimmer's ultimate goals for *Te Ao Hou,* like the government's, went well beyond simply allowing Maori to speak "in their own voice."

15   Keith Sinclair, "Te Ao Hou (The New World)—No. 1," 42.

16   The first literary competition was announced in issue 5 (Spring 1953) in a bilingual advertisement for "Story Competition/He Whaka Tae Tae Tuhituhi." The ad asks that entries address contemporary Maori life, whether set in the country, town, or city; it is hoped that such stories will "increase awareness of what Maori life today really is"; and the ad asserts that these "real" stories will be the "greatest help for the future." Despite these high aims, the first competition produced no results. By comparison, the second competition, announced in issue 14 (April 1956), was a considerable success, producing one Maori and several English language texts suitable for publication. Schwimmer devotes his editorial for issue 14 to "Our Literary Competition," and he uses the event to promote his views on the importance of writing for Maori. The Maori's future, he contends, will depend upon how "well" they think about themselves in the present.

17   Gerald Vizenor, "Socioacupuncture: Mythic Reversals and the Striptease in Four Scenes," in *Crossbloods,* 83–97.

18   See "*Te Ao Hou,* and the Space Between," in Francis Pound, *The Space Between.*

19   It is likely that Hineira is a pseudonym for Arapera Hineira Blank, author of "Yielding to the New" discussed above.

20   Translation by I. H. Kawharu in *Waitangi: Maori and Pakeha Perspectives of the Treaty of Waitangi,* ed. I. H. Kawharu, 321.

21   Ibid., 319 n. 7.

22   After 1769, when Captain James Cook and the crews of his ships first landed in Aotearoa/New Zealand, dysentery, sexually transmitted diseases, tuberculosis, influenza, whooping cough, and other European diseases were introduced into the Maori population, increasing Maori death rates and decreasing Maori fertility. In addition, by the 1820s muskets were introduced widely into Maori society, inciting the so-called Musket Wars, in which newly and suddenly more powerfully armed Maori groups sought revenge against traditional enemies. New Zealand historians and health experts believe that the Maori population was cut in half by 1850. In the 1860s, in addition to Maori deaths that resulted from a series of "Land Wars" fought against the British, regional epidemics of typhoid, measles, whooping cough, and influenza claimed more Maori lives. At the close of the nineteenth century, the Maori population hit a low point, an estimated 42,000 people.

23   Following the bitter land wars of the 1860s, Maori delegations traveled to England in 1882 and 1884, hoping to petition the Crown to uphold its Treaty promises. Neither delegation was granted a royal audience. (It is interesting to note, as an aside, that political scientists locate the beginnings of international indigenous minority political activism in these early Maori attempts to gain audiences with the British Crown. See, for example, Franke Wilmer, *The Indigenous Voice In World Politics,* 211.) A third Maori delegation traveled to England in 1914. Though Te Rata, the delegation's Tainui leader, secured an audience with King George V, the deputation nevertheless "returned home empty handed." Ten years later, in 1924, yet another Maori leader, W. T. Ratana, traveled to England to argue Treaty rights. His attempt to meet with George V was blocked by the New Zealand high commissioner, and Ratana was forced to return home to seek internal solutions to Maori grievances (Walker, *Ka Whawhai Tonu Matou,* 160–65, 183–84).

24   My translation is based on *The Revised Dictionary of Modern Maori,* put together by R. M. Ryan (3d ed., 1989), which gives "text" as the first definition of *kupu,* followed by "word" and "message." Ryan is obviously following H. W. Williams's authoritative *Dictionary of the Maori Language* (7th ed., 1971), which defines the noun *kupu* as "anything said," "saying," "message," "word," "talk." In the *English-Maori Dictionary,* put together by H. M. Ngata (1993), *text* is translated into Maori as "kupu tuhi," literally, "written word" (tuhi = to write). Ngata translates *policy* as "kaupapa," as does the dictionary of recent Maori neologisms, *Te Matatiki:*

Contemporary Maori Words (1996), put together by the Maori Language Commission/Te Taura Whiri i te Reo Maori.

25 Here I am following Ngata's *English-Maori Dictionary.*

26 Quoted in Robert J. C. Young, *Colonial Desire: Hybridity in Theory, Culture and Race,* 20.

27 Ibid., 23.

28 Rua's name may also allude to the early-twentieth-century Tuhoe prophet and charismatic political leader Rua Kenana, who organized a utopian community, Hiruharana Hou/New Jerusalem, in the Urewera mountains. See Walker, *Ka Whawhai Tonu Matou,* 181–83.

29 Terence Barrow, *An Illustrated Guide to Maori Art,* 32.

30 Ibid., 78.

31 Bob's interior monologue recalls the image that dominates *Te Ao Hou*'s first cover, a carved waka taua (war canoe): "Yes, he'd gone away, left the old life and ways, but did not the world ahead hold the same challenges as it had in the past—even back to the great fleet [of Polynesian ancestors who migrated to Aotearoa/New Zealand]? Bob had prepared himself well, and prevailed; as the old people had done through the ages." In his references to the great fleet, Bob reclaims a Polynesian tradition of courage, skill, adventure, and innovation as a source of strength for meeting contemporary Maori challenges.

2   Indian Truth

1 Neihardt is best known for writing the as-told-to biography *Black Elk Speaks* (1932) and a series of epic poems about the American west.

2 Much has been written about Hayes's tragic life and early death after returning home from the war to a still highly segregated Arizona. The so-called cult of the Suribachi flag-raising was aided by the 1949 film *Sands of Iwo Jima,* starring John Wayne. For an account of the making of the film as U.S. Marine Corps propaganda and of the controversy surrounding the accuracy of the famous photographs of Hayes's participation in the flag-raising, see Garry Wills, *John Wayne's America,* 149–57. Marder's article, quoted at the head of this chapter, rehearses the history of the Navajo "code talkers" and lists their impressive accomplishments. He states that the marines chose Navajo over other Indian languages because "Navajos were the only Indian group in the United States not infested with German students during the 20 years prior to 1941, when the Germans had been studying tribal dialects under the guise of art students, anthropologists, etc." (25). In this version, indigenous languages are unwitting victims of a sinister, anti-American force; Navajo stands out as the one language resilient against German infestation. Marder thus transforms one of the

Indian languages—all of which were viewed prior to the war as impediments to assimilation—into a secret *American* weapon. In February 2000, Hasbro added a "Navajo Code Talker" to its series of classic G.I. Joe action figures. Navajo G.I. Joe is equipped to speak seven phrases recorded in Navajo by former code talker Sam Billison. For a copy of the official Navajo Code used by the Marines (recently declassified), see Margaret T. Bixler, *Winds of Freedom: The Story of the Navajo Code Talkers of World War II.*

3   Renato Resaldo, in *Culture and Truth: The Remaking of Social Analysis,* defines "imperialist nostalgia" as "a mourning for what one has destroyed" (69). Robert F. Berkhofer Jr., in *The White Man's Indian: Images of the American Indian From Columbus to the Present,* demonstrates the power, appeal, and frequency of images of "the dying Indian" in American art and literature since the eighteenth century.

4   In the 1940s and 1950s, Orland Kay Armstrong, a veteran of World War I, published as a freelancer articles on a wide range of topics in popular journals like the *Reader's Digest, Christian Century,* and *Nation's Business,* as well as in a number of newspapers. Between 1945 and 1959, the *Reader's Digest* published additional articles by Armstrong that address Indian issues. Like "Set the American Indians Free!," these argue for "emancipation" from federal services and advocate integration into mainstream American life. See "Let's Give the Indians Back to the Country" (April 1948), "Indians Are Going to Town" (January 1955, written with Marjorie Armstrong), "Give the Indians an Even Chance!" (November 1955), and "The Navajos Feel the Wind of Progress" (March 1959, condensed from the *Denver Post* [15 February 1959]). For a response to "Set the American Indians Free!," see "Freedom Or Exploitation! Is Mr. O. K. Armstrong's Recent Solution of the American Indian Problem Sound?" by Haven Emerson, M.D., then president of the American Association on Indian Affairs, published in the AAIA's journal, the *American Indian* (fall 1945). The New York–based AAIA began publishing its quarterly journal in 1943; it ran until 1959 and featured the work of a number of well-known writers on Indian cultures and affairs, including Oliver LaFarge, Clyde Kluckhohn, D'Arcy McNickle, Felix S. Cohen, and Sol Tax.

5   Both Collier's personal philosophy and the official policies he implemented emphasized developing Indian economies and civil rights by preserving Indian cultures and by supporting the development of separate Indian identities on the reservations. Collier's opponents accused him of romanticizing Indians and the Indian past and of holding back contemporary Indians' "progress." Under the pressure of such criticisms of himself and of the Indian Reorganization Act he had successfully lobbied Congress to pass in 1934, Collier resigned from his post as commissioner of Indian affairs in January 1945. His romantic ideals and his philosophy of cultural pluralism, however, were not so easily ousted.

6 Riegert was educated at the Haskell Institute, one of the BIA's vocational boarding schools located in Lawrence, Kansas. In 1946 he served as senior clerk at the Red Lake Agency in Minnesota.

7 Alison Bernstein, *American Indians and World War II: Toward a New Era in Indian Affairs,* 58. Bernstein mistitles the poem in her footnote. The lines she quotes are these: "We bind each other's wounds and eat the same ration. / We dream of our loved ones in the same nation."

8 In its retelling of Indian history, the poem appears to be another possible antecedent and possible literary source for the World Council of Indigenous People's 1975 "Solemn Declaration," which I discuss in the Conclusion.

9 Originally, NCAI was to stand for the National Council of American Indians, but the name was changed to the National Congress of American Indians to avoid confusion with an earlier NCAI of that name, founded in 1926 by Gertrude Bonin (Zitkala-Sa) (Sioux). For an account of the original NCAI, see Hazel Hertzberg, *The Search for an American Indian Identity: Modern Pan-Indian Movements,* 207–8. Also see Thomas Cowger, *The National Congress of American Indians: The Founding Years,* 19.

10 Cowger notes in *The National Congress of American Indians* that roughly 80 percent of the founding members of the NCAI had ties to the BIA and that at least four had also been founding members of the Society of American Indians (SAI) in 1911 (41). Greatest participation came from members of the Oklahoma and northern Plains tribes, especially the Sioux (40). Cowger gives a complete list of NCAI officers and members of the executive council (44). Whereas only 10 percent of the original delegates were women, by 1950 women would represent more than half of NCAI membership. At the 1945 convention in Montana, a resolution was passed to elect annually at least one woman to the executive council (41, 53). The NCAI's first national secretary and one of its founding members from Oklahoma was Dan Madrano (Caddo), who had been educated at the Riverside Indian School at Anadarko, Oklahoma, at the Carlisle Indian School at Carlisle, Pennsylvania, and at the National School of Law at Washington, D.C. In 1955 Madrano published a book of humor, *Heap Big Laugh,* that pokes fun at Indians, members of the NCAI, and bureaucrats in Indian Affairs.

11 In late February 1954, for example, the NCAI organized an Emergency Conference in Washington, D.C., to demonstrate Indian opposition to termination legislation. *Indian Truth* reported that two hundred Indian delegates from twenty-one states attended (March–May 1954, 2). The NCAI did not, however, offer radical alternatives. Hoping only to slow the pace of termination, they focused on the specific details of proposed legislation and lobbied for informed Indian consent. See also Cowger, *The National Congress of American Indians,* 114.

12 See Cowger, *The National Congress of American Indians,* 74–75, 157–58.

13   In her youth, Bronson aligned herself with Protestant Christian organizations that ministered to Indians. While attending the University of Kansas, for example, she worked as a student counselor at the Methodist Home for Indian Girls in Lawrence. She joined the federal Indian Service in 1925 after completing her degree at Mount Holyoke College. Her long career with the Office of Indian Affairs included work as an English teacher at the Haskell Institute, also located in Lawrence, and as student guidance officer for the entire Indian Service. Bronson also worked in the area of Indian health education for the Public Health Service. During Deloria's childhood, her father served as an Episcopal priest among the Teton Sioux at St. Elizabeth's Church at Wakpala, South Dakota, on the Standing Rock Reservation. Deloria attended Christian schools in South Dakota; she began her college career at the University of Chicago and Oberlin College and then transferred to Columbia Teachers College, where she earned her bachelor of science degree and began her work with the anthropologist Franz Boas. In 1919 Deloria accepted a position with the YWCA as health education secretary for Indian schools and reservations. In 1923 she went to work at the Haskell Institute in Lawrence, Kansas, where Bronson was also employed in the mid-1920s. Deloria resumed her work with Boas in 1927. Biographical information on Deloria is taken from Agnes Picotte's "Biographical Sketch of the Author" and Raymond J. DeMallie's afterword in the published edition of *Waterlily*, as well as from Vine Deloria Jr.'s introduction to the 1998 edition of *Speaking of Indians*.

14   Deloria began *Waterlily* in 1942 and completed the novel by 1948, although it was not published until 1988.

15   By the mid-1940s, Bronson had aligned herself with the Indian Rights Association, one of the best-known "friends of the Indians" organizations, accepting a position on the Board of Directors and becoming the IRA's Washington correspondent. Founded in Philadelphia in 1882, the IRA described itself during this period as a "nonsectarian and nonpartisan" watchdog organization that sought "to promote the spiritual, moral, and material welfare of the Indians and to protect their Legal Rights" (*Indian Truth*, January/February 1946). Bronson actively promoted the IRA's causes, especially those involving collaboration with Christian missions (see *Indian Truth*, May–June 1944 and May–September 1945). In addition, Bronson also served as secretary and executive director of the NCAI and edited that organization's newsletter, the *Washington Bulletin*. The January–April 1947 issue of *Indian Truth* reports that in her NCAI capacity, Bronson traveled to Alaska in October and November 1946 to offer the Indians there "the resources of [the NCAI] in their fight to establish their property rights in Alaska" (1). Bronson's interest in the Alaskan land, fishing, trapping, and timber rights situation eventually drew accusations

of Communist leanings, and she was subject to a formal congressional investigation (*Indian Truth,* January–April 1960, 2). See also Cowger, *The National Congress of American Indians,* 57, 59. For a fuller description of the IRA and its journal, *Indian Truth,* see Daniel F. Littlefield Jr. and James W. Parins, eds., *American Indian and Alaska Native Newspapers and Periodicals,* 1:235–42.

16 While completing her teaching degree at Columbia University, Deloria met anthropologist Franz Boas and many of his students, including Ruth Benedict, an introduction that would greatly affect the trajectory of her writing career. Until Boas's death in 1942, Deloria worked with him on a range of anthropological and linguistic projects, resulting in a number of published articles and several books, including *Dakota Texts* (1932), *Dakota Grammar* (1941), and *Speaking of Indians* (1944). In the late 1930s and early 1940s, Deloria also was involved in academic projects among the Navajo and the Lumbee sponsored by the BIA. And, like Bronson, Deloria became during this period a popular figure on the Indian lecture circuit. See DeMallie, afterword to *Waterlily,* 238–39.

17 Moreover, Deloria's book is dedicated to one of her former teachers and "a great missionary." In her acknowledgments, she lists another missionary teacher (who served as the YWCA secretary for Indian work) and the Missionary Education Movement as important influences. Throughout the body of the text, Deloria also acknowledges the influence of Boas, several times quoting his work at length.

18 Deloria's imaginative account of migration from Asia anticipates a similar imaginative account written by Deloria's contemporary D'Arcy McNickle in his first book-length work of nonfiction, *They Came Here First: The Epic of the American Indian* (1949); see the first chapter of McNickle's book and my discussion below. Deloria's account also anticipates N. Scott Momaday's controversial statement that he has "a [personal] sense of the Kiowas' existence as a people from the time they lived in Asia to the present day." "There are times," Momaday states further, "when I think about people walking on ice with dogs pulling travois, and I don't know whether it's something that I'm imagining or something that I remember. But it comes down to the same thing"; see Charles L. Woodard, *Ancestral Voice: Conversations with N. Scott Momaday,* 21–22, and my discussion in chapter 4.

19 James Clifford, *The Predicament of Culture: Twentieth-Century Ethnography, Literature, and Art,* 93.

20 In his afterword, DeMallie reports that Ruth Benedict's sudden death in 1948 "deprived Deloria of the professional assistance she needed" to get *Waterlily* published (240). In any event, Deloria's own attempts to publish the novel in the late 1940s and early 1950s failed. Both commercial and university presses returned the manuscript, praising its ethnographic material but worrying that there was not a large enough reading public for

such a book (240–41). After Deloria's death in 1971, the manuscript was
entrusted to the Dakota Indian Foundation in Chamberlain, South Dakota. Agnes Picotte, director of the Ella C. Deloria Project, also in Chamberlain, brought the manuscript to the attention of the University of
Nebraska Press in the 1980s.

21 DeMallie, for instance, places *Waterlily* in the context of Boasian anthropology in the 1930s and 1940s. He notes Deloria's unique "insider's perspective" and praises the novel as "a major contribution to understanding
women in traditional Sioux culture." What makes the novel of interest
today, he writes, is that "It represents a blurring of categories: in conception it is fundamentally a work of ethnographic description, but in its
method it is narrative fiction, a plot invented to provide a plausible range
of situations that reveal how cultural ideals shaped the behavior of individual Sioux people in social interactions." It is clear which category
DeMallie considers of paramount importance: "For above all, Ella Deloria's work . . . has provided the data and insight from which we can come to
understand the Sioux people of the last century in the way that she intended, as fellow human beings" (DeMallie, afterword to *Waterlily,* 233,
241, 243).

22 Clifford, *The Predicament of Culture,* 110.

23 See my discussion in chapter 4.

24 See my discussions in chapters 4 and 3, respectively.

25 See Virginia H. Mathews, introduction to *Sundown,* ix; A. LaVonne
Brown Ruoff, *American Indian Literatures: An Introduction, Bibliographic
Review, and Selected Bibliography,* 58; Robert Allen Warrior, *Tribal Secrets:
Recovering American Indian Intellectual Traditions,* 25; Louis Owens, *Other
Destinies: Understanding the American Indian Novel,* 50.

26 Warrior, *Tribal Secrets,* 60; N. Scott Momaday, "The Man Made of
Words," 52.

27 Mathews's "activism," such as it was, was distinctly local. He was well
educated, with degrees from the University of Oklahoma and Oxford, and
he was well traveled beyond the confines of the reservation where he had
been born and raised. But, unlike Bronson and Deloria or their contemporary D'Arcy McNickle, he was not heavily involved with national Indian rights organizations, government bureaus, or religious institutions.
From 1934 until 1942 he served on the Osage Tribal Council, regularly
making trips to Washington, D.C., to attend to the business of the people.
He also was responsible for the creation of a tribal museum and the
"conservation" of artifacts, including the commissioning of an artist to
paint portraits of Osage elders.

28 By the time Mathews was a child, the Osage had already largely converted
from the "religion of Wah'Kon-Tah" to the syncretic peyote religion,
which Mathews clearly views as nontraditional, despite its incorporation

of older Osage elements as well as elements of Christianity. Mathews describes the work of the Christian missions in colonizing and militaristic terms: "this cleaning-up activity of militant, devouring Christianity . . . the cleaning-out of the machine-gun nests of the native religion, and the gradual roundup of the guerrillas left in odd corners as the advance sweeps on" (84). He also comments that the Osage elders no longer like to speak of the old religion, because it "failed before the stronger religion of the white man, [and] it can do no more than cause death; it has nothing to do with living now" (85).

29 Like Bronson and Deloria, McNickle had strong ties to powerful public institutions. John Collier hired him to work for Indian Affairs in 1936; he became an outspoken supporter of Collier's ideals and continued to serve in various capacities in Indian Affairs even after Collier's resignation, until 1954. At different points in his career, McNickle worked as an educator in both community and university settings.

30 Paul Chaat Smith and Robert Allen Warrior, *Like a Hurricane: The Indian Movement from Alcatraz to Wounded Knee,* 40.

31 See John Lloyd Purdy, *Word Ways: The Novels of D'Arcy McNickle,* 86; Jay Hansford C. Vest, "A Legend of Culture: D'Arcy McNickle's *Runner in the Sun,*" 160; and Alfonso Ortiz, afterword to *Runner in the Sun,* 239, 242.

32 Deloria's *Speaking of Indians* follows a similar division of American Indian history.

33 Many readers will recognize Quail's tattoo—"a small circle, with parallel lines shooting away in the four directions"—as the American Indian sun symbol used as an official emblem by the state of New Mexico. Perhaps this is McNickle's subtle connection between prehistory and the present. If so, McNickle invites readers to expand their vision of "America" even further, to accommodate ongoing trade and movement between the Americas into their conception of American history.

34 See Cowger, *The National Congress of American Indians,* 135–36, for an account of Indian opposition to the NCAI's involvement in the AICC, particularly from several eastern tribal groups, who objected to the NCAI's emphasis on U.S. citizenship and "white" institutional practices.

35 The IRA promoted the creation of U.S.-style tribal governments and tribal constitutions and encouraged Indian nations to hold referenda to decide whether or not they wished to adopt new policies.

36 The *Declaration* argues that its recommendations are "comparable in scope and purpose to the Indian Trade and Intercourse Act of June 30, 1834 . . . and the Indian Reorganization Act of June 18, 1934, which recognized the inherent powers of Indian Tribes" (5).

37 Indians also served in the Korean War (1950–53) but their participation in this conflict, like that of other Americans, appears to have been celebrated much less than their participation in the earlier war.

38 It is useful to recall that Bronson's involvement in Alaskan Indian affairs roused suspicion of her having Communist leanings.

39 The Southwest Regional Indian Youth Council was a pan-Indian organization founded in 1955 in New Mexico to promote Indian education.

An Indigenous Renaissance

1   Rupert Costo, "Moment of Truth for the American Indian," 5–6.

2   M. Annette Jaimes Guerrero, "Academic Apartheid: American Indian Studies and 'Multiculturalism,'" 56.

3   Elizabeth Cook-Lynn, "Intellectualism and the New Indian Story," 127. Cook-Lynn makes similar statements in her *Anti-Indianism in Modern America.*

4   Ranginui Walker, "Capitalism v. Tangata Whenua," *New Zealand Listener,* 24 July 1982; reprinted in Walker, *Nga Tau Tohetohe: Years of Anger,* 221.

5   In her introduction to Kaplan and Pease, eds., *Cultures of United States Imperialism,* Amy Kaplan argues that "The critical force of multiculturalism thus may lay itself open to recuperation by a renewed version of 'consensus'" (15). For more extended critiques of multiculturalist paradigms, see Chidi Okonkwo, *Decolonization Agonistics in Postcolonial Fiction,* esp. 7–10, and E. San Juan Jr., *Beyond Postcolonial Theory,* esp. chapter 4, "The Multicultural Imaginary: Problematizing Identity and the Ideology of Racism."

6   In "Multicultural Conditions," the introduction to his edited volume *Multiculturalism: A Critical Reader,* David Theo Goldberg states that "Movement and migration, it could be said, are the defining sociohistorical conditions of humanity" (22). While this statement may be true at a high level of abstraction, its use as a justification for a multiculturalist paradigm implicitly devalues any contemporary claim to the moral and political priority of indigenous (nation) status, and it tends to obscure rather than illuminate particular historical conditions. Seemingly neutral terms like "movement" and "migration" too easily become euphemisms for what are, from an indigenous minority perspective, histories of violent conquest, theft, and aggressive settlement.

7   Some activists and scholars argue that this description should include Chicanos as well as American Indians in the United States.

8   Wendy Brown, "Wounded Attachments," 59.

9   Stuart Hall, "The Local and the Global: Globalization and Ethnicity," 28.

10 See, for instance, Charles Taylor's celebrated 1992 essay "The Politics of Recognition."

11 Paul Havemann, ed., *Indigenous Peoples' Rights in Australia, Canada, and New Zealand,* 472. Havemann (473) quotes Will Kymlicka's suggestion of

three types of supplemental citizenship rights for indigenous peoples: (1) self-government rights, (2) polyethnic rights, and (3) special representation rights.

12 Ranginui Walker, *Ka Whawhai Tonu Matou*, 207.

13 Ibid., 211. In 1971 Nga Tamatoa had warned the government "that unless the Treaty was ratified the Maori would declare Waitangi a day of mourning" (Ranginui Walker, "The Treaty of Waitangi as the Focus of Māori Protest," 276). In 1973 the Treaty remained unratified and Parliament changed the official name of the holiday, which is held on 6 February, from Waitangi Day to New Zealand Day, prompting the protest action (Walker, *Ka Whawhai Tonu Matou*, 211). Although the Treaty remains unratified, due largely to conflicting points of view about the relationship among its versions and about the potential ramifications of its implementation, the holiday's original name has been restored.

14 See above, n. 23 of chapter 1.

15 Based on its findings, the Waitangi Tribunal was authorized to make nonbinding recommendations to Parliament for settlement. However, the initial legislation authorized the tribunal only to investigate claims for Treaty violations that occurred after 1975. It would take another decade before a legislative amendment extended the tribunal's jurisdiction back to 1840. Over time, the Waitangi Tribunal has developed in its official reports a number of principles for interpreting the Treaty. These "relevant principles" state, among other things, that the tribunal should "treat neither text as superior but . . . give considerable weight to the much more numerously signed Maori version (this was supported by the American Supreme Court's 'indulgent rule' by which treaties with indigenous peoples should be construed in the sense in which these people would have understood them)" and that the tribunal should "apply the 'contra proferentum rule' by which ambiguities should be construed *against* the party framing the provision in question" (W. H. Oliver, *Claims to the Waitangi Tribunal*, 78).

16 In the 1990s Ihimaera continued his commitment to bring a wide range of Maori voices to large audiences by editing the ambitious, five-volume *Te Ao Marama* (world of light) series of anthologies, which presents not only contemporary Maori fiction, poetry, and drama but also nonfiction essays and political writing, plus writing specifically for children.

17 Tom Holm, *Strong Hearts, Wounded Souls: Native American Veterans of the Vietnam War*, 122.

18 In its introduction to *Voices from Wounded Knee, 1973, in the Words of the Participants*, the editorial collective of Akwesasne Notes remarks that "All of us were involved in the anti-war movement; one of us is a Vietnam veteran" (2). Throughout the text, the editors identify American Indian and other participants in the occupation who were Vietnam veterans;

several veterans were interviewed about the connections they saw between Vietnam and Wounded Knee (194–201).

19 For a full account, see Troy R. Johnson, *The Occupation of Alcatraz Island: Indian Self-Determination and the Rise of Indian Activism,* 16–27.

20 It is important to note the high level of disagreement among American Indian leaders, scholars, and activists over the meaning and usefulness of the term "Red Power." Some conservative Indians, for instance, worried about the term's potential Communist connotations. Others thought "Red Power" described a Black Power–style militancy, whereas to them a term like "Indian Power" described action guided by more traditional American Indian methods. See Beatrice Medicine, "Red Power: Real or Potential?"

21 "Statement of Policy," *Indian Historian* 1.1 (October 1964).

22 "Days to Remember," *Indian Historian* 2.2 (Summer 1969): 37.

23 "Statement of Policy," *Indian Historian* 1.1 (October 1964).

24 See Ruth Roessel (Navajo), *Navajo Studies at Navajo Community College,* for a description of the early focus and curriculum of the college.

25 Vine Deloria Jr., *Behind the Trail of Broken Treaties: An Indian Declaration of Independence,* 35. Also see Littlefield and Parins, *American Indian and Alaska Native Newspapers and Periodicals,* vol. 2, 8–10.

26 Sidney Mills, "I Choose to Serve My People." See also "Statement by Sid Mills."

27 Shirley Hill Witt and Stan Steiner have reprinted several statements of American Indian anti–Vietnam War sentiment in *The Way: An Anthology of American Indian Literature*; see 202–8.

28 The same issue contains an editorial titled "Genocide," which states, "Indian people were horrified but not surprised at the revelation of the Mi Lai Massacre in South Vietnam. Seeing the bloody mutilated bodies in *Life* magazine brought back the memory of events in the not too distant past of this country" (2).

29 Wendy Rose, "The Long Root," reprinted in her *Bone Dance: New And Selected Poems, 1965–1993,* 4.

30 American Indian activists targeted Plymouth Rock in Massachusetts for Thanksgiving Day protest in 1972.

31 Joane Nagel, "The Political Mobilization of Native Americans," 43.

32 Deloria notes the controversy over Chief Red Fox's Indian authenticity in *God Is Red,* 307 n. 4. Red Fox was also accused of plagiarism; see Henry Raymont, "Doubt Is Cast on McGraw-Hill's 'Memoirs of Red Fox.' "

33 *Wassaja,* the national newspaper produced by the Indian Historical Society, was particularly critical of the mass media's portrayal of the Wounded Knee occupation. See Jeannette Henry, "The Mass Media on Wounded Knee." In its March 1976 issue, the newspaper published a letter to the editor from Maurice D. Bird, a Maori living in Rotorua, Aotearoa/New

Zealand. A regular subscriber to *Wassaja,* Bird reports on the 1975 Maori
Land March and makes connections between that event and Indian activism in the United States.

34 Robert Allen Warrior argues that, like John Joseph Mathews in the previous generation, Deloria "contend[s] in [his] work that the success or
failure of American Indian communal societies has always been predicated
not upon a set of uniform, unchanging beliefs, but rather upon a commitment to the groups and the groups' future" (*Tribal Secrets: Recovering
American Indian Intellectual Traditions,* xx). Deloria has remained a prolific writer and commentator on Indian affairs, and he played a significant
role in the development of the growing field of American Indian legal and
political studies in the 1980s and 1990s.

35 See Daniel Littlefield and James Parins, *American Indian and Alaska Native Newspapers and Periodicals.* Some of the more than eight hundred
publications continue to be produced, while many others were short-
lived. In the appendix I list several that were of national significance.

3 Rebuilding the Ancestor

1 Hone Tuwhare, "On a Theme by Hone Taiapa," in *Deep River Talk:
Collected Poems,* 87.

2 Maori poet and scholar Hirini Melbourne makes the similar point that
"The ancient Maori were surrounded by writing in their daily life: the
carvings on posts and houses, the marks on cloaks, the very architecture of
the great meeting houses. The fact that texts—compositions, speeches,
ritual replies, and so forth—were memorized, not written down, does not
mean that the ancient Maori inhabited a world from which writing was
absent" ("Whare Whakairo: Maori 'Literary' Traditions," 132).

3 Whina Cooper, now deceased, received knighthood in 1981 and is often
referred to as Dame Whina Cooper. A group of Maori protestors, feeling
Cooper had "sold out," attempted to stop her investiture ceremony.

4 Anne Salmond, "Nga Huarahi O Te Ao Maori: Pathways in the Maori
World," 112.

5 Cleve Barlow, *Tikanga Whakaaro: Key Concepts in Maori Culture,* 175.

6 Salmond, "Nga Huarahi O Te Ao Maori," 112.

7 See Joan Metge, *The Maoris of New Zealand: Ruatahi*; Erik Schwimmer,
ed., *The Maori People in the Nineteen-Sixties: A Symposium*; and Anne
Salmond, *Hui: A Study of Maori Ceremonial Gatherings.*

8 I. H. Kawharu, personal communication, 23 June 1994.

9 Melbourne, "Whare Whakairo: Maori 'Literary' Traditions," 135–36.

10 See my discussion of *Waterlily* in chapter 2.

11 *Facts New Zealand,* 117.

12 Bruce Biggs, "Humpty-Dumpty and the Treaty of Waitangi," 308.

13 I. H. Kawharu, *Waitangi: Maori and Pakeha Perspectives of the Treaty of Waitangi,* 320 n. 8.

14 Mason Durie, "The Treaty of Waitangi—Perspectives on Social Policy," 282.

15 Sidney Moko Mead, "Nga Timunga Me Nga Paringa O Te Mana Maori: The Ebb and Flow of Mana Maori and the Changing Context of Maori Art," 21–23.

16 David V. Williams, "Te Tiriti o Waitangi—Unique Relationship Between Crown and Tangata Whenua?" 81.

17 Biggs, "Humpty-Dumpty and the Treaty of Waitangi," 307.

18 W. H. Oliver, *Claims to the Waitangi Tribunal,* 26.

19 Ibid., 66–67.

20 Terrence Barrow, *An Illustrated Guide to Maori Art,* 90–92.

21 Ihimaera's description of the patu pounamu swimming through water also draws on a Maori tradition that certain spiritually potent objects carved from greenstone possess the ability to travel through water of their own volition.

22 Barlow, *Tikanga Whakaaro,* 147.

23 Ihimaera includes the detail that the young woman and her Pakeha husband live in one of Wellington's many suburbs, Porirua, which translates into English as "two peoples"—another possible reference to treaty discourse.

24 As a noun, Toki's name translates into English as "axe" or "adze" (traditionally made of stone), suggesting, perhaps, Toki's identification with the taonga in this scene. As a verb, *toki* can translate into English as "chop" (as with an axe) but also as "fetch," the latter being consonant with Toki's role in this scene in relation to the taonga.

25 Hemi is a transliteration of James; as a noun, Roimata translates into English as "tears" or "present made to bereaved persons."

26 Birth order is highly significant in Maori traditions. As Margaret Orbell points out, Maui, like other heroes in mythology, "acts vigorously to overcome his low status as the youngest son" (*A Concise Encyclopedia of Maori Myth and Legend,* 84). In addition to his status and the circumstances of his birth, other details of Toko's life align with the Maui stories.

27 See Ranginui Walker, *Ka Whawhai Tonu Matou: Struggle without End,* 15; Queenie Rikihana Hyland, *Paki Waitara: Myths and Legends of the Maori,* 19–23; Antony Alpers, *Maori Myths and Tribal Legends,* 28–36; Orbell, *A Concise Encyclopedia of Maori Myth and Legend,* 83–84.

28 Rongopai is an actual meeting house, located in the village of Waituhi on the North Island's east coast, Witi Ihimaera's family home. Built in 1887 in anticipation of a visit to the east coast by the Maori prophet and "rebel" leader Te Kooti, Rongopai is one of a number of meeting houses built after 1870 that include figurative paintings in their decorations in place of

traditional carvings of ancestors. Rongopai remains one of the best examples of what is considered the "second phase" of Maori figurative painting, which began about 1885. The strangeness of the paintings rendered the house tapu (restricted) until 1963, with the result that no one was allowed to alter any of the paintings. Since the lifting of the tapu, many of Rongopai's deteriorating paintings have been restored. See Roger Neich's discussion of Rongopai in *Painted Histories: Early Maori Figurative Painting.*

29 Though far more elaborately developed, the plot of Ihimaera's novel *Tangi* is reminiscent of the plot of J. H. Moffatt's short story "The Homecoming," published in issue 56 of *Te Ao Hou* (September 1966), which I discuss at the end of chapter 1.

30 This aspect of *Whanau* can be read as a reworking of the plot of Ihimaera's short story "The Whale," which I discuss above.

31 In his 1975 statement titled "Why I Write," Ihimaera says that "Mine is not essentially an activist approach and I have been accused of not being 'political' enough or critical enough of our Pakeha-dominated society. . . . But I say my work is political because it is exclusively Maori, the criticism of Pakeha society is implicit in the representation of an exclusively Maori values system, and I am concerned with the greatest problem we have—that of retaining our emotional identity—rather than the more individual but also very real social problems some of us face today. My concern is for the roots of our culture, the culture we carry within ourselves and which makes us truly Maori" (117).

32 Like Toko in *Potiki,* Simon is a Maui figure, a mysterious mute Pakeha boy Joe found washed up on the beach.

33 John Rangihau, in "Being Maori," states that "Maoris have a saying that you walk into a meeting house and you feel the warmth of it because you know that meeting house is named after an ancestor. And you are amidst people who have passed on. All the things they have said over the years are echoing through the meeting house and you immediately feel a warmth" (170).

34 For example: "Every day the sounds came closer until one day we could see the yellow cuttings that the yellow machines had made, and the yellow clothes and the yellow hard hats that the men wore who worked the yellow machines" (106). Though written entirely in English, this passage draws attention because of its repetition of "yellow," which connects the destruction of the "yellow" land to the "yellow" machines and "yellow" men causing that destruction. For the bilingual reader, the repetition is suggestive on another level as well. One of the Maori words for yellow is renga. As an adjective, *renga* can mean "yellow" or "light-colored," but also, when discussing water, it can mean "discolored" or "turbid"—a reference to earlier scenes in the novel when the developers pollute the ocean with runoff from their digging in the hills and when they dam the stream with rocks in order to flood the family's gardens and cemetery with muddy

water. As an adjective *renga* can also mean "scattered about"—a reference to the developers' attempts to dislocate the Maori through their various tactics. When used as a verb, *renga* means to "overflow" or "fill up"— another reference to the flooding. *Renga* can also be doubled as *rengarenga*. As an adjective, in addition to "scattered about," *rengarenga* can mean "crushed," "pounded," "destroyed," and "beaten," as well as "strident" and "raucous." All of these meanings resonate in the specific scene and in the novel as a whole. Grace's bilingual punning creates a third text in the interplay between the meanings *yellow* accrues in this scene and the potential meanings of *renga.*

35 Bill Ashcroft, Gareth Griffiths, and Helen Tiffin, in *The Empire Writes Back,* describe the insertion of this type of vernacular into a "postcolonial" text "as a linguistic variant to signify the insertion of the outsider into the discourse" (57).

36 Literally, tihei mauriora translates as "the sneeze of life." In English, this "sneeze" is referred to as a baby's first cry.

37 Barrow, *An Illustrated Guide to Maori Art,* 35–36.

38 The god of war is also named Tu or Tumatauenga.

39 Although less than 15 percent of the total population, Maori make up nearly half of New Zealand's prison population. In addition, the New Zealand Department of Statistics reports that "In 1990, 6% of Maori men aged 20 to 24 were received into prison under sentence, compared to 0.7% of the equivalent non-Maori population. Among women aged 20 to 24 years, 8% of Maori were received into prison under sentence, compared with 5% of non-Maori"; see *Facts New Zealand,* 124.

40 I am rephrasing a point made in Homi Bhabha's *The Location of Culture:* "Such art does not merely recall the past as social cause or aesthetic precedent; it renews the past, refiguring it as a contingent 'in-between' space, that innovates and interrupts the performance of the present" (7).

41 Salmond, "Nga Huarahi O Te Ao Maori," 120.

42 Tama or Tamatea appears frequently as a protagonist in the work of Ihimaera as well as Stewart. These may be references to one of the many Tamas in Maori myth and legend traditions; see Orbell, *A Concise Encyclopedia of Maori Myth and Legend,* 140–44.

43 Mead, "Nga Timunga Me Nga Paringa O Te Mana Maori," 23.

44 Judith Binney, "Maori Oral Narratives, Pakeha Written Texts: Two Forms of Telling History," 17.

4 Blood/Land/Memory

1 "NIYC Dictionary," *Americans Before Columbus* 3.2 (August–October 1971): 6. More recently, Elizabeth Cook-Lynn (Sioux), in *Why I Can't Read Wallace Stegner and Other Essays,* reiterates Deloria's and the NIYC's points

about Indian invisibility and stereotypes, writing that "Indigenous peoples are no longer in charge of what is imagined about them, and this means that they can no longer freely imagine themselves as they once were and as they might become" (143).

2   See especially Kenneth Lincoln, *Native American Renaissance;* A. LaVonne Brown Ruoff, *American Indian Literatures: An Introduction, Bibliographic Review, and Selected Bibliography;* Louis Owens, *Other Destinies: Understanding the American Indian Novel;* Robert Allen Warrior, *Tribal Secrets: Recovering American Indian Intellectual Traditions;* Jace Weaver, *That the People Might Live: Native American Literatures and Native American Community;* and Kenneth M. Roemer, introduction to *Native American Writers of the United States.*

3   The proclamation was published under the title "We Hold the Rock" in *Alcatraz Indians of All Tribes Newsletter* 1.1 (January 1970); it was reprinted as an appendix to Vine Deloria Jr.'s *God Is Red,* 317–18, and in Shirley Hill Witt and Stan Steiner's *The Way: An Anthology of American Indian Literature,* 232–35, as well as in other publications. The proclamation itself is reprinted in the National Indian Youth Council's journal *Americans Before Columbus* 2.1 (December 1969–January 1970), 8; and in *Red Power: The American Indians' Fight for Freedom,* 2d ed., ed. Alvin M. Josephy Jr., Joane Nagel, and Troy Johnson, 39–43. Josephy et al. include a list of references for accounts of the occupation.

4   See "Introduction" n. 26.

5   See Robert A. Williams Jr., *Linking Arms Together: American Indian Treaty Visions of Law and Peace, 1600–1800,* for a detailed analysis of the "identifiable idioms, symbols, and metaphors that proliferate in the treaty literature involving some of the major Indian tribal groupings of eastern North America during the seventeenth and eighteenth centuries" (38–39).

6   In his *American Indians, Time, and the Law: Native Societies in a Modern Constitutional Democracy,* Wilkinson describes the complexity of treaty documents and their negotiations: "These documents, and the discussions leading up to them, have an opaque quality that evidences the obstacles facing federal and tribal representatives in the field. The difficulties far outstripped the fact that the negotiations usually were required to be conducted through interpreters. Well beyond that, these negotiators were people with radically different world views. They had fundamentally divergent ways of conceptualizing the very things that had forced them together: land, religion, trade, political power, family, and natural resources. . . . In the largest sense, there was a gulf that no document could bridge" (15).

7   Article 1, Treaty with the Creeks, Washington [D.C.], 1866, in *Rifle, Blanket and Kettle: Selected Indian Treaties and Laws,* ed. Frederick E. Hosen, 109. Similarly, Article 1 of the Treaty with the Western Shoshoni, 1863, begins "Peace and friendship shall be hereafter established and main-

tained between the Western Shoshonee nation and the people and Government of the United States" (105). Article 1 of the Treaty with the Blackfeet, 1855, begins "Peace, friendship and amity shall hereafter exist between the United States and the aforesaid nations and tribes of Indians, parties to this treaty, and the same shall be perpetual" (99).

8 Treaty with the Sioux and Arapaho, 1868, in *Rifle, Blanket and Kettle,* ed. Hosen, 124.

9 Ibid., 123.

10 Ibid., 128.

11 Treaty with the Western Shoshoni, 1863, in *Rifle, Blanket and Kettle,* ed. Hosen, 105.

12 Treaty with the Oto and Missouri Indians, 1854, in *Documents of United States Indian Policy,* 2d ed., ed. Francis Paul Prucha, 89.

13 In *American Indians, Time, and the Law,* Wilkinson notes that even President Andrew Jackson, who opposed making treaties with Indian nations on principle and who was largely responsible for the implementation of Indian removal policies, "found nothing anomalous about recognizing and protecting tribal self-government in the new homelands. Thus he said that the Indians were to have 'governments of their own choice, subject to no other control from the United States than such as may be necessary to preserve peace on the frontier and between the several tribes' " (17).

14 Williams argues in *Linking Arms Together* that "kinship terms had precisely understood meanings" for American Indians who negotiated treaties during the Encounter era (early 16th through the late 18th centuries) and that these terms for kinship "were used to define the expected forms of behavior among treaty partners" (71). Obviously, precise meanings for kinship terms have been lost in the developing tradition of language use popularly associated with treaties.

15 In the American Indian Historical Society's volume *Textbooks and the American Indian,* Rupert Costo and Jeannette Henry present the findings of their examination of more than three hundred textbooks then in use in public primary and secondary schools. "Not one," they report, "could be approved as a dependable source of knowledge about the history and culture of the Indian people in America" (11). Describing a government and citizenship textbook used not only in public schools but also in schools run by the Bureau of Indian Affairs, they report that "There is no mention of treaties and treaty making with the Indians" (124). In a subsequent volume, *Indian Treaties: Two Centuries of Dishonor,* Costo and Henry write, "There is no knowledge on the part of the general public, and little understanding on the part of the educational community, of the treaties. . . . This is due to the wretched poverty of this nation's educational system, a state of illiteracy frightening to behold" (v).

16 I examine a specific example in "Hero With Two Faces: The Lone Ranger as Treaty Discourse."

17 See, for example, Costo and Henry, *Indian Treaties,* x. The American Indian International Treaty Council was created in 1974; in 1977, it was granted nongovernmental organization (NGO) status in the United Nations; see Vine Deloria Jr. and Clifford Lytle, *The Nations Within: The Past and Future of American Indian Sovereignty,* 241.

18 Williams, in *Linking Arms Together,* details a number of the rituals by which a treaty document might become a "sacred text" (47) and a "living reality" during the Encounter era (61). Indian individuals and groups, however, have always disagreed over the sacredness of treaties. In the Canadian context, for example, Howard Adams (Métis) argues in *Prison of Grass: Canada from the Native Point of View* that treaties are "contracts of continuing oppression," and that "When Indians hold the treaties as sacred testaments, the process of colonization is indeed complete" (73).

19 Deloria and Lytle explain in *The Nations Within* "how the idea of the treaty became so sacred to Indians that even today, more than a century after most of the treaties were made, Indians still refer to the provisions as if the agreement were made last week. The treaty, for most tribes, was a sacred pledge made by one people to another and required no more than the integrity of each party for enforcement. That the United States quickly insisted that the treaties should be interpreted rigidly as strictly legal documents has galled succeeding generations of Indians and made permanent peace between Indians and the federal government impossible" (8). D'Arcy McNickle explores how American Indians responded to the threat of termination policies in *Native American Tribalism: Indian Survivals and Renewals.* "A suggestion that their treaties might be denounced brought consternation to the Indians," McNickle writes, "for the treaties, like the land base itself, had acquired a symbolic value with which the tribes could associate their continuing existence. The treaties made them a distinctive people, the abrogation of which would cut them off from their own past" (105–6).

20 See Deloria and Lytle, *The Nations Within,* 236; Prucha, *American Indian Treaties,* 411.

21 See Vine Deloria Jr., *Behind the Trail of Broken Treaties: An Indian Declaration of Independence,* 77–78; Prucha, *American Indian Treaties,* 415–16. The autobiography of American Indian activist Russell Means (Sioux), *Where White Men Fear to Tread,* written with Marvin J. Wolf, features copies of original pages from the 1868 Fort Laramie Treaty as endpapers. Means asserts his authority to speak by literally placing his words between the leaves of this historical document.

22 Prucha, *Documents of United States Indian Policy,* 110.

23 Prucha, *American Indian Treaties,* 283. See also Vine Deloria Jr., "The Theological Dimension of the Indian Protest Movement," in *For This Land: Writings on Religion in America,* 32–33.

24 Similarly, a brief article published in the December 1969–January 1970

issue of the National Indian Youth Council's journal *Americans Before Columbus* employs the metaphors popularly associated with the U.S. government's treaty promises for the purposes of emphasizing American Indian decline and re-recognizing American Indian sovereignty. See Tommy Belt (Cherokee), " 'For as Long as the Rivers Shall Run, and the Grasses Shall Grow.' " Hanay Geiogamah, in his play "Foghorn," originally performed in 1973, emphasizes this decline with a recitation of part of the Alcatraz Proclamation, as well as with a parodic scene in which a list of specific treaties is written on a roll of toilet paper. *Akwesasne Notes,* the national newspaper produced by the Mohawk nation, published a number of political cartoons lampooning the federal government's inability to honor its treaty promises. In September 1969 it published a cartoon by Soop titled "A Dark Picture of Treaties." Against a black background, one Indian says, "Limping Bear, the water ain't moving!" His friend replies, "Dat not all—ain't no grass growin'!" In January 1973 it published a cartoon by G.B.M. in which a BIA official, sitting under a portrait of General Custer and at a desk covered with documents spilling into a wastebasket, asks a group of Indians, "Why should we honor these treaties? We have what we want now. What more can you give us?" The three Indians respond, "Trouble. And we keep our promises." And in late spring 1978 the newspaper published a cartoon by R. Diggs in which a treaty document is drawn as a large rug. The Indian standing on it asks, "What's this! ANOTHER new treaty?" The white man about to pull the rug out from under him replies, "Yes, but THIS time we'll keep our word!" *Wassaja,* the national newspaper published by the American Indian Historical Society, reprinted the text of the Treaty of 1868 in April–May 1973 and again in July 1973 as part of a special supplement on Indian treaties. In its October 1976 issue it reprinted an article from the Cheyenne newspaper *Tsistsistas Press,* titled "Indians on Mars?" The article describes the testing of the Viking I Mars probe on Cheyenne land and reports that an older Cheyenne claims there are Indians on the red planet; he wants to record a message to be carried by Viking I that translates into English: "Be cautious of these men, they will try to make a treaty with you" (6). *Wassaja* published cartoons by Jim Hathaway in May and June 1978 that continue these themes. In the May cartoon an overweight White politician uses a document marked "Indian Treaty" to light his cigar. In the June cartoon a U.S. cavalry officer tells his sergeant, "I wouldn't worry too much about the extra ammo, Sgt., just be sure we got plenty of blank Indian treaties!" In 1978 the San Francisco-based Indian activist group United Native Americans echoed the Alcatraz Proclamation in a parodic statement titled "Bureau of Caucasian Affairs."

25   Martin A. Link, ed., *Navajo: A Century of Progress, 1868–1968.* Link also assisted with the production of a commemorative pamphlet, *Treaty Be-*

tween the United States of America and the Navajo Tribe of Indians, With a Record of the Discussions that Led to its Signing (1968).

26   In this period the Navajo nation produced other texts that commemorate the Long Walk and the internment at Fort Sumner, including *Navajo Stories of the Long Walk Period,* a collection of oral histories published by the Navajo Community College Press in 1973.

27   The chapters that follow (in *Navajo: A Century of Progress, 1868–1968*) record the progress—along with the setbacks—of the Navajo since the signing of the treaty, including the return of additional lands and the expansion of the reservation in 1878, 1880, 1882, and 1884 (11). The final chapter pointedly contrasts the actions of the self-governing Navajo nation with the actions of protestors: "these programs . . . are being accomplished by determination and hard work—not by resorting to riots, sit-ins, and flower waving!" (55).

28   Momaday's literary achievement has meant that most critics have been uninterested in Chief Eagle's work. An exception is Charles R. Larson, who includes a discussion of *Winter Count* in his early study *American Indian Fiction;* see especially 100–112. In *Medicine Talk: A Guide to Walking in Balance and Surviving on the Earth Mother,* Brad Steiger includes an interview he conducted with Chief Eagle in 1973 (this interview is the basis for much of Larson's commentary). Steiger reports that Chief Eagle wrote *Winter Count* over a period of four years and that he is also an accomplished painter. Chief Eagle was born on the Rosebud Sioux Reservation in South Dakota. During World War II, he served in the U.S. Marine Corps from 1942 until 1945. At the time of the interview with Steiger, Chief Eagle was living in Pierre, South Dakota, working as director of tourism for the Development Corporation of the United Sioux Tribes of South Dakota.

29   Evensigh is constructed explicitly as an orphaned White rather than as a White captive.

30   Welch's horrific details of the massacre evoke the more infamous tragedy of the Southern Cheyenne at Sand Creek, Colorado, on 29 November 1864. Black Kettle's attempt to shield his people behind President Lincoln's verbal promise of friendship, the raised stars and stripes, and a white flag of peace ended in a similar slaughter.

31   Welch recounts the events leading up to the massacre on the Marias in more detail and describes his and friends' successful efforts to locate the massacre site in 1985 in his nonfiction work, written with Paul Stekler, *Killing Custer: The Battle of the Little Bighorn and the Fate of the Plains Indians;* see 25–47. The available historical record supports Welch's depiction of this event on the Marias. John C. Ewers reports, in *The Blackfeet: Raiders on the Northwestern Plains,* that "The Indians have claimed that as soon as Heavy Runner learned troops were approaching [his camp on the

Marias River], he walked out alone to meet them, and that he was holding up his hands and waving his identification paper when a soldier shot him dead" (250). Other American Indian novelists have followed Welch's lead in depicting the cavalry's disregard for treaties. See, in particular, Thomas King's (Cherokee) 1993 comic novel, *Green Grass, Running Water,* 150.

32 More recently, Diane Glancy (Cherokee) has coupled the discourse of treaties with the discourse of marriage in her 1996 novel, *Pushing the Bear: A Novel of the Trail of Tears.*

33 Amos Bad Heart Bull, *A Pictographic History of the Oglala Sioux,* 24, 26.

34 Ibid., 23.

35 Hertha Wong's *Sending My Heart Back across the Years: Tradition and Innovation in Native American Autobiography* also addresses the conventions of pictographic narratives; see chapters 2 and 3 of that volume.

36 Photographs of the declaration are included in Troy R. Johnson, *The Occupation of Alcatraz Island: Indian Self-Determination and the Rise of Indian Activism,* and in Paul Chaat Smith and Robert Allen Warrior, *Like A Hurricane: The Indian Movement from Alcatraz to Wounded Knee.*

37 The original Viking hardback and the subsequent Penguin paperback editions of *Ceremony* include an illustration of the "star map" on 179. The original Viking hardback and the Penguin paperback editions of *Fools Crow* include six winter count illustrations by the artist Dana Boussard.

38 Bad Heart Bull, *A Pictographic History of the Oglala Sioux,* xx.

39 When Bad Heart Bull's sister, Dollie Pretty Cloud, died in 1947, the ledger book was interred with her body as a cherished personal possession, according to Sioux custom.

40 Chief Eagle states in his novel's dedication and acknowledgements that "Approximately sixty-five percent of WINTER COUNT uses Indian thoughts and language which has been interpreted into English." In his interview with Steiger, Chief Eagle attributes his bilingualism to his upbringing. Since he was orphaned as a child, Chief Eagle told Steiger, he was raised by his Sioux elders: "Those who brought me up taught me not to accept the non-Indian ways of life. They would not even let me learn English" (114).

41 M. Annette Jaimes, "Federal Indian Identification Policy: A Usurpation of Indigenous Sovereignty in North America," 126. Jaimes quotes American Indian activist Russell Means, who claimed in 1985, in a speech he gave at the law school of the University of Colorado at Boulder, that "Our treaties say nothing about your having to be such-and-such a degree of blood in order to be covered. No, when the federal government made its guarantee to our nations in exchange for our land, it committed to provide certain services to us as *we* defined ourselves" (130).

42 Jack Forbes repeats this frequently asked question in his poem "Beyond the Veil":

> Are you a real Indian
> they sometimes ask
> Children in
> school classrooms
> Wondering why I don't
> scalp someone.
> How much Indian blood do you have? (105)

43 Such policies began changing in the 1990s—a fact that is both celebrated and lamented in American Indian communities. An Associated Press article published in the *Arizona Daily Star* reports that, because of "generations of intermarriage . . . many tribes are easing membership requirements just to survive." So that their own children and grandchildren will qualify as tribal members, the article reports, some tribes are reducing blood quantum requirements of one-half, one-quarter, or even one-eighth down to one-sixteenth. In addition to survival as distinct communities, the article cites American Indian casino profits as a possible motive for increased numbers of Americans of marginal Indian blood quantum claiming Indian status; see "Tribes Have New Look With Mixed Bloodlines."

44 The hyphenated term "re-membering" is generally attributed to American Indian scholar Paula Gunn Allen (Laguna/Sioux); it is meant to suggest the idea of putting pieces back together.

45 Momaday's trope has incited considerable controversy among scholars of American Indian literatures. In particular, blood memory has drawn a rather biting critique from Arnold Krupat, who describes the phrase as "absurdly racist" (*The Voice in the Margin: Native American Literature and the Canon*, 13; see also Krupat's *The Turn to the Native: Studies in Criticism and Culture*, 60, 62). H. David Brumble discusses what he terms Momaday's "racialist" ideas in *American Indian Autobiography*, 173–80. For a fuller discussion of the controversy over blood memory and American Indian responses, especially Vizenor's in *The Heirs of Columbus*, see my "Blood (and) Memory."

46 For a critique of the Indian authenticity of Momaday's work based on the fact that Momaday is not fluent in an indigenous language and does not write in traditional indigenous genres, see Karl Kroeber, "Technology and Tribal Literature."

47 Momaday also reprints this poem and gives another prose version of the story of the giveaway ceremony in his 1997 collection *The Man Made of Words: Essays, Stories, Passages.*

48 Garrick Mallery provides illustrations of Dakota (Sioux) pictographs for the 1833 meteor shower in his detailed interpretations of nineteenth-century winter counts drawn by Lone Dog, a Dakota of the Yanktonais

tribe, and Battiste Good, a Brule. See Mallery's *Picture-Writing of the American Indians,* vol. I, especially 280 (fig. 218, 1833–'34, "The stars fell") and 320 (fig. 390, 1833–'34, "Storm-of-stars winter").

49 Joy Harjo reports a similar exchange with "the old, old Creek one who comes in here and watches over me [while I write]" in her autobiographical essay "Ordinary Spirit." Harjo writes: "I tell him that it is writing these words down, and entering the world through the structure they make, that has allowed me to see him more clearly, and to speak. And he answers that maybe the prayers, songs and his belief in them has allowed him to create me" (266). There are obvious parallels here, too, to the relationship represented between ancestors and contemporary indigenous minorities in Apirana Taylor's poem "Sad Joke on a Marae," which I discuss in chapter 3.

50 In the New Zealand Maori context, historian Judith Binney has noted that "In the oral form of telling history, the narrative *belongs* to the narrator. This can be seen most clearly when the narrator tells the story as events in which he or she participated, but which occurred before the narrator was born" ("Maori Oral Narratives, Pakeha Written Texts: Two Forms of Telling History," 24). Binney attributes the term "kinship I" to anthropologist J. Prytz Johansen, *The Maori and His Religion in Its Non-Ritualistic Aspects,* ixxx.

51 The document's tabulation of Momaday's official blood quantum of seven-eighths is inaccurate. His father was a full-blood Kiowa, his mother a one-eighth Cherokee.

52 See, for example, Lincoln, *Native American Renaissance;* Ruoff, *American Indian Literatures;* Owens, *Other Destinies.*

53 Reprinted in Duane Niatum, ed., *Harper's Anthology of 20th Century Native American Poetry,* 189.

54 For Vizenor's own definitions of this term, see his "Trickster Discourse" and "*Trickster Discourse:* Comic Holotropes and Language Games."

55 Louis Owens makes a similar point in his discussion of *Bearheart* in *Other Destinies:* "In the oral tradition a people define themselves and their place within an imagined order, a definition necessarily dynamic and requiring constantly changing stories" (238).

56 For a fuller discussion of *The Heirs of Columbus* and its connections to Momaday's work, see my "Blood (and) Memory."

57 From the introduction to *The Memoirs of Chief Red Fox* (1971): "CHIEF RED FOX, as this, his book, goes to press, prevails among the Sioux Indians as a statuesque, historical figure, an advocate of their ancestral rights and a recorder of their place among the races of man. Born on July 11, 1870 . . . Here is the recital of his long and interesting life as a lone Red Man drifting across the prairies of White civilization and exchanging greetings with kings, scientists, writers, and artists who were flexing their intellectual and physical muscles in the cultural centers of the world" (vii).

Conclusion

1 Douglas E. Sanders, *The Formation of the World Council of Indigenous Peoples,* 20, 22.

2 Ibid., 11.

3 My use of the term *autoethnography* follows Mary Louise Pratt's usage in *Imperial Eyes: Travel Writing and Transculturation:* "instances in which colonized subjects undertake to represent themselves in ways that *engage with* the colonizer's own terms" (7).

4 Stuart Hall, "The Local and the Global: Globalization and Ethnicity," 52–53.

5 Gayatri Chakravorty Spivak, *The Post-Colonial Critic: Interviews, Strategies, Dialogues,* 11–12; Bart Moore-Gilbert, *Postcolonial Theory: Contexts, Practices, Politics,* 179.

6 At the time, Michael Posluns was a freelance broadcaster and writer associated with the national American Indian newspaper *Akwesasne Notes.*

7 Deloria writes that he too "was considering writing a book to illustrate the relationship between the various aboriginal peoples of the globe" when Manuel "called me and asked me to write a foreword to *his* book" (ix).

8 Manuel names the "destructive forces" of the West as "the state through the Indian agent; the church through the priests; the church and state through the schools; the state and industry through the traders" (69).

9 See especially 70–89.

10 NIYC Dictionary.

11 Manuel's language here appears to purposefully echo the language of John F. Kennedy's 1961 Inaugural Address, in which the new U.S. president declared that "this hemisphere intends to remain the master of its own house."

12 Financial and logistical problems prevented indigenous peoples from Asia and Africa from attending the preparatory and subsequent meetings. The WCIP's attempts to contact indigenous peoples in eastern Europe and China mostly failed. No doubt because of George Manuel's and the NIB's founding influence, during these early years the WCIP focused primarily on issues facing indigenous minorities residing in First World nations. It is important to note, however, that not all indigenous minority activists embraced the Fourth World movement or the WCIP. Some, like certain members of the U.S. American Indian Movement (AIM), were leery of an international organization that might dilute their own attempts to argue for nationally based treaty rights before the international community (Paul Chaat Smith, personal communication, 25 October 1999). In the 1980s North American groups lost effective control of the WCIP's leadership, and the organization turned its energies more toward the particular political situations facing South and Central American Indians.

13 WCIP Report 1974. I am indebted to Ranginui Walker for allowing me access to his WCIP files while I was studying at Auckland University on an IIE Fulbright Fellowship in 1994. Walker served as a Maori delegate to the WCIP during the 1970s and 1980s, and his files include copies of original typescripts of the reports, motions, notes, and minutes generated during the Preparatory, Policy Board, and First and Second General Assembly meetings of the WCIP, as well as drafts and final versions of WCIP documents and formal resolutions. All references to WCIP materials are to these files. The 1974 definition is also quoted in full in Sanders, *The Formation of the World Council of Indigenous Peoples*, 12.

14 James Clifford, *The Predicament of Culture: Twentieth-Century Ethnography, Literature, and Art*, 17.

15 Drawing on the work of Edward Said, Bill Ashcroft, Gareth Griffiths, and Helen Tiffin argue in *The Empire Writes Back: Theory and Practice in Post-Colonial Literatures* that "all post-colonial societies realize their identity in difference rather than in essence" (167).

16 See Sanders, *The Formation of the World Council of Indigenous Peoples*, 14–18.

17 Bracketed additions on the manuscript of the draft declaration.

18 Bracketed additions on the manuscript of the draft declaration.

19 My use of the term *invention* follows Roy Wagner's usage in *The Invention of Culture*. Wagner views invention as a natural, "positive and expected component of human life" (xvi) and as a function of "observing and learning"—and thus making "visible"—any phenomenon, including one's own culture or a culture different from one's own (4). According to Wagner, the specific instance of inventing cultures occurs "whenever and wherever some 'alien' or 'foreign' set of conventions is brought into relation with one's own" (10). Delegates to the WCIP invent the Fourth World, I am arguing, through two such operations, which occur not sequentially but of necessity more or less simultaneously: first, by bringing into relation the many different indigenous cultures represented at the First General Assembly and second, by bringing into relation that invented collectivity—Indigenous Peoples with a capital "I" and capital "P"—and the so-called First World of settler-invaders.

20 John Bierhorst, ed., *Four Masterworks of American Indian Literature*, 332. Other variations in the Night Chant include

> With beauty before me, I walk.
> With beauty behind me, I walk.
> With beauty above me, I walk.
> With beauty below me, I walk.
> With beauty all around me, I walk.
> It is finished in beauty. (329–30)

21 See ibid., 281–83. Versions of the Navajo Night Chant and especially its lines about "walking in beauty" appear to have been well known among American Indian writers and scholars prior to 1975. N. Scott Momaday includes an extended passage from the Night Chant, in English translation, in his novel *House Made of Dawn,* published in 1968 (146–47). Ruth Muskrat Bronson includes four lines from the Night Chant as a chapter epigraph in her nonfiction work *Indians Are People, Too,* published in 1944. And various anthologies of American Indian literature include excerpts from the Night Chant, such as *Literature of the American Indian,* compiled by Thomas E. Sanders and Walter W. Peek, published in 1973 (364–65).

22 Harald Gaski, "The Sami People: The 'White Indians' of Scandinavia," 115.

23 Albert Barunga (Mowanjum) describes an Australian Aboriginal understanding of the relationship between human cultures and the earth in his poem "My People": "A race of people who rose with the sun, / As strong as the sun they had laws, / Traditions co-existing with nature." Quoted in Jennifer Isaacs, ed., *Australian Dreaming: 40,000 Years of Aboriginal History,* 294.

24 WCIP Resolutions 1975. The final version of the Solemn Declaration is reprinted in Sanders, *The Formation of the World Council of Indigenous Peoples,* 17–18, and in Roger Moody, ed., *The Indigenous Voice: Visions and Realities,* 2:61–62.

25 The Solemn Declaration now opens with a formal preamble establishing its intended audience, "all nations," which is subsequently referred to as "the concert of nations," suggesting specifically the UN but also, implicitly, expanding that "concert" to include indigenous "nations" as yet unrecognized by the UN. The preamble is also notable for how it echoes both the preamble to the U.S. Constitution and the preamble to the Charter of the United Nations.

26 A number of comparisons can be made with the U.S. Declaration of Independence, including the submission of specific "proofs" of the oppressor's tyranny "to a candid world," the appeal to a higher power, the claim to speak on behalf of the people, and, of course, the assertion of independence.

27 This maneuver is reminiscent of Ruth Muskrat Bronson's hemispheric enumeration of American Indians in the 1940s; see chapter 2.

28 For a definition of "emblems of differentiation," see Jocelyn Linnekin and Lin Poyer, introduction to *Cultural Identity and Ethnicity in the Pacific,* 4.

29 WCIP Resolutions 1977.

30 For a brief history of the UN's Working Group on Indigenous Populations, see John Stevens, "Indigenous Activism at the U.N."

31 The UN designated 1993 as the International Year of the World's Indige-

nous People and the period 1995–2004 as the International Decade of the World's Indigenous People; for every year during the decade, the UN has designated 9 August as the International Day of the World's Indigenous People.

32 The efforts of the Working Group can be seen as an extension of work begun by the International Labour Office (ILO), which initiated its first programs on behalf of indigenous peoples in 1926 and which published its monumental study *Indigenous Peoples: Living and Working Conditions of Aboriginal Populations in Independent Countries* in 1953. Already in 1953, the authors of the ILO study noted the difficulty of defining indigenous identity: "there is no unanimity regarding the standards to be used in this regard among experts in indigenous questions. Some are in favour of a linguistic and others of a cultural criterion; others prefer that of 'group consciousness'; others a functional criterion and still others a combination of two or more of the above, together, in some cases, with one based on physical characteristics" (15). The Working Group's efforts can also be seen as an extension of the work of the UN's Sub-Commission on Prevention and Protection of Minorities, which appointed a special rapporteur in 1971 to make a comprehensive study of discrimination against indigenous populations. The special rapporteur's report was submitted during the years 1981–84. See United Nations, *The Rights of Indigenous Peoples*, 5–6.

33 UN Document E/CN.4/Sub.2/L.566, chap. 11. Quoted in Franke Wilmer, *The Indigenous Voice in World Politics: From Time Immemorial*, 216. The Working Group completed a draft Declaration of Indigenous Peoples Rights in 1993. For the full text, see *Voice of Indigenous Peoples: Native People Address the United Nations.* In 1996 the Working Group released a definition of indigenous peoples that adds to the earlier emphasis on objective criteria a discourse of self-definition: "priority in time; voluntary perpetuation of their cultural distinctiveness; self-identification as indigenous; and experience of subjugation, marginalisation, dispossession, exclusion, and discrimination by the dominant society" (UN Document E/CN.4/Sub.2/AC.4/1996/2; quoted in Paul Havemann, ed., *Indigenous Peoples' Rights in Australia, Canada, and New Zealand*, 5–6).

34 Stevens, "Indigenous Activism at the U.N."

35 An exception may be Maori activist and scholar Ranginui Walker, who was a delegate to the WCIP's early general assemblies.

36 It is certainly possible that I have missed marks of specific indigeneity in the final version of the Solemn Declaration. The "Sons of the Sun" at the end of stanza three, for instance, may refer to the Sami story that their people are descended from the sun (see Harold Gaski, "Introduction," 15–19). If it is, the phrase, embedded as it is in the middle of the declaration, is too ambiguous for most non-Sami audiences and lacks the force of the repetition of "walking in Beauty" in the draft version.

37 See Linda Tuhiwai Smith, *Decolonizing Methodologies: Research and Indigenous Peoples,* 186.

38 Jack Forbes, "Colonialism and Native American Literature: Analysis," 19, 20, 23.

39 Gerald Vizenor, *Manifest Manners: Postindian Warriors of Survivance,* 11.

40 Elizabeth Cook-Lynn, *Why I Can't Read Wallace Stegner and Other Essays: A Tribal Voice,* 82.

41 Elizabeth Cook-Lynn, introduction to *The Politics of Hallowed Ground: Wounded Knee and the Struggle for Indian Sovereignty,* 7.

42 Elizabeth Cook-Lynn, "Intellectualism and the New Indian Story," 124.

43 Hirini Melbourne, "Whare Whakairo: Maori 'Literary' Traditions," 129.

44 Merata Mita, "Indigenous Literature in a Colonial Society," 314.

45 Timoti Karetu, "Te Ngahurutanga: A Decade of Protest, 1980–1990," 162.

46 See, for example, James Ruppert, *Mediation in Contemporary Native American Fiction,* and Catherine Rainwater, *Dreams of Fiery Stars: The Transformations of Native American Fiction.*

47 Greg Sarris, *Keeping Slug Woman Alive: A Holistic Approach to American Indian Texts,* 6, 7.

48 Craig Womack, *Red on Red: Native American Literary Separatism.*

49 Barry Barclay, *Our Own Image*; Linda Tuhiwai Smith, *Decolonizing Methodologies,* 187–88.

BIBLIOGRAPHY

Adams, Howard. *Prison of Grass: Canada from the Native Point of View.* Toronto: New Press, 1975.

Ahmad, Aijaz. *In Theory: Classes, Nations, Literatures.* London: Verso, 1992.

Akwesasne Notes. Mohawk Nation. 1968–.

"Alcatraz Island Reclaimed by Indians." *Americans Before Columbus* 2.1 (December 1969–January 1970): 8.

Allen, Chadwick. "Blood (and) Memory." *American Literature* 71.1 (March 1999): 93–116.

——. "Blood as Narrative/Narrative as Blood: Declaring a Fourth World." *Narrative* 6.3 (October 1998): 236–55.

——. "Hero With Two Faces: The Lone Ranger as Treaty Discourse." *American Literature* 68.3 (September 1996): 609–38.

——. "Postcolonial Theory and the Discourse of Treaties." *American Quarterly* 52.1 (March 2000): 59–89.

Allender, Robert. "Disordered Cinema." *Landfall* 5.4 (December 1951): 296–304.

Allison, Harvey. "I Am an Indian." *Indians at Work,* 1 July 1936, 23–25.

Alpers, Antony. *Maori Myths and Tribal Legends.* 2d ed. Auckland: Longman, 1996.

The American Indian. American Association on Indian Affairs. 1943–59.

"The American Indian Historical Society." *Wassaja* 2.8 (September 1974): 12.

Anderson, Benedict. *Imagined Communities: Reflections on the Origin and Spread of Nationalism.* Rev. ed. London: Verso, 1983.

Armstrong, O. K. "Give the Indians an Even Chance!" *Reader's Digest,* November 1955, 101–5.

——. "Indians Are Going to Town." *Reader's Digest,* January 1955, 39–43.

——. "Let's Give the Indians Back to the Country." *Reader's Digest,* April 1948, 129–32.

——. "The Navajos Feel the Wind of Progress." *Reader's Digest,* March 1959, 203–6+.

——. "Set the American Indians Free!" *Reader's Digest,* August 1945, 47–52.

Arvidson, Ken. "Aspects of Contemporary Maori Writing in English." In *Dirty Silence: Aspects of Language and Literature in New Zealand,* ed. Graham McGregor and Mark Williams, 117–28. Auckland: Oxford University Press, 1990.

Ashcroft, Bill, Gareth Griffiths, and Helen Tiffin. *The Empire Writes Back: Theory and Practice in Post-Colonial Literatures.* London: Routledge, 1989.

——, eds. *The Post-Colonial Studies Reader.* London: Routledge, 1995.

Atencio, Steve. "Native American Brotherhood President Plans World Organization of Aboriginal Peoples as Answer to Need for Unity." *Wassaja* 2.10 (November–December 1974): 13.

Bad Heart Bull, Amos. *A Pictographic History of the Oglala Sioux.* Text by Helen H. Blish; introduction by Mari Sandoz. Lincoln: University of Nebraska Press, 1967.

Baker, Heretaunga Pat. *Behind the Tattooed Face.* Wellington: Cape Catley, 1975.

Barclay, Barry. *Our Own Image.* Auckland: Longman Paul, 1990.

Barlow, Cleve. *Tikanga Whakaaro: Key Concepts in Maori Culture.* Auckland: Oxford University Press, 1991.

Barnes, Jim. *This Crazy Land.* Tempe, Ariz.: Porch, 1980.

Barrow, Terence. *An Illustrated Guide to Maori Art.* Auckland: Reed, 1984.

Basic Call to Consciousness. Mohawk Nation/Rooseveltown, N.Y.: Akwesasne Notes, 1978.

Bedford, Denton R. *Tsali.* San Francisco: Indian Historian Press, 1972.

Belt, Tommy. " 'For as Long as the Rivers Shall Run, and the Grasses Shall Grow.' " *Americans Before Columbus* 2.1 (December 1969–January 1970): 6.

Berkhofer, Robert F., Jr. *The White Man's Indian: Images of the American Indian from Columbus to the Present.* New York: Vintage, 1978.

Bernstein, Alison R. *American Indians and World War II: Toward a New Era in Indian Affairs.* Norman: University of Oklahoma Press, 1991.

Between Sacred Mountains: Navajo Stories and Lessons from the Land. Chinle, Ariz.: Rock Point Community School, 1982.

Bhabha, Homi K. *The Location of Culture.* London: Routledge, 1994.

Bierhorst, John, ed. *Four Masterworks of American Indian Literature.* New York: Farrar, Straus and Giroux, 1974.

Biggs, Bruce. "Humpty-Dumpty and the Treaty of Waitangi." In *Waitangi: Maori and Pakeha Perspectives of the Treaty of Waitangi,* ed. I. H. Kawharu, 300–12. Auckland: Oxford University Press, 1989.

——. *Let's Learn Maori: A Guide to the Study of the Maori Language.* Rev. ed. Auckland: Reed, 1973.

——. "The Maori Language Past and Present." In *The Maori People in the Nineteen-Sixties,* ed. Erik Schwimmer, 65–84. Auckland: Blackwood, 1968.

Binney, Judith. "Maori Oral Narratives, Pakeha Written Texts: Two Forms of Telling History." *New Zealand Journal of History* 21.1 (1987): 16–28.

Bird, Maurice D. Letter. *Wassaja* 4.3 (March 1976): 19.

Bixler, Margaret T. *Winds of Freedom: The Story of the Navajo Code Talkers of World War II.* Darien, Conn.: Two Bytes Publishing Company, 1992.

Blaeser, Kimberly M. *Gerald Vizenor: Writing in the Oral Tradition.* Norman: University of Oklahoma Press, 1996.

Blank, Arapera. "Yielding to the New." *Te Ao Hou* 28 (September 1959): 8–10.

Blue Cloud, Peter. *Turtle, Bear, and Wolf.* Mohawk Nation/Rooseveltown, N.Y.: Akwesasne Notes, 1976.

———. *White Corn Sister.* New York: Strawberry, 1977.

———, ed. *Alcatraz Is Not an Island.* Berkeley: Wingbow Press, 1972.

Blythe, Martin. *Naming the Other: Images of the Maori in New Zealand Film and Television.* Metuchen, N.J.: Scarecrow Press, 1994.

Bossley, Pete. *Te Papa: An Architectural Adventure.* Wellington: Te Papa Press, 1998.

Bronson, Ruth Muskrat. *Indians Are People, Too.* New York: Friendship Press, 1944.

———. "Indian Home and Family Life." *Indian Truth* 22.2 (May–September 1945): 6.

———. "Much Work Needed." *Indian Truth* 37.1 (January–April 1960): 1–5.

———. "Shall We Repeat Indian History in Alaska?" *Indian Truth* 24.1 (January–April 1947): 1–9.

Brøsted, Jens, et al., eds. *Native Power: The Quest for Autonomy and Nationhood of Indigenous Peoples.* Bergen, Norway: Universitetsforlaget, 1985.

Brown, Dee. *Bury My Heart at Wounded Knee: An Indian History of the American West.* New York: Holt, 1970.

Brown, Wendy. "Wounded Attachments." In *States of Injury: Power and Freedom in Late Modernity.* Princeton: Princeton University Press, 1995.

Bruchac, Joseph. *This Earth Is a Drum.* Austin, Tex.: Cold Mountain Press, 1977.

———. *There Are No Trees inside the Prison.* Brunswick, Maine: Blackberry Press, 1978.

———. *Translator's Son.* Merrick, N.Y.: Cross-Cultural Communications, 1980.

Brumble, H. David, III. *American Indian Autobiography.* Berkeley: University of California Press, 1988.

Buck, Peter. *The Coming of the Maori.* Wellington: Maori Purposes Fund Board, 1949.

Burger, Julian. *Report from the Frontier: The State of the World's Indigenous Peoples.* London: Zed Books, 1987.

Burlingame, Lori. "Cultural Survival in *Runner in the Sun.*" In *The Legacy of D'Arcy McNickle: Writer, Historian, Activist,* ed. John Lloyd Purdy, 136–51. Norman: University of Oklahoma Press, 1996.

Bush, Barney. *My Horse and a Jukebox.* Los Angeles: University of California Press, 1979.

Chapman, Abraham, ed. *Literature of the American Indians: Views and Interpretations: A Gathering of Indian Memories, Symbolic Contexts, and Literary Criticism.* New York: Meridian, 1975.

Cheyfitz, Eric. *The Poetics of Imperialism: Translation and Colonization from The Tempest to Tarzan.* Expanded ed. Philadelphia: University of Pennsylvania Press, 1997.

Chief Eagle, Dallas. *Winter Count*. 1967. Reprint, Denver: Golden Bell, 1968.

Clifford, James. *The Predicament of Culture: Twentieth-Century Ethnography, Literature, and Art*. Cambridge, Mass.: Harvard University Press, 1988.

Cohen, Felix S. *Handbook of Federal Indian Law*. Washington: Government Printing Office, 1942.

Collier, John. "The Coming of Dr. Saenz." *Indians at Work,* 1 November 1933, 1–3.

——. "Talk to the Students of Bacone College, Oklahoma, March 22, 1934." *Indians at Work,* 1 May 1934, 30–32.

Coltelli, Laura. *Winged Words: American Indian Writers Speak*. Lincoln: University of Nebraska Press, 1990.

Cook-Lynn, Elizabeth. *Anti-Indianism in Modern America: A Voice from Tatekeya's Earth*. Urbana: University of Illinois Press, 2001.

——. "Intellectualism and the New Indian Story." In *Natives and Academics: Researching and Writing about American Indians,* ed. Devon A. Mihesuah, 111–38. Lincoln: University of Nebraska Press, 1998.

——. Introduction to *The Politics of Hallowed Ground: Wounded Knee and the Struggle for Indian Sovereignty,* ed. Mario Gonzalez and Elizabeth Cook-Lynn. Urbana: University of Illinois Press, 1999.

——. *Then Badger Said This*. New York: Vintage, 1977.

——. *Why I Can't Read Wallace Stegner and Other Essays: A Tribal Voice*. Madison: University of Wisconsin Press, 1996.

Cornell, Stephen. *The Return of the Native: American Indian Political Resurgence*. New York: Oxford University Press, 1988.

Costo, Rupert. "Indian Treaties: The Basis for Solution of Current Issues." *Wassaja Special Supplement* July 1973: 1.

——. "Moment of Truth for the American Indian." In *Indian Voices: The First Convocation of American Indian Scholars,* 3–8. San Francisco: Indian Historian Press, 1970.

Costo, Rupert, and Jeannette Henry. *Indian Treaties: Two Centuries of Dishonor*. San Francisco: Indian Historian Press, 1977.

——. *Textbooks and the American Indian*. San Francisco: Indian Historian Press, 1970.

Cowger, Thomas W. *The National Congress of American Indians: The Founding Years*. Lincoln: University of Nebraska Press, 1999.

Dansey, Harry. "Of Two Races." *Te Ao Hou* 28 (September 1959): 6–8.

——. *Te Raukura / The Feathers of the Albatross*. Auckland: Longman, 1974.

Debo, Angie. *A History of the Indians of the United States*. Norman: University of Oklahoma Press, 1970.

de Certeau, Michel. *The Practice of Everyday Life*. Trans. Steven F. Rendall. Berkeley: University of California Press, 1984.

"A Declaration of Apache Bill of Rights." *Wassaja* 1.7 (October 1973): 6.

Declaration of Continuing Independence. International Indian Treaty Council.

Standing Rock, Sioux Indian Country, 1974. Reprint, *Akwesasne Notes* 6.3 (July 1974): 9.

Declaration of Indian Purpose. American Indian Chicago Conference. University of Chicago, 1961.

Deloria, Ella Cara. *Speaking of Indians.* Vermillion: University of South Dakota Press, 1944.

———. *Waterlily.* Lincoln: University of Nebraska Press, 1988.

Deloria, Vine, Jr. *Behind the Trail of Broken Treaties: An Indian Declaration of Independence.* New York: Delacorte, 1974.

———. *Custer Died for Your Sins: An Indian Manifesto.* New York: Macmillan, 1969.

———. *For This Land: Writings on Religion in America.* New York: Routledge, 1999.

———. *God Is Red.* New York: Grosset, 1973.

———. *The Indian Affair.* New York: Friendship Press, 1974.

———. Introduction to *Speaking of Indians,* by Ella Cara Deloria. Lincoln: University of Nebraska Press, 1998.

———. *The Metaphysics of Modern Existence.* San Francisco: Harper and Row, 1979.

———. "The Subject Nobody Knows." *American Indian Quarterly* 19.1 (Winter 1995): 143–47.

———. *We Talk, You Listen: New Tribes, New Turf.* New York: Macmillan, 1970.

———, ed. *Of Utmost Good Faith.* San Francisco: Straight Arrow, 1971.

Deloria, Vine, Jr., and Clifford Lytle. *The Nations Within: The Past and Future of American Indian Sovereignty.* New York: Pantheon, 1984.

DeMallie, Raymond J. Afterword to *Waterlily,* by Ella Cara Deloria. Lincoln: University of Nebraska Press, 1988.

Dennis, R. "To the Race—A Son." *Te Ao Hou* 48 (September 1964): 6–9.

Diggs, R. "What's This! ANOTHER New Treaty?" Cartoon. *Akwesasne Notes* 10.2 (Late Spring 1978): 4.

Dodge, Robert K., and Joseph B. McCullough, eds. *Voices from Wah'kon-tah: Contemporary Poetry of Native Americans.* New York: International Publishers, 1974.

Durie, E. T. J. "The Treaty in Maori History." In *Sovereignty and Indigenous Rights: The Treaty of Waitangi in International Contexts,* ed. William Renwick, 156–69. Wellington: Victoria University Press, 1991.

Durie, Mason. "Dreamer's Return." *Te Ao Hou* 28 (September 1959): 18–21.

———. "I Failed the Test of Life." *Te Ao Hou* 14 (April 1956): 22–24.

———. "The Treaty of Waitangi—Perspectives on Social Policy." In *Waitangi: Maori and Pakeha Perspectives of the Treaty of Waitangi,* ed. I. H. Kawharu, 280–99. Auckland: Oxford University Press, 1989.

Dyck, Noel. "Aboriginal Peoples and Nation-States: An Introduction to the Analytical Issues." In *Indigenous Peoples and the Nation-State: "Fourth*

World" Politics in Canada, Australia, and Norway.* Social and Economic Papers, 14. St. John's: Institute of Social and Economic Research, Memorial University of Newfoundland, 1985.

———, ed. *Indigenous Peoples and the Nation-State: "Fourth World" Politics in Canada, Australia, and Norway.* Social and Economic Papers, 14. St. John's: Institute of Social and Economic Research, Memorial University of Newfoundland, 1985.

Eastman, Charles A. *From the Deep Woods to Civilization: Chapters in the Autobiography of an Indian.* 1916. Reprint, Lincoln: University of Nebraska Press, 1977.

"Emancipating the Indian." *Indian Truth* 25.3 (May–August 1948): 4–5.

Emerson, Haven. "Freedom or Exploitation! Is Mr. O. K. Armstrong's Recent Solution of the American Indian Problem Sound?" *American Indian* 2.4 (fall 1945): 3–7.

Evers, Larry, ed. *The South Corner of Time: Hopi, Navajo, Papago, Yaqui Tribal Literatures.* Tucson: University of Arizona Press, 1980.

Ewers, John C. *The Blackfeet: Raiders on the Northwestern Plains.* Norman: University of Oklahoma Press, 1958.

Facts New Zealand. Wellington: Department of Statistics, 1992.

Fiorentino, Daniele. "The American Indian Writer as a Cultural Broker: An Interview with N. Scott Momaday." *Studies in American Indian Literatures* 8.4 (winter 1996): 61–72.

"The First International Conference of Indigenous Peoples Meet at Tseshaht B.C." *Akwesasne Notes* 7.5 (early winter 1975): 34.

Fixico, Donald L. *Termination and Relocation: Federal Indian Policy, 1945–1960.* Albuquerque: University of New Mexico Press, 1986.

Fleras, Augie, and Jean Leonard Elliott. *The "Nations Within": Aboriginal-State Relations in Canada, the United States, and New Zealand.* Toronto: Oxford University Press, 1992.

Forbes, Jack. "Beyond the Veil." In *Ceremony of Brotherhood,* ed. Rudolfo A. Anaya and Simon J. Ortiz, 105–13. Albuquerque: Academia, 1981.

———. "Colonialism and Native American Literature: Analysis." *Wicazo Sa Review* 3 (1987): 17–23.

———, ed. *The Indian in America's Past.* Englewood Cliffs, N.J.: Prentice-Hall, 1964.

Gandhi, Leela. *Postcolonial Theory: A Critical Introduction.* New York: Columbia University Press, 1998.

Gaski, Harold. Introduction to *In the Shadow of the Midnight Sun: Contemporary Sami Prose and Poetry,* ed. Harold Gaski, 9–41. Karasjok, Norway: Davvi Girji, 1997.

———. "The Sami People: The 'White Indians' of Scandinavia." *American Indian Culture and Research Journal* 17.1 (1993): 115–28.

Gates, Henry Louis, Jr. *The Signifying Monkey: A Theory of African-American Literary Criticism.* New York: Oxford University Press, 1988.

Geiogamah, Hanay. *New Native American Drama: Three Plays.* Norman: University of Oklahoma Press, 1980.

Giago, Tim. *The Aboriginal Sin: Reflections on the Holy Rosary Indian Mission School.* San Francisco: Indian Historian Press, 1978.

Glancy, Diane. *Pushing the Bear: A Novel of the Trail of Tears.* New York: Harcourt Brace, 1996.

Goldberg, David Theo, ed. *Multiculturalism: A Critical Reader.* Oxford: Blackwell, 1994.

Grace, Patricia. *The Dream Sleepers and Other Stories.* Auckland: Longman, 1980.

——. *Mutuwhenua: The Moon Sleeps.* Auckland: Longman, 1978.

——. *Potiki.* Auckland: Penguin, 1986.

——. *Waiariki.* Auckland: Longman, 1975.

Grace, Patricia, and Witi Ihimaera. "The Maori in Literature." In *Tihe Mauri Ora: Aspects of Maoritanga,* ed. Michael King, 80–85. Auckland: Methuen, 1978.

Gridley, Marion. *Contemporary American Indian Leaders.* New York: Dodd, Mead, 1972.

Guerrero, M. Annette Jaimes. "Academic Apartheid: American Indian Studies and 'Multiculturalism.'" In *Mapping Multiculturalism,* ed. Avery F. Gordon and Christopher Newfield, 49–63. Minneapolis: University of Minnesota Press, 1996.

Gutmann, Amy. Introduction to *Multiculturalism: Examining the Politics of Recognition,* ed. Amy Gutmann. Princeton: Princeton University Press, 1994.

Hale, Janet Campbell. *Custer Lives in Humboldt County.* Greenfield Center, N.Y.: Greenfield Review Press, 1978.

——. *Owl's Song.* 1974. New York: Avon, 1976.

Hall, Stuart. "The Local and the Global: Globalization and Ethnicity." In *Culture, Globalization, and the World-System: Contemporary Conditions for the Representation of Identity,* rev. ed., ed. Anthony D. King, 19–39. Minneapolis: University of Minnesota Press, 1997.

Harjo, Joy. "Ordinary Spirit." In *I Tell You Now: Autobiographical Essays by Native American Writers,* ed. Brian Swann and Arnold Krupat, 263–70. Lincoln: University of Nebraska Press, 1987.

——. *She Had Some Horses.* New York: Thunder's Mouth Press, 1983.

——. *What Moon Drove Me to This?* New York: I. Reed, 1979.

Hathaway, Jim. "Indian Treaty." Cartoon. *Wassaja* 6.4 (May 1978): 3.

——. "I Wouldn't Worry Too Much About the Extra Ammo, Sgt., Just Be Sure We Got Plenty of Blank Indian Treaties." Cartoon. *Wassaja* 6.5 (June 1978): 8.

Hau, P. W. "Maori-Tanga." *Te Ao Hou* 62 (March–May 1968): 24.

Havemann, Paul, ed. *Indigenous Peoples' Rights in Australia, Canada, and New Zealand.* Auckland: Oxford University Press, 1999.

"A Helpful Interpretation." Review of *They Came Here First,* by D'Arcy McNickle. *Indian Truth* 26.2 (June–October 1949): 7.

Henare, Manuka. "Colonials at the Helm." In *Mana Tiriti: The Art of Protest and Partnership,* 38–39. Wellington: Daphne Brasell Associates Press, 1991.

Henry, Jeannette. "The Mass Media on Wounded Knee." *Wassaja* 4.3 (March 1976): 16.

Hertzberg, Hazel W. *The Search for an American Indian Identity: Modern Pan-Indian Movements.* Syracuse: Syracuse University Press, 1971.

Hineira. "The Visitors." *Te Ao Hou* 38 (March 1962): 5–9.

Hobsbawm, Eric, and Terence Ranger. *The Invention of Tradition.* Cambridge: Cambridge University Press, 1983.

Hobson, Geary, ed. *The Remembered Earth: An Anthology of Contemporary Native American Literature.* 1979. Albuquerque: University of New Mexico Press, 1981.

Hogan, Linda. *Calling Myself Home.* Greenfield Center, N.Y.: Greenfield Review Press, 1978.

Holm, Tom. *Strong Hearts, Wounded Souls: Native American Veterans of the Vietnam War.* Austin: University of Texas Press, 1996.

Hosen, Frederick E., ed. *Rifle, Blanket, and Kettle: Selected Indian Treaties and Laws.* Jefferson, N.C.: McFarland, 1985.

Hulme, Keri. *The Bone People.* 1984. Reprint, Baton Rouge: Louisiana State University Press, 1985.

——. *The Silences Between (Moeraki Conversations).* Auckland: Auckland University Press, 1982.

Hunn, J. K., *Report on Department of Maori Affairs with Statistical Supplement.* 1960. Wellington: Government Printer, 1961.

Hyland, Queenie Rikihana. *Paki Waitara: Myths and Legends of the Maori.* Auckland: Reed, 1997.

Ihimaera, Witi. *Maori.* Wellington: Government Printer, 1975.

——. *The Matriarch.* Auckland: Heinemann, 1986.

——. *Pounamu, Pounamu.* Auckland: Heinemann, 1972.

——. *Tangi.* Auckland: Heinemann, 1973.

——, ed. *Te Ao Mārama: Contemporary Māori Writing.* 5 vols. Auckland: Reed, 1992–96.

——. *The Whale Rider.* Auckland: Heinemann, 1987.

——. *Whanau.* Auckland: Heinemann, 1974.

——. "Why I Write." *World Literature Written in English* 14.1 (April 1975): 117–19.

Ihimaera, Witi, and D. S. Long, eds. *Into the World of Light: An Anthology of Maori Writing.* Auckland: Heinemann, 1982.

Indian Historian. American Indian Historical Society. 1964–.

Indians at Work. U.S. Department of the Interior, Office of Indian Affairs. 1933–45.

Indians in the War. Chicago: U.S. Department of the Interior, Office of Indian Affairs, 1945.

"Indians on Mars?" *Tsistsistas Press* [Cheyenne newspaper]. Reprinted in *Wassaja* 4.10 (October 1976): 6.

Indian Truth. Indian Rights Association. 1924–.

Indian Voices: The First Convocation of American Indian Scholars. San Francisco: Indian Historian Press, 1970.

International Labour Office. *Indigenous Peoples: Living and Working Conditions of Aboriginal Populations in Independent Countries.* Studies and Reports, New Series, no. 35. Geneva: ILO, 1953.

Isaacs, Jennifer, ed. *Australian Dreaming: 40,000 Years of Aboriginal History.* Sydney: Lansdowne, 1980.

Jackson, Michael D. "Literacy, Communications and Social Change: A Study of the Meaning and Effect of Literacy in Early Nineteenth Century Maori Society." In *Conflict and Compromise: Essays on the Maori since Colonization,* ed. I. H. Kawharu, 27–54. Wellington: Reed, 1975.

Jaimes, M. Annette. "Federal Indian Identification Policy: A Usurpation of Indigenous Sovereignty in North America." In *The State of Native America,* ed. M. Annette Jaimes, 123–38. Boston: South End, 1992.

Johansen, J. Prytz. *The Maori and His Religion in Its Non-Ritualistic Aspects.* Copenhagen: Munksgaard, 1954.

Johnson, Troy R. *The Occupation of Alcatraz Island: Indian Self-Determination and the Rise of Indian Activism.* Urbana: University of Illinois Press, 1996.

Josephy, Alvin M., Jr. *Red Power: The American Indians' Fight for Freedom.* New York: McGraw, 1971.

Josephy, Alvin M., Jr., Joane Nagel, and Troy Johnson, eds. *Red Power: The American Indians' Fight for Freedom.* 2d ed. Lincoln: University of Nebraska Press, 1999.

Kaplan, Amy, and Donald Pease, eds. *Cultures of United States Imperialism.* Durham, N.C.: Duke University Press, 1993.

Karetu, Timoti S. "Te Ngahurutanga: A Decade of Protest, 1980–1990." In *Dirty Silence: Aspects of Language and Literature in New Zealand,* ed. Graham McGregor and Mark Williams, 159–76. Auckland: Oxford University Press, 1990.

Kawharu, I. H., ed. *Waitangi: Maori and Pakeha Perspectives of the Treaty of Waitangi.* Auckland: Oxford University Press, 1989.

Kickingbird, Kirke, and Karen Ducheneaux. *One Hundred Million Acres.* New York: Macmillan, 1973.

King, Michael. "Between Two Worlds." In *Oxford History of New Zealand,* 2d ed., ed. Geoffrey W. Rice, 285–307. Auckland: Oxford University Press, 1992.

——, ed. *Pakeha: The Quest for Identity in New Zealand.* Auckland: Penguin, 1991.

——, ed. *Te Ao Hurihuri/The World Moves On: Aspects of Maoritanga*. 1975. Auckland: Oxford University Press, 1977.

King, Thomas. *Green Grass, Running Water*. New York: Bantam, 1993.

Kohere, Reweti T. *The Autobiography of a Maori*. Wellington: Reed, 1951.

Koru: The New Zealand Maori Artists and Writers Annual Magazine. Vol. 1 (1976); vol. 2. (1978).

Kroeber, Karl. "Technology and Tribal Narrative." In *Narrative Chance: Postmodern Discourse on Native American Indian Literatures,* ed. Gerald Vizenor, 17–37. 1989. Reprint, Norman: University of Oklahoma Press, 1993.

Krupat, Arnold. "Postcolonialism, Ideology, and Native Literature." In *The Turn to the Native: Studies in Criticism and Culture,* 30–55. Lincoln: University of Nebraska Press, 1996.

——. "Postcoloniality and Native American Literature." *Yale Journal of Criticism* 7.1 (spring 1994): 163–80.

——. *The Turn to the Native: Studies in Criticism and Culture*. Lincoln: University of Nebraska Press, 1996.

——. *The Voice in the Margin: Native American Literature and the Canon*. Berkeley: University of California Press, 1989.

Krupat, Arnold, and Brian Swann. "Of Anthologies, Translations, and Theory: A Self-Interview." *North Dakota Quarterly* 57.2 (spring 1989): 137–47.

LaDuke, Winona. *All Our Relations: Native Struggles for Land and Life*. Cambridge, Mass.: South End, 1999.

Lame Deer, John (Fire), and Richard Erdoes. *Lame Deer: Seeker of Visions*. New York: Simon and Schuster, 1972.

Larson, Charles R. *American Indian Fiction*. Albuquerque: University of New Mexico Press, 1978.

Laughton, J. G. "Maoritanga." Part I, *Te Ao Hou* 8 (winter 1954): 10–12. Part II, *Te Ao Hou* 9 (spring 1954): 17–18.

Levine, Stuart, and Nancy Oestreich Lurie, eds. *The American Indian Today*. Deland, Fla.: Everett Edwards, 1968.

Lincoln, Kenneth. *Native American Renaissance*. Berkeley: University of California Press, 1983.

Link, Martin A., ed. *Navajo: A Century of Progress, 1868–1968*. Window Rock, Ariz.: Navajo Tribe, 1968.

Linnekin, Jocelyn, and Lin Poyer. Introduction to *Cultural Identity and Ethnicity in the Pacific,* ed. Jocelyn Linnekin and Lin Poyer. Honolulu: University of Hawaii Press, 1990.

Littlefield, Daniel F., Jr., and James W. Parins, eds. *American Indian and Alaska Native Newspapers and Periodicals*. 3 vols. Westport, Conn.: Greenwood Press, 1984–86.

Loomba, Ania. *Colonialism/Postcolonialism*. London: Routledge, 1998.

M., G. B. "Why Should We Honor These Treaties?" Cartoon. *Akwesasne Notes* 5.1 (January 1973): 9.

Madrano, Dan M. *Heap Big Laugh.* Illus. Roland Whitehorse. Tulsa: Western Printing, 1955.

Mallery, Garrick. *Picture-Writing of the American Indians.* 2 vols. 1893. New York: Dover, 1972.

Manuel, George, and Michael Posluns. *The Fourth World: An Indian Reality.* New York: Free Press, 1974.

Maori Language Commission/Te Taura Whiri I Te Reo Maori. *Te Matatiki: Contemporary Maori Words.* Auckland: Oxford University Press, 1996.

Marae Magazine. Auckland: Marae Publications Ltd., 1974.

Marder, Murrey. "Navajo Code Talkers." In *Indians in the War,* 25–27. Chicago: U.S. Department of the Interior, Office of Indian Affairs, 1945.

Martin, Calvin, ed. *The American Indian and the Problem of History.* New York: Oxford University Press, 1987.

Mathews, John Joseph. *Life and Death of an Oilman: The Career of E. W. Marland.* Norman: University of Oklahoma Press, 1951.

———. *The Osages: Children of the Middle Waters.* Norman: University of Oklahoma Press, 1961.

———. *Talking to the Moon.* 1945. Reprint, Norman: University of Oklahoma Press, 1981.

———. *Sundown.* 1934. Reprint, Norman: University of Oklahoma Press, 1988.

———. *Wah'Kon-Tah: The Osage and the White Man's Road.* Norman: University of Oklahoma Press, 1932.

Mathews, Virginia H. Introduction to *Sundown,* by John Joseph Mathews. Norman: University of Oklahoma Press, 1988.

Matthiessen, Peter. *In the Spirit of Crazy Horse.* New York: Viking, 1983.

McClintock, Anne. "The Angel of Progress: Pitfalls of the Term 'Postcolonialism.'" In *Colonial Discourse/Postcolonial Theory,* ed. Francis Barker, Peter Hulme, and Margaret Iversen, 253–66. Manchester: Manchester University Press, 1994.

McFarland, Ron, ed. *James Welch.* Lewiston, Idaho: Confluence Press, 1986.

McFarlane, Peter. *Brotherhood to Nationhood: George Manuel and the Making of the Modern Indian Movement.* Toronto: Between the Lines, 1993.

McKenzie, D. F. *Oral Culture, Literacy and Print in Early New Zealand: The Treaty of Waitangi.* Wellington: Victoria University Press, 1985.

McNickle, D'Arcy. *The Hawk Is Hungry and Other Stories.* Ed. Birgit Hans. Tucson: University of Arizona Press, 1992.

———. "Indian Expectations." *Indian Truth* 38.1 (June 1961): 1–6.

———. *The Indian Tribes of the United States: Ethnic and Cultural Survival.* London: Oxford University Press, 1962.

———. *Native American Tribalism: Indian Survival and Renewals.* New York: Oxford University Press, 1973.

——. *Runner in the Sun.* 1954. Reprint, Albuquerque: University of New Mexico Press, 1987.

——. *The Surrounded.* 1936. Reprint, Albuquerque: University of New Mexico Press, 1978.

——. *They Came Here First: The Epic of the American Indians.* 1949. Reprint, New York: Octagon, 1975.

——. *Wind from an Enemy Sky.* San Francisco: Harper and Row, 1978.

McNickle, D'Arcy, and Harold E. Fey. *Indians and Other Americans: Two Ways of Life Meet.* New York: Harper, 1959.

Mead, Sidney Moko [Hirini Moko]. "Nga Timunga Me Nga Paringa O Te Mana Maori: The Ebb and Flow of Mana Maori and the Changing Context of Maori Art." In *Te Maori: Maori Art from New Zealand Collections,* ed. Sidney Moko Mead, 20–36. New York: Abrams, 1984.

——. "Show Us the Way/Whakaaturia Mai Te Huarahi." *Te Ao Hou* 38 (March 1962): 14–18.

——. "Te Tupu Te Toi Whakairo Ki Aotearoa: Becoming Maori Art." *Te Maori: Maori Art from New Zealand Collections,* ed. Sidney Moko Mead, 63–75. New York: Abrams, 1984.

Means, Russell, with Marvin J. Wolf. *Where White Men Fear to Tread: The Autobiography of Russell Means.* New York: St. Martin's, 1995.

Medicine, Beatrice. "Red Power: Real or Potential?" In *Indian Voices: The First Convocation of American Indian Scholars,* 299–331. San Francisco: Indian Historian Press, 1970.

Melbourne, Hirini. "Whare Whakairo: Maori 'Literary' Traditions." In *Dirty Silence: Aspects of Language and Literature in New Zealand,* ed. Graham McGregor and Mark Williams, 129–41. Auckland: Oxford University Press, 1990.

Metge, Joan. *The Maoris of New Zealand: Ruatahi.* Rev. ed. London: Routledge, 1976.

——. *A New Maori Migration: Rural and Urban Relations in Northern New Zealand.* London School of Economics Monographs on Social Anthropology, 27. London: Athlone, 1964.

Mills, Sidney. "I Choose to Serve My People." *Renegade* [Survival of American Indians Association] 1.1 (May 1969). Reprinted in *The Way: An Anthology of American Indian Literature,* ed. Shirley Hill Witt and Stan Steiner, 208–10. New York: Knopf, 1974.

Mita, Merata. "Bastion Point Day 507" [documentary aired on TVNZ's "Contact" program]. Wellington, 1981.

——. "Indigenous Literature in a Colonial Society." *The Republican,* November 1984, 4–7.

Mitcalfe, Barry. "The Best of Both Worlds." *Te Ao Hou* 31 (June 1960): 45–48.

Mitchell, Emerson Blackhorse, and T. D. Allen. *Miracle Hill: The Story of a Navaho Boy.* Norman: University of Oklahoma Press, 1967.

Moffatt, J. H. "The Homecoming." *Te Ao Hou* 56 (September 1966): 7.

Momaday, N. Scott. *The Ancient Child.* New York: Doubleday, 1989.

——. *Angle of Geese and Other Poems.* Boston: Godine, 1974.

——. *The Gourd Dancer.* New York: Harper and Row, 1976.

——. *House Made of Dawn.* New York: Harper and Row, 1968.

——. *In the Presence of the Sun: Stories and Poems, 1961–1991.* New York: St. Martin's, 1992.

——. "The Man Made of Words." In *Indian Voices: The First Convocation of American Indian Scholars,* 49–84. San Francisco: Indian Historian Press, 1970.

——. *The Man Made of Words: Essays, Stories, Passages.* New York: St. Martin's, 1997.

——. *The Names: A Memoir.* New York: Harper and Row, 1976.

——. "Personal Reflections." In *The American Indian and the Problem of History,* ed. Calvin Martin, 156–61. New York: Oxford University Press, 1987.

——. *The Way to Rainy Mountain.* Albuquerque: University of New Mexico Press, 1969.

Moody, Roger, ed. *The Indigenous Voice: Visions and Realities.* Vol. 2. London: Zed Books, 1988.

Moore-Gilbert, Bart. *Postcolonial Theory: Contexts, Practices, Politics.* London: Verso, 1997.

Morris, Glenn T. "International Law and Politics: Toward a Right to Self-Determination for Indigenous Peoples." In *The State of Native America: Genocide, Colonization, and Resistance,* ed. M. Annette Jaimes, 55–86. Boston: South End, 1992.

Murphy, James E., and Sharon M. Murphy. *Let My People Know: American Indian Journalism.* Norman: University of Oklahoma Press, 1981.

Nagel, Joane. "The Political Mobilization of Native Americans." *Social Science Journal* 19.3 (July 1982): 37–45.

Navajo Stories of the Long Walk Period. Supervised by Ruth Roessel. Tsaile, Ariz.: Navajo Community College Press, 1973.

Neich, Roger. *Painted Histories: Early Maori Figurative Painting.* Auckland: Auckland University Press, 1993.

Neihardt, John G. *Black Elk Speaks: Being the Life of a Holy Man of the Oglala Sioux.* 1932. Reprint, Lincoln: University of Nebraska Press, 1961.

New Zealand in Profile 1998. Wellington: Statistics New Zealand/Te Tari Tatau, 1998.

Ngata, H. M. *English-Maori Dictionary.* Wellington: Learning Media/Te Pou Taki Korero, 1993.

Niatum, Duane. *Ascending Red Cedar Moon.* New York: Harper and Row, 1974.

——. *Digging Out the Roots.* New York: Harper and Row, 1977.

——, ed. *Carriers of the Dream Wheel: Contemporary Native American Poetry.* New York: Harper and Row, 1975.

——, ed. *Harper's Anthology of 20th Century Native American Poetry.* San Francisco: Harper and Row, 1988.

"NIYC Dictionary." *Americans Before Columbus* 3.2 (August–October 1971): 6.

Okonkwo, Chidi. *Decolonization Agonistics in Postcolonial Fiction.* New York: St. Martin's, 1999.

Oliver, W. H. *Claims to the Waitangi Tribunal.* Wellington: Department of Justice, 1991.

Orange, Claudia. *The Treaty of Waitangi.* Wellington: Allen and Unwin, 1987.

Orbell, Margaret. *A Concise Encyclopedia of Maori Myth and Legend.* Christchurch: Canterbury University Press, 1998.

——. *Traditional Maori Stories.* Auckland: Reed, 1992.

——. *Waiata: Maori Songs in History.* Auckland: Reed, 1991.

——, ed. *Contemporary Maori Writing.* Auckland: Reed, 1970.

Ortiz, Alfonso. Afterword to *Runner in the Sun,* by D'Arcy McNickle. Albuquerque: University of New Mexico Press, 1987.

Ortiz, Simon. *Going for the Rain.* New York: Harper and Row, 1976.

——. *A Good Journey.* Tucson: University of Arizona Press, 1977.

——. *The Howbah Indians.* Tucson: University of Arizona Press, 1978.

——. "Towards a National Indian Literature: Cultural Authenticity in Nationalism." 1981. Reprinted in *Critical Perspectives on Native American Fiction,* ed. Richard F. Fleck, 64–68. Washington, D.C.: Three Continents Press, 1993.

Owens, Louis. *Other Destinies: Understanding the American Indian Novel.* Norman: University of Oklahoma Press, 1992.

Paine, Robert. "The Claim of the Fourth World." In *Native Power: The Quest for Autonomy and Nationhood of Indigenous Peoples,* ed. Jens Brøsted et al., 49–66. Bergen: Universitetsforlaget, 1985.

——. "Ethnodrama and the 'Fourth World': The Sami Action Group in Norway, 1979–81." In *Indigenous Peoples and the Nation-State: "Fourth World" Politics in Canada, Australia, and Norway,* ed. Noel Dyck, 190–235. Social and Economic Papers 14. St. John's: Institute of Social and Economic Research, Memorial University of Newfoundland, 1985.

Parker, Dorothy R. "D'Arcy McNickle: An Annotated Bibliography of His Published Articles and Book Reviews in a Biographical Context." In *The Legacy of D'Arcy McNickle: Writer, Historian, Activist,* ed. John Lloyd Purdy, 3–29. Norman: University of Oklahoma Press, 1996.

——. "D'Arcy McNickle's *Runner in the Sun:* Content and Context." In *The Legacy of D'Arcy McNickle: Writer, Historian, Activist,* ed. John Lloyd Purdy, 117–35. Norman: University of Oklahoma Press, 1996.

——. *Singing an Indian Song: A Biography of D'Arcy McNickle.* Lincoln: University of Nebraska Press, 1992.

Parry, Benita. "Resistance Theory/Theorising Resistance: or Two Cheers for Nativism." In *Colonial Discourse/Postcolonial Theory,* ed. Francis Barker, Peter Hulme, and Margaret Iversen, 172–96. Manchester: Manchester University Press, 1994.

Pearson, Bill. "The Maori and Literature 1938–65." In *The Maori People in the Nineteen-Sixties: A Symposium,* ed. Erik Schwimmer, 217–56. Auckland: Blackwood, 1968.

——. "Witi Ihimaera and Patricia Grace." In *Critical Essays on the New Zealand Short Story,* ed. Cherry Hankin, 166–84. Auckland: Heinemann, 1982.

Pertusati, Linda. *In Defense of Mohawk Land: Ethnopolitical Conflict in Native North America.* Albany: State University of New York Press, 1997.

Philp, Kenneth R. *Termination Revisited: American Indians on the Trail to Self-Determination, 1933–1953.* Lincoln: University of Nebraska Press, 1999.

Pound, Francis. *The Space Between: Pakeha Use of Maori Motifs in Modernist New Zealand Art.* Auckland: Workshop Press, 1994.

Powers, William K. *Oglala Religion.* Lincoln: University of Nebraska Press, 1975.

Pratt, Mary Louise. "Arts of the Contact Zone." *Profession 1991* (1991): 33–40.

——. *Imperial Eyes: Travel Writing and Transculturation.* London: Routledge, 1992.

Prucha, Francis Paul. *American Indian Treaties: The History of a Political Anomaly.* Berkeley: University of California Press, 1994.

——, ed. *Documents of United States Indian Policy.* 2d ed. Lincoln: University of Nebraska Press, 1990.

Purdy, John Lloyd. *Word Ways: The Novels of D'Arcy McNickle.* Tucson: University of Arizona Press, 1990.

——, ed. *The Legacy of D'Arcy McNickle: Writer, Historian, Activist.* Norman: University of Oklahoma Press, 1996.

Rainwater, Catherine. *Dreams of Fiery Stars: The Transformations of Native American Fiction.* Philadelphia: University of Pennsylvania Press, 1999.

Rangihau, John. "Being Maori." In *Te Ao Hurihuri/The World Moves On: Aspects of Maoritanga,* ed. Michael King, 165–75. 1975. Reprint, Auckland: Oxford University Press, 1977.

Raymont, Henry. "Doubt Is Cast on McGraw-Hill's 'Memoirs of Red Fox.'" *New York Times,* 10 March 1972.

Red Fox, William. *The Memoirs of Chief Red Fox.* With an introduction by Cash Asher. New York: McGraw-Hill, 1971.

Renwick, William, ed. *Sovereignty and Indigenous Rights: The Treaty of Waitangi in International Contexts.* Wellington: Victoria University Press, 1991.

Revard, Carter. *Ponca War Dancers.* Norman, Okla.: Point Riders Press, 1980.

Rice, Geoffrey W., ed. *The Oxford History of New Zealand.* 2d ed. Auckland: Oxford University Press, 1992.

Riegert, William A. "What Are We, 'The American Indian,' Fighting For?" *South Dakota Historical Collections* 22 (1946): 26–27.

Roemer, Kenneth M. Introduction to *Native American Writers of the United States,* ed. Kenneth M. Roemer. Dictionary of Literary Biography, vol. 175. Detroit: Gale Research, 1997.

Roessel, Ruth, ed. *Navajo Studies at Navajo Community College.* Many Farms, Ariz.: Navajo Community College Press, 1971.

Rosaldo, Renato. *Culture and Truth: The Remaking of Social Analysis.* Boston: Beacon, 1989.

Rose, Wendy. *Bone Dance: New and Selected Poems, 1965–1993.* Tucson: University of Arizona Press, 1994.

——. *Lost Copper.* Banning, Calif.: Malki Museum Press, 1980.

——. "Neon Scars." In *I Tell You Now: Autobiographical Essays by Native American Writers,* ed. Brian Swann and Arnold Krupat, 251–61. Lincoln: University of Nebraska Press, 1987.

Rosen, Kenneth, ed. *The Man to Send Rain Clouds: Contemporary Stories by American Indians.* New York: Vintage, 1974.

——, ed. *Voices of the Rainbow: Contemporary Poetry by American Indians.* New York: Seaver Books, 1975.

Rothenberg, Jerome, ed. *Shaking the Pumpkin: Traditional Poetry of the Indian North Americas.* New York: Doubleday, 1972.

Ruoff, A. LaVonne Brown. *American Indian Literatures: An Introduction, Bibliographic Review, and Selected Bibliography.* New York: Modern Language Association, 1990.

Ruppert, James. *Mediation in Contemporary Native American Fiction.* Norman: University of Oklahoma Press, 1995.

Ryan, P. M. *The Revised Dictionary of Modern Maori.* 3d ed. Auckland: Reed Education, 1989.

Said, Edward W. *Orientalism.* New York: Vintage, 1978.

Salmond, Anne. *Eruera: The Teachings of a Maori Elder.* 1980. Reprint, Oxford: Oxford University Press, 1990.

——. *Hui: A Study of Maori Ceremonial Gatherings.* Wellington: Reed, 1975.

——. "Maori Epistemologies." In *Reason and Morality,* ed. Joanna Overing, 240–63. London: Tavistock, 1985.

——. "Nga Huarahi O Te Ao Maori: Pathways in the Maori World." In *Te Maori: Maori Art from New Zealand Collections,* ed. Sidney Moko Mead, 109–37. New York: Abrams, 1984.

——. "Theoretical Landscapes: On Cross-Cultural Conceptions of Knowledge." In *Semantic Anthropology,* ed. David Parkin, 65–87. London: Academic Press, 1982.

——. "Tribal Words, Tribal Worlds: The Translatability of Tapu and Mana." University of Auckland, 1987.

Sanders, Douglas E. *The Formation of the World Council of Indigenous Peoples.* IWGIA Document 29. Copenhagen: IWGIA 1977.

Sanders, Thomas E., and Walter W. Peek, comps. *Literature of the American Indian.* New York: Glencoe Press, 1973.

San Juan, E., Jr. *Beyond Postcolonial Theory.* New York: St. Martin's, 1998.

Sarris, Greg. *Keeping Slug Woman Alive: A Holistic Approach to American Indian Texts.* Berkeley: University of California Press, 1993.

Schubnell, Matthias. *N. Scott Momaday: The Cultural and Literary Background.* Norman: University of Oklahoma Press, 1985.

Schwimmer, Erik, ed. *The Maori People in the Nineteen-Sixties: A Symposium.* Auckland: Blackwood, 1968.

——. "The Story of the Modern Marae." *Te Ao Hou* 2 (spring 1952): 23–24+.

——. *The World of the Maori.* Wellington: Reed, 1966.

Sciascia, Piri. "Ka Pu Te Ruha, Ka Hao Te Rangatahi: As the Old Net Piles Up on Shore, the New Net Goes Fishing." In *Te Maori: Maori Art from New Zealand Collections,* ed. Sidney Moko Mead, 156–66. New York: Abrams, 1984.

Shoemaker, Adam. *Black Words, White Page: Aboriginal Literature, 1929–1988.* St. Lucia, Queensland: Queensland University Press, 1989.

Shorris, Earl. *The Death of the Great Spirit: An Elegy for the American Indian.* New York: Simon and Schuster, 1971.

Shunatona, Chief Joe [Joseph Bayhylle Shunatona]. *Skookum's Laugh Medicine: Indian Humor from the Great Sooner State.* Illus. Brummet Echohawk and Will Cloud. Tulsa: Oklahoma 50th Anniversary Celebration, 1957.

Silko, Leslie Marmon. *Ceremony.* New York: Viking, 1977.

——. *Laguna Woman.* Greenfield Center, N.Y.: Greenfield Review Press, 1974.

Sinclair, Keith. "Te Ao Hou (The New World)—No. 1." *Here and Now* 2.12 (September 1952): 42.

Smith, Linda Tuhiwai. *Decolonizing Methodologies: Research and Indigenous Peoples.* London: Zed Books, 1999.

Smith, Martin Cruz. *Nightwing.* New York: Norton, 1977.

Smith, Paul Chaat, and Robert Allen Warrior. *Like a Hurricane: The Indian Movement from Alcatraz to Wounded Knee.* New York: New Press, 1996.

Soop. "A Dark Picture of Treaties." Cartoon. *Akwesasne Notes* 1.8 (September 1969): 38.

Spivak, Gayatri Chakravorty. *The Post-Colonial Critic: Interviews, Strategies, Dialogues.* Ed. Sarah Harasym. New York: Routledge, 1990.

Stam, Robert and Ella Shohat. "Contested Histories: Eurocentrism, Multiculturalism, and the Media." In *Multiculturalism: A Critical Reader,* ed. David Theo Goldberg, 296–324. Oxford: Blackwell, 1994.

"Statement by Sid Mills." *Akwesasne Notes* 1.6 (June 1969): 47.

Stead, C. K. "Ihimaera: Old Wounds and Ancient Evils." 1986. Reprinted in *Answering the Language: Essays on Modern Writers,* 189–195. Auckland: Auckland University Press, 1989.

——. "Keri Hulme's 'The Bone People,' and the Pegasus Award for Maori Literature." *Ariel,* October 1985, 101–8.

Steiger, Brad. *Medicine Talk: A Guide to Walking in Balance and Surviving on the Earth Mother.* New York: Doubleday, 1975.

Steiner, Stan. *The New Indians.* New York: Delta, 1968.

Stevens, John. "Indigenous Activism at the U.N.: The Working Group on Indigenous Populations." *Native Americas* 15.1 (Spring 1998): 46–53.

Stewart, Bruce. *Tama and Other Stories.* Auckland: Penguin, 1989.

Storm, Hyemeyohsts. *Seven Arrows.* New York: Harper and Row, 1972.

Sturm, Terry, ed. *The Oxford History of New Zealand Literature in English.* Auckland: Oxford University Press, 1991.

Sutherland, I. L. G., ed. *The Maori People Today: A General Survey.* Auckland: Oxford University Press, 1940.

Swann, Brian, and Arnold Krupat, eds. *I Tell You Now: Autobiographical Essays by Native American Writers.* Lincoln: University of Nebraska Press, 1987.

Tall Mountain, Mary. *Nine Poems.* San Francisco: Friars, 1977.

Tapahonso, Luci. *Blue Horses Rush In: Poems and Stories.* Tucson: University of Arizona Press, 1997.

——. *Sáanii Dahataał/The Women Are Singing.* Tucson: University of Arizona Press, 1993.

Tauroa, Hiwi. *Te Kawa o te Marae/A Guide to Marae.* Wellington: Trade Union Education Authority, 1989.

Taylor, Apirana. *Eyes of the Ruru.* Wellington: Voice, 1979.

Taylor, Charles. "The Politics of Recognition." 1992. Reprinted in *Multiculturalism: Examining the Politics of Recognition,* ed. Amy Gutmann, 25–73. Princeton: Princeton University Press, 1994.

Te Ao Hou/The New World. Wellington: Department of Maori Affairs, 1952–75.

Te Awekotuku, Ngahuia. *Mana Wahine Maori: Selected Writings on Maori Women's Art, Culture, and Politics.* Auckland: New Women's Press, 1991.

Te Kaea. Wellington: Department of Maori Affairs, 1979–81.

Te Waru-Rewiri, Kura. "The Covenant." In *Mana Tiriti: The Art of Protest and Partnership,* 46. Wellington: Daphne Brasell Associates Press, 1991.

"This is Vietnam, 1972." *Akwesasne Notes* 4.3 (April 1972): 34.

Thom, Mel. "The New Indian Wars." *American Aborigine* 3.1 (n.d.): 2–8. Reprinted in *The Way: An Anthology of American Indian Literature,* ed. Shirley Hill Witt and Stan Steiner, 102–7. New York: Knopf, 1974.

Thomas, Robert K. "Pan-Indianism." In *The American Indian Today,* ed. Stuart Levine and Nancy O. Lurie, 77–85. Deland, Fla.: Everett Edwards, 1968.

Thornton, Russell. "Introduction and Overview." In *Studying Native America: Problems and Prospects,* ed. Russell Thornton, 3–14. Madison: University of Wisconsin Press, 1998.

Tirohia. "Goodbye." *Te Ao Hou* 27 (June 1959): 14–16.

Treaty Between the United States of America and the Navajo Tribe of Indians, With a Record of the Discussions that Led to its Signing. Introduction by Martin A. Link. Las Vegas, Nevada: K. C. Publications, 1968.

"Treaty with the Sioux: 1868." *Wassaja* 1.3 (April–May 1973): 7, 22.

"Treaties Made, Treaties Broken: New Legal Strategies for Subverting Indian Rights." *Akwesasne Notes* 10.5 (winter 1978) 12, 13.

"Tribes Have New Look with Mixed Bloodlines." *Arizona Daily Star* (Tucson), 27 January 1997.

Trouillot, Michel-Rolph. *Silencing the Past: Power and the Production of History.* Boston: Beacon, 1995.

Turner, Frederick W., III, ed. *The Portable North American Indian Reader.* New York: Viking, 1974.

Tuwhare, Hone. *Deep River Talk: Collected Poems.* Auckland: Godwit, 1993.

———. *No Ordinary Sun.* 1964. 3d ed., Dunedin: John McIndoe, 1977.

United Nations. *The Rights of Indigenous Peoples.* Fact Sheet, no. 9. Geneva: United Nations, 1997.

———. *Seeds of a New Partnership: Indigenous Peoples and the United Nations.* New York: United Nations, 1994.

United Native Americans. "Bureau of Caucasian Affairs." San Francisco: 1978. American Native Press Archives, University of Arkansas, Little Rock.

Velie, Alan R., ed. *American Indian Literature: An Anthology.* Norman: University of Oklahoma Press, 1979.

Vest, Jay Hansford C. "A Legend of Culture: D'Arcy McNickle's *Runner in the Sun.*" In *The Legacy of D'Arcy McNickle: Writer, Historian, Activist,* ed. John Lloyd Purdy, 152–65. Norman: University of Oklahoma Press, 1996.

Vizenor, Gerald. *Crossbloods: Bone Courts, Bingo, and Other Reports.* Minneapolis: University of Minnesota Press, 1990.

———. "Crows Written on the Poplars: Autocritical Autobiographies." In *I Tell You Now: Autobiographical Essays by Native American Writers,* ed. Brian Swann and Arnold Krupat, 101–9. Lincoln: University of Nebraska Press, 1987.

———. *Darkness in Saint Louis Bearheart.* 1977. Reprinted as *Bearheart: The Heirship Chronicles.* Minneapolis: University of Minnesota Press, 1990.

———. *Empty Swings: Haiku in English.* Minneapolis: Nodin Press, 1967.

———. *Fugitive Poses: Native American Indian Scenes of Absence and Presence.* Lincoln: University of Nebraska Press, 1998.

———. *The Heirs of Columbus.* Hanover, N.H.: Wesleyan University Press, 1991.

———. *Manifest Manners: Postindian Warriors of Survivance.* Hanover, N.H.: Wesleyan University Press, 1994.

———. *Seventeen Chirps: Haiku in English.* Minneapolis: Nodin Press, 1964.

———. *Tribal Scenes and Ceremonies.* Minneapolis: Nodin Press, 1976.

———. "Trickster Discourse." *American Indian Quarterly* 14 (Summer 1990): 277–87.

———. "*Trickster Discourse:* Comic Holotropes and Language Games." In *Narrative Chance: Postmodern Discourse on Native American Indian Literatures,* ed. Gerald Vizenor, 187–211. 1989. Reprint, Norman: University of Oklahoma Press, 1993.

———. *Wordarrows: Indians and Whites in the New Fur Trade.* Minneapolis: University of Minnesota Press, 1978.

———, ed. *The Everlasting Sky: New Voices from the People Named the Chippewa.* New York: Macmillan, 1972.

Vogel, Virgil J. *This Country Was Ours: A Documentary History of the American Indian.* New York: Harper and Row, 1972.

Voices from Wounded Knee, 1973, in the Words of the Participants. Mohawk Nation/Rooseveltown, N.Y.: Akwesasne Notes, 1974.

Voice of Indigenous Peoples: Native People Address the United Nations. Sante Fe, N.M.: Clear Light, 1994.

Wagner, Roy. *The Invention of Culture.* Rev. ed. Chicago: University of Chicago Press, 1981.

Walker, Ranginui J. "The Genesis of Maori Activism." *Journal of the Polynesian Society* 93.3 (September 1984): 267–81.

———. "Indigenous Counter-Culture." *New Zealand Listener,* 13 August 1973. Reprinted in Walker, *Nga Tau Tohetohe: Years of Anger,* 210–13. Auckland: Penguin, 1987.

———. *Ka Whawhai Tonu Matou: Struggle without End.* Auckland: Penguin, 1990.

———. "Marae: A Place to Stand." In *Te Ao Hurihuri/The World Moves On: Aspects of Maoritanga,* rev. ed., ed. Michael King, 21–30. New Zealand: Methuen, 1977.

———. *Nga Tau Tohetohe: Years of Anger.* Auckland: Penguin, 1987.

———. "The Politics of Voluntary Association." In *Conflict and Compromise: Essays on the Maori since Colonization,* ed. I. H. Kawharu, 167–86. Wellington: Reed, 1975.

———. "The Treaty of Waitangi as the Focus of Māori Protest." In *Waitangi: Maori and Pakeha Perspectives of the Treaty of Waitangi,* ed. I. H. Kawharu, 263–79. Auckland: Oxford University Press, 1989.

———, comp. *Bastion Point,* 1980. Auckland University.

———, comp. *He Taua and the Haka Party,* 1980. Auckland University.

———, comp. *Land March Newsletters,* 1980. Auckland University.

———, comp. *Nga Tamatoa Newsletters,* 1980. Auckland University.

———, comp. *Te Hokioi Newsletters,* 1980. Auckland University.

Warrior, Robert Allen. *Tribal Secrets: Recovering American Indian Intellectual Traditions.* Minneapolis: University of Minnesota Press, 1995.

Watkins, Arthur V. [Senator Watkins on Termination Policy.] *Annals of the*

American Academy of Political and Social Science 311 (May 1957): 47–50, 55. Reprinted in *Documents of United States Indian Policy,* 2d ed., ed. Francis Paul Prucha, 238–39. Lincoln: University of Nebraska Press, 1990.

Weaver, Jace. "From I-Hermeneutics to We-Hermeneutics: Native Americans and the Post-Colonial." In *Native American Religious Identity: Unforgotten Gods,* ed. Jace Weaver, 1–25. Maryknoll, N.Y.: Orbis Books, 1998.

——. *That the People Might Live: Native American Literatures and Native American Community.* New York: Oxford University Press, 1997.

Weewish Tree. American Indian Historical Society. 1971–.

" 'We Hold the Rock': Alcatraz Proclamation to the Great White Father and His People." *Alcatraz Indians of All Tribes Newsletter* 1.1 (January 1970). Reprinted in *The Way: An Anthology of American Indian Literature,* ed. Shirley Hill Witt and Stan Steiner, 232–35. New York: Knopf, 1974.

Welch, James. *The Death of Jim Loney.* New York: Harper and Row, 1979.

——. *Fools Crow.* New York: Penguin, 1986.

——. "Poetics and Politics." Unpublished transcript of a classroom visit. Tucson: University of Arizona, 23 March 1992.

——. *Riding the Earthboy 40.* 1971. Reprint, Lewiston, Idaho: Confluence, 1990.

——. *Winter in the Blood.* New York: Viking, 1974.

Welch, James, and Paul Stekler. *Killing Custer: The Battle of the Little Bighorn and the Fate of the Plains Indians.* New York: Norton, 1994.

Whispering Wind Magazine. Louisiana Indian Hobbyist Association. 1967–.

White, James L., ed. *The First Skin around Me: Contemporary American Tribal Poetry.* Moorhead, Minn.: Territorial Press, 1976.

Wiget, Andrew. *Native American Literature.* Boston: Twayne, 1985.

Wikiriwhi, H. Te M. "He Korero Hararei/A Holiday Story." *Te Ao Hou* 14 (April 1956): 16–21.

Wilkinson, Charles F. *American Indians, Time, and the Law: Native Societies in a Modern Constitutional Democracy.* New Haven: Yale University Press, 1987.

Williams, David V. "Te Tiriti o Waitangi—Unique Relationship between Crown and Tangata Whenua?" In *Waitangi: Maori and Pakeha Perspectives of the Treaty of Waitangi,* ed. I. H. Kawharu, 64–91. Auckland: Oxford University Press, 1989.

Williams, H. W. *Dictionary of the Maori Language.* 7th ed. Wellington: GP Publications, 1971.

Williams, Mark. "Witi Ihimaera and the Politics of Epic." In *Leaving the Highway: Six Contemporary New Zealand Novelists.* Auckland: Auckland University Press, 1990.

Williams, Robert A., Jr. *Linking Arms Together: American Indian Treaty Visions of Law and Peace, 1600–1800.* New York: Oxford University Press, 1997.

Wills, Garry. *John Wayne's America.* New York: Simon and Schuster, 1997.

Wilmer, Franke. *The Indigenous Voice in World Politics: From Time Immemorial. Violence, Cooperation, Peace, 7.* Newbury Park, Calif.: Sage, 1993.

Witt, Shirley Hill, and Stan Steiner, eds. *The Way: An Anthology of Indian Literature.* New York: Knopf, 1974.

Womack, Craig. *Red on Red: Native American Literary Separatism.* Minneapolis: University of Minnesota Press, 1999.

Wong, Hertha Dawn. *Sending My Heart Back across the Years: Tradition and Innovation in Native American Autobiography.* New York: Oxford University Press, 1992.

Woodard, Charles L. *Ancestral Voice: Conversations with N. Scott Momaday.* Lincoln: University of Nebraska Press, 1989.

World Council of Indigenous Peoples. "Coordinator's Notes Re: Recommended Program and Agenda." International Conference of Indigenous Peoples, 27–31 October 1975.

——. "Draft 'Solemn Declaration.'" First General Assembly, Port Alberni, B.C., Canada, 27–31 October 1975.

——. "Indigenous Struggle in the Pacific." Pacific Region Conference, Canberra, Australia, 25–27 June 1984.

——. "Motions of the Policy Board Meeting Held in Copenhagen, Denmark from June 16–18 1975."

——. "Report of the Secretariat to the Policy Board at Copenhagen Meeting (June 16–20, 1975) Reporting on Period from May 1st 1974 to June 6th 1975."

——. "Report on the Preparatory Meeting of the International Conference of Indigenous People Held in Georgetown, Guyana, April 8–11, 1974."

——. "Resolutions." First General Assembly, Port Alberni, B.C., Canada, 27–31 October 1975.

——. "Resolutions." Second General Assembly, Kiruna, Sweden, 24–27 September 1977.

——. "Resolutions." Third General Assembly, Canberra, Australia, 27 April–2 May 1982.

Worthington, Mikaere. "Back to the Mat." *Te Ao Hou* 40 (September 1962): 11–15.

Young Bear, Ray A. *Winter of the Salamander: The Keeper of Importance.* San Francisco: Harper and Row, 1980.

Young, Robert J. C. *Colonial Desire: Hybridity in Theory, Culture, and Race.* London: Routledge, 1995.

INDEX

Third World, 9, 216, 245 n.11; critique of, 201–2
Thom, Mel, 106–7
Tiffin, Helen, 18, 29–32, 243 n.24, 245 n.13, 264 n.35, 274 n.15
Tirohia, 52–54
Trail of Broken Treaties, 122
Transgenerational address, 181, 188, 192
Treaties, 3, 12, 17, 111, 219; Fort Laramie, 118, 166–67, 169, 219, 267 n.21, 267 n.24; Navajo, 167; NCAI, 80; United States, 3–4, 19–21, 78, 117–18, 163–66, 193, 243 n.26, 265 nn.5 and 6, 266 nn.13 and 14, 267 nn.18 and 19. *See also* Treaty of Waitangi
Treaty discourse, 14, 17–22, 30, 45, 50, 57–65, 76, 80, 104–6, 109, 117, 121, 146, 161–71, 175, 178, 197, 207, 211, 267 n.24, 270 n.32; as allegory, 19–20, 65, 137–46, 243 n.28, 262 n.23; as metaphor and metonymy, 20–21, 165, 167, 169–70, 172
Treaty of Waitangi, 3, 5, 19–20, 37, 50, 57, 59–65, 111, 114–15, 117, 128, 137–46, 243 n.27, 250 n.23, 259 n.13
Trickster discourse, 190
Turangawaewae (standing place), 47
Tuwhare, Hone, 115, 127

United Nations, 6, 28–29, 193, 197, 212, 214–15, 244 n.9, 275 n.25, 275 n.31, 276 n.32; Decolonization Mandate, 28–29, 244 n.9; International Non-Governmental Organizations Conference on Indigenous Peoples in the Americas, 214; Sub-Commission on Prevention and Protection of Minorities, 276 n.32; Treaty on Genocide, 193; Working Group on Indigenous Populations, 214–15, 276 n.32, 276 n.33
United Native Americans, 120, 267 n.24

Vicarious honor, 89–90, 181
Victoria, Queen, 61–62
Vietnam War, 108, 117–18, 120–21, 123, 259 n.18, 260 nn.27 and 28

Vizenor, Gerald, 1–2, 23, 27, 56, 86–87, 124, 161, 178, 190–92, 217, 245 n.11, 271 n.45, 272 n.54
Voices from Wounded Knee, 1973, 123, 259 n.18

Wagner, Roy, 274 n.19
Waitangi Day, 114, 122, 259 n.13
Waitangi Tribunal, 115, 137–39, 144, 259 n.15
Walker, Ranginui, 111, 113, 127, 274 n.13, 276 n.35
Walters, Gordon, 57
War Memorial Museum, 12–13
War on Poverty programs, 122
Warrior, Clyde, 106
Warrior, Robert Allen, 91, 122, 261 n.34
Wassaja, 126, 260 n.33, 267 n.24
Watene, Neil A., 195
Watkins, Arthur V., 25
Weaver, Jace, 32
Weewish Tree, 126
Welch, James, 23, 33, 125, 161, 168–72, 175–76, 188–89, 269 n.30
Whakapapa. *See* Genealogy
Whare tipuna, 47–48, 56–57, 69–72, 128, 130–35, 146–59, 218, 263 n.33; as literary tradition, 135, 218
Wilkinson, Charles F., 163–65, 265 n.6, 266 n.13
Williams, David, 138
Williams, Robert A., 265 n.5, 266 n.14, 267 n.18
Winter count, 170–75, 178, 183; personal, 172–73. *See also* Pictographic discourse
Womack, Craig, 219
Women: in Maori culture, 142
Woodard, Charles, 187–88
World Council of Churches, 199
World Council of Indigenous Peoples, 7, 23, 195–215, 218, 273 n.12, 274 nn.13 and 19, 276 n.35; draft Solemn Declaration, 203–7, 210, 212, 216; First General Assembly of, 203, 207, 274 n.19; Second General Assembly of, 213–14; Solemn Declaration, 203,

Chadwick Allen is an assistant professor

in the Department of English at

Ohio State University.

Library of Congress Cataloging-in-Publication Data

Allen, Chadwick.
Blood narrative: indigenous identity in American
Indian and Maori literary and activist texts /
Chadwick Allen.
p. cm. — (New Americanists)
Includes bibliographical references and index.
ISBN 0–8223–2929–8 (cloth: alk. paper)
ISBN 0–8223–2947–6 (pbk.: alk. paper)
1. American literature—Indian authors—History and
criticism. 2. New Zealand literature—Maori authors
—History and criticism. 3. Literature, Comparative
—American and New Zealand. 4. Literature,
Comparative—New Zealand and American.
5. Maori (New Zealand people)—Intellectual life.
6. Indians of North America—Intellectual life.
7. Indian activists—Intellectual life. 8. Identity
(Psychology) in literature. 9. Indigenous peoples in
literature. 10. Group identity in literature. I. Title.
II. Series.
PS153.I52 A45 2002
810.9'897—dc21   2002001660